Abandoned house, Cherokee, Alabama, 2023 (photograph by Luke Spinelli).

The Lizard People Don't Want You to Read This

Essays on Conspiracy Theory in Popular Culture

Edited by ROBERT SPINELLI

McFarland & Company, Inc., Publishers
Jefferson, North Carolina

This book has undergone peer review.

LIBRARY OF CONGRESS CATALOGING-IN-PUBLICATION DATA

Names: Spinelli, Robert, 1980– editor
Title: The lizard people don't want you to read this : essays on conspiracy theory in popular culture / edited by Robert Spinelli.
Description: Jefferson, North Carolina : McFarland & Company, Inc., Publishers, 2025. | Includes bibliographical references and index.
Identifiers: LCCN 2025037107 | ISBN 9781476694856 paperback ∞
ISBN 9781476656250 ebook
Subjects: LCSH: Conspiracy theories in popular culture | LCGFT: Essays
Classification: LCC P96.C6575 L59 2025
LC record available at https://lccn.loc.gov/2025037107

ISBN (print) 978-1-4766-9485-6
ISBN (ebook) 978-1-4766-5625-0

© 2025 Robert Spinelli. All rights reserved

No part of this book may be reproduced or transmitted in any form or by any means, electronic or mechanical, including photocopying or recording, or by any information storage and retrieval system, without permission in writing from the publisher.

Front cover image © Shy Radar/Shutterstock

Printed in the United States of America

McFarland & Company, Inc., Publishers
 Box 611, Jefferson, North Carolina 28640
 www.mcfarlandpub.com

Acknowledgments

There are many people to thank when it comes to constructing a book of this kind. First, I want to thank all of the contributors to this volume; this has been a long process, and everyone has been so generous in their support and dedication to seeing the project to completion. Thank you all for your willingness to continue putting it all together. I am grateful to the Southwest Popular/American Culture Association, where I first presented research in 2022 and began to determine what kind of contribution I could make to the study of conspiracy theories. Thank you to the administration of American Baptist College for letting me explore these themes in my classes.

On a personal note, I thank everyone who has encouraged me to continue to pursue this work despite the various obstacles that have come up in the past several years. It has been helpful to have this work to return to time and again. Last, thank you to my kids, who make all the extra work worthwhile. I hope you will one day read this book and understand what I have spent my free time doing.

Table of Contents

Acknowledgments   v

Introduction
    Robert Spinelli   1

Part I: Literature and Text

Of Witches and Witch-Hunts: An Interdisciplinary
Approach to Conspiracy Theories
    Julia Siwek *and* Florian Zitzelsberger   9

A Symbol for Hope: Superman's Battle with the KKK
as a Model for Effective Cultural Engagement
with Conspiracy Theories
    Colin McRoberts   25

Morphology of the Conspiracy Theory
    Matthew N. Hannah   40

The Hellfire Club: Secret Societies in the Fiction of Marvel
Comics and Real-World Parallels
    Sean Thomas Milligan   60

The End Is Near: Doomsday Conspiracy Theories
and Apocalyptic Paranoia
    Daniel P. Compora   80

Part II: Cultural Mythology and Social Media

Conspiring to Be an Ethical All-American
    Hasmet M. Uluorta   95

From Candy to Contact Killer: Moral Panic and the Fentanyl
Contact Overdose Myth
    Kat Albrecht *and* Andrew Burns   110

It's a Bird, It's a Plane, It's a Manifestation of Grief:
How Sightings of Mothman Reveal the Grief Behind Conspiracy
  MICHELLE DRAKE ... 124

The Material Ephemera of QAnon "True Believers":
A Constitutive Rhetoric
  HOLLY T. HAMBY ... 142

Anti-Semitic Conspiracy Theories in Popular Culture: Blame It on "the Jews"
  JAMES WEATHERFORD ... 154

Memes, Schemes, and Conspiracy Machines: How Viral Disinformation Produces a Shadow-Marketplace of Ideas
  CHELSEA L. HORNE ... 169

Part III: Film and TV

A Transmission of the Times: HIV/AIDS Conspiracies and Denialism in Historical Dramas
  GORDON ALLEY-YOUNG ... 185

Gendered Extremism and Horror Cinema: Immersive Depictions of Far-Right Radicalization in *Soft & Quiet*
  TARA HEIMBERGER ... 201

How Conspiracy Theories Manifest Anthropocenic Anxieties: A Post-Human Critique of Humanism Through the Lens of *Inside Job*
  SUTIRTHO ROY ... 215

"We're now living in a post-cover-up, post-conspiracy age": *The X-Files* and the Changing Forms of Conspiratorial Culture
  BETHAN JONES ... 234

About the Contributors ... 251
Index ... 255

Introduction

Robert Spinelli

When I was young, I spent a lot of time at the local library. On the second floor, down a wind-filled corridor, was the nonfiction section, which contained a few rows of books on strange topics: the occult, alien abduction narratives, cryptids, paranormal investigations, and conspiracy theories. Being someone interested in offbeat topics and "spooky" subject matter, I gravitated toward this section and eventually read most of the books contained on those shelves. While I read these with a skeptical eye, the temptation to believe in the subject matter was great and reading such a plethora of material about these topics meant it was quite easy to understand the allure of fringe beliefs. It is far more interesting to imagine running into Bigfoot in the woods nearby than just run-of-the-mill wildlife. Seeing lights in the sky at night and imagining that they were indicators of extraterrestrial life both excited and terrified me.

When I was growing up in the nineties, my favorite TV show was, undoubtedly, *The X-Files*. Each week, my best friend and I would call each other after the latest episode and discuss either the monster of the week, which was often a topic I had read about in books taken out from the library, or the latest set of conspiratorial subplots in the show. While this was a deep source of entertainment for us, we both knew that the real pleasure of the show was its entertainment value and that these stories were not sources of fact or meaning. Indeed, the most core theme in *The X-Files* is its exploration of epistemology and its juxtaposition with faith. As I matured and moved on to other topics of study in college and beyond, my fascination with these topics waned and fell into the background of my thought processes.

After 9/11, I was surprised to see that variations on the ideas that I had read about as a teenager were starting to appear as supposedly credible headlines. Government cover-ups, secret organizations, demonic faces in smoke were all being spoken about as potential truths existing in the wake of the World Trade Center attacks. Although I had not taken the Y2K and millennial concerns seriously, the reappearance of these tropes with a more vitriolic and organized bent to them were now apparent, and it was shocking to see not only how commonplace they had become but also how alluring they were to many people. In 2009, while teaching a critical thinking course, I did a lecture about conspiracy theories. Students were asked to present an idea of their choosing and then the class would discuss and, theoretically, debunk the theory. This format worked until one student presented a detailed overview of 9/11 truther views that incorporated some of the anti–Obama birther views as well. Several of the students present argued against these ideas, but many determined that they supported and agreed with the points of the 9/11 conspiracy theorists. As discussion was getting heated, I had to shut down the conversation, but I was surprised to see just how quickly the students fell into alignment with conspiratorial thinking and how determined they were that these ideas were true, leading them to shut off hearing opposing viewpoints.

The divisions that I saw play out in the classroom setting became extremely blatant in the lead-up to the 2016 election. As has been well documented by other researchers and plenty of news media, the mainstreaming of conspiracy theories found its figurehead with Donald Trump. Although many of the conspiratorial themes being floated at this time, and in succeeding years, are not new, the visibility of these ideas in popular culture, social media and the political realm meant that conspiracy theories gained a veneer of credibility that they had not enjoyed up to this point. While the discussions and readings of my adolescence were engaged in for entertainment reasons, the mixture of paranoid ideas and political unrest made for a different sense of actual danger that has played out in different forms since this time.

Since the early 2000s, there has been an increasing number of scholarly books dealing with the topic of conspiracy theories. These studies have come from a number of disciplines—political science, cultural studies, folklore, media studies and sociology are a few of the fields most represented in analysis of contemporary conspiratorial culture and the problem of misinformation in the political realm. While much has been written about the mainstreaming of what used to be fringe ideas and the apparent increase in the presence of conspiracy theories in headlines due to the influence of Donald Trump and QAnon, there is a gap in the literature when it comes to examining the role of popular culture in reflecting and disseminating conspiracy theories. This collection has been assembled to fill in some of those gaps and to illustrate the wide range of formats in which conspiracy theories have appeared in the media that we consume.

The breadth of popular culture studies became clear to me upon attending the Southwest Popular/American Culture Association conference in 2022. During a panel discussion surrounding conspiracy theories, it was further cemented to me just how much the topic has woven its way into the fabric of society. Popular culture analysis offers a unique view of how pervasive a set of ideas may be in the minds of consumers. Although there may not be consensus as to what ideas are most widely shared or believed, their presence in the contemporary mindset is revelatory of the degree to which systems of thought have become mainstreamed. To gain a thorough overview of the ways in which conspiratorial themes were prevalent in many forms of media, I decided that an edited collection would be the best way to explore the multifaceted appearances of these thought patterns. After placing a call for contributors on various platforms, I selected sixteen for inclusion in the final volume. These scholars come from a variety of fields, some established researchers and others early-career writers who bring a fresh perspective to the work. It is my hope that this volume will be useful in a number of disciplines and that it will find an audience among non-academics as well.

Conspiracy theories are attractive for a multitude of reasons, one of the primary being that they offer simplified solutions to complex issues. These theories eschew nuance in their explanations of events and postulate elaborate explanations normally involving sinister plots and secret alliances (Knight 2000). "Conspiracy theory" or "conspiracy theorist" are terms typically used in a negative way, utilized to cast doubt on those who would voice such absurd and implausible ideas and call them into question as reliable sources. However, conspiracy theorists also display characteristics that are usually seen as positive: they are individualistic, unafraid to question ideas presented by authorities and are resistant to dominant epistemological narratives. Conspiracists self-identify as "truthers," as in the case of those who seek to vindicate 9/11 theories supporting the idea that the attacks were an inside job, or as "citizen sleuths," as those researchers into the JFK assassination termed themselves (Olmstead 2008). In popular culture, no character exemplifies the cool mystique surrounding conspiracists as much as Fox Mulder. Mulder is an attractive, clearly intelligent, and qualified FBI investigator who is well known for thinking differently than his peers, earning him the nickname "Spooky." Of course, in the context of the show, Mulder's eccentric ideas are often found to be correct, which only exacerbates the vision of the conspiracist as someone who is destined to reveal uncomfortable truths about the world around them.

The conspiratorial narrative places the Mulderesque figure in the role of an operative trying to see beyond the official version of events given by mainstream media, governmental figures, or untrustworthy scientists. QAnon, specifically, played into this aspect of conspiracy culture, exemplified by the crossover of online theorizing into real life with Pizzagate. When Edgar Welch fired upon Comet Ping Pong, he did so under the false belief that he was bringing freedom to imprisoned children being held under a Hillary Clinton–run ring of traffickers. In the contemporary mythology of the conspiracist, Welch saw himself as performing heroic actions based on esoteric knowledge gained from an online community of fellow truth seekers. Rachel Runnels focuses on the idea that conspiracy narratives echo the hero's journey as described by Joseph Campbell. In Campbell's archetypal scheme, the hero embarks upon a journey based on a desire to uncover or reveal truths. No longer apt to remain a recipient of others' truths, the hero becomes a participant in a quest of their own (Runnels 2019). Peter Knight (Knight 2021) argues that conspiracy-centered fictional narratives encourage the reader to identify with rugged, lone wolf detective–style characters, which correlates directly to the archetype of the hero setting off on their own path of exploration and discovery. This tendency of the conspiracist to place themselves in the center of their own heroic narrative has its contemporary reflection in the predominantly online formation of the QAnon movement, with its devotees acting as digital warriors spreading the truths of the movement via social media sites and traditional message boards.

Mark Fenster directly describes this conspiratorial take on hero-making as a "conspiracy narrative" due to its tendencies toward moralism, black-and-white thinking and attempts to describe events within a framework with its own sense of coherence (Fenster 2008). Tracing conspiracy narratives through various films and books, Fenster illustrates the ease with which these stories can offer explanations that tempt with their ability to explain away larger issues, yet which fall apart under scrutiny. If we are to view conspiracy theories as a form of storytelling, with their own series of familiar narrative arcs and inherent drama, perhaps the value of these theories isn't in their status as "truth" but in their ability to provide meaning in the face of grief and traumatic events (Birchall 2006). While a devout belief in conspiracy theories can and does lead to dangerous circumstances, particularly as they mix with politics and ideologues who seek to capitalize on paranoia to stir up their devotees, a study of the ways in which conspiratorial thinking has presented itself in various forms of media can reveal other aspects of conspiratorial culture.

The essays collected in this volume take a multitude of approaches to explore the impact of conspiratorial thinking on the world we inhabit. The aim of this collection is not to condemn these thoughts but to explore them in an attempt to achieve a different level of understanding of how they function, where they come from and how pervasive they are in the media we consume.

The Essays

The first section explores instances of conspiratorial thinking and how it manifests in the realm of literature and text. Julia Siwek and Florian Zitzelsberger take a historical approach to examining the ways the complex web of history, culture, and media in which conspiracy theories surrounding witches were and are created, disseminated, (re)framed, and instrumentalized, ultimately drawing tentative conclusions about how conspiracy theories as a historical phenomenon have been touched, and transformed, by digital media and new forms of (non-literary) communication. Colin McRoberts examines early Superman comic books and their depictions of and struggles with the KKK and white supremacy and contrasts this treatment with the ways in which contemporary comic media portray similar themes today. Matthew N. Hannah maps the textual structure of various conspiracy theories in order to demonstrate that the popularity of fiction such as Dan Brown's *Da Vinci Code* can be attributed to the pervasive cultural fascination with the shadowy plots, secret cabals, complex symbolism, and narrative revelation that have historically structured American conspiracism. Taking on the role of secret societies such as the Illuminati, Sean Thomas Milligan uses examples from the X-Men comic book series to discuss the historical roots of organizations that remain in the background of political and social influence. Finally, Daniel P. Compora explores prominent doomsday prophecies and conspiracies, focusing on religious and secular narratives to provide both historical and religious contexts. Focusing primarily on project Blue Beam, the discussion progresses from historical examples (e.g., Nostradamus prophecies) to more recent ones, including QAnon and Covid-19 conspiracy theories.

The second section takes on the themes of cultural mythology and social media. Hasmet M. Uluorta takes a Lacanian approach to examining the role of conspiracy theories in creating a sense of personal identity, leading to the designation of the Ethical All-American as an ideal to measure oneself against. Kat Albrecht and Andrew Burns approach the study of the fentanyl craze as an example of contemporary cultural mythology that takes real-world issues and plays upon fears to create moral panics surrounding drug overdoses. Michelle Drake takes a folkloric approach to the study of Mothman and how its appearances lead to a connection between mourning and identity and how these constructs combine to create reasonings for the unexplainable in the world. Holly T. Hamby examines everyday material ephemera—including apparel, bumper stickers and flags—as physical representations of belonging to conspiracy and white nationalist communities. James Weatherford traces the historical trajectory of anti–Semitic conspiracy theories from the beginning of the Common Era into the contemporary age and considers how cultural representations have undeniably reinforced and propagated such myths resulting in violence and discrimination against Jews. Chelsea L. Horne applies an interdisciplinary approach to consider the role of network effects, virality, and internet design and architecture in providing a forum for robust information sharing—of both "good" content as well as problematic content like disinformation and conspiracy theories.

The final section covers several instances of how conspiracy theories are present in the realms of film and TV. Gordon Alley-Young examines historical dramas to connect the current resurgence in HIV/AIDS and other conspiracy theories to how both conspiracy theories and healthcare have historically been tools for stigmatizing and marginalizing individuals from LGBTQAI+ and/or BIPOC communities. Using the horror film *Soft & Quiet* as a springboard, Tara Heimberger delves into the alt-right "Trad-Wife" movement and exposes the insidious facets inherent in the "soft" and "quiet" nature of female white nationalism in a scholarly examination of ethical spectatorship and the use of stylized long takes to intricately navigate prolonged scenes of violence. In examining the TV show *Inside Job*, Sutirtho Roy poses a meta-narrative counter-gaze to the very insecurities which lead people to formulate, propagate and cling to conspiracy theories. His essay analyzes such theorizing as a post-modern form of mythopoeic storytelling that arises from mankind's uneasy relationship with the environment and non-human creatures. Bethan Jones concludes the collection with an exploration of the cultural context in which *The X-Files* emerged and the particular political, social and economic factors that contributed to the conspiratorial narratives that underlined the show's success.

References

Birchall, Clare. (2006). *Knowledge Goes Pop: From Conspiracy Theory to Gossip.* Berg.
Fenster, Mark. (2008). *Conspiracy Theories: Secrecy and Power in American Culture.* Regents of the University of Minnesota.
Knight, Peter. (2021). "Conspiracy Theories: Linked to Literature | UNESCO." Accessed April 26, 2024. https://www.unesco.org/en/articles/conspiracy-theories-linked-literature-0.
Olmsted, Kathryn S. (2009). *Real Enemies: Conspiracy Theories and American Democracy, World War I to 9/11.* Oxford University Press.
Runnels, Rachel. (2019). "Conspiracy Theories and the Quest for Truth." *Digital Commons @ ACU Electronic Theses and Dissertations* (Paper 180). https://digitalcommons.acu.edu/etd/180.

Part I
Literature and Text

Of Witches and Witch-Hunts
An Interdisciplinary Approach to Conspiracy Theories
Julia Siwek *and* Florian Zitzelsberger

History Matters: A Call for (More) Literacy

While it is tempting to conceive of conspiracy theories as a phenomenon of "our time," a by-product of social media or developments in digitization more broadly, this essay is premised on the idea that conspiratorial thought and narratives have pervaded western societies since the Early Modern period. What changed is the status of conspiracy theorizing as a form of knowledge production on the one hand and the attention given to conspiratorial narratives on the other.* Michael Butter (2018), for example, argues that up until the second half of the twentieth century, conspiratorial thought was considered *legitimate* knowledge that eventually got relegated to a marginal position within dominant discourse before resurfacing with a new connotation of constituting improper or illegitimate knowledge (141; 144). This new (hyper-) visibility partly is due to the changed media landscape, with social media and their algorithms creating a fertile ground for the spreading of conspiratorial narratives within specific groups and allowing them to seep into mainstream discourses, reaching more people than in the preceding decades (Butter 2018, 180). This spreading is rapid and often uncontrolled, with hardly any mechanisms in place to differentiate between fact and fiction.

Rather than speaking of conspiracy theories as an entirely new

---

*We broadly follow Butter's (2014; 2018) terminology in this essay. However, in some cases we opt for conspiratorial narrative rather than conspiracy theory because it designates both a specific discourse or epistemic modality (like the conspiracy theory; we also use conspiratorial thought to specify the latter) and the concrete form in which conspiratorial thought manifests. See also our discussion of dramatizations of conspiratorial thought in the second half of the essay.

9

phenomenon, then, we may consider these recent developments as indicative of a renaissance of a specific epistemic modality. Especially in the context of western societies, conspiratorial narratives are regarded as conducive to an increased polarization and populism: The more people believe in large-scale conspiracies, the more difficult it will become to find common ground, as a society, to engage in meaningful dialogue and find consensus as to what is "true" and not, and to remain open to the (democratic) processes through which participants of a society negotiate community and their cohabitation (Butter 2018, 218; 233). As a consequence, it is a necessity to enable individuals to engage critically with conspiratorial narratives and attendant phenomena such as disinformation and propaganda. The kind of *literacy* this requires is not an end in itself, nor does it exist solely in the classroom; it "prefigures qualities of responsible citizenship" and as such is tied to "political education" in the classroom and beyond (Holze and Zitzelsberger 2021, 80).

Butter (2018) acknowledges this complexity in his call for more *social literacy* in schools and universities, which he sees as inextricably linked to *historical and media literacies*, to ensure a responsible engagement with such phenomena (299). While media literacy can be broadly conceived as the ability to assess and evaluate media content (for example, the trustworthiness of news accounts as well as their sources) and the construction and potential distortion of meaning through media (Butter 2018, 229–230; see also Pollak et al. 2018), historical literacy in Butter's formulation more specifically speaks to the distinction of what is commonly termed conspiracy *theory* as opposed to historically documented cases of *conspiracies*. The comparison of the two highlights that actual conspiracies usually happen on a much smaller scale and with less efficacy than conspiracy theorists assume. Notably, investing in social, media, and historical literacy is a first step toward critical awareness and informed judgement grounded in assumptions about human nature and social processes that conspiracy theories usually lack or overlook (Butter 2018, 230–31).

In this essay, we share an interdisciplinary perspective on conspiratorial narratives situated at the nexus of the social, medial, and historical. Focusing on narratives surrounding witches as well as the (political) metaphor of the witch-hunt, we demonstrate how a diachronic orientation to the subject matter sheds light on contemporary conspiracy theories. Combining insights from medieval German studies and American studies, we trace a web of WITCHES—a designation of a discursive construct in conspiratorial thought as well as its dramatizations as supposed enemy or scapegoat rather than "actual" witches—across temporal, geographical, and medial borders. The goal is to become attuned to and sensitized for continuities that allow for a more nuanced perspective on contemporary conspiracy theories on the one hand and that help demystify some of the assumptions and anxieties surrounding them by highlighting historical precedent on the other. Because conspiratorial narratives blur the line between fact and fiction, we suggest that a first step to (en)counter conspiratorial thought and foster literacy in the classroom is through textual analysis.

We first collaborated on this topic during a class we designed for aspiring teachers at the University of Passau, Germany, in 2021. The class examined the historical, cultural, and medial contexts and functions of conspiratorial narratives, disinformation, and propaganda from the perspectives of medieval German studies and American studies. The design of this class will serve as a brief contextualization of our research at the outset of this essay, especially regarding productive overlaps of the two disciplines, which at first glance make an unusual pairing. Our collaboration was based on a seminar concept developed at the University of Passau, the "Information and Media Literacy Think Tank" (Makeschin 2018; see also Fitz and Zitzelsberger 2023), which aims at offering students an open forum for discussing topics in an interdisciplinary fashion at eye level with experts in the field. For this iteration, we invited colleagues from history and history education, linguistics, media and art education, and experts on anti–Semitism research and prevention, and supplemented in-person discussion with a digital whiteboard used by students to document the class and visualize connections among the individual contributions, core themes, and case studies (see Zitzelsberger and Siwek 2023). Over the course of the semester, a diachronic, transmedial, and transnational web emerged that made apparent not only how the individual phenomena—conspiratorial narratives, disinformation, propaganda—are related, but also how the different disciplinary perspectives mutually enrich each other, such that neither discipline could have generated the same kind of knowledge alone.

Roughly the first half of the class was thematically focused on WITCHES as an object of study shared by both core disciplines. The belief in witches in central Europe is often perceived as the first modern conspiracy theory (Tschacher 2001, 66; Butter 2018, 145). It represents one of the most consequential manifestations of conspiratorial thought, which led to successive waves of persecution of alleged witches in the Early Modern period. Based solely on trial records, approximately 50,000 executions of individuals accused of witchcraft can be documented in Europe. However, accounting for victims of lynching as well as social consequences including the ostracization of the accused, the dark figure is much higher (Dillinger 2007, 91). With the first European settlements in New England came the import of this kind of conspiratorial thought to the North American continent, and even though the circumstances of accusations of witchcraft may differ in both contexts, it appears that the image of the WITCH used to legitimate the persecution of the accused has been relatively stable. To understand the stability and pervasiveness of this discourse—from Central Europe in the fifteenth century to Puritan New England to the adoption of the witch-hunt metaphor in twentieth-century politics and contemporary mutations—our class turned to various (literary and non-literary) texts, in line with a new historicist understanding of the textuality of culture (Greenblatt 1995). In doing so, central motifs were delineated, and an analysis was conducted on how these were updated, reinterpreted, and functionalized in various historical-cultural contexts and medial regimes.

Below, we follow the same path by illustrating how diachronically oriented, historically informed textual analysis can uncover connecting threads spanning centuries, mapping an overarching discourse. We demonstrate that narratives and motifs associated with WITCHES are found in current examples of conspiratorial thought as well and consider the characteristics of this latest update against the backdrop of radically transformed communication forms.

From Conspiratorial Narrative to Political Metaphor: The Witch in Diachronic Perspective

The most infamous text in the history of European witch persecution is the *Malleus maleficarum* (Hammer of Witches) (Kramer 2001 [c. 1486]) by the Dominican monk and inquisitor Heinrich Kramer, also known as Institoris. Kramer composed his treatise in 1486 as a kind of compendium of witchcraft (Dillinger 2007, 47) and simultaneously as a manual for witch trials, which he sought to promote with his writing. In doing so, he aligned himself with a demonological discourse that had undergone a decisive turn in the first half of the fifteenth century. Thus, in the western Alpine region, the idea of a secretive, malevolent witch sect acting against Christianity emerged, as outlined by the Dominican Johannes Nider in his *Formicarius* in 1437. At the same time, certain notions were associated with the concept of the witch around 1400, which can already be identified as patterns in witch trials around 1430–40 (Blauert 2004, 122) and subsequently were to shape the image of the WITCH over centuries: pacts and sexual relations with the devil (or demons), harmful sorcery, witch's flight, and the witch's sabbath—elements that co-constitute the so-called "elaborate" or cumulative concept of witchcraft (Dillinger 2007, 20–21). The "new phenomenon" of the witch sect drew ideologically from various sources.

On the one hand, in the population, there was a widespread belief in wizards and sorceresses who could bring about both good and evil through magical practices. On the other hand, the alleged offenses of the Cathars and Waldensians persecuted as heretics—devil worship, nocturnal orgiastic gatherings, and child sacrifice—were transferred to witches. The ritual murder of infants and children was also attributed to Jews in the Middle Ages. The adoption of anti–Jewish prejudices was most visibly reflected in the designation of the solemn witches' gathering as the "sabbath" (Voltmer and Irsigler 2002, 31; Jerouschek and Behringer 2001, 12).

Kramer took up Nider's cautionary discourse regarding witches proficient in harmful sorcery, thus embarking on precarious intellectual terrain, given the canonical theological tradition's repudiation of popular conceptions concerning harmful magic and night flights as demonic delusions (Bailey 2002, 123–125). Consequently, the initial two parts of the *Malleus maleficarum* endeavor to establish the veracity and peril of witches while delineating the spectrum of transgressions they perpetrate. To substantiate these assertions, Kramer collates biblical exegeses alongside the writings of church fathers and theologians, deploying scholastic methodology (Jerouschek and Behringer 2001, 10). Doubts pertaining to the existence of witches' arch-heresy are thus framed as a form of heresy in themselves (69). The modus operandi of witches is explicated in the prefatory *Apologia*, wherein the author contends that they "voluntarily subject themselves through a covenant with the devil" and operate "with the divine sanction and demonic agency" (1^r; our translation*). Heinrich Kramer subscribed to the belief in the imminent end of the world and the devil's efforts to turn as many people as possible to the witch heresy before the apocalypse. This heresy was purportedly more prevalent among women (1^r). Consequently, the text adopts another aspect of the *Formicarius*: Nider's treatise, structured in the form of a dialogue, allocated one interlocutor, *Theologus*, to expound upon the vulnerability of women to the crime of witchcraft. Ostensibly, this was an attempt to rationalize the burgeoning trend whereby accusations of witchcraft predominantly targeted women by the early fifteenth century, contrasting with the predominantly male demographic indicted for sorcery during the

---

*A brief explanation of these discipline-specific conventions of citation: Medieval manuscripts and early modern prints do not feature the same kind of pagination as bound books. When quoting from such sources, instead of referencing a page number, one usually indicates the sheet (e.g., of paper) on which the quoted passage is printed; the superscript letters indicate whether the passage is located on the front (*r* for *recto*) or the back (*v* for *verso*). For example, the notation 1^r means that the reproduced text can be found on the front of the first sheet of the manuscript. Additional letters may be used to indicate the column in which the quoted passage occurs (also in superscript, e.g., $1^{r,a}$) or give further information about foliation (as in the tract by Ulrich Molitor quoted below, e.g., $\underline{e}3^v$.

fourteenth century (Bailey 2002, 120; 122–23). Kramer epitomizes this development by exclusively focusing on women as practitioners of harmful sorcery (*maleficarum*) in the title of his treatise. The misogynistic orientation of the text culminates in the sixth question of the first part, wherein the distinct susceptibility of women to the enticements of the devil is elucidated: Citing biblical passages, theological tracts, and ancient writings, women are attributed with various vices, including avarice, faithlessness, moral weakness, malevolence, envy, vanity, and, above all, lust (21ra–23ra). Kramer underscores the presumed fragility of female faith through an alleged etymological derivation of *femina* from *fides* (faith) and *minus* (21vb). His verdict concludes: "Consequently, woman is inherently wicked, since she doubts faith more quickly, and also denies faith more quickly. This is the basis for witches" (21vb; our translation). Notably, male practices of magic (e.g., necromancy) are tangentially addressed in the *Malleus maleficarum* and are classified and exculpated as separate from witches (39rb–39va; see also Broedel 2002, 136). Grounded in inherited convictions regarding the inferiority of the female gender, the *Malleus maleficarum* unprecedentedly and unambiguously establishes witchcraft as a crime perpetrated by women.

In the further course of his argumentation, Kramer presents an array of exempla illustrating the manifold witchcraft crimes, placing emphasis on harmful sorcery, known as *maleficium*. The accusations range from inhibiting fertility, transforming humans into animals, causing diseases in both humans and animals, and demonic possession, to the killing and sacrifice of children, as well as weather magic that jeopardizes the livelihoods of predominantly rural communities (e.g., 46ra–46rb). Furthermore, he discusses other elements of the cumulative concept of witchcraft (48rb–56rb), although surprisingly, the witches' sabbath receives relatively little attention despite serving as the nucleus of the notion of a formed witch sect and thus being more strongly emphasized in older treatises (Jerouschek and Behringer 2001, 12–13). Additionally, this gathering can be regarded as the primary framework for the further transgressions of the witches—including the flight to the assembly site, entering into a pact with the devil, and sealing it through sexual intercourse with demons. Within the context of his depiction of the witches' sabbath, Kramer identifies an elite group of witches who, unlike the others, practice all forms of *maleficium* and also sacrifice children and devour them (48va). The demon also demands from its adepts the production of an ointment made from the bones and limbs of children, which is used to perform witchcraft (48vb). Kramer particularly emphasizes the role of "witching midwives" in this context, who surpass all others in their malice (20va). They are primarily responsible for the killing of fetuses in the womb, infants, and young children. They drink their blood and devour them (32rb–32va). Kramer also highlights the danger posed by midwives collaborating conspiratorially with expectant mothers, many of whom are themselves witches (69vb).

Although the *Malleus maleficarum* allocates relatively little space to the witches' sabbath, as previously noted, its role in the development of conspiratorial thought surrounding witches in the fifteenth century is nevertheless pivotal. The motif of the witches' sabbath shapes the group of conspirators, forming a sect through their collective worship of the devil and the performance of abhorrent rituals. It can be surmised that Institoris sought primarily to demonstrate the breadth and, due to the numerous examples cited, the seemingly overwhelming evidence of *maleficium*, as belief in forms of harmful magic was widespread in the population, making it a plausible accusation and a means to intensify the persecution of witches.

The *Malleus maleficarum* likely fueled witch-hunts. The advent of the printing press facilitated the dissemination of Kramer's treatise within a limited, literate, and Latin-proficient audience, enabling its impact to unfold (Voltmer and Irsigler 2002, 31; 33). Approximately 30 editions were printed by 1669, making the *Malleus maleficarum* arguably the most widely distributed systematic demonology until the first half of the seventeenth century (Jerouschek and Behringer 2001, 11; 16). While suspicions against groups such as Jews or Waldensians had existed in the Middle Ages, and individuals had already been convicted of practicing magic, the consequential conspiracy narrative surrounding a witch sect needs to be seen in the context of the new medial regime (Butter 2018, 145–146). In addition to its syncretistic nature described earlier (see also Tschacher 2001, 66), the belief in witchcraft constitutes a metaphysical conspiracy theory situated within a Christian worldview (Butter 2018, 146). Kramer markedly inscribed a misogynistic imprint onto the notion of witches in league with the devil (Bailey 2002, 128; see 128n8 for an overview of studies on the gendered nature of witchcraft). While his theses were not uncontested, the extreme gendering of the WITCH espoused by him remained influential in scholarly discourse.

The treatise *De laniis et phitonicis mulieribus*, printed in 1489 and authored by the Constance jurist, notary, and ducal councilor Ulrich Molitor (Molitoris), similarly portrays witchcraft as a crime committed by women. However, there is a significant reinterpretation of the WITCH: here, it is a woman who is deceived by devilish illusions, merely *believing* to attend witch sabbaths or to cause harm with the aid of demons. In the early modern German edition published before 1500, titled *Von den unholden oder hexen* (Molitor 1997 [1508]), the conclusion states they are "in jrm vnglauben betrogen" (e3^v). As well, then, in Molitor's perspective, they deserve death for their heresy, apostasy, and allegiance to the devil (e4ʳ). Molitor's work demonstrates how witchcraft was a crime taken seriously as a concern of scholars of the law as well as secular courts. Notably, woodcuts depicting witches expanded the audience, potentially including illiterate individuals. At first glance, the witches appear to act independently and could have opened up an interpretation of witchcraft contrary to the treatise's direction. However, the rimmed eyes of the figures may have been intended to indicate the delusional nature of witchcraft activities (Gold 2016, 278). The depiction of the witches' sabbath in the second German edition (published by Johann Otmar in Augsburg) shows a group of three women sitting outside at a covered table. The woodcut in no way resembles the traditional descriptions of orgiastic gatherings but rather stages a communal meal.*

In a stark contrast, a pamphlet titled *Zauberey* (published nearly 130 years later in 1626) represents a culmination of all facets of the cumulative concept of witchcraft in the image of the witches' sabbath (Jakob 2020, 629).† Visually "flooded" with a multitude of characters, the pamphlet posits witchcraft as a communal crime predominantly involving women but also men. The visual representation is characterized by obscenity (especially in the motif of the coupling with the devil) and vividness—in the foreground on the right, bones and corpses of infants lie at the feet of a group engaged in practices of *maleficium*. Notably, the image also depicts a demon summoning by a magician, a genuinely male practice of sorcery (Jakob 2020, 632; 631–32 for a detailed description of the image). The pamphlet contextualizes the print graphic using two captions, one in Latin and a longer one in German: on the one hand, the pamphlet emphasizes the verisimilitude of the represented events and situates them in a specific location, the Blocksberg (see the inscription *B.Berg*), and on the other hand, the captions exhibit strategies of emotionalization and reception guidance—through direct address and an anticipation of an affective reaction to what is seen ("So dreadful [...] That whoever sees it may weep with sorrow"; our translation). Thus, the pamphlet possesses tremendous propagandistic potential. Through the interplay of image and text, the activities of the witch sect are propagated as a real threat to individuals and society. With its combination of a print graphic and Latin and German texts, the pamphlet can appeal to recipients of varying levels of education. The emergence of the pamphlet falls within the peak phase of witch-hunts between 1580 and 1650, a period when the notion of the witches' sabbath

---

*See the digital version at München, Bayerische Staatsbibliothek—Res/4 H.g.hum. 16 o: https://www.digitale-sammlungen.de/de/view/bsb10897899?page=60).

†See the digital version at the Germanisches Nationalmuseum HB802: http://objektkatalog.gnm.de/objekt/HB802.

frequently surfaced among the primary charges in witch trials (Voltmer and Irsigler 2002, 32).

* * *

We now turn to the adoption of the image of the WITCH in New England's Puritan theocracy and later the United States as an example of the pervasiveness of this image to show (1) that it outlasted the metaphysical conspiracy theory with which it originally has been associated and (2) how the legacy of Puritanism ties the witch to conspiratorial thought in such a way that it becomes a versatile metaphor that is readily taken up by new conspiratorial narratives, regardless of whether they are connected to "actual" witches. The metaphysical conspiracy theory discussed above found fertile ground in the Puritans' belief system in the seventeenth century, which rests upon a binary division of the world into "good" and "evil," and their doctrine of predestination, according to which witches, usually women considered to be corrupted by the devil, were sent upon Puritan society as a trial to endure.* For the Puritans, the alleged existence of witches—seen as responsible for bad harvests, etc.—is a reminder of their *own* decline, God's reaction to their sinfulness (Butter 2014, 51). However, as Butter notes, the fact that God would allow a conspiracy to ensue ultimately "indicated that [Puritans] were still the chosen people; it reaffirmed the covenant between them and God" (51) because this trial was seen as a sign of God's grace, a chance at redemption.

This metaphysical conspiracy theory most infamously culminated in the Salem witch trials of 1692–93 during which nineteen people, most of them women, were executed after being convicted for their alleged practice of witchcraft. As Perry Miller (1983) asserts, within Puritan society, the trials were a logical consequence, not superstition, of "the afflictions of New England," which included disease and death among colonists: "an appearance of witchcraft […] was from the beginning as much to be anticipated as Indian raids; by 1692 several instances had been encountered, and a more organized assault was altogether predictable" (192). In addition, the Salem witch trials happened at a time when Puritan theocracy was in a state of

---

*Puritans believed that they were God's "chosen people" and that everything that happened was according to God's will. What we describe here regarding witches is an actualization of a pattern that also undergirds the settlers' attitude toward indigenous populations who in early accounts were often characterized as devilish (see, e.g., Rowlandson 2003 [1682]). The genre of captivity narratives comes to mind as an early example of literary production with high propagandistic potential. Notably, and similar to the discourse surrounding witches, these texts were centrally concerned with female sexuality and religion: "with the female captive came the threat of rape, or—even worse according to Puritan beliefs—of intermarriage with a member of a tribe that had adopted Catholicism" (Sivils 2014, 87–88; see also Reed 2007, 225).

crisis, and the persecution of women as witches made sense according to this logic because it meant restoring the "transcendental, the economic, and the sexual orders" undergirding Puritanism, all of which intersect in—and were threatened by—the highly gendered image of the WITCH (Reed 2007, 219). Not unlike the misogyny of the *Malleus maleficarum*, this logic is based on a discursive link between femininity and "the Devil's constant, present temptations of body and soul" (210–11). While the Salem witch trials are commonly understood as the "final chapter" of systematic witch-hunts and more generally the belief in witches on North American territory, Owen Davies (2013) highlights that the logic that made these trials possible merely got displaced and that accusations of witchcraft and their consequences continued to affect disenfranchised groups in particular (3).

Davies turns to archival material—including legal records and newspapers—as well as folklore in his research. Here, we are interested in how the image of the WITCH, rather than the belief in "actual" witches, survived the end of Puritan theocracy. To this end, we identify the WITCH as a *topos* in literature and how this image remains tied to conspiratorial thought in such dramatizations.* The underlying argument is that the WITCH could stay relevant and present in the cultural imaginary because of such dramatizations or fictionalizations and that it is this image, shaped by the demonological discourse of the Early Modern period, that is taken up in conspiracy theories today rather than contemporary notions of witches and witchcraft.

Nathaniel Hawthorne's short story "Young Goodman Brown" (1835), for example, imagines a secret congregation of Puritans in the woods, discovered by the protagonist, who cannot believe his eyes: Some of the most pious people from his village, including goody Cloyse, who taught him catechism, and even the village's minister, have gathered in the woods for a satanic "worshipping assembly" (Hawthorne 2003, 1271). The text dramatizes conspiratorial thought through its focalizer Goodman Brown, who "suspects everybody living in Salem Village of being part of the devilish conspiracy" (Butter 2014, 109), which Hawthorne uses to address Puritan hypocrisy. "Young Goodman Brown" does not paint a picture of Puritans as God's chosen people who are threatened by an outside force. The text turns allegedly devout Puritans into conspirators against the purported foundational beliefs of Puritanism, showing that the piety Goodman Brown witnesses in the village (also after his return, which makes him wonder if he had only dreamed about the terrifying events [Hawthorne

---

*Butter distinguishes "between discursive texts that expose an alleged conspiracy by gathering and presenting evidence that is supposed to convince readers that a dangerous conspiracy exists, and texts that dramatize conspiracy scenarios" (25).

2003, 1272]) is merely a cover for the actual motives of the villagers, whatever those may be. Notably, despite the spatio-temporal setting of the story and the use of historical names, the text makes no mention of the Salem witch trials. However, Butter (2014) maintains that "Young Goodman Brown" is set in a "world permeated by the knowledge of and fears about witchcraft that fueled the trials" (106). We see this most prominently in the way the text draws on elements of the cumulative concept of witchcraft discussed above, such as satanic worship (Hawthorne 2003, 1271), or hints at them, as is the case with the witch's flight (goody Cloyse's "broomstick" had disappeared [1266]). In "Young Goodman Brown," the recourse to Puritanism not only implies an uptake of a specific belief system; it also makes conspiratorial thought as a specific epistemic modality "experienceable" through narrative.

Another example more frequently discussed in this context is Arthur Miller's 1953 play *The Crucible*, which not only dramatizes the Puritan metaphysical conspiracy theory surrounding witches, but was written in response to another conspiracy theory—or at least a sense of paranoia and fear permeating the United States in the 1950s—through allegory: the Second Red Scare, also often called a "communist witch-hunt," under Republican senator Joseph McCarthy (Meyers 1999). The comparison between the Second Red Scare and the time of the Salem witch trials was based in part on the modus operandi of McCarthy, whose baseless accusations of government officials, teachers, professors, journalists, etc., as communist allies planning to subvert the government ("McCarthyism" n.d.) are reminiscent of the hysteria and seeming volatility with which people were denounced as witches in the seventeenth century. While the plot of *The Crucible* begins with accusations by afflicted children, whose perceptible ailments and later testimony are considered a form of "proof," the characters eventually begin to spiral and denounce each other to deflect from their own accusations. Similar to how "Young Goodman Brown" allows the reader to perceive the world through the eyes of a conspiracy theorist (Butter 2014, 109), *The Crucible* stages the compulsive search for connections in willing suspension of contingency characteristic of conspiracy theorizing.

Narrative passages inserted in the first act, beginning with "A Note on the Historical Accuracy of this Play," make this allegorical reading explicit. Initially providing context about the setting of the play, including information about Puritans and their theocratic society as well as the historical background of the Salem witch trials, the paratext shifts its focus as the plot progresses:

> Our difficulty in believing the [...] political inspiration of the Devil is due in great part to the fact that he is called up and damned not only by our social antagonists but by our own side, whatever it may be. [...] In the countries of

the Communist ideology, all resistance of any import is linked to the totally malign capitalist succubi, and in America any man who is not reactionary in his views is open to charge of alliance with the Red hell. [...] A political policy is equated with moral right, and opposition to it with diabolical malevolence. Once such an equation is effectively made, society becomes a congeries of plots and counterplots, and the main role of government changes from that of the arbiter to that of the scourge of God. [...] The analogy, however, seems to falter when one considers that, while there were no witches then, there are Communists and capitalists now, and in each camp there is certain proof that spies of each side are at work undermining each other [Miller 1990, 54–57].

As with "Young Goodman Brown," the recourse to Puritanism is functional for the text's representation of a specific conspiratorial narrative. With its binary worldview, the Puritan ideology lends itself as a foil for negotiating conspiracy thinking ("plots and counterplots") and the way the United States legitimates this kind of thinking by juxtaposing self and other, good and bad, "moral right" and "diabolical malevolence," in a way that aligns with American exceptionalism. If not for witches per se, think about the abundance of references to ideas like the "city upon a hill" in political speeches that also support this idea of the morally righteous, superior position of the United States that dates back to an era when that sense of election was used to legitimate violence against indigenous populations and, among the settlers themselves, alleged witches.

At first glance, the paratextual elements support the idea that the WITCH has, over time, become a variable signifier detached from "actual" witches, a symbol of transgression threatening the existing (social) order. However, the explanatory passages at the same time show how certain connotations survive their translation to a new context. When conjuring the image of the "Red hell," for example, Miller highlights how in contemporary uses of the WITCH, secular and metaphysical conspiracy theories partly converge through the use of religious rhetoric. In addition, as we will see in contemporary examples, the image of the WITCH—which carries with it a history of misogyny and femicide on the one hand and a history of conspiracy theorizing on the other—continues to be a strategy of undermining or attacking women.

Denunciation, Delegitimization, Deflection: The WITCH and Contemporary Conspiratorial Narratives

A recent example for the resurfacing of the WITCH in line with the narratives and motifs discussed here is the Pizzagate conspiracy theory, which links older rumors about the involvement of the Clintons in child pornography with Satanism and cannibalism. Pizzagate emerged on the internet forum 4chan, where several anonymous users scoured leaked private emails from John Podesta, Hillary Clinton's campaign manager, for alleged evidence of prominent Democratic Party members' involvement in a child pornography ring. Among these emails was one from performance artist Marina Abramovic, a friend of Podesta's, mentioning an upcoming "Spirit Cooking" event. The 4chan users fashioned from this the narrative of a satanic pedophile ring, allegedly operating from a pizzeria in Washington (Tuters et al. 2018). Shortly thereafter, a confidant of Donald Trump spread the rumor that at the Spirit Cooking event, John Podesta consumed the blood and other bodily fluids of children (Bleakley 2023). Abramovic subsequently faced defamation on social media, being labeled a Satanist and witch. In a telephone interview with *The New York Times*, the artist recounted the harassment she endured and clarified: "There was no human blood, or baby serving, or sex orgies" (Marshall 2020, n.p.).

Elements of the cumulative concept of witchcraft are here integrated into a new macro-narrative, which forms the nexus of a network of several conspiratorial narratives. Additionally, conspiracy rumors are disseminated without substantiation for the accusations—a characteristic feature, according to Butter (2018), of contemporary conspiracy thinking (181). The centuries-old motif of the witches' sabbath is updated and now serves the purpose of defaming political opponents and a specific form of elite criticism. Ultimately, this also reveals an interesting parallel to early modern witch-hunts, which were often similarly instrumentalized for the resolution of economic, social, and political conflicts (Tschacher 2001, 50).*

Notably, however, when the witch-hunt is used as a metaphor for describing a dynamic of persecution within the context of a specific political (rather than metaphysical) conspiracy theory, it is often used *by* elite groups or individuals belonging to a hegemonic group to delegitimize their opponents or minorities. Donald Trump has repeatedly invoked this metaphor, claiming to be the target of the greatest witch-hunt of all time (Münger 2023). Likewise, in the #MeToo debate in German-speaking countries, the witch-hunt metaphor was frequently used as a counteraccusation against allegations of sexual abuse perpetrated by men (Stokowski

---

*"The allegations of Satanic abuse were not entirely a fabrication of contemporary non-factual news producers, however. There is a lengthy history in the United States, and globally, of organized child abuse being linked to Satanic rituals, dating back to at least the early 1980s" (Bleakley 2023, 518). The circular logic of conspiracy theorizing becomes particularly evident if one considers how conspiracy theories such as those surrounding the "Pizzagate" are subsequently taken up by other conspiracy theories, for example, by the QAnon movement.

2018). In both cases, the metaphor is employed to deflect or refute justified accusations (against men). While *men* take up this image to criticize their own alleged prosecution, which they consider unjustified and baseless, the metaphor never leaves its gendered place since the witch-hunt ultimately remains a rhetorical tool of delegitimizing *women*. That is, even in cases that seemingly invert the logic, the image of the WITCH remains tied not necessarily to women per se, but to its misogynistic roots that facilitated the link between women and witches in the first place.

* * *

The diachronic examination of the interplay of historical and cultural contexts in which conspiracy theories about witches/WITCHES have been developed, disseminated, reinterpreted, and instrumentalized, and continue to be, along with the transmedial and comparatist analysis of significant case studies, elucidates overarching principles of conspiracy thinking. On the one hand, our examples revealed the characteristic linking of disparate events, people, and structures to perceived parts of the same large-scale conspiracy inherent in conspiracy thinking. On the other, the diachronic approach allowed us to map a discursive network spanning several centuries regarding witches, which, through the adoption of motifs and the updating of narratives associated with witches/WITCHES in ever-new media and under changing medial regimes, has produced its own manifestations of the WITCH over time, continuing to do so into our present day.

By implementing the perspective outlined here in the classroom, students are able to develop a deepened awareness of history by tracing the long duration of communication forms such as propaganda and forms of disinformation, and their frequent utilization for conspiracy theories over several centuries and in their dissemination across continents. We maintain that textual analysis can become a first step in developing media and historical literacies, with hope that such an effort will translate to social literacy outside the classroom and continue to make us all less susceptible to conspiratorial narratives.

REFERENCES

Primary Sources

Hawthorne, Nathaniel. (2003 [1835].) "Young Goodman Brown." In *The Norton Anthology of American Literature: 1820–1865 (Vol. B)*, edited by Nina Baym, 1263–72. New York: Norton.

Kramer, Heinrich (Institoris). (2001 [c. 1486]). *Der Hexenhammer: Malleus Maleficarum*. Translated by Wolfgang Behringer, Günter Jerouschek, and Werner Tschacher, edited by Günter Jerouschek and Wolfgang Behringer. München: dtv. Digital version at München,

Bayerische Staatsbibliothek—2 Inc.s.a. 836: https://www.digitale-sammlungen.de/view/bsb00043229?page=20%2C21.
Miller, Arthur. (1990 [1953]). *The Crucible*. Stuttgart: Reclam.
Molitoris, Ulrich. (1997 [1508]). "Von den unholden oder hexen." In *Ulrich Molitoris: Schriften*, edited by Jörg Mauz, 138–180. Konstanz: Verlag am Hockgraben. Digital version of the German treatise at München, Bayerische Staatsbibliothek—Res/4 H.g.hum. 16 o: https://www.digitale-sammlungen.de/de/view/bsb10897899?page=60).
Rowlandson, Mary White. (2003 [1682]). "A Narrative of the Captivity and Restoration of Mrs. Mary Rowlandson." In *The Norton Anthology of American Literature: Literature to 1820 (Vol. A)*, edited by Nina Baym, 309–40. New York: Norton.
Zauberey ([1626]). Pamphlet with print graphic by Michael Herr, Latin text by Johann Ludwig Gottfried, German text by anon., and edited by Matthäus Merian der Ältere. Digital version at the Germanisches Nationalmuseum—HB802: http://objektkatalog.gnm.de/objekt/HB802.

Secondary Sources

Bailey, Michael David. (2002). "The Feminization of Magic and the Emerging Idea of the Female Witch in the Late Middle Ages." In *Essays in Medieval Studies* 19: 120–134.
Blauert, Andreas. (2004). "Frühe Hexenverfolgungen in der Schweiz, am Bodensee und am Oberrhein." In *Wider alle Hexerei und Teufelswerk: Die europäische Hexenverfolgung und ihre Auswirkungen auf Südwestdeutschland*, edited by Sönke Lorenz and Jürgen Michael Schmidt and the Institut für Geschichtliche Landeskunde und Historische Hilfswissenschaften of the Universität Tübingen, 119–130. Ostfildern: Jan Thorbecke Verlag.
Bleakley, Paul. (2023). "Panic, Pizza and Mainstreaming the Alt-Right: A Social Media analysis of Pizzagate and the Rise of the QAnon Conspiracy." *Current Sociology* 71 (3): 509–525. https://doi.org/10.1177/00113921211034896.
Broedel, Hans Peter. (2002). "To Preserve the Manly Form from so Vile a Crime: Ecclesiastical Anti- Sodomitic Rhetoric and the Gendering of Witchcraft in the Malleus Maleficarum." In *Essays in Medieval Studies* 19: 135–148.
Butter, Michael. (2014). *Plots, Designs, and Schemes: American Conspiracy Theories from the Puritans to the Present*. Berlin: De Gruyter.
_____. (2018). *"Nichts ist, wie es scheint": Über Verschwörungstheorien*. Berlin: Suhrkamp Verlag.
Davies, Owen. (2013). *America Bewitched: The Story of Witchcraft After Salem*. Oxford: Oxford University Press.
Dillinger, Johannes. (2007). *Hexen und Magie: Eine historische Einführung*. Frankfurt am Main: Campus Verlag.
Fitz, Karsten, and Florian Zitzelsberger. (2023). "Viral Media: American Studies, Information and Media Literacy, and the COVID-19 Pandemic." In *Innovative Lehrkräftebildung, digitally enhanced*, edited by Ines Brachmann et al., 85–144. Passau: Pressbooks. https://oer.pressbooks.pub/skilldeopenbook/chapter/viral-media-american-studies-media-literacy-and-the-covid-19-pandemic/.
Gold, Julia. (2016). *'Von den vnholden oder hexen': Studien zu Text und Kontext eines Traktats des Ulrich Molitoris*. Hildesheim: Weidmann.
Greenblatt, Stephen. (1995). "Culture." In *Critical Terms for Literary Study*, edited by Frank Lentricchia and Thomas McLaughlin, 225–232. Chicago: University of Chicago Press.
Holze, Regina, and Florian Zitzelsberger. (2021). "Teaching as Sharing: Hashtag Activism and Information and Media Literacy." *F&E Edition* 27: 79–90.
Jakob, Hans-Joachim. (2020). "Michael Herr, Matthäus Merian der Ältere und Johann Klaj: Bild und Text im Flugblatt *Eigentlicher Entwurf und Abbildung deß Gottlosen und verfluchten Zauber Festes*." In *Johann Klaj (um 1616-1656): Akteur—Werk—Umfeld*, edited by Dirk Niefanger and Werner Wilhelm Schnabel, 625–644. Berlin: De Gruyter. https://doi.org/10.1515/9783110669480-023.
Jerouschek, Günter, and Wolfgang Behringer. (2001). "'Das unheilvollste Buch der Weltliteratur?' Zur Entstehungs- und Wirkungsgeschichte des Malleus Maleficarum und

zu den Anfängen der He-xenverfolgung." In Heinrich Kramer (Institoris), *Der Hexenhammer: Malleus Maleficarum*, translated by Wolfgang Behringer, Günter Jerouschek, and Werner Tschacher, edited by Günter Jerouschek and Wolfgang Behringer, 9–98. München: dtv.

Makeschin, Sarah. (2019). "Der Information-and-Media-Literacy-Think-Tank: Eine Forderung nach neuem Denken und Partizipation in der universitären Lehre im digitalen Zeitalter." *PAradigma* 9: 166–180.

Marshall, Alex. (2020). "Marina Abramovic Just Wants Conspiracy Theorists to Let Her Be." *New York Times*, April 21. https://www.nytimes.com/2020/04/21/arts/design/marina-abramovic-satanist-conspiracy-theory.html.

"McCarthyism and the Red Scare." (n.d.). *Miller Center*. Accessed March 20, 2024. https://millercenter.org/the-presidency/educational-resources/age-of-eisenhower/mcarthyism-red-scare.

Meyers, Kevin. (1999). "Miller Recounts McCarthy Era, Origins of 'The Crucible.'" *The Harvard Crimson*. Accessed March 20, 2024. https://www.thecrimson.com/article/1999/5/12/miller-recounts-mccarthy-era-origins-of/.

Miller, Perry. (1983). *The New England Mind: From Colony to Province*. Cambridge: Harvard University Press.

Münger, Felix. (2023). "Schiefe historische Parallelen—Trumps Mär von der 'grössten Hexenjagd aller Zeiten.'" *Radio SRF2 Kultur*, October 6. https://www.srf.ch/kultur/gesellschaft-religion/schiefe-historische-parallelen-trumps-maer-von-der-groessten-hexenjagd-aller-zeiten.

Pollak, Guido, Jan-Oliver Decker, Karsten Fitz, Alexander Glas, Viola Huang, Dorothe Knapp, Sarah Makeschin, et al. (2019). "Interdisziplinäre Grundlagen der Information und Media Literacy (IML): Theoretische Begründung und (hochschul-)didaktische Realisierung—Ein Positionspapier." *PAradigma* 9: 14–129.

Reed, Isaac. (2007). "Why Salem Made Sense: Culture, Gender, and the Puritan Persecution of Witchcraft." *Cultural Sociology* 1(2): 209–234.

Sivils, Matthew. (2014). "Indian Captivity Narratives and the Origins of American Frontier Gothic." In *A Companion to American Gothic*, edited by Charles Crow, 84–95. Hoboken: Wiley.

Stokowski, Margarete. (2018). "Hexen, überall Hexen?" *Spiegel Online*, January 23. https://www.spiegel.de/kultur/gesellschaft/hexenjagd-ist-was-anderes-ihr-memmen-kolumne-von-margarete-stokowski-a-1189301.html.

Tschacher, Werner. (2001). "Vom Feindbild zur Verschwörungstheorie: Das Hexenstereotyp." In *Verschwörungstheorien: Anthropologische Konstanten—historische Varianten*, edited by Ute Caumanns and Mathias Niendorf, 49–74. Osnabrück: fibre Verlag.

Tuters, Marc, Emilija Jokubauskaitė, and Daniel Bach. (2018). "Post-Truth Protest: How 4chan Cooked Up the Pizzagate Bullshit." *M/C Journal* 21 (3). https://doi.org/10.5204/mcj.1422.

Voltmer, Rita, and Franz Irsigler. (2002). "Die europäischen Hexenverfolgungen der Frühen Neuzeit: Vorurteile, Faktoren und Bilanzen." In *Hexenwahn. Ängste der Neuzeit. Begleitband zur gleichnamigen Ausstellung des Deutschen Historischen Museums, Berlin, Kronprinzenpalais 3. Mai bis 6. August 2002*, edited by Rosmarie Beier-de Haan, Rita Voltmer and Franz Irsigler, 30–45. Wolfratshausen: Edition Minerva.

Zitzelsberger, Florian, and Julia Siwek. (2023). "Mit der Denkfabrik gegen das Querdenken: "Propaganda, Verschwörungsmythen, Fake News in historischer Perspektive"—Ein interdisziplinäres Format zur Stärkung der historical literacy in der Lehrkräftebildung." *DiLab Blog*. Accessed March 20, 2024. https://blog.dilab.uni-passau.de/propaganda-verschwoerungsmythen-und-fake-news-in-historischer-perspektive-interdisziplinaerer-think-tank-zur-information-and-media-literacy-iml/.

A Symbol for Hope

Superman's Battle with the KKK as a Model for Effective Cultural Engagement with Conspiracy Theories

COLIN MCROBERTS

Introduction

Popular culture overflows with heroes and villains imported from the real world. As consumers gravitate towards these characters mass media passively becomes a map of contemporary attitudes. Indiana Jones fights Nazis and Neo fights conformity because their writers saw those things as natural villains; because audiences agree, the stories become enduring. Modern popular culture treats conspiracy theories far more sympathetically. Audiences have a high tolerance for even very toxic irrational beliefs, despite the real and dramatic harm they do, and popular culture reflects that passive acceptance. This passive mapping of popular culture to prevailing attitudes is not the only path forwards, though. Precedent shows that writers can consciously choose to use their creations to shift public perception.

This essay presents one such example, when the writers of the 1940s Superman radio serial used their stories and their audience to confront the real Ku Klux Klan. They created hugely popular stories that focused audiences on the damage the Klan did and its hateful, cynical beliefs instead of its carefully cultivated, self-aggrandizing mythology. Their success is impossible to quantify, but they challenged public apathy and helped prevent the Klan's resurgence. Modern popular culture, though, has largely failed to do the same for the conspiracy theories that grew out of the Klan's motivating beliefs. The essay concludes by comparing the two approaches. If more contemporary creators were to make the same choice the Superman writers did, it could similarly help refocus public perceptions on the harm done by toxic, irrational communities rather than dignifying them.

An Action Hero as a Tool for Action

The 1940s radio serial *The Adventures of Superman* was a charming mixture of cereal ads and family-friendly drama. Mid–Atlantic accents narrated the walloping victories of Superman and various gutsy lawmen, intrepid reporters, and precocious kids over a succession of mostly imaginary villains. From early on, though, the writers occasionally used Superman to fight proxy battles against real-world evils. He famously trounced the Nazis in *Look* magazine, seizing Hitler (and Stalin, in a two-panel afterthought) for extrajudicial rendition to the League of Nations (Siegel and Shuster 1940). The comic drew scorn from one of the most popular newspapers in Nazi Germany, *Das Schwarze Korps*—the official publication of the *Schutzstaffel* and the "most widely feared organ of the National Socialist press" (Combs 1982, 11, 14; Hoehne 1971, 248). Its dismal review sneered at the Nazi characters' poor German and Superman's lack of "strategic sense and tactical ability, storming the West Wall in shorts."* But the main complaint of the SS was that Superman was subverting "the noble yearnings of American children" by seeding "suspicion, evil, laziness, and criminality in their young hearts" ("Jerry Siegel Attacks!" n.d.). What higher praise could there be for Superman or his creators, Jerry Siegel and Joe Shuster? The Nazis despised them, and not just because they were Jewish. Himmler's propagandists understood that their stories were a true threat.

Nazis figured less prominently in the radio serial. They crept in from time to time as spies and mad scientists, but the show focused more on mobsters, smugglers, pirates, and occasionally corrupt businessmen and government officials. Especially with the end of the war there was room for an enemy worthy of Superman: something vile enough to fit into the simple moral geometry of a radio serial and real enough to carry weight. The writers found the Ku Klux Klan.

The Klan, founded in 1865, had already reinvented itself twice by those post-war years. Defeated Confederates created it as a guerrilla force and weapon for white supremacy, but they overreached. Their heinous violence provoked public outrage and aggressive responses from Congress, including the Ku Klux Klan Act of 1871—portions of which are still

---

**Das Schwarze Korps* 1940; "Jerry Siegel Attacks!," n.d. It is hardly the worst sin of the review, but Superman's brief, bold, and tight shorts are an artistic triumph.

critical elements of modern civil rights legislation.* Not long afterwards, as Reconstruction drew to a close, the weakened Klan simply became less relevant. It existed to curb Black political and economic power with the threat of violence, but Southern state governments were increasingly able to do it through the statehouse (SPLC 2011, 15). That first and most militant version of the Klan lived its life in the nineteenth century and withered shortly before the patenting of the telephone.

Entrepreneurs revived the Klan in the early twentieth century. A preacher and his followers reconsecrated it at Stone Mountain, near Atlanta, in 1915. They erected a burning cross to mark the occasion, echoing a notorious lynch mob that had, in turn, lifted the symbol from the novel that inspired the film *Birth of a Nation* (Bulger 1992, 182). The Klan understood the powers of symbolism and popular culture very well. And this iteration of it was phenomenally successful for a time. In the mid-1920s, the Klan claimed over five million members—nearly one in twenty white Americans (Bulger 1992, 183).

This wave would also recede. Slow economic, demographic, and political shifts probably did the most damage, but erupting scandals around a prominent KKK leader played a significant part. David Stephenson was the Grand Dragon for Indiana, a Klan stronghold, and one of the chief recruiters for the entire organization. He helped elect the governor in 1925, then savagely raped and murdered a woman he met at the inaugural ball (Abbott 2012). His prominence and the fact that his victim was white brought his crimes to the attention of a country that had paid far too little attention to the Klan's violence against marginalized victims.

At the time, many white Americans saw the Klan as an upstanding civic organization, and its members often "passed as honorable citizens" (Gordon 2018, 18). The Stephenson scandal undermined that fiction and membership collapsed (Mitchell 2018). It took a dramatically public story, though, to make white America pay attention to what Klan leaders really stood for. Before that, and to a somewhat lesser extent afterwards, the Klan was able to leverage its skill at mythmaking and public relations to create a more benign image for itself. The blow to that image was a turning point that marked a sharp decline in their power.

The Klan resurged again in 1946, when it returned to Stone Mountain. The site is deeply significant to the Klan, which had helped organize the creation of its enormous monument. The mountain hosts the largest bas-relief carving in the world, twelve thousand square feet honoring Confederate heroes and champions of slavery. The project's backers supported the Klan in turn, and but for a shortfall in funding the monument

---

*See, e.g., 42 U.S.C. § 1983.

might have included hooded night riders (Miranda 2023). So, in 1946, a new generation of Klan leaders chose the site for the re-reconsecration of the KKK. This time, the ceremony included dire threats of death for any who would give up the organization's secrets (Bowers 2012, 128).

This iteration of the Klan was not as powerful as the second wave, but it was still the insidious Invisible Empire. It did not need massive membership drives and access to mainstream politicians to attack, torture, and murder Americans. It did need a public image and cachet to spread its ideology, recruit members, and motivate violence. It built that image using "invented traditions and folklore" (Bulger 1992, 192). This wave of the Klan, like the last, was adept at building a powerful and transmissible cachet. If it was less monolithic than the previous version, it was also more enduring. This fragmented but virulent Klan, with deep roots and a talent for survival, was the enemy Superman found for those transformative post-war years.

Putting Superman into Action Against the Klan

The link between the writers of Superman and the Klan runs through a complicated man, William Stetson Kennedy. Kennedy was born to privilege, but he was a "traitor to his race and class" (Roberts 2011). He spent years working with a New Deal initiative that employed writers to record the country's folklore. He uncovered and documented "such living traditions as bawdy songs, prostitute narratives, urban traditions, and the folklore of the Florida tourism industry" (Bulger 1992, 22). He was decades ahead of many of the experts in his field, who would take a generation to catch up to his understanding of popular culture (Bulger 1992, 22). His experiences helped build in him a deep contempt for racism, and particularly the Ku Klux Klan.

Kennedy was a complicated man, and there is a great deal of uncertainty about the veracity of his exploits. He was certainly a resolute enemy of the Klan. He worked with various collaborators to infiltrate it, and by the time the Klan kicked off its third wave, Kennedy had already begun exposing their violence and peculiar rituals (Bowers 2012, 111). When the Klan reinvented itself in the second Stone Mountain ceremony, he was allegedly there undercover (Bulger 1992, 192). From the very beginning, his expertise in folklore and culture helped him understand how dependent it was on its image. That understanding would be vital in his campaign against it (Bulger 1992, 193).

Kennedy worked against the Klan in many ways, launching legal attacks on local chapters' charters and feeding information about their violence to other journalists and law enforcement (Bulger 1992, 204–05). These efforts had a real impact, but the Klan was resilient to op eds, lawsuits and criminal trials. Even in its diminished state it was well-resourced, popular, and politically influential in its strongholds. Searching for a way to affect public opinion more broadly, Kennedy turned to his expertise in popular culture.

> The Superman idea came one day when I saw a group of small boys playing with secret passwords in much the same way that grown men played with them in the Klan. Why not get the Klan's secret password into the mouths of kids? It would make a laughing stock out of the Klan's gobbledygook rigamarole! But to do any good this would have to be done all across the country. It was then that I thought of Superman. The radio version of this fabulous, jet-propelled character ... had already won national recognition for going after real villains, including hate-mongers [Kennedy 2011, 92].

Kennedy writes here about sharing the Klan's passwords, and he told wonderful stories about how the Klan fumbled to change them in secret meetings (Kennedy 2011, 91–94). One suggestion was supposedly "Damn Superman!" so that censors would keep the serial from airing it (Kennedy 2011, 94). But these accounts are not completely true. The show does not seem to have used any Klan passwords, and Kennedy later acknowledged taking creative liberties with his accounts (Patton 2006; Bulger 1992, 207).

Wherever the line between truth and fiction is, Kennedy did work with the Superman serial to attack the Klan. Contemporary reports describe him as a consultant hired to add authenticity to its stories (Bulger 1992, 319). He has even been credited with proposing the storyline in the first place (Kennedy 2011, 3). This was consistent with his campaign against the Klan overall. He disclosed Klan secrets through other channels, such as a confidante who was also a prominent columnist and radio broadcaster (Bulger 1992, 205). In 1946, the Georgia governor affirmed that his investigations "facilitated Georgia's prosecution of the Ku Klux Klan" (Patton 2006). The most telling witness of all must be the Klan itself. It found him troubling enough to put a bounty on "the traitor's ass" (Bulger 1992, 207). Kennedy was a real threat to the Klan, and Superman was an important part of that work.

The serial addressed the Klan in 1946 with a series of episodes called "*The Clan of the Fiery Cross*."* It never mentioned the KKK by name, but there was no mistaking the villains as anything else. The fictitious Clan's leaders included a "Grand Scorpion" and "Grand Imperial Mogul," clear

---

**The Hate Monger's Organization* was another Superman arc that aired earlier that year. In it, the "Guardians of America" planned to use divisive lies to pit Americans of different races and religions against each other. It spoke to similar themes as *The Clan of the Fiery Cross* but is not as well remembered today.

references to the real Klan's menagerie of Grand Cyclopses, Grand Dragons, Grand Ensigns, Grand Exchequers, Grand Giants, Grand Magi, Grand Marshals, Grand Monks, Grand Schubladens, Grand Scribes, Grand Sentinels, Grand Titans, Grand Turks, and Grand Wizards.* The subtle changes were likely just a ploy to avoid legal complications with a defensive, well-connected, and well-resourced Klan (Bowers 2012, 136).

The story in *The Clan of the Fiery Cross* is as straightforward as a 1940s radio drama can be. A young white baseball player complains to his uncle because his Chinese American teammate is outshining him. The uncle turns out to be the Grand Scorpion of the Clan of the Fiery Cross, kicking off a variety of violent and racist plots. Superman and his friends at the Daily Planet thwart the evildoers and redeem the young player, who gives the paper valuable intelligence about the Clan. The racist uncle flees to his superior, the Grand Imperial Mogul, but they end up fighting amongst themselves. The Scorpion kills the Mogul, then tries to assassinate Superman's friend Jimmy Olsen. Superman foils the plan and delivers him to the police. In the end, the Scorpion's nephew redeems himself and the boys' team wins the big game.

If these episodes lacked genuine secret passwords, they revealed more important truths: the Klan was petty, unamerican, and a fraud. Despite its pomp and circumstance, it was not an ancient and impressive organization—it was a club for thugs that milked its gullible members to feed the con artists at the top. The confrontation between the Grand Scorpion and the Grand Imperial Mogul is not subtle:

> Mogul: Now, in addition to the police, you've got Superman looking for us. Do you realize what that means? Just when we were launching a huge new membership drive? This will cost us 10,000 new members.
> Scorpion: Maybe not, Wilson.
> Mogul: Maybe, nothing! Your fool stunt cost us ten thousand new members who would have paid us $100 apiece for initiation fees and another $25 for robes and hoods. That means over $1 million we would have split.
> Scorpion: Oh, what's money got to do with the spot we're in now?
> Mogul: What's money got to do with it?
> Scorpion: Yes, after all we're not in this only for money.
> Mogul: No? What have you been doing with the 25% cut you get on all new members to the Metropolis chapter and the 10% cut on their robes? Giving it to charity?
> Scorpion: Certainly not. I like money, sure, but aside from that I'm also working to purify America, to clean it of foreigners.
> Mogul: Oh, come now, Riggs.... Wait a minute. Is it possible that you really

---

*See, e.g., Lester and Wilson 1905.

believe all that stuff about getting rid of the foreigners? That one race, one religion, one color hokum? ... Well, I'll be. I thought you had brains, Riggs, but obviously something's happened to you. You've become drunk on the slop we put up for the suckers.

SCORPION: Suckers? Who are you calling—

MOGUL: Our members, Riggs. The poor fish who want to hate and blame somebody else for their failures in life. The saps who believe drivel such as a man is a dangerous enemy because he goes to a different church. The little nobodies who want to believe some of the races inferior so they can feel superior. The jerks who go for that "100% American"* rot.

SCORPION: Rot? You mean you don't believe?

MOGUL: Of course not. You must know there is no such thing as what we call a hundred percent American. Everyone here except the Indians is descended from foreigners.... I'm running a business, Riggs, and so are you. We deal in one of the oldest and most profitable commodities on earth: hate. Your mistake was when you forgot you were a businessman and began believing your own sales talk ["*The Clan of the Fiery Cross*, Episode 14" 1946 (transcribed by the author)].

This was an insightful indictment of the Klan. It was a business, and particularly in its second iteration—the high-water mark of its membership and power—a spectacularly profitable one. Before his fall, David Stephenson earned more than twice as much as Babe Ruth (Fryer and Levitt 2007, 33). The money came from initiation and other fees, such as the sale of members' signature robes. Cheaply made and sold to Klansmen at a huge markup, they turned a large profit for the Klan's leaders (Fryer and Levitt 2007, 30). Membership fees came from an enormous customer base, as anywhere from five to fourteen percent of the eligible population may have been members at one point (Fryer and Levitt 2007, 8–9).

Economists have argued that, rather than a supervillain, the Klan at its peak would be "better described as a wildly successful pyramid scheme" (Fryer and Levitt 2007, 4). Of course, it was not just a pyramid scheme. Its lasting impact comes from the violence it committed and the hate it spread, not its business success.

By the 1940s, when the Superman serial took aim at the Klan, its membership had decayed considerably. It was not dying, though, but transforming into the smaller and more clandestine gang it is today. There was a reason it transformed instead of simply dissolving into new daughter organizations; its image, derived partly from the memory of its powerful heights, was a powerful tool. It needed its victims, supporters, and bystanders all to see it as mysterious, determined, and inevitable. Without

---

*"100% American" was a prominent Klan slogan (Gordon 2018). For example, one of the Klan's moneymaking schemes was selling a "Kluxer's Knifty Knife," a "real 100 percent knife for 100 percent Americans" (Rice 1972, 18–19).

that weight behind it, it would have been a much less terrifying force and less attractive to potential members. It bolstered that image with "invented traditions and folklore" to reinforce its cachet as a powerful and dignified institution (Bulger 1992, 192). Superman was a perfect tool for attacking that image.

The Impacts on the Klan and the Culture

Kennedy saw the subtle and powerful blow that Superman dealt to the Klan. "I knew that the millions of kids who had listened to Superman were not likely to grow up to be Klansmen" (Kennedy 2011, 94). It exercised the influence of popular culture on the people standing at the margins: not just children, but anyone casually familiar with the Klan and not yet possessed of strong feelings about it. People directly tied to the Klan—as enthusiastic supporters or as victims—would have inflexible beliefs about it. Those on the margin, though, would be more open to a narrative framework that cast it as a buffoonish, cynical, for-profit, and utterly debased gang of murderers. Their later encounters with the KKK would always come in the context of that early impression, making for a much more significant and long-lasting stamp.

It is highly likely, given the show's young audience and Kennedy's direct reference to them, that this was the strategy. The Klan understood the threat. It put a bounty on Kennedy for the same reason that *Das Schwarze Korps* attacked his collaborators' anti–Nazi work. These organizations were fighting more than just a culture war, but their real-world power depended in part on the power of their image and reputation. Superman helped push an enormous change in how mainstream America perceived the Klan. The impact on the Klan's membership and influence is not quantifiable, but the show was very popular with the generation that would grow up to increasingly reject it. The serial boasted four million listeners even before *The Clan of the Fiery Cross* debuted, and the success of that arc made the show "the undisputed leader in children's radio" (Bowers 2012, 118, 143). There were other and greater drivers of the KKK's decline, of course, but the Superman arc reached an audience few other tactics could. Over a generation the country progressed from a nation where hooded night riders were seen as heroes fit for major motion pictures and national monuments to one in which the Klan was as much an unambiguous villain as the Nazis. Popular culture was not just the venue where that change happened. It consciously helped lead that change, as part of a considered and rational strategy to make a difference.

Lessons for Engagement with the Culture of Conspiracy Theories

The KKK was and is more than just a nexus of conspiracy theories, and not all conspiracy theories are dangerous, prejudiced, or even false.* But its attacks on vulnerable minorities always relied on manufacturing and spreading lies about them.† The point was to create fear (Gordon 2018, 55). That project still exists and serves the interests of the Klan's fellow travelers. Relatively few people are willing to admit to being explicit racists, compared to the Klan's heyday, but extremists will still march with torches to act out their manufactured fear of the "Great Replacement." Their refrain betrays the bigotry behind the conspiracy theory: "Jews will not replace us."‡ The conspiracy theory is inseparable from the bigotry. Its evangelists are promoting the conspiratorial fear that hidden powers are intentionally importing non-white people and cultures to supplant white America—and it has become a mainstay of conspiracy theory culture.§

Popular culture has not responded to the spread of such conspiracy theories with the same muscle that Siegel and Shuster did in the 1940s. That is not to say that it has not responded to the spread of conspiracy theories at all. There are far more conspiracy theorist characters in modern popular culture than there were Klansmen in 1940s radio serials, so it may seem unfair to say that the issue has gone unaddressed. In fact, that would be saying too little. Modern entertainment elevates and celebrates conspiracy theories more often than it confronts the damage they do.

The clearest example of this are characters like Fox Mulder of *The X-Files*. He represents a common trend in the portrayal of conspiracy theorists: the crusader. These characters see plots in the shadows because those plots exist. The audience knows that the protagonist is right about everything and sympathizes with their noble struggle against both the conspirators and doubters. Skeptics exist so the conspiracy theorist can win them over, or as dupes, or as villains; their skepticism is an obstacle the hero overcomes.

Characters like Mulder are heroes to conspiracy theorists because they are idealized. They represent the best possible case for someone whose identity becomes bound up in believing impossible things: they are gifted,

---

*For an insightful discussion of true conspiracy theories, and conspiracy theories used by marginalized groups instead of against them, see chapter two of Anna Merlan's *Republic of Lies* (Merlan 2019).
†See, e.g., Gordon 2018, 48–49.
‡https://www.nytimes.com/2023/04/18/us/charlottesville-rally-indictment.html.
§See, e.g., Rose 2022; Wilson and Flanagan 2022; Confessore and Yourish 2022; "'The Great Replacement': An Explainer" 2021.

righteous, brave, misunderstood, and destined for vindication despite the attacks of unreasonable skeptics. They have some flaws, such as when stories gesture towards the isolation of characters like Mulder or Rorschach, the antihero of the *Watchmen* graphic novel and film. Even these wrinkles become marks of nobility, implied to be the price the characters pay for their purity and insight. These ennobling narratives hardly convey the real damage conspiracy theory culture does to believers who become deeply immersed in it, though, much less the damage to others. If Mulder's obsession sets him back, he will have recovered by the next episode. The real people he is loosely patterned after are less resilient.

Real conspiracy theorists do not experience the vindication inherent to a protagonist. In the wake of the initial Covid-19 vaccines, for example, would-be Mulders confidently predicted that the immunizations were "clot shots" that would slaughter millions. One leading anti-vaccine conspiracy theorist announced to a huge audience, "It's over for humanity. There will be nothing left but lone survivors" (Merlan 2020). They were, thankfully and utterly predictably, wrong. Vaccines saved millions of lives (Agrawal, Sood, and Whaley 2023). Side effects were overwhelmingly mild and handled publicly and forthrightly by experts and authorities. (See, e.g., Blumenthal et al. 2023.) But there is no readily available cultural model for a story where the government was right and the underdog was wrong, capturing the damage done when conspiracy theorists persuaded their friends and family to reject life-saving medicine. (See, e.g., Farhart et al. 2022.) Popular culture gives those conspiracy theorists a heroic archetype to apply to themselves: there is no need to account for the failure of their theories, only to wait for vindication. Heroes persist, they do not tally up the harm they've done and reassess their beliefs.

Some media does cast conspiracy theorists as villains. This is relatively unusual, though, particularly for major characters—and it still tends to ennoble them. For example, the film *Contagion* featured a conspiracy theorist named Krumwiede, who convinces his followers to reject a life-saving vaccine in favor of an herbal remedy. The writers could not resist implying that he might actually be right. A producer explained, "you're not really sure about him. Is the government really hiding something and does the herbal remedy he's talking about really work? I think we all suspect at one time or another that we're not getting the whole truth, and in that sense, Krumwiede represents the audience's point of view" (Warner Bros. 2011). This spin is common for conspiracy theorist characters, not only because the ambiguity is interesting, but also because villains are more compelling when they have power, virtue, or a good argument on their side.

Real conspiracy theorists are far more often marginalized individuals. (See, e.g., Douglas, Sutton, and Cichocka 2017.) They come to their beliefs as a way of explaining and grappling with a world that does not suit them, and that is not a mindset particularly common to the rich and powerful, who find reality more to their liking. But what would be the point of powerless villains? Popular culture inflates them, with ambiguity or coolness or a secret nous, to make them a more compelling threat. Krumwiede would be less interesting as a dangerous opportunist or an irrational anti-vaxxer, so the story preserves the possibility that he has a point.

In between the heroes and the villains are the holy fools, to borrow a term from Orthodox Christianity. In that context, the madness of a holy fool is only a mask for their "sanity and high morality, even pious intent" (Ivanov 2006, 1). Popular culture often puts a similar spin on conspiracy theorists, asking audiences to sympathize with characters who seem deranged on the surface. They are lovable and well-intentioned goofs or irascible but secretly wise madmen, and because they are outside the norm they can carry insights that straightforward characters cannot. The audience can neither take them at face value nor discount them completely.

Randy Quaid's conspiracy theorist in the film *Independence Day* is a holy fool. The movie introduces him as a parody of the tinfoil-hatted conspiracy theorist ranting about alien abductions, but he turns out to have been right all along. His heroic self-sacrifice saves the world that disbelieved and disrespected him. Dale Gribble from the TV series *King of the Hill* is a barely functional lunatic, but his mania and delusions are a major driver of the character's enduring popularity. Joe Rogan's character from the series *NewsRadio* similarly became an audience favorite, presaging the actor's own arc. Characters like these have irrational beliefs that deeply degrade their believers in the real world, but in their fictional context turn out to be literally true or noble quirks. Because these characters' beliefs empower them, they are not accurate portrayals of conspiracy theorists. At the same time, because holy fools are still fools, they are not role models to real conspiracy theorists. Given their popularity, though, they may be the most effective evangelists for real-world conspiracy theories.

Consider, for example, Alex Jones. There are few more prominent conspiracy theorists alive, and none who have been so thoroughly exposed and debunked. His vicious attacks on the parents of murdered children, leading to a billion-dollar defamation judgment and humiliating bankruptcy, were merely one lowlight of a long and shameful career as a professional liar. In contrast to the obscurity of most individual conspiracy theorists, Jones is a household name. His public image is far more positive than his horrific and humiliating record because popular culture has largely adopted him as a holy fool. He appeared in the Richard Linklater movies *Waking Life* (passionately reciting abstract platitudes) and *A Scanner Darkly* (as a street prophet who sees hidden truths). These performances predated his most widely known misdeeds, but even at the time he was a prolific huckster and disseminator of dangerous, hateful lies. More recently an artist skillfully remixed one of his trademark rants into a chill folk song (Swanson 2017). The video was deft, silly, and popular. Jones praised it, shared it, and asked for more; in a calculated trade, the boost it gave his image far outweighed whatever injury it did to his dignity (Ohlheiser 2017; Roettgers 2017). While classic holy fools demonstrated their piety by suffering real degradations, Jones offered only the appearance of humility. Since the appearance of sincerity is all he needed in return, it was a profitable trade. It was only possible because the popular culture criticism to which he was responding highlighted the amusing absurdity of his work instead of showing the damage that he does.

That damage is terrible, and not dissimilar to that done by the Klan in its various incarnations. This essay is far too short to describe the damage of conspiracy theorists in general, Jones's career shows how dangerous they can be. He practices what has been described as "stochastic terrorism, or the use of mass media to provoke random acts of ideologically motivated violence that are statistically predictable but individually unpredictable" (Hamm and Spaaij 2017, 84). Researchers have tied his influence to lethal shootings. (See, e.g., Hamm and Spaiij 2017, 86, 113, 138.) He and his devotees have done enormous non-violent harm as well, such as the well-documented persecution of the parents of children slain at Sandy Hook Elementary School. (See, e.g., Williamson 2022.) Those devotees are victims themselves; as they fall into the well of conspiracy theory culture, they become less able to engage meaningfully and productively with the world around them. Jones contributes to their alienation and isolation, as many conspiracy theory leaders do, because they would reject his alternative realities if they were more able to manage the real world.

What if popular culture focused on those aspects of conspiracy theories, instead of making conspiracy theorists out to be self-sacrificing prophets or lovable clowns? The Superman serial chose to tell the truth about the Klan, speaking directly both to its bigotry and the cynical profit motive driving the organization. Modern popular culture has failed to do the same with regards to conspiracy theorists. It sugarcoats them, serving them to audiences as noble heroes and delightful buffoons. The truth is that while not all conspiracy theories are dangerous, there are many that are and that have devoted followings. Those believers undermine public health and democratic institutions and help sow exactly the kind of discord the Klan championed. (See, e.g., Jolley, Marques, and Cookson 2022.)

The Superman serial had an advantage over modern pop culture. It had a huge audience and relatively few competitors (Bowers 2012, 143). Modern fiction can hardly aspire to the same kind of dominance. Pop culture has grown in every way: more makers creating more villains and heroes for more consumers across more distribution channels. The sheer number of stories in circulation has exploded into an immensely more complex cultural environment. Virtually no modern production is ever going to be as powerful as the Superman serials were. Modern creators appealing to more niche audiences may actually find that such messaging helps distinguish them from their competitors.

Any impact the Superman serial had, or could have had, traces back to one decision its makers made: they were willing to try. They had no shortage of villains. They could have invented an endless stream of pirates and gangsters to populate their scripts. They chose to use their fictional characters to speak about, and to, the real world in a way that would not have been possible without taking a risk. They could have failed. The Klan's message was popular in white America, and they might have alienated audiences and sponsors. They might have been pilloried for using a children's show to address mature themes. They might even have suffered violence; Kennedy faced real threats to his life. But they realized that they had a tool at hand that could accomplish something that virtually no one else could. They intentionally used it to do work that could not have been done in any other way. And they did not fail.

Partly for that reason, modern productions are hardly shy about speaking to real social ills; popular culture bursts at the seams with positive messages about any number of serious issues, both because their creators do care about such things and because it can help build sympathetic audiences. Conspiracy theories should be one of those issues. Popular culture can turn its eye on the culture of conspiracy theories in the same way that it once put a spotlight on the culture of the Klan, showing audiences the truth. Modern culture leaders must make the same choice, to win the same victory.

References

Abbott, Karen. (2012). "'Murder Wasn't Very Pretty': The Rise and Fall of D.C. Stephenson." *Smithsonian Magazine*, August 30. Accessed January 4, 2024. https://www.smithsonianmag.com/history/murder-wasnt-very-pretty-the-rise-and-fall-of-dc-stephenson-18935042/.
Agrawal, Virat, Neeraj Sood, and Christopher Whaley. (2023). "The Impact of the Global COVID-19 Vaccination Campaign on All-Cause Mortality." w31812. Cambridge, MA: National Bureau of Economic Research. https://doi.org/10.3386/w31812.
Blumenthal, Kimberly G., Matthew Greenhawt, Elizabeth J. Phillips, Nancy Agmon-Levin, David B.K. Golden, and Marcus Shaker. (2023). "An Update in COVID-19 Vaccine Reactions in 2023: Progress and Understanding." *The Journal of Allergy and Clinical Immunology: In Practice* 11 (11): 3305–18. https://doi.org/10.1016/j.jaip.2023.06.057.
Bowers, Rick. (2012). *Superman versus the Ku Klux Klan: The True Story of How the Iconic Superhero Battled the Men of Hate.* Washington, D.C: National Geographic.

Bulger, Margaret Anne. (1992). "Stetson Kennedy: Applied Folklore and Cultural Advocacy." University of Pennsylvania.

Carolina, A. Miranda. (2023). "How Stone Mountain Weaponized Art against Black People, in a Compelling New Documentary." *Los Angeles Times*, January 12. https://www.latimes.com/entertainment-arts/story/2023-01-12/monument-untold-story-stone-mountain-examines-largest-confederate-monument.

"Clan of the Fiery Cross, Episode 14." (1946). *The Adventures of Superman*.

Combs, William L. (1982). "The Voice of the SS: A History of the SS Journal Das Schwarze Korps." Purdue University.

Confessore, Nicholas, and Karen Yourish. (2022). "A Fringe Conspiracy Theory, Fostered Online, Is Refashioned by the G.O.P.", May 16, sec. U.S. https://www.nytimes.com/2022/05/15/us/replacement-theory-shooting-tucker-carlson.html.

Das Schwarze Korps. (1940). "Jerry Siegel Greift Ein!" April 25.

Douglas, Karen M., Robbie M. Sutton, and Aleksandra Cichocka. (2017). "The Psychology of Conspiracy Theories." *Current Directions in Psychological Science* 26 (6): 538–42. https://doi.org/10.1177/0963721417718261.

Farhart, Christina E., Ella Douglas-Durham, Krissy Lunz Trujillo, and Joseph A. Vitriol. (2022). "Vax Attacks: How Conspiracy Theory Belief Undermines Vaccine Support." *Progress in Molecular Biology and Translational Science* 188: 135–69. Elsevier. https://doi.org/10.1016/bs.pmbts.2021.11.001.

Fryer, Roland, and Steven Levitt. (2007). "Hatred and Profits: Getting Under the Hood of the Ku Klux Klan." w13417. Cambridge, MA: National Bureau of Economic Research. https://doi.org/10.3386/w13417.

Gordon, Linda. (2018). *The Second Coming of the KKK: The Ku Klux Klan of the 1920s and the American Political Tradition*. New York: Liveright.

"'The Great Replacement': An Explainer." (2021). ADL. April 19, 2021. https://www.adl.org/resources/backgrounder/great-replacement-explainer.

Hamm, Mark S., and Ramón Spaaij. (2017). *The Age of Lone Wolf Terrorism*. New York: Columbia University Press.

Heinz, Hoehne. (1971). *The Order of the Death's Head: The Story of Hitler's SS*. New York: Ballantine.

Ivanov, S.A. (2006). *Holy Fools in Byzantium and Beyond*. Oxford: Oxford University Press.

"Jerry Siegel Attacks!" (n.d.). German Propaganda Archive. Accessed November 13, 2023. https://research.calvin.edu/german-propaganda-archive/superman.htm.

Jolley, Daniel, Mathew D. Marques, and Darel Cookson. (2022). "Shining a Spotlight on the Dangerous Consequences of Conspiracy Theories." *Current Opinion in Psychology* 47 (October): 101363. https://doi.org/10.1016/j.copsyc.2022.101363.

Kennedy, Stetson. (2011). *The Klan Unmasked*. Tuscaloosa: University of Alabama Press.

Lester, John C., and D.L. Wilson. (1905) *Ku Klux Klan: Its Origin, Growth and Disbandment*. https://www.gutenberg.org/ebooks/31819/pg31819-images.html.

Merlan, Anna. (2019). *Republic of Lies: American Conspiracy Theorists and Their Surprising Rise to Power*. First edition. New York: Metropolitan Books/Henry Holt.

Merlan, Anna. (2020). "The Coronavirus Is an Exciting Opportunity for Conspiracy Theorists." *Vice*, January 27. https://www.vice.com/en/article/pkeayk/the-coronavirus-is-an-exciting-opportunity-for-conspiracy-theorists.

Mitchell, Dawn. (2018). "Murdering Madge Oberholtzer: Rape, Poison and the KKK." *The Indianapolis Star*, November 14. https://www.indystar.com/story/news/history/retroindy/2018/11/14/murder-madge-oberholtzer-rape-poison-and-kkk-d-c-stevenson/1978705002/.

Ohlheiser, Abby. (2017). "In the Great 'Meme Wars,' Alex Jones Doesn't Care If He Makes Them or Is Them." *Washington Post*, July 19. https://www.washingtonpost.com/news/the-intersect/wp/2017/07/19/in-the-great-meme-wars-alex-jones-doesnt-care-if-he-makes-them-or-is-them/.

Patton, Charlie. (2006). "KKK Book Stands up to Claim of Falsehood." *The Florida Times-Union*, January 29. https://web.archive.org/web/20170826113628/http://jacksonville.com/tu-online/stories/012906/met_20943923.shtml#.WaFdQnbP1qY.

Rice, Arnold S. (1972). *The Ku Klux Klan in American Politics*. New York: Haskell House.
Roberts, Diane. (2011). "Stetson Kennedy, Unmasker of the Klan." *The Guardian*, September 2, sec. World news. https://www.theguardian.com/commentisfree/cifamerica/2011/sep/02/protest-florida.
Roettgers, Janko. (2017). "Alex Jones Challenges the Internet to Remix His Videos." *Variety* (blog), July 18. https://variety.com/2017/digital/news/alex-jones-super-deluxe-mashup-1202498877/.
Rose, Steve. (2022). "A Deadly Ideology: How the 'Great Replacement Theory' Went Mainstream." *The Guardian*, June 8, sec. World news. https://www.theguardian.com/world/2022/jun/08/a-deadly-ideology-how-the-great-replacement-theory-went-mainstream.
Siegel, Jerry, and Joe Shuster. (1940). "How Superman Would End the War." *Look*, February 27. https://archive.org/details/HowSupermanWouldEndTheWar/page/n1/mode/2up.
Southern Poverty Law Center. (2011). *Ku Klux Klan: A History of Racism and Violence*. Sixth edition. https://www.splcenter.org/sites/default/files/Ku-Klux-Klan-A-History-of-Racism.pdf.
Swanson, Kelly. (2017). "This Is What Alex Jones Rants Sound Like When Turned into a Bon Iver Song." *Vox*, July 14. https://www.vox.com/policy-and-politics/2017/7/14/15972948/alex-jones-bon-iver-song-super-deluxe.
Warner Bros. (2011). CONTAGION Production Notes. https://web.archive.org/web/20170907213408/http://www.visualhollywood.com/movies_2011/contagion/notes.pdf.
Williamson, Elizabeth. (2022). "Here's What Jones Has Said about Sandy Hook." *New York Times*, September 22. https://www.nytimes.com/2022/09/22/us/politics/heres-what-jones-has-said-about-sandy-hook.html.
Wilson, Jason, and Aaron Flanagan. (2022). "The Racist 'Great Replacement' Conspiracy Theory Explained." Southern Poverty Law Center, May 17. https://www.splcenter.org/hatewatch/2022/05/17/racist-great-replacement-conspiracy-theory-explained.

Morphology of the Conspiracy Theory

MATTHEW N. HANNAH

> "Everyone loves a conspiracy."
> —Dan Brown, *The Da Vinci Code*
>
> "I have come to believe that the whole world is an enigma, a harmless enigma that is made terrible by our own mad attempt to interpret it as though it had an underlying truth."
> —Umberto Eco, *Foucault's Pendulum*

Introduction

Conspiracy theories are everywhere in American culture, from television to books to social media. Some conspiracy theories have become acceptable within polite society—such as belief in UFO cover-ups—while others are dangerous and extreme—such as the Great Replacement conspiracy theory, which posits that whites are being replaced by migrants as a political plot. As more people turn to social media as their primary source for information and news, conspiracy theories have increasingly become an integral part of American political life. But what is it about conspiracy theories that continue to entertain and entrap us in their webs? And can we better understand the impact of conspiracy theories if we answer that question? I argue that conspiracy *theories* can be productively understood as conspiracy *narratives*, as stories we tell ourselves to explain mysterious or traumatic events. Reconfiguring conspiracy theory as conspiracy narrative provides a space to intervene in the very real epidemic of conspiracism that plagues our world today. Rather than analyze the conspiracy *qua* theory, I develop a morphology of conspiracy narratives to account for their diversity and persistence as explanatory mechanisms. Such a structural approach can provide insights into the stories people tell themselves about events but may also provide keys to understanding the nature of conspiracy theories themselves.

Scholars have long assessed the presence of conspiracy theories in literature and popular culture. Peter Knight (2000) characterizes these materials as part of a broader conspiracy culture, which gives voice to cultural anxieties that the "normal order of things itself amounts to a conspiracy" (3). "The rise of a cultural fascination with conspiracy as an undeniably plausible working assumption in the last few decades," Knight argues, "cannot be separated from the emergence of what might be termed a culture *of* conspiracy" (28). Certainly, such a culture of conspiracy can be seen in films but is present in literature as well, especially with the transition to postmodern literature after 1945, with its turn toward inherent instabilities of meaning and authority alongside loss of faith in institutions. "Modernist styles thereby become postmodernist codes," states Fredric Jameson (1992, 17). In a postmodern age, codes become the predominant symbolic order. It is no wonder that conspiracy theories became one of the narrative modes *par excellence* after 1945. Authors such as Umberto Eco, Thomas Pynchon, Don DeLillo, Norman Mailer, and Dan Brown mined the conspiracy theory for literary inspiration, and such novels rely on the same mixture of complex plots and obscure codes that inform conspiracy theories themselves.

Literature provides a perfect vehicle for narrating conspiracies because both operate according to similar structural features. Peter Knight (2021) argues that "conspiracy fiction does not merely show the inner workings of the conspiracy in a way that eludes the paper trails of more supposedly factual versions. It also often encourages readers to identify with an individual character—usually a lone, heroic detective figure" (n.p.). These heroic figures are easy to translate into literature because they implement central structural features of character with the complexity of clues and symbols. Svetlana Boym (1999) argues that "the terms of conspiracy and of narrative overlap: in both cases one speaks about plots and plotting" (97). The persistence and popularity of conspiracy theories in film and literature reflects the fact that American audiences enjoy stories about heroic figures confronting convoluted plots with shadowy actors, that these narratives themselves are enjoyable because they strike a familiar chord with readers.

Conspiracy theories might prove so popular due to the same dynamics that make literary narratives about them so enjoyable. Indeed, the persistence of conspiracism may be directly connected to the fact that they are so narrative in structure. Rachel Runnels (2019) argues that conspiracy theories function as familiar cultural narratives, structured according to what Joseph Campbell called "the hero's journey" (65). Applying Campbell's typography of myth to the study of conspiracy theories, Runnels argues that conspiracism's popularity is a direct result of their familiarity as cultural stories. After all, so many of the founding documents of conspiracy theories are themselves fiction passing itself off as real. From the *Protocols of the Elders of Zion* to the *Turner Diaries*, conspiracy theories have always maintained a strange and problematic relationship to fiction. Conspiracy fiction masquerades as historical fact, and, in many ways, such documents function as drivers of conspiracy theory because individuals don't read them carefully enough. If the popularity of conspiracy theories can be linked to their structure as narratives, we can use narrative theory to understand how they function as narratives, which may reveal key insights about their popularity and persistence.

Analyzing conspiracy *qua* narrative offers a new method with which to understand their persistence and popularity in American culture. Such an approach may yield key insight into the process by which individuals come to believe in them as factual rather than fictional stories. Such an approach also provides an additional set of tools derived from literary theory, which can be deployed to understand the structural and semiotic parameters of contemporary conspiracism and may supplement existing methodologies from information studies and media studies. Tracing the topography of conspiracy narratives will reveal much about how people conceptualize their social and political lives, what Fredric Jameson (1990) calls "cognitive mapping" in postmodernity: "Conspiracy, one is tempted to say, is the poor person's cognitive mapping in the postmodern age; it is the degraded figure of the total logic of late capital, a desperate attempt to represent the latter's system, whose failure is marked by its slippage into sheer theme and content" (360). Conspiracy narrative might be said to be an attempt to tell the story of social totality, to communicate a cognitive map of the characters and events perceived to structure the whole.

The communicative power of conspiracy narrative is an essential feature of conspiracy theory itself: it is the narrative which circulates the theory by condensing the random stew of data into a narrative structure, which I discuss elsewhere as a "conspiracy of data" (Hannah 2021). Philosopher Slavoj Žižek (2004) argues that conspiracy as cognitive mapping is an attempt to make stable meaning without the tools to do so: "when individuals lack the elementary cognitive mapping capabilities and resources that would enable them to locate their place within a social totality, they invent conspiracy theories that provide an ersatz mapping, explaining all the complexities of social life as the result of a hidden conspiracy" (319). In this account, conspiracy narrative locates an individual within the story as the main hero or protagonist but also, in the internet age, as the author too (Habermas 2022).* If this similarity holds true, such narrative similarities provide an opportunity to intervene in this conspiracist space.

Conspiracy narratives are the product of semiotic production within a larger narrative structure, which provides the contours for signs to take on conspiracist meanings. Drawing on literary theory, Mark Fenster ([1999] 2008) describes conspiracy theories as an interpretive practice of meaning-making predicated on the proliferation of signs: "As an interpretive practice, conspiracy theory represents an impossible, almost utopian drive to seize and fetishize individual signs in order to place them within vast interpretive structures that unsuccessfully attempt to stop the signs' unlimited meaning production" (96).† Conspiracy theories are an interpretive practice whereby the theorist arrests and halts the endless significatory potential of signs by placing them within an existing structure (the theory itself). The seizure that Fenster theorizes could be said to reflect the precise moment in which theory becomes narrative. Indeed the "vast interpretive structures" could be imagined as narrative structures, which order the signs in particular ways so as to communicate with others. Certainly, conspiracy *qua* theory is ideological too, reflecting the particular social and political beliefs of individual subjects, but ideology itself is often communicated through narrative, and conspiracy narratives may contain a dialectic of ideology and narrative within them.‡

Structures of Conspiracy Narratives

In his master's thesis, novelist Kurt Vonnegut speculated about the shape of stories. All stories in Western civilization, in his account, could be reduced to eight basic structures that can be read by a computer (Johnson 2022). His analysis of the shape of stories can be understood as part of a larger movement within literary criticism known as structuralism (Sturrock 2003; Robey 1973). While many literary theories could be applied to conspiracy narratives, I focus on the structural approach in order to trace the morphology of conspiracy narratives as a set of structural features and

---

*It is no mistake that postmodern novels often feature the author as a character in the story.
†Fenster's discussion of signs derives from Ferdinand de Saussure's analysis of the sign as comprised of both signifiers, or sound-images, and signifieds, or the concept produced by the signifier.
‡A compelling example of this narrative structure of ideology can be found in Žižek's documentary on ideology in cinema: *The Pervert's Guide to Ideology.* Jameson (1972) also makes this point: "We may therefore understand the Structuralist enterprise as a study of superstructures, or, in a more limited way, of ideology" (101).

semiotic codes. In this approach, I hope to unearth a structure underlying these theories and determine some common principles for better understanding what Naomi Klein (2020) has called the "conspiracy smoothie." While the smoothie metaphor has explanatory potential for explaining the bizarre theories, codes, and symbols that swirl together in extremely paranoid online spaces where conspiracy theories breed, the metaphor occludes that most conspiracy theories rely on similar infrastructural principles and that such structures allow for perpetual recirculation of the same semiotic codes. Articulating these structural features as narrative features will allow me to map the contours of what Michael Barkun (2003) has called the "superconspiracy" (6).

The premise of structuralism is that literary narratives can be reduced to underlying and recurring structures and that we can map relations between the elements that structure such stories.* According to Terence Hawkes (1977), structuralism is a "way of thinking about the world which is predominately concerned with the perception and description of structures" (17). Rather than seeing the world as consisting of "independently existing objects," structuralists recognize the inherently relational nature of things: "At its simplest, [structuralism] claims that the nature of every element in any given situation has no significance by itself, and in fact is determined by its relationship to all the other elements involved in that situation" (18). According to Hawkes, such relationships are emblematic of a "morphological approach" to literature that ignores the texts' message, history, sociological, biographical, or psychological aspects, focusing instead on the text as literary structure (61). For my purposes, we might apply structuralism to consider the conspiracist components of a narrative—what makes a narrative conspiratorial—rather than its literary aspects.

Of the structuralist critics who are most salient for the study of conspiracy narratives, the most useful is found in the analysis of folktales by the Russian critic Vladimir Propp. His morphological analysis of the structures of folk narratives is especially resonant for structurally analyzing conspiracism as a set of relational structures that can be deployed and remixed in various permutations. In his pivotal text, *The Morphology of the Folktale*—which inspired the title of this essay—Propp ([1968] 1994)

---

*Prominent thinkers in the structuralist mode include the linguist Ferdinand de Saussure, anthropologist Claude Lévi-Strauss, and literary scholars Victor Schlovsky, Boris Eichenbaum, Roman Jakobson—members of the Russian formalist school—and Roland Barthes. In his seminal *Structural Anthropology* (1963), Lévi-Strauss provides an example of the structuralist approach: "An alternative approach is to break down cultures into abstract elements and to establish, between elements of the same type in different cultures, rather than between cultures themselves, the same kind of relationships of historical descent and progressive differentiation which the paleontologist sees in the evolution of species" (4).

argues that morphology is essential to understand history, that understanding events must be linked to understanding how constitutive parts relate to one another: "We shall insist that as long as no correct morphological study exists, there can be no correct historical study. If we are incapable of breaking the tale into its components, we will not be able to make a correct comparison" (15). Understanding the folktale morphologically is thus an essential feature of historical analysis. This suggests that a similar morphological study of conspiracy narratives is essential to understanding extreme politics and may reveal the underlying epistemological contours of conspiracism and paranoia within political discourse.

Propp's approach to folktales is significant because it reduces the complexity and diversity of the various folktales to elements that can be related to one another within the larger structure. Propp argues that such a relational approach reveals repeated narrative patterns: "For the sake of comparison we shall separate the component parts of fairy tales by special methods; and then, we shall make a comparison of tales according to their components" (19). Through such a reduction of the whole to its constituent parts, Propp maps the contours of the folktale as a function of certain recurring dynamics. "From this we can draw the inference that a tale often attributes identical actions to various personages," Propp continues, "This makes possible the study of the tale *according to the functions of its dramatis personae*" (original emphasis, 20). Hawkes sums up Propp's project as an attempt to understand lateral linkages between elements such as characters as drivers of narrative: "the fairy tale is seen primarily to embody a syntagmatic, 'horizontal' structuring, rather than the associative 'vertical' structuring represented by the lyric" (68). Analyzing the horizontal connections between characters or events can thus be mapped as functions of narrative.

Because structuralism is focused on the relation between the various pieces of a text or narrative within the whole, it can reveal much about the perception and processing of knowledge within the larger conspiracist community. Fredric Jameson (1972) describes structuralism as an attempt to work out a "philosophy of models." Such a philosophy assumes that the larger structure is epistemological in nature and constrains or expands thought: "the presupposition here is that all conscious thought takes place within the limits of a given model and is in that sense determined by it" (101). The underlying argument here is that language, and its structuring, constrain what is possible to think. For the structuralists, the structure of narrative determines what it is possible to conceptualize. For understanding conspiracy narratives, this is essential whether we accept the totalizing impulse that all conscious thought is determined by language. Conspiracy theory may only be possible because the language models used to create conspiracy narratives exist and function according to certain narrative rules.

Propp's analysis reduces the complexity of folktales to modular functions by a set of characters, which reveals the commonalities among various tales. These functions "constitute the basic elements of the tale" and, taken together relationally, are the fundamental infrastructure on which "the course of the action is built" (71). Characters are understood according to the basic function they play in such action, and Propp identifies a limited set with specific roles to play. Propp discovers seven "spheres of action" with thirty-one functions performed by seven characters listed in Table 1. According to Hawkes, "one character may be involved in several spheres of action" but that "the number of spheres of action occurring in the fairy tale is finite." The limited range of action for the set of characters common to folktales reveals "discernible and repeated structures which, if they are characteristic of so deeply rooted a form of narrative expression may ... have implications for all narrative" (Hawkes 69). The broader implications of structural approaches to narrative can also be extended to conspiracy narrative, and such a morphology is instructive for better understanding the underlying impulse to believe in conspiracism.

Table 1: Propp's Morphology

Character	Functions
The villain	Villainy, reconnaissance, deception, harms family, fighting with hero, pursuit
The donor (provider)	Preparation of magical agent, provision to hero of magical agent
The helper	Liquidation of misfortune or lack, rescue from pursuit, solution of difficult tasks, transfiguration of hero
The princess (sought person)	Branding, exposure, recognition, punishment of second villain, marriage
The dispatcher	Dispatch
The hero	Dispatched, search or quest, reaction to donor, wedding, fighting with villain, returns
The false hero	Search or quest followed by reaction to donor, presents unfounded claims, exposure

Propp's unique insight in charting the modular function of repeating features reveals that folktales rely on a certain number of possible plots, and this insight suggests important aspects of narrative itself. The structural features of narrative may be limited, which reveals how and why narratives are especially popular, palatable, and salient for representing human experience and knowledge. Mapping the cartography of narratives reveals the underlying epistemological features of stories themselves; the "shapes of stories" reveal the shape of cultural production and epistemology. Adapting Propp's morphology for the study of conspiracy narratives may prove important for understanding the underlying appeal of such narratives as explanatory mechanisms for narrating the political and social events around us. In other words, a structuralist approach to conspiracy narratives may tell us much for their enduring popularity as a mode of cognitive mapping.

Toward a Morphology of Conspiracy Theories

Adapting Propp's insight—that folktales can be dissected into structural elements with correspondences that reveal how such tales are structured—and applying it to the study of conspiracy narratives reveals the underlying relations of such narratives. And because conspiracy narratives are similar in composition to folktales, myths, mysteries and other formative cultural narratives, they provide an ideal test case for structural analysis (Chlup 2023; Fritze 2022; Tangherlini et al. 2023). Literary scholar Christian Sieg (2023) articulates the particular narrative stakes of conspiracy theories:

> In the storyworld of conspiracy theorists, conspirators differ from all other groups because of the power and moral ruthlessness attributed to them. The dichotomous order of the storyworld, where the group of conspirators faces the morally honest people, also explains why conspiracy narratives are so attractive to populist parties. Such attributions gain plausibility in times when moralistic views dominate and powerful groups of people are trusted with running everything. The villains of such narratives are well known: the CIA, Mossad, "the Russians," or even Donald Trump. The plausibility of conspiracy narratives is based on numerous other fictional and factual narratives that depict actors in a way that conspiracy theorists can relate to. The narratological concept of a transmedial storyworld conceptualizes this link [n.p.].

Conspiracy narrative is thus theorized as the ordering structure of the "storyworld" in which the conspirators function as villains, the conspiracy theorists function as narrator-heroes, and the overarching story is comprised of both factual information and fictive elements organized within the context of the narrative itself. Thus, conspiracy narratives exhibit a complex structural interplay among many narrative elements, symbols, and codes in superposition as both true and false, fact and fiction, and localized in politics and history.

The morphology of conspiracy narratives can be mapped along different axes, which reveal the structural and epistemological features of these narratives. Runnels (2019) argues that conspiracy theories build credibility through "a narrative based on an age-old structure to make their positions seem more persuasive to readers" (60). Her analysis of conspiracy theories implementing the "hero's journey" structure to convey legitimacy is an example of certain structuralist principles being used to understand conspiracy narrative. Drawing on Joseph Campbell's theory, the hero's journey includes seventeen possible steps with multiple archetypes, which reappear in Western storytelling with some frequency (66). Such stories are dominant as structural features, appearing in cultural narratives as varied as Homer's *Odyssey* or *Star Wars*. Runnels argues that conspiracy narratives deploy the familiar structural features of the hero's journey to construct a persuasive story, which is compelling to believers (Table 2).

Table 2: The Hero's Journey

Feature of the Hero's Quest	Conspiracy Narrative
Becoming the hero	Reader should engage in some activity as a protagonist; break free of convention; think freely; do your own research; opposing and recognizing evil
Taking on mentor role	Provide resources, maps, and keys for newcomers; guide new believers; holders of wisdom; share truths and knowledge
Challenging tradition	Discredit traditional epistemologies; expose traditional media; rejecting orthodoxy; thinking freely

Certainly, Runnels is correct that such structural motifs may prove especially persuasive, but there are equally important structural aspects of the conspiracy narrative beyond the hero's journey. Indeed, one might imagine conspiracy narrative as the "villain's journey" instead. There is also more at stake in analyzing the structural features of conspiracism than simply understanding these narratives as persuasive. In a time of increasing income inequality, loss of faith in authority, and social unrest, conspiracy narratives may have even more salience as explanatory mechanisms for the way the world operates. Jean-François Lyotard characterizes our postmodern moment as a "crisis of narratives" in which the Enlightenment certainty in metanarratives that certify knowledge has been severely called into question ([1979] 1984, xxiv–xxv). Conspiracy narratives may appear more palatable because they are familiar at a time when the impossibility of "master narratives" that can organize our lives seems especially significant. Into the ensuing void, conspiracy narrative has stepped, providing an ordering principle for knowledge, politics, and society.

One approach to understanding conspiracy narratives structurally is to seek archetypes and myths on which such stories are based. Jesse Walker (2013) offers such an archetypical reading of conspiracism as fundamentally tied to American mythology and ideology. "By using the word myths, I don't mean to suggest that these stories are never true," Walker

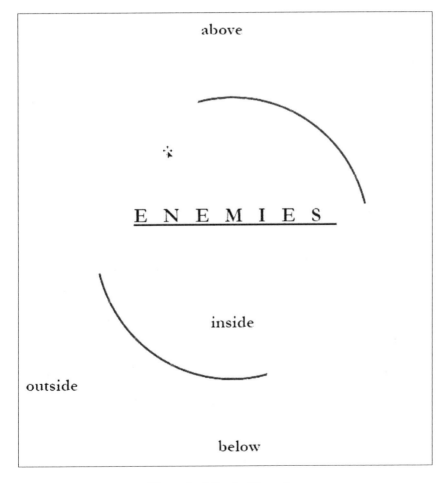

Figure 1a. Wheel of Enemies.

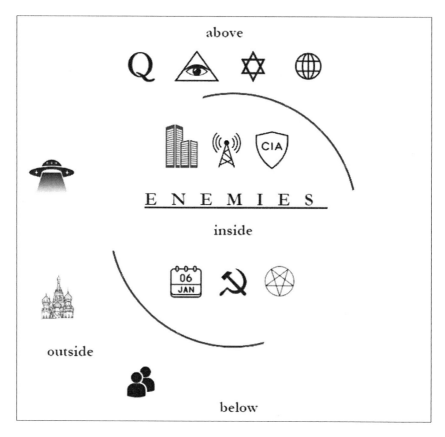

Figure 1b. Wheel of Enemies with Prominent Conspiracy Narratives.

argues, "I mean that they're culturally resonant ideas that appear again and again when Americans communicate with one another: archetypes that can absorb allegations, true or not, and arrange them into a familiar form" (16). Myths about the relationship between Americans and forces deemed hostile to the social order, for example, structure many conspiracy narratives. Walker distinguishes five central myths of conspiracism based on the villain-function within the conspiracy narrative: the enemy inside, the enemy outside, the enemy from above, the enemy from below, and the benevolent conspiracy (16). Ignoring the fifth primal myth, focused on benevolent conspiracy, we can visualize Walker's central myths as a wheel of relations on which to plot conspiracy narratives (Figure 1a and 1b).

This map of the fundamental American myths undergirding conspiracy theories visualizes the structural components of the prominent conspiracy narratives that currently spread across the internet. For example, we can chart the coordinates of conspiracy narratives based on the functional role of the enemy or conspirators. In the lower left corner, for example, are located the Russian agent conspiracy theory (Kremlin icon) and the Great Replacement narrative (people icon) which both posit outside forces (Trump as Russian agent, immigrants) as causal agents for sociopolitical upheavals. Narratives about conspirators undermining the social order from within include January 6 conspiracy narratives (calendar icon) from both the right and left, the Red Scare in which Communists are hidden among us (hammer and sickle icon), the Satanic Panic wherein children are influenced or abused by Satanic forces (pentagram icon), 9/11 conspiracy theories (towers icon), CIA conspiracy narratives (badge icon), and Covid/5G (broadcast icon) conspiracy narratives which purport that our own bodies are controlled by domestic communications infrastructure. Conspiracy narratives with villains operating through global control include QAnon (Q icon) in which a Satanic child-trafficking conspiracy is led by a global cabal, the Great Reset (globe icon) facilitated by the World Economic Forum to dominate the world, the Illuminati (pyramid icon) who controls historical events, and antisemitic narratives about the Rothschilds and George Soros (Star of David icon). Such a topography is imperfect, of course, because each conspiracy narrative could occupy multiple zones, and I have placed each icon close to potential additional zones. Thus, UFO (saucer icon) conspiracy narratives could be said to originate from outside but also from above with global government cover-ups.*

Because conspiracy narratives are driven by actors operating in certain prescribed ways, mapping the topography of action can also be useful for understanding the structure of conspiracy narrative. As spy novelist Ian Fleming once wrote, "Once is happenstance. Twice is coincidence. The third time it's enemy action" ([1959] 2002, 166). Enemy action is a key component to the structure of conspiracy narrative because the enemy can often only be identified through symptomatic readings of clues, symbols, and events. Indeed, the very nature of conspiracy in these stories is that they are both secret and public: the members of the Illuminati cannot be identified, yet they deploy obvious symbolism in music videos (Dice 2013). Another example might be the way in which QAnon is structured so digital soldiers can decode the cryptic Q drops through internet research. Q reiterates throughout the drops: "symbolism will be their downfall" (Q !!HslJq13jV6). The agents of a conspiracy are narratively structured so that their behavior is publicly visible while their identities as conspirators

---

*There are many possible primary sources for this array of conspiracy narratives so I will mention an example from each as support for my assessment of each narrative's enemies. See Glenn Beck (2022), David Icke (2019), David Icke (1999), Renaud Camus (2012), Dave Hayes (2020), Pat Robertson (1991), Lawrence Pazder and Michelle Smith (1980), Craig Unger (2021).

are secret. Michael Barkun (2003) visualizes the spaces of such action in which organizations and their activities can be visualized along as secret, not secret axis (Figure 2a and 2b), and such a mapping reveals the various ways in which activities are performed by characters within conspiracy narratives.

Barkun's chart reveals the structural aspects of enemy action within conspiracy narratives. For example, we can plot the CIA, Great Reset, Covid 5G, 9/11, and Russian conspiracy narratives as actions by groups who are not secret but who operate in secret ways. Narratives about Satanists, UFO coverups, QAnon, and the Illuminati can be charted as secret groups operating in secret ways. But there are some groups whose members are well known and whose behavior is not secret, and here we might include the January 6 Capitol riot, the anti–Semitic conspiracy theories, and the Great Replacement. Conspiracy narratives in this zone know their enemies and know what they want. Into the zone of secret groups behaving in not-secret ways I have placed the Red Scare conspiracy narratives. We don't know who the Communist infiltrators are, but we

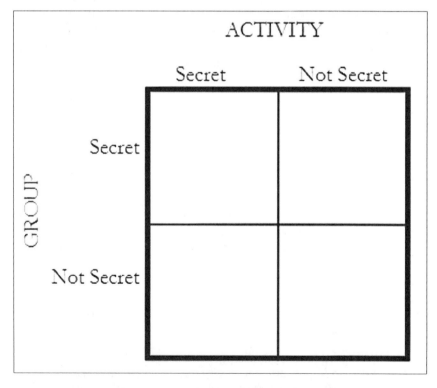

Figure 2a. Michael Barkun's Chart of Group Activities.

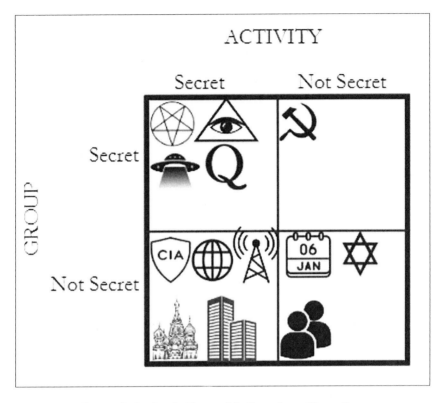

Figure 2b. Barkun's Chart with Conspiracy Narratives.

know what they want: the overthrow of American capitalism. While each of these specific conceptions can be contested in various cases, this structural mapping demonstrates potential approaches to understanding conspiracy narratives as such.

Conspiracy narratives can thus be analyzed structurally as a rotating set of characters with specific functions and certain structural features that provide the narrative movement of the conspiracy theory. Combining Walker's description of myths about enemies to the social order with Barkun's analysis of action, while adding structural elements that appear with regularity across conspiracy narratives, I provide an overarching morphology (Table 3). In this morphology, we can see the key actors at work in "doing the research," unearthing the conspiracy, and opposing the evildoers. Some conspiracy narratives foreground this function as constitutive (QAnon) while others are structured on the overdetermination of enemy agents. In addition, we can assess the particular dynamics of power within the narrative: who has it and how do they wield it? We can also determine the role of symbolism within the conspiracy narrative: does it employ or analyze maps, symbols, and graphics as explanatory mechanisms? Finally, what psychological fears does the narrative activate (Douglas, Sutton, and Cichocka 2017?) Such fear can be the product of existential dread or anxiety but can also be a source of *jouissance* (van Proojien et al. 2022). After all, who doesn't like to be scared?

Table 3: Morphology of the Conspiracy Narrative

Narrative	Actors	Agents	Power	Symbolism	Fear Locus
	Unknown	Members of Illuminati; celebrities; Vatican	Cultural; Economic; Social; Political	Yes	Global domination
	Victims	Doctors; Big Pharma; Big Tech	Medical	No	Bodily autonomy; Domestic authority
	Unknown	CIA operatives; MK Ultra	Cultural; Political; Medical	No	Domestic authority; Bodily autonomy
	Jan 6ers; Democrats	Federal agents; Antifa; Donald Trump	Political; Epistemological	No	Domestic authority; Political norms
	Gentiles	Bankers	Economic; Cultural; Political	Yes	Global domination; Economic anxiety; Sociocultural erosion
	Democrats	Russian agents; Donald Trump	Political	No	Domestic authority; Political norms
	Truthers; activists	Deep State	Political; Epistemological	No	Domestic authority
	Patriots	Communist agents; spies; infiltrators	Political; Economic; Social	Yes	Domestic authority; Sociocultural erosion

Narrative	Actors	Agents	Power	Symbolism	Fear Locus
🛸	Abductees; UFOlogists	Deep State; alien races	Political; Epistemological	No	Bodily autonomy; Authoritarianism
Q	Patriots; anons	Deep State, Hollywood, Democrats	Political	Yes	Global domination; Domestic authority
👥	Patriots	Migrants; Democrats	Political; Economic	No	Sociocultural erosion; Economic anxiety
⛤	Parents; Christians	Children; cultists; music industry	Cultural; Social; Religious	Yes	Sociocultural erosion

Structural approaches to conspiracy narratives must also take into account the role of actors within these conspiracy narratives. A.J. Greimas distinguished the character-functions in narrative as that between actors and actants. In his analysis, actors are "recognizable in the particular discourses in which they are manifested" and actants are characterized by the "narrative syntax" ([1970] 1987, 106). Whereas actors can occupy different roles in the narrative as subjects or objects, they serve as actual characters whereas actants serve to help or hinder the actor (Felluga 2011). Within the storyworld of conspiracy narratives, such roles are a bit more complicated because the actors are often implied and collective, defined negatively by the actants (which I call agents). The dialectic of the individual and the collective within conspiracy narratives is an essential aspect of conspiracism more generally (Melley 2000). That is, the actor is often the conspiracy theorist, and such an actor is protean in that each individual could be interpellated as an actor through engagement with the agents of the conspiracy narrative (Althusser [1971] 2008, 47). The agents are more stable but also complicated by the fact that their existence is both known and unknown. The Illuminati are both everywhere and nowhere. QAnon battles a Deep State whose agents are implicated and yet not proven to be participatory. Indeed, the very function of the conspiracy narrative is to provide the narrative elements that reveal the existence of agents and, by extension, of actors.

These actors are often members of specific groups who are both targeted by and victims of the conspiracy narrative. For example, we might consider parents as actors in the "Satanic Panic" or envision vaccine recipients as actors in the Covid-19 conspiracy narratives. Some actors are far more diffuse and potentially dangerous such as the patriots who come to believe in the Great Replacement and who may join extremist groups or white-power movements. Perhaps the most interesting actors are located within the QAnon conspiracy theory as they comprise an active research community with a coherent collective identity as "anons" (Sommer 2023). QAnon, in particular, represents a new modality for actors to coalesce from the disparate ideological space into a collective and militant cadre of conspiracy theorists with extensive narratives and symbolic systems. Such symbolic systems include conspiracy maps and graphics as a core set of narrative clues, and many of the conspiracy narratives above include such symbolic objects.

But I have also identified the actants, or the agents, as the cabal or collective that drives the conspiracy narrative through their existence and operation on the narrative. Thus, we see agents such as the secret members of the Illuminati, the global cabal of Jewish bankers, the World Economic Forum, the Democratic Party, and the Satanists as various versions of the same enemy but with subtly unique functions within each narrative, which drives the fear at the center of the narrative. For example, within the Covid conspiracy community, medical doctors and Big Pharma are colluding with the tech companies to infiltrate human bodies with fraudulent vaccines. Thus, the activity of the agents is directly related to the fear: loss of bodily autonomy through the power of the medical industrial complex (Knight and Butter 2023). Conspiracy narratives about global shadowy groups such as the Illuminati or the cabal of pedophiles in QAnon are tied to fears about authoritarianism and global domination, i.e., loss of American democracy and prestige. Each agent is connected to the locus of power and the underlying fear or anxiety within the social order, which drives the conspiracy narrative much like the plot of a novel.

Conclusion

Approaching conspiracy narratives structurally reveals the elements that comprise such stories and suggests repeating patterns of American conspiracism. Reconfiguring conspiracy theories as narratives with a recurring set of features, characters, and elements can open a space to intervene and undermine the development of such narratives because the underlying features become clear as interlocking, interoperable features. Showcasing the fictive elements of conspiracy narratives as a repeated and formulaic structure undermines their status as factual accounts of historical events; positioning the conspiracy narrative as a fictional story which is ideologically substituted for actual events may excavate the conspiracy theory of its explanatory power and infuse it with the same status as other cultural forms such as mythology and fairy tales.

Recognizing the literary structures within conspiracy narratives may help extremism researchers to intervene in conspiracist movements by offering a robust set of tools and talking points for demonstrating the fictiveness of conspiracy theories while also acknowledging the entertainment potential. Structural approaches can present unique opportunities to understand the collapse of storytelling into political ideology and may allow us to better design political and social interventions as well. "If conspiracy can be fictional," Svetlana Boym speculates, "can fiction conspire to undo it?" (97). Can we adapt lessons from literary studies which will provide new models for intervention? Perhaps readers resonated with the Dan Brown novels because they were already so invested in conspiracy theories, and we can use that entertainment value to showcase how reductive such narratives are for explaining the truly complex and random events that actually occur.

Furthermore, revealing the structural components of conspiracy narrative may offer opportunities to substitute other narratives that satisfy the same psychological and emotional needs but offer more healthy responses to social ills. For example, identifying the agents within conspiracy narratives produces a set of character-functions that can be replaced with actual critique of the actors responsible for social problems. After all, such structural analysis can demonstrate the ways in which cultural narratives fit into a superstructure, which operates in relation to an economic base that structures our storyworlds—and lifeworlds—in various ways (Schaff 1977). Rather than seek conspiracist narratives to explain why events occur, we can point to more material causal mechanisms in the hopes of building solidarity among those desperate for explanations. Conspiracy narratives may thus turn out to be inadequate to explain the real world in all its terrible beauty.

References

Althusser, Louis. (1971) 2008. *On Ideology*. London: Verso.
Barkun, Michael. (2003). *A Culture of Conspiracy: Apocalyptic Visions in Contemporary America*. Berkeley: U of California P.
Beck, Glenn. (2022). *The Great Reset: Joe Biden and the Rise of Twenty-First Century Fascism*. Brentwood, TN: Forefront Books and Mercury Ink.
Boym, Svetlana. (1999). "Conspiracy Theories and Literary Ethics: Umberto Eco, Danilo Kiš and The Protocols of Zion." *Comparative Literature* 51 (2): 97–122. https://doi.org/10.2307/1771244.
Brown, Dan. (2003). *The Da Vinci Code*. New York: Doubleday.

Camus, Renaud. (2018). *You Will Not Replace Us!* Chez l'auteur.
Chlup, Radek. (2023). "Conspiracy Narratives as a Type of Social Myth." *International Journal of Politics, Culture, and Society*, June 10: 1–23. https://doi.org/10.1007/s10767-023-09454-1.
Clarke, Simon. (1981). *The Foundations of Structuralism: A Critique of Lévi-Strauss and the Structuralist Movement*. Harvester Studies in Philosophy. Brighton: Harvester Press.
"Conspiracy Theories: Linked to Literature | UNESCO." (2024). Accessed January 11. https://courier.unesco.org/en/articles/conspiracy-theories-linked-literature-0.
Dice, Mark. (2013). *Illuminati in the Music Industry*. Createspace.
Douglas, Karen M., Robbie M. Sutton, and Aleksandra Cichocka. (2017). "The Psychology of Conspiracy Theories." *Current Directions in Psychological Science* 26 (6): 538. https://doi.org/10.1177/0963721417718261.
Eco, Umberto. (1989). *Foucault's Pendulum*. New York: Harcourt.
Felluga, Dino. (2011). "Modules on Greimas: On Plotting." *Introductory Guide to Critical Theory*. Purdue U. Accessed February 12, 2024. http://www.purdue.edu/guidetotheory/narratology/modules/greimasplot.html.
Fenster, Mark. (1999) 2008. *Conspiracy Theory: Secrecy and Power in American Culture*. Minneapolis: U of Minnesota P.
Fiennes, Sophia, dir. *A Pervert's Guide to Ideology*. New York: Zeitgeist Films, 2013.
Fleming, Ian. (1959) 2002. *Goldfinger*. London: Penguin.
Fritze, Ronald H. (2022). *Hope and Fear: Modern Myths, Conspiracy Theories and Pseudo-History*. London: Reaktion Books.
Greimas, Algirdas Julien. (1987). *On Meaning: Selected Writings in Semiotic Theory*. Theory and History of Literature, vol. 38. Minneapolis: U of Minnesota P.
Habermas, Jürgen. (2022). "Reflections and Hypotheses on a Further Structural Transformation of the Political Public Sphere." *Theory, Culture & Society* 39 (4): 145–71. https://doi.org/10.1177/02632764221112341.
Hannah, Matthew N. (2021). "A Conspiracy of Data: QAnon, Social Media, and Information Visualization." *Social Media + Society* 7 (3): 20563051211036064. https://doi.org/10.1177/20563051211036064.
Hawkes, Terence. (1977). *Structuralism and Semiotics*. Berkeley: U of California P.
Hayes, Dave. (2020). *The Great Awakening*. DHayes Media.
Icke, David. (1999). *The Biggest Secret: The Book That Will Change the World*. David Icke Books.
Icke, David. (2019). *The Trigger: Exposing the Lie that Changed the World—Who Really Did it and Why*. Ickonic Publishing.
Jameson, Fredric. (1972). *The Prison-House of Language: A Critical Account of Structuralism and Russian Formalism*. Princeton UP. https://doi.org/10.2307/j.ctv10crf9x.
Jameson, Fredric. (1990). "Cognitive Mapping." *Marxism and the Interpretation of Culture*. Eds. Cary Nelson and Lawrence Grossberg. Urbana: U of Illinois P. 347–57.
Jameson, Fredric. (1992). *Postmodernism or the Cultural Logic of Late Capitalism*. Durham: Duke UP.
Johnson, Stephen. (2022). "Kurt Vonnegut on the 8 'Shapes' of Stories." *Big Think* (blog), June 13. https://bigthink.com/high-culture/vonnegut-shapes/.
Klein, Naomi. (2020). "The Great Reset Conspiracy Smoothie." *The Intercept*, December 8. https://theintercept.com/2020/12/08/great-reset-conspiracy/.
Knight, Peter. (2000). *Conspiracy Culture: From Kennedy to the X-Files*. London: Routledge.
Knight, Peter. (2021). "Conspiracy Theories: Linked to Literature | UNESCO." Accessed January 11. https://courier.unesco.org/en/articles/conspiracy-theories-linked-literature-0.
Knight, Peter, and Michael Butter. (2023). *Covid Conspiracy Theories in Global Perspective*. Conspiracy Theories Series. New York: Routledge.
Lévi-Strauss, Claude. (1974). *Structural Anthropology*. New York: Basic Books.
Lyotard, Jean-François. (1979) 1984. *The Postmodern Condition: A Report on Knowledge*. Translated by Geoff Bennington and Brian Massumi. Minneapolis: U of Minnesota P.
Melley, Timothy. (2000). *Empire of Conspiracy: The Culture of Paranoia in Postwar America*. Ithaca: Cornell UP.

Pazder, Lawrence, and Michelle Smith. 1980. *Michelle Remembers*. New York: Congdon and Lattés.
Prooijen, Jan-Willem van, Joline Ligthart, Sabine Rosema, and Yang Xu. (2022). "The Entertainment Value of Conspiracy Theories." *British Journal of Psychology* 113 (1): 25–48. https://doi.org/10.1111/bjop.12522.
Propp, Vladimir. (1968) 1994. *Morphology of the Folktale*. Translated by Louis Wagner. Austin: Uof Texas P. Q !!HslJql3jV6 ID: bbb895. (2020). Oct. 7. 8kun.net. https://8kun.top/qresearch/res/10972547.html#10973205.
Robertson, Pat. (1991). *The New World Order*. Dallas: Word.
Robey, David. (1973). *Structuralism: An Introduction*. Wolfson College Lectures. Oxford: Clarendon Press.
Runnels, Rachel. (2019). "Conspiracy Theories and the Quest for Truth." *Digital Commons @ ACU Electronic Theses and Dissertations* (Paper 180). https://digitalcommons.acu.edu/etd/180.
Schaff, Adam. (1977). *Structuralism and Marxism*. Oxford: Pergamon Press.
Sieg, Christian. (2023). "Conspiracy Theories as Narratives." Accessed January 31, 2024. https://www.uni-muenster.de/Religion-und-Politik/en/aktuelles/schwerpunkte/epidemien/05_thema_verschwoerung.html.
Sommer, Will. (2023). *Trust the Plan: The Rise of QAnon and the Conspiracy that Unhinged America*. New York: Harper.
Sturrock, John. (2003). *Structuralism*. 2nd ed. Oxford: Blackwell.
Tangherlini, Timothy R., Shadi Shahsavari, Pavan Holur, and Vwani Roychowdhury. (2023). "QAnon, Folklore, and Conspiratorial Consensus: A Case Study in the Computational Analysis of Conspiracy Theory Narratives." In *The Social Science of QAnon: A New Social and Political Phenomenon*, edited by Monica K. Miller, 234–51. Cambridge: Cambridge UP.
Unger, Craig. (2021). *American Kompromat: How the KGB Cultivated Donald Trump, and Related Tales of Sex, Greed, Power, and Treachery*. New York: Dutton.
Walker, Jesse. (2013). *The United States of Paranoia: A Conspiracy Theory*. New York: Harper.
Žižek, Slavoj. (2004). "The ongoing "soft revolution." *Critical Inquiry* 30 (2): 292–323.

The Hellfire Club
Secret Societies in the Fiction of Marvel Comics and Real-World Parallels

SEAN THOMAS MILLIGAN

Introduction

Conspiracy theories are becoming increasingly problematic at this juncture in American culture and politics. From misinformation about the efficacy and safety of vaccines to falsehoods regarding the integrity of our elections, to paranoia about secret cabals controlling the world from the shadows, conspiracy theories are a great source of anxiety in the public psyche. Indeed, conspiracy theories have the potential to result in real-world harm, which is an unfortunate reality that can be seen playing out today with vaccine hesitancy and political violence. Research such as that conducted by Salazar-Fernández et al. shows that "beliefs in conspiracy theories may temporally precede beliefs in vaccine effectiveness for COVID-19" (2023). For the influence of belief in conspiracy theories on political violence, one need look no further than the January 6, 2021, attack on the U.S. Capitol. Suresh et al. find that "social media platforms offer fertile ground for the widespread proliferation of conspiracies during major societal events, which can potentially lead to offline coordinated actions and organized violence" (2023). Dickey (2023, 315) examines several such cases of violence, explaining that the 2018 Tree of Life Congregation synagogue attack in Pittsburgh, the 2019 Walmart shooting in El Paso, and the 2022 Tops massacre in Buffalo were all perpetrated by individuals who consumed media espousing racist and antisemitic conspiracy theories such as the Great Replacement theory. The tangible dangers of conspiratorial belief are clear.

Conspiracy theories have roots not only in the real world, but also in the fictional realm of comic books and superheroes. Conspiracies can be found as a central plot point in countless comic books and graphic novels, from Alan Moore's *V for Vendetta* to Warren Ellis' *Transmetropolitan*. Indeed, the ever-popular caped crusader, Batman, often finds himself putting his detective skills to the test to uncover various plots and machinations as he wages war against the seedy underbelly of Gotham City. Comic books feature a tremendous variety of stories not only of conspiracies, but also stories about those who fight back and try to shine a revealing light upon the conspirators. A particularly poignant example of one such group of conspirators is Marvel Comics' Hellfire Club, a group of powerful elites who pull the strings from behind the scenes to further their own nefarious agendas. This clandestine organization often clashes with superhero groups like the X-Men.

Interestingly, the Hellfire Club of Marvel's storylines draw inspiration from the historical clubs of the same name which arose in eighteenth-century Britain and Ireland. The Hellfire Clubs from our own reality were the subject of rumors, and perhaps some truths, about unsavory and controversial activities. The historical Hellfire Club's legacy lives on, not only in the comic books they inspired, but also in contemporary conspiracy theories which posit that secret societies are at the heart of American policymaking. Gulyas (2016, 25) tells us that "secret societies … have long played a significant role in conspiracy theories and political paranoia." Hypothesized groups like the New World Order, the Deep State, or Illuminati can in some ways trace their lineage back to certain chapters of the Hellfire Club. These types of conspiracy theories about secret organizations are pervasive in American history. After all, as Dickey (2023, 3) puts it, "from the earliest European settlers to reach this land to the present day, we have mused about secret plots, hidden conspirators, invisible groups that threaten to control us." Or, more simply put, "the United States was born in paranoia" (Dickey 2023, 3).

This essay examines the intriguing interplay between reality and fiction when it comes to Marvel's Hellfire Club. I will argue that the fictional Hellfire Club reflects very real cultural and societal anxieties about secret groups manipulating and controlling various aspects of politics and economics, as well as the everyday lives of ordinary citizens. Through this lens, we can examine the Hellfire Club and see how comics, as a medium, provide a particularly appealing playground for authors and artists to represent our deep-rooted fears of nefarious cabals and puppeteering overlords. This is especially true in the case of comic books in the superhero genre.

The Historical Hellfire Club

Perhaps fittingly for such exclusive and secretive societies, relatively little information can be easily found about the historical Hellfire Clubs of England and Ireland. A handful of books have been written on the subject, including titles such as *The Hell-fire Clubs: Sex, Satanism, and Secret Societies* by Evelyn Lord (2010) and *Blasphemers & Blackguards: The Irish Hellfire Clubs* by David Ryan (2012). My research turned up even fewer academic articles. Furthermore, many of the journalistic articles written about the Hellfire Club hedge their claims with hesitant, uncertain phrasing, the result of which is a glut of stories saying that the club "may have" done this or was "rumored" to do that. What they actually did is surprisingly difficult to determine. This proves to be a frustrating experience when trying to separate fact from fiction. Therefore, the topic of the hellfire clubs is tantalizingly ripe for additional research and writing. Indeed, this tension between fact and fiction, between what the club was rumored to do and what they did, is likely a major reason why the Hellfire Club and similar organizations generate so much discussion and mistrust. When the lines between myth and truth are blurred, it is little wonder that people turn to conspiracy theories to help make sense of things. This essay does not intend, however, to provide a full and detailed history of the Hellfire Club. Neither does it seek to examine at length the causes and factors behind conspiratorial thinking. These things will be touched on only as necessary to develop an understanding of how comic books as a medium act as a venue for manifesting conspiratorial anxieties and nightmares. The overall aims of this essay are to track an intriguing parallel in secret societies which coexist in both the real world and fiction and to showcase the unique potential of comics for engaging with conspiracies.

Although others have already given more thorough histories of the Hellfire Club than can be accomplished in the scope of this essay, a brief overview of the club's activities and public perceptions of the club is necessary. The hellfire clubs (multiple different organizations borrowed the name), despite their cultural and societal impact, were relatively short-lived groups, more like a flash in the pan than an enduring movement. Mostly, the clubs existed for a few decades in the eighteenth century (Lord 2010, 66; Ryan 2012, 3). The first Hellfire Club is believed to have been started in London around 1720, though there were precursor groups operating under different names in earlier years, including "The Damned Crew," "The Baller's Club," "The Mohocks," and others (Lord 2010, 1–44; Ryan 2012, 2). While the original Hellfire Club began in London, groups operating under that moniker soon followed elsewhere, including the Dublin Hellfire Club in 1737 (Ryan 2012, 3).

A few common threads connect the various groups that are known as hellfire clubs. Firstly, the club members were all decidedly upper-class elites. The first English Hellfire Club, for example, was founded by Philip, the Duke of Wharton. The Whartons, indeed, were so wealthy that "by the age of twelve Philip had his own string of racehorses" (Lord 49). Similarly, Ryan (2012) describes the Irish chapters as being "exclusive," with "a membership drawn from fashionable, upper-class circles" (2). Furthermore, the club members "were generally ... propertied men" (Ryan 2012, 7). This is the first of many parallels to contemporary conspiracy theories centered around secret societies—modern beliefs about such groups consistently hypothesize that their membership consists of the ruling elite.

Another commonality among the hellfire clubs is the public perception—accurate or not—of debauchery, blasphemy and violence. Here is where it gets difficult to separate fact from fiction. At the time, it was widely believed that the Dublin Hellfire Club, for example, "engaged in rampant orgies, excessive drinking and gambling, and sinister Satanic rituals" (Ryan 2012, 1). While excesses and moral transgressions like gambling and drinking were certainly not outside the realm of possibility, tales also circulated of a much more sinister nature. Ryan (2012), writing about the Irish Hellfire Club, goes on to tell of a piece of folklore which postulates that a card game being played by club members was interrupted by the appearance of the Devil (1). Speculation also held that the club engaged in grisly murders and sacrifices. To these points, Ryan (2012) points out that "no documented evidence has been found to support any of these claims" (2). These charges were not levied at only the Irish club; Lord (2010) describes similar rumors of Satanism and sexual impropriety which circulated about the London Hellfire Club founded by Wharton (57).

The biggest reason it is so difficult to determine the truth about the hellfire clubs is that rumors were rampant, and journalists at the time were quick to fan the flames. It was beneficial to journalists to have a sensational story to sell, and indeed "once the existence of the club became common knowledge journalistic hacks quickly embellished what happened at its meetings, so that fact and fiction became merged" (Lord 2010, 52). Gossip, spurred on by newspapers at the time, may have started the hellfire furor, but interest in the clubs was kept alive by public interest. Ryan (2012) explains that "over the ensuing 200 years [since the end of the clubs], a growing body of myth and legend served to sustain the memory of the Irish hellfire clubs" (4). It seems that people are simply drawn to stories about secret, nefarious societies. Ryan (2012) points out that these centuries of "myth and legend" have only served to further obscure the "true nature" of the Hellfire Club (4). It has become very difficult to separate fact from fiction when it comes to these clubs as a result of sensationalized journalism and the long-term propagation of legend.

Although challenging to determine the truth, there are some available facts and verifiable falsehoods about the clubs. The most sensational accounts are, of course, false (or highly likely to be false). So, if the clubs did not engage in wanton murder, Satanic rituals, and other sinister things, what exactly *did* they do? While it seems unlikely that the hellfire clubs were ever visited by the devil, they did sometimes engage in behaviors which mocked and eschewed the established religious order at the time. For example, one group, known as the Medmenham Monks (they never referred to themselves as the Hellfire Club but were later known as such) held "mock religious ceremonies" (Ryan 2012, 3). Ryan (2012) is quick to point out, though, that "there is no evidence that they actually practised devil worship" (3). The hellfire clubs and their precursors were, however, seen as blasphemous and violent, and there was a basis in truth for much of this. As Ryan (2012) recounts, one member of the Dublin Hellfire Club "killed a servant in a drunken rage" while other clubs that followed "engaged in violent and aggressive conduct" (3). Additionally, a group called the "Holy Fathers" was said to utter "vile oaths, imprecations and blasphemies" (O'Connor, qtd. in Ryan 2012, 4). The original Hellfire Club of 1721 "met together to toast the devil and indulge in other sacrilegious actions" (Lord 2010, 51). Other related groups like the Pinkindindies engaged in violent acts such as "assaults, rapes, robberies, and acts of vandalism" (Ryan 2012, 4). It is clear that the hellfire clubs and related groups did conduct themselves in such a way that, while the stories written about them may have been embellished, the public was justified to some degree in thinking them violent and blasphemous.

Apart from the violence and perceived blasphemy of some clubs, what the hellfire clubs really offered their members was an opportunity for self-indulgence among like-minded peers. Ryan (2012) explains that "drink and drinking vessels feature prominently in the group portraits" of the Irish hellfire clubs. Indeed, "hellfire clubs offered gentlemen companionship and the opportunity to drink heavily, gamble unrestrainedly and behave in a boisterous manner" (Ryan 2012, 16). The bulk of their activities seem to have revolved around drinking, gambling, and other social excesses. But this has not stopped the perpetuation of rumor, myth, and legend.

Ultimately, bearing in mind the challenges of identifying what is historical reality and what is sensationalism, we do know a few things about the hellfire clubs. Members were generally wealthy men, though some clubs counted women among their ranks. The primary activities of the clubs seemed to be drinking and gambling. While the more fanciful stories are likely myth and legend, many hellfire clubs and their members did engage in sacrilegious behavior. Members of certain groups also acted violently at times, resulting in injury or even death. It is easy to see why the clubs' activities captured the attention of both the public and the newspapers, and why the hellfire clubs have maintained a lasting legacy of mystique and intrigue. With at least a basic understanding of the history of these clubs, we can shift our attention to Marvel's reimagining of the Hellfire Club.

Marvel's Hellfire Club and Real-World Inspirations

Marvel's Hellfire Club does feature in a fair number of comics but is not one of the most pervasive groups of characters in Marvel comics. Their most prominent appearance is probably in Chris Claremont's (1980) *The Dark Phoenix Saga*, where the club made its first appearance. There also exists a lesser-known four-issue run called *The Origin of the Inner Circle*, written by Ben Raab (2000). The Hellfire Club and its members also make appearances or are otherwise referenced in a handful of video games and television and film adaptations. The Hellfire Club in Marvel comics is a fictional society that engages in excess, much like the real-world club, but also a group of villains and supervillains who frequently oppose the X-Men.

Among their members are Sebastian Shaw, Emma Frost, Harry Leland, and Jason Wyngarde. According to Tim Webber (2023), writing an article on "The History of the Hellfire Club" for Marvel's website, "the Hellfire Club brought together a secret society for the wealthy and elite. Thanks to leaders like Emma Frost and Sebastian Shaw, it also evolved into one of the most important mutant-run institutions in the Marvel Universe." Webber (2023) explains that the club uses sociopolitical power and clout, along with their impressive finances, to compel others to carry out their commands. This parallels the historical Hellfire Club. Webber (2023) goes on to point out that "many members use it [the Hellfire Club] as an elite social club" while the secretive Inner Circle wields the true power. Marvel's Hellfire club departs from the historical club in that it has ambitions for world domination, but the influence is clear. The Hellfire Club in Marvel comic books pays homage to its real-world counterpart, as they throw parties at which partygoers dress in old-fashioned Victorian outfits (Webber 2023).

Let's return to the leadership of Marvel's Hellfire Club: Sebastian Shaw and Emma Frost. Certainly, there are other big players in the club— Leland and Wyngarde play prominent roles in many stories. But Shaw and Frost are unquestionably at the top; or rather, at the center of the inner circle which consists of the most powerful Hellfire Club members. Both Sebastian Shaw and Emma Frost are mutants in the world of the X-Men. Shaw's power involves the absorption of energy to increase his own strength, while Frost (sometimes portrayed as a hero instead of a villain) possesses powerful telepathic abilities, as well as the useful trait of turning her flesh into organic diamond—rendering her extremely durable and strong.

Both, in addition to their mutant powers, are also cunning and extremely intelligent, with Shaw maintaining a public image as a businessman while secretly pulling the strings behind the scenes of the Hellfire Club. It is their superpowers, however, that are most interesting when considered in the context of conspiracy theories and secret cabals. Their superpowers reinforce their natural talents for subterfuge, manipulation, and deceit. As previously mentioned, Shaw can absorb energy that is directed towards him. At one point in *The Dark Phoenix Saga*, Shaw is battling with X-Men member and fellow mutant Cyclops, who fires powerful beams of energy from his eyes. Shaw taunts Cyclops, saying, "Your vaunted optic blasts mean nothing to a man capable of absorbing all forms of kinetic energy. The harder you hit me—with anything—the stronger I get!" (Claremont 1980, 99). It is fitting (in several ways) that a villain who is the head of a secret, nefarious organization possesses this power. Firstly, Shaw's absorption power echoes the greed and lust for power that he displays throughout the story. Rather than being granted a unique power of his own, he relies on stealing the energy produced by others. Secondly, it is interesting that Shaw's power grows as others attempt to harm him.

This seems to parallel the nature of conspiracies themselves—whether theory or actual conspiracy—in which attempts to reveal them for what they are can often prove frustrating. This is in part because, according to van Prooijen and Douglas (2018), conspiracy theories are "emotional given that negative emotions and not rational deliberations cause conspiracy beliefs." Indeed, "Conspiracy beliefs … do not appear to be grounded in controlled, analytic mental processes" (van Prooijen and Douglas). Shermer (2022) speaks to this as well, noting that "as cognitive dissonance theory predicts, true believers [of QAnon] doubled down on their belief [after President Biden's inauguration], as has happened historically when facts failed to support a conspiracy theory." This favoring of emotional mental processing over analytical thinking is precisely what gives conspiracy theories their slippery tendency to evade attempts at disproving them. Anyone who has tried to argue with a conspiracy theorist online has probably had the following experience: a conspiracy theorist demands evidence. The respondent provides the requested evidence, only for the conspiracy theorist to move the goalposts. The credibility of the evidence is called into question, the topic is changed, or the conspiracy theorist demands additional evidence. This cycle will continue with the conspiracy theorists rarely conceding that the evidence disproves their theory. Dickey puts it this way:

The conspiracy theory posits at its core an unshakable tenet: the Jews are behind everything, the government has evidence of UFOs, etc. That tenet must be absolutely impervious to any counter-indicative evidence; everything and anything must be made to "prove" the central tenet. But this is a difficult rhetorical and logical position to maintain, and thus it requires the constant shifting and reinterpretation of the past, present, and future. To maintain a conspiracy theory in the absence of evidence, particularly as more time elapses, requires an increasingly extreme contortion of reality and the past [6–7].

Just as it can be difficult to disprove a conspiracy theory, as its proponents will often continually shift to new explanations, so too does it prove frustrating for the heroes in *The Dark Phoenix Saga* to battle Shaw. After all, as Shaw tells us, the harder you hit him, the stronger he becomes.

Similarly, Emma Frost's character and abilities are fitting for someone deep within the inner circle of such a powerful group. There is perhaps no superpower more well-suited to such a character than telepathy. Frost can read thoughts, control minds, and plant false memories, among other things. She need not rely on manipulation through old-fashioned tactics like persuasive speech, bribes, and threats. Rather, she can simply force others to do her will, violate their privacy by invading their thoughts, and make them think and feel things that are not aligned with reality. Gulyas (2016, 99) highlights the prominence of mind control narratives in conspiracy theories, explaining that these types of anxieties have roots in the Cold War and can range from "sinister forces targeting individuals and turning them into mind-controlled slaves" to "our entire culture ... being manipulated through mind control on a massive scale." But mind control and telepathy are not Frost's only powers—she also has the ability to transform her body into diamond. In addition to becoming stronger and resistant to damage, this diamond form represents her wealth and greed. It is hard to think of a more fitting set of powers for a conspiratorial supervillain than mindreading, mind controlling, and taking on a form composed of the same matter as a literal gemstone representing wealth and status.

Just as their powers are well-suited to the members of the Hellfire Club, so too are their supervillain aliases appropriate for the inner circle of a secret cabal. Emma Frost is also known as the White Queen, again signaling status. Sebastian Shaw has been called the Black King, the Lord Imperial, and the Black Bishop. Again, these monikers are symbolic of his wealth and status, but we also see the establishment of the game of chess as a theme in these comic book stories. Of course, we have all seen chess, or the idea of a chess match, used as a metaphor for business dealings, politics, and other activities that the Hellfire Club plays a role in. Jason Wyngarde, another Hellfire Club member with the powers of memory alteration and producing psionic illusions, goes by "Mastermind." From the eighteenth century-inspired outfits to the superpowers, to the aliases signaling power, status, and manipulation, the influence of the historical Hellfire Club and other rumored secret societies on Marvel's iteration of the club is clear.

Comics as a Venue for Exploring Conspiratorial Anxieties

The actions of Marvel's Hellfire Club reflect anxieties about manipulation and the invasion of privacy, mirroring anxieties about supposed real-world secret societies. A common theme in conspiracy theories today is that of privacy—specifically, many conspiracy theories explore the possibility of the government or some other organization peering into the private lives of citizens. The story of *The Dark Phoenix Saga* deals heavily with both themes of manipulation and the loss of privacy. One part of the Hellfire Club's plan in this story is to gain mental control over the X-Men character Jean Grey, also known as Phoenix. Jean Grey is incredibly powerful, with extraordinary psychic abilities and, at times, pyrokinesis and even immortality.

The Hellfire Club wishes to use Jean, or Phoenix, to their own advantage. In order to achieve this mental dominance over Phoenix, Hellfire Club member Mastermind plants illusions and false memories in Phoenix's mind. Mastermind provides us with a commentary on his plans with Phoenix through the use of thought bubbles in the comic book, saying, "I'm merely giving her a taste of some of her innermost—forbidden—needs and desires" (Claremont 1980, 8). Mastermind's phrasing is interesting, as accessing one's "innermost … needs and desires" reflects the debauchery and self-indulgence of the real-world hellfire clubs. The subsequent panels of the comic reveal even further the abusive nature of Mastermind's power, as Jean believes herself to be in a fantasy world. The narrator paints a picture for us: "When at last she opens her eyes, the 'Blackbird' [a jet plane used by the X-men] and her friends are gone. For her, time has apparently slipped backwards two hundred years and she is once more Lady Jean Grey, now en route to America with the man she loves and will soon marry" (Claremont 1980, 8). The "man she loves and will soon marry" is revealed to be Mastermind, the very one planting these false experiences in her mind. Mastermind creates an entire illusionary world for Phoenix, even inserting himself into her life as her soon-to-be husband.

But that's not all—the Hellfire Club seeks to exert their influence not only on individual mutants but, eventually, mutants and non-mutants alike across the globe. It is revealed that the Hellfire Club has somehow hacked, or "tapped" into Cerebro, the device designed by Professor Xavier in order to identify and locate both humans and mutants alike around the world. Cerebro is a sort of supercomputer that works by detecting brainwaves. Mastermind muses on the potential of Cerebro, saying, "Poor Xavier. If only he knew ... that the Hellfire Club has a tap on his precious Cerebro, and that every scrap of data in its memory banks is ours for the asking" (Claremont 1980, 13). Professor Xavier usually uses Cerebro to identify and track down potential mutants in order to recruit them to Professor Xavier's School for Gifted Youngers—the X-Men's campus for training young mutants. The Hellfire Club's plan is to recruit mutants themselves by reaching them before the X-Men can. Thus, the Hellfire Club uses technology with complete disregard for privacy in order to fill their ranks in secrecy.

The Dark Phoenix Saga is certainly the most influential and prominent story featuring Marvel's iteration of the Hellfire Club. The club may play a role in other stories but is not often the focal point. The four-issue run *The Origin of the Inner Circle* provides a richer history of the club, including its origins in the Salem Witch Trials. Many of the themes here echo those found in *The Dark Phoenix Saga*. Above all else, the club seeks power and status for its members. In issue #4, new initiates to the club are told "your outstanding achievements have set you all above the rank and file of common society. The time has come to assume your rightful places among the world's elite, the architects of tomorrow" (Raab 2000). This is perhaps one of the clearest statements in Marvel's fiction of the Hellfire Club's ethos and motivations. The members seek to be elevated above the mere ordinary and to hold true power and influence over the affairs of the world. This too is one of the characteristics of Marvel's Hellfire Club most representative of the fears and anxieties of real-world conspiracy theorists—the anxiety that these secret societies exist and that their chief ambition is to grow more powerful and to determine the fates of others from behind the scenes, to be the "architects of tomorrow" (Raab 2000).

We have built some background knowledge of the historical Hellfire Clubs of eighteenth-century England and Ireland, and also explored the Marvel Comics supervillain group of the same name. We have established an interesting parallel between the historical clubs that inspired the fiction of the comic books. However, there is more at play here than comic books simply drawing inspiration from the past. The superhero genre of comic books specifically provides a unique platform for writers and artists to depict societal fears and anxieties about conspiracy theories, and, more specifically, conspiracy theories about secret societies.

One of the reasons this is true has already been hinted at. Superhero comic books are often over-the-top and campy, allowing for an environment where it does not seem unusual to have villains with such on-the-nose names as "Mastermind" for the ones pulling the strings behind the scenes. The superhero genre allows for characters whose superpowers directly reflect the character's motivations, ambitions, personality, and morality. Superhero comics create a space in which the reader can see their anxieties play out on the page. In real life, the reader might be worried about the extent to which the media they consume contains verified information versus propaganda, whether they are being lied to and manipulated or not, and so on. In the pages of a comic book or graphic novel like *The Dark Phoenix Saga*, the reader sees these concerns given life in the form of villains conjuring lifelike illusions out of thin air, exerting full control over the mind and actions of their victim, and more. And while these fears are given life on the page, it is a safe space to let these fears play out. The over-the-top camp of superhero stories allows for the reader to navigate these worries without the actual threat of conspiracy.

Certainly, this is not limited to characters in the Hellfire Club. It is no mistake that villains like Mysterio and Loki have been big players in recent years in both television and cinema. There are dozens and dozens, if not hundreds, of characters across comics media with similar abilities. Of course, these characters are not found only in the Marvel universe; rather, they can be seen in the works of essentially any comics publisher. These characters represent our fears about being manipulated, manifested on the page.

Superhero Comics and Reader Agency

The reason we fear, and resist manipulation is because we want to maintain agency. In the real world, the idea of shadowy groups controlling the world behind the scenes threatens our sense of agency. If we are made to believe that the New World Order is rigging an election or deciding on a winner for us, it renders our vote obsolete. If we think the Deep State is conducting false flag events meant to mislead us, our belief in our own agency is damaged this way as well.

However, in a way that at first seems contradictory, conspiracy theories about secret societies also provide believers with a way to regain that sense of agency. Schöpfer et al. (2023) explain that conspiracy theories can allow believers to gain a "sense of coherence" in which conspiracy theories "help their followers make sense of the complexity of the world by providing them with simple, overarching narratives" (2). Furthermore, conspiracy theories may help believers to feel their lives have meaning because "what they are doing matters in the grand scheme of things" (Schöpfer et al. 2023, 2). Schöpfer et al. acknowledge that, upon initial consideration, conspiracy theories about secret societies controlling the world would seemingly result in a loss of agency. However, these conspiracy theories allow people to believe in a narrative that is likely simpler than the complexities of reality (often, a single conspiracy theory works to connect and explain a multitude of events). Additionally, believers may feel that they matter and that they can make a difference. As Schöpfer et al. (2023) put it, "conspiracy theories might provide people who usually feel they are powerless with the illusion that they can make a difference. Indeed, because conspiracy theories purport to identify the 'real' enemy behind all societies' problems … they can provide them with the feeling that they too can fight for the common good" (2). This line of thinking is also established by Shermer (2022, 2), who underscores the feelings of happiness and empowerment that believers in QAnon express thanks to believing they are "in possession of … secret knowledge." Believers in conspiracy theories may feel less like members of a fringe group, as they can join social media groups, sign petitions, engage in activism, and otherwise try to get their message of what they perceive to be truth out to a wider audience. In this way, conspiracy theories create this semi-paradoxical effect in which the imagined secret society removes one's agency, while simultaneously creating order out of a chaotic world and giving one the feeling they can fight back, that they can help to shine a light on the truth.

People gravitate towards superhero comics that feature stories about these types of conspiracies as well. Comics allow us to see these fears about a loss of agency laid bare on the page, but there are other important characteristics of the superhero comic book that make the experience of reading stories about these fears a cathartic and empowering experience. Just as conspiracy theories about secret societies provide a simplified narrative for very complicated events, so too can comic books. As previously mentioned, superhero comic books can be very obvious and in-your-face with their messaging, with characters whose powers and aliases give away their true nature and motivation. Of course, there are numerous exceptions to the rule, with comic books and graphic novels that tackle complicated subjects with great care and nuance. However, the genre has roots in very black and white, good versus evil storytelling. At their heart, superhero stories are about this struggle. Even when the details of the story are nuanced, anyone can immediately follow the basic premise of good against evil. And just as real-life conspiracy theories paradoxically grant us the very agency they at first remove, so too do superhero comics provide us a sense of agency in the form of emotional catharsis seeing these conflicts play out on the page. The reader roots for the X-Men and for the downfall of the Hellfire Club because this type of story engages our craving for simplicity and agency in the same ways that conspiracy theories do. And, after all, in a world where supervillains exist, so too must superheroes. The iconic image of the superhero provides us with a model of who we want to be and who we could be. It is no coincidence that so many superheroes, prior to gaining their powers, were ordinary people just like us.

The message to the average person is clear: anyone can make a difference. Anyone can help in the ongoing cosmic battle between good and evil. This idea is further enhanced by the fact that so many superheroes are, as described by Costello (2009, 10), "flawed heroes or antiheroes." Costello (2009, 10) points to Benjamin Grimm, also known as the Thing, as being "blessed with strength but cursed with ugliness." Several other characters are touched upon, including Spider-man, who struggles with bearing responsibility for his uncle's death, and Thor, "who was condemned to live on Earth rather than Asgard because of his lack of humility" (Costello 2009, 11). A similar sentiment is echoed by DiPaolo (2011, 219), who writes that "Marvel comic books have long invited direct reader identification with Marvel heroes, who are designed to be as flawed and 'human' as the reader." These characters show that people can resist the typical stereotypes of what a hero looks like, and they can make mistakes, while still possessing great power and the ability to make a difference in the world. Importantly, many superheroes are also people with disabilities. Representation matters, and the fact that readers can look to characters like Barbara Gordon, who uses a wheelchair, or Daredevil, the blind crimefighter (to name just two out of a minimum of several dozen) is tremendously valuable in helping readers with disabilities feel like there are heroes out there who they can relate to. This is one of many ways in which superhero comics allow readers to develop, strengthen, and maintain a sense of agency. This effect is only compounded when it comes to superhero stories that deal with conspiracies.

There is no better venue for portraying this perpetual conflict than the superhero comic book. Comics are an artform that is especially well-suited to depicting political and ideological tension. As McAllister, Sewell, and Gordon (2001) explain, "Comic art combines printed words and pictures in a unique way. The complex nature of this combination allows for much flexibility in the manipulation of meaning" (3). Intriguingly, this interplay of word and image creates an environment which encourages "multiple interpretations, even ones completely oppositional to any specific artistic intent" (McAllister, Sewell, and Gordon 2001, 4). This is another reason why people might turn to superhero comics in an attempt to reclaim a sense of agency. Comics, perhaps more than artforms which consist purely of word or image alone, allow for ambiguity and a multitude of textual interpretations. This gives the reader the power to engage in meaning-making independent of authorial intent. Comics readers can often superimpose their own ideological preferences onto comics because of the agency and freedom of interpretation afforded by the medium.

Marginalization in the X-Men Universe and Comics as a Marginalized Medium

Several conflicts exist within the X-Men universe. As previously discussed, these showcase tensions between good and evil as well as between various classes, as the Hellfire Club represents the secretive, wealthy, and powerful elite. Another conflict central to the X-Men mythos is the marginalization of mutants. A recurring plot point throughout X-Media is the attempt to oppress mutants, strip them of their rights, and in some cases even slaughter them in acts of genocide. In many ways, such X-Men storylines serve as an allegory for historical atrocities such as American slavery, racial segregation, and the Holocaust. This is made explicit with the character of Magneto, generally depicted in the canon as a Holocaust survivor who vows never to allow something like that to happen to him again. As Magneto states in Chris Claremont's iconic story *X-Men: God Loves, Man Kills*, "I have lived under a dictatorship and seen my family butchered by its servants. When I rule, it will be for the betterment of all" (1982).

The brutal oppression and hate faced by mutants in the X-Men universe is further elucidated for readers right from the opening pages of the *God Loves, Man Kills* storyline, which sees a pair of nine and eleven-year-old youths executed in cold blood by an anti-mutant group calling themselves the Purifiers. Other mutants find themselves called "muties," a slur in the X-Men canon. During the climax of the story, X-Men member Cyclops confronts the Rev. William Stryker, the leader of the Purifiers, asking, "Are arbitrary labels more important than the way we live our lives, what we're supposed to be more important than what we actually are?!" (Claremont 1982). Cyclops goes on to exclaim, "For all you know, we could be the real human race, and the rest of you, the mutants" (Claremont 1982). Stryker responds, pointing at Nightcrawler, another X-Men member known for his devilish appearance, with blue-black skin, yellow eyes, and a barbed tail, "Human?! You dare call that … thing— human?!?" (Claremont 1982).

The X-Men in Marvel's comics face Othering processes caused by ignorance, fear, hatred, and, importantly, the spreading of lies and conspiracy theories which results in harm and violence. This directly echoes but inverts the real-world dangers posed by the spread of hateful theories like the Great Replacement theory. This is a far-right conspiracy theory which posits that demographic change, namely a decline in white birth rates, is the result of intentional actions (such as mass migration and other sociopolitical factors) in an effort to bring about demographic changes such that whites become a minority demographic (Beydoun and Sediqe 2023; Goetz 2021). Indeed, Beydoun and Sediqe (2023, 72) explain that proponents of the Great Replacement theory see "the influx of immigrants and rising influence of Black culture" as the primary mechanisms of these demographic shifts. This racist conspiracy theory is problematic for a number of reasons: it frames racial and ethnic demographic fluctuations as a problem to be dealt with, it presents these fluctuations as intentional and even genocidal, and it places blame on minority racial and ethnic groups. In this way, the Great Replacement theory preys on what Beydoun and Sediqe (2023, 72) call "mounting white anxiety" and presents minority groups as the Other, and even an outright enemy. Beydoun and Sedique (2023, 72) go on to draw a direct link between belief in these types of racist conspiracy theories and terrorist attacks which target Muslim, Jewish, black, and Latinx groups. The alienating and discriminatory effects of conspiracy theories like this are clear. It is also clear how the comic world of the X-Men takes inspiration from Othering ideologies like this to depict this kind of hateful discrimination and terrorism. However, rather than becoming a space where the reader becomes more fearful of the Other, *X-Men: God Loves, Man Kills* showcases the dangers of falling victim to conspiracy theories built on marginalization.

The examples shown in *X-Men: God Loves, Man Kills* demonstrate comics as a medium adept at portraying the capacity of conspiracy theories to Other and marginalize groups of people for immutable characteristics over which they have no control. As opposed to traditional media like film and literature, which rely on image or word alone, comics utilize both in order to create something original. The interplay of image and word allows the reader to become a more active participant in the reading experience, as the reader imagines the action that occurs in the gutters between and outside of the comic book panels.

Comics as a medium, though, are inextricably linked with the concept of marginalization, as comic books themselves have historically been treated as lesser in comparison to traditional media. Berninger, Ecke, and Haberkorn (2010, 1) even make the argument that comics are "certainly older than moving pictures." Despite this claim, however, the authors note that comics "have received less critical attention than either" (Berninger, Ecke, and Haberkorn 2010, 1). They continue to argue that "comics have long been marginalized by critics and academics" and that "they have been described as a fringe phenomenon" (Berninger, Ecke, and Haberkorn 2010, 4). Pustz (1999, 22–23) further discusses the marginalization and isolation of comic book fandom, citing "conflict among its members" as well as "boundaries between all comic book readers and outsiders." These "boundaries" come in a variety of forms. Comic books themselves can feel intimidating for someone new to the genre to get into—how does one know where to start reading a superhero comic like Batman, Superman, or Spider-man when there might be hundreds or even thousands of issues already published? And as Pustz (1999, 221–23) points out, comic book shops themselves act as a sort of "clubhouse" for the comic book readership, offering a comforting and welcoming environment for the in-group but sometimes creating an atmosphere that is "so intimidating that new readers, especially women, can find it difficult to become involved." Comic books, including their culture and fandom, are at once increasingly influential drivers of popular culture, yet also closed-off and inaccessible to the general public.

These aspects of comic books offer a medium where unique artistic techniques as well as the isolated and marginalized nature of comic culture itself allows authors and artists to depict marginalization as well as conspiracy theories in which the marginalized are targeted. When Magneto rages against the evil machinations of the Reverend Stryker and his Purifiers attempt to commit genocide against mutantkind, so too does the reader share in this rage while also fostering a great sense of empathy with the marginalized mutants. Similarly, as the X-Men battle against the Hellfire Club and their schemes, the reader is given heroes to root for. The readership wants nothing more than to see the X-Men shine the light of truth on the shadowy Hellfire Club, unraveling their plots and bringing the conspirators to justice. This is in no small part because the reader aligns with the marginalized X-Men, and the power of comics allows us to see the battle of good and evil play out in a satisfying way. And just as conspiracy theories may allow members of a fringe group to feel more like they are part of an exclusive in-group, comic books likewise see their fandom enjoying the comforts of shared culture.

Conclusion: The Proliferation of Conspiracy Theories and the Role of Comics

It may feel like belief in conspiracy theories is becoming increasingly commonplace. Research refutes the idea that more people believe in conspiracy theories than ever before (Uscinski et al. 2022). Perhaps the prevalence of social media and other forms of mass media has simply shifted fringe beliefs to the forefront of public discourse. Interestingly, the emergence of the coffee house in the eighteenth century played a similar role to social media today. Ryan (2012) discusses the importance of the coffee house not in propagating conspiracy theories but in helping Enlightenment philosophy, an important precursor to the hellfire clubs, to spread (6). As Ryan (2012) explains, "the most important development [for the establishment of clubs] was the increased proliferation of coffee houses and taverns as locations in which men could meet and mingle" (6). The author goes on to tell us that "the coffee house environment facilitated the spread of Enlightenment philosophy, which advocated a more sophisticated society based on scientific and rational principles" (Ryan 2012, 6). This embrace of science and rationality is part of the cultural shift that allowed hellfire clubs to take root and engage in the exchange of what were deemed to be blasphemous ideas. Just as the coffee house and tavern of the eighteenth century allowed for the accelerated exchange of ideas, social media today plays a similar role. While belief in conspiracy theories may not be rapidly increasing, it is possible that social media allows for increasingly fringe ideas to become commonplace and centered in the media diet of the average person.

Still, even if belief in conspiracies has remained roughly constant, it seems difficult to argue that these theories are harmless. Even if the amount of people subscribing to conspiratorial beliefs has remained roughly constant, social media provides a platform where these beliefs can reach wide audiences and continue to spread. As Shermer puts it, "In the age of social media, what counts is not evidence so much as retweets, re-posts, and likes" (2020). Conspiracy theories today seem to possess a dangerous undercurrent, as believers in anti-vaccination conspiracy theories might choose to forgo vaccinations and actively advocate against their use, and we have seen belief in conspiracy theories about electoral fraud result in incidents like the January 6 U.S. Capitol attack.

Clearly, conspiratorial thinking has the potential to result in real-world harm. But for some, conspiracy theories offer a way of explaining the chaos of the world in a manner that simplifies things and presents an opportunity for the average person to feel like they matter and can make meaningful contributions—even if those contributions are misguided. If true evil exists in the world, or if supervillains exist who can violate our right to privacy via mind-reading telepathy or dictate our thoughts and actions through the power of mind control, so too must goodness exist in the form of superheroes.

It seems conceivable that one might wonder, since belief in conspiracy theories can be dangerous and harmful, whether comic books depicting conspiracies also have the potential for harm. The answer to this is clearly

The Hellfire Club (Milligan) 77

no. It often feels like every type of emerging media or culture is forced to withstand attacks like this. There are still debates about video games causing violence, despite evidence showing they do not (Ferguson 2015; Markey, Markey, and French 2015). Dungeons & Dragons faced accusations of Satanism. Certainly, various genres of music from rock to heavy metal to rap and hip-hop have seen similar criticisms. Similarly, comic books could be (and have been) derided as harmful. To the contrary, what comic books do is allow us to see our fears play out in a safe, controlled, fictional setting. People who have anxieties about the potential loss of agency resulting from secret societies ruling the world can explore these anxieties through comics. The juxtaposition of conspiracies with other fantastical elements present in superhero comics will, if anything, make conspiracy theories seem like just more fantasy.

Comic books can help us to differentiate reality from fiction, but this is not to say that they cannot have real-world impacts. It is just that those impacts, in my view, tend to be beneficial rather than harmful. As already stated, comics allow us to see our anxieties play out in a controlled environment. The superhero genre also establishes a dynamic of clear-cut good versus evil, and provides the reader not just with villains, but also heroes to look up to and to emulate in our lives. The world of Marvel comics displays a reimagining of the real-world Hellfire Club, where the true history of the club and its members is exaggerated and warped to give the reader a picture of the definitive secret society bent on world domination. In reality, the members of the historical hellfire clubs of eighteenth-nineteenth-century England and Ireland gathered to drink, to gamble, and to speak their mind about the church in a way that was seen as blasphemous. Yes, occasionally the boisterous, alcohol-fueled club activities could turn violent and the clubs, in some cases, deservedly earned a poor reputation. But their more lasting impact is seen through the spreading of myth and legend. Thus, the Hellfire Club established a lore which is kept alive in Marvel comics today. Just as the Hellfire Club's mythical nature helped to inspire the idea of secret societies and shadowy cabals, so too does the fictionalized version in the X-Men universe help to keep the legend alive. Today, many believers in conspiracy theories continue to fret over imagined groups like the Deep State, the Illuminati, or the New World Order. These people likely fear a loss of agency and may feel overwhelmed by the complexities of the world, and so turn to conspiracy theories. After all, "conspiracy theorists believe that in uncovering and exposing an evil cabal, they are doing the world a positive service" (Shermer 2022, 86). This provides believers with a sense of agency as well as a mechanism for ordering and making sense of the world. The genre and medium of superhero comic books mirrors this dynamic by playing on these anxieties and giving them form on the page in both text and image. Like conspiratorial thinking, superhero comics provide an opportunity to make sense of a chaotic world and to believe in real heroes. Comics are also relatable when it comes to fears of marginalization by oppressive groups because of their own past as a marginalized artform. While conspiracy theories can in certain cases be dangerous, superhero comics should be embraced as a safe environment to explore anxieties about marginalization and loss of agency further.

References

Berninger, Mark, Jochen Ecke, and Gideon Haberkorn. (2010). *Comics as a Nexus of Cultures: Essays on the Interplay of Media, Disciplines, and International Perspectives*. Jefferson: McFarland.
Beydoun, Khaled A., and Nura A. Sediqe. (2023). "The Great Replacement Theory: White Supremacy as Terrorism?" *Harvard Civil Rights—Civil Liberties Law Review* 58, no. 1.
Claremont, Chris. (1980). *The Uncanny X-Men: The Dark Phoenix Saga*. 3rd ed., New York: Marvel Worldwide.
Claremont, Chris. (1982). *X-Men: God Loves, Man Kills*. New York: Marvel Comics.
Costello, Matthew J. (2009). *Secret Identity Crisis: Comic Books & the Unmasking of Cold War America*. New York: Continuum International.
Dickey, Colin. (2013). *Under the Eye of Power: How Fear of Secret Societies Shapes American Democracy*. New York: Viking/Penguin Random House.
DiPaolo, Marc. (2011). *War, Politics, and Superheroes: Ethics and Propaganda in Comics and Film*. Jefferson: McFarland.
Ellis, Warren. (2009). *Transmetropolitan Vol. 1: Back on the Street*. New York: DC Comics.
Ferguson, Christopher J. (2015). "Does Movie or Video Game Violence Predict Societal Violence? It Depends on What You Look at and When." *Journal of Communication* 65, no. 1. https://doi.org/10.1111/jcom.12142.
Goetz, Judith. (2021). "'The Great Replacement': Reproduction and Population Policies of the Far Right, Taking the Identitarians As an Example." *Journal of Diversity and Gender Studies* 8, no. 1. https://doi.org/10.21825/digest.v8i1.16944.
Gulyas, Aaron John. (2016). *Conspiracy Theories: The Roots, Themes, and Propagation of Paranoid Political and Cultural Narratives*. Jefferson: McFarland.
Lord, Evelyn. (2010). *The Hell-Fire Clubs: Sex, Satanism, and Secret Societies*. New Haven: Yale University Press.
Markey, Patrick M., Charlotte N. Markey, and Juliana E. French. (2015). "Violent Video Games and Real-World Violence: Rhetoric versus Data." *Psychology of Popular Media Culture* 4, no. 4. https://doi.org/10.1037/ppm0000030.
McAllister, Matthew P., Edward H. Sewell, Jr., and Ian Gordon. (2001). *Comics and Ideology*. New York: Peter Lang.
Moore, Alan. (1988). *V for Vendetta*. New York: DC Comics.
Pustz, Matthew J. (1999). *Comic Book Culture: Fanboys and True Believers*. Jackson: University Press of Mississippi.
Raab, Ben. (2000). *X-Men The Hellfire Club: The Origin of the Inner Circle*. New York: Marvel Comics.
Ryan, David. (2012). *Blasphemers & Blackguards: The Irish Hellfire Clubs*. Dublin: Merrion.
Salazar-Fernández, Camila, María José Baeza-Rivera, Diego Manríquez-Robles, Natalia Salinas-Oñate, and Malik Sallam. (2023). "From Conspiracy to Hesitancy: The Longitudinal Impact of COVID-19 Vaccine Conspiracy Theories on Perceived Vaccine Effectiveness." *Vaccines* 11, no. 7. http://dx.doi.org/10.3390/vaccines11071150.

Schöpfer, Céline, Angela Gaia F. Abatista, Joffrey Fuhrer, and Florian Cova. (2023). "'Where There Are Villains, There Will Be Heroes': Belief in Conspiracy Theories as an Existential Tool to Fulfill Need for Meaning." *Personality and Individual Differences* 200: 111900–.

Shermer, Michael. (2020). "Why People Believe Conspiracy Theories." *Skeptic* 25, no. 1: 17.

Shermer, Michael. (2022). *Conspiracy: Why the Rational Believe the Irrational.* Baltimore: Johns Hopkins University Press.

Suresh, Vishnuprasad Padinjaredath, Gianluca Nogara, Felipe Cardoso, Stefano Cresci, Silvia Giordano, and Luca Luceri. (2023). "Tracking Fringe and Coordinated Activity on Twitter Leading Up To the US Capitol Attack." Proceedings of the 18th International Conference on Web and Social Media, 2024. https://doi.org/10.48550/arXiv.2302.04450.

Uscinski, Joseph, Adam Enders, Casey Klofstad, Michelle Seelig, Hugo Drochon, Kamal Premaratne, and Manohar Murthi. (2023). "Have Beliefs in Conspiracy Theories Increased Over Time?" *PLoS ONE* 17, no. 7: 1–19. e0270429. https://doi.org/10.1371/journal.pone.0270429.

van Prooijen, Jan-Willem, and Karen M. Douglas. (2018). "Belief in Conspiracy Theories: Basic Principles of an Emerging Research Domain." *European Journal of Social Psychology* 48, no. 7. 10.1002/ejsp.2530.

Webber, Tim. (2023). "The History of the Hellfire Club." Marvel. https://www.marvel.com/articles/comics/hellfire-club-history-members-inner-circle-explained.

The End Is Near
Doomsday Conspiracy Theories and Apocalyptic Paranoia

DANIEL P. COMPORA

Introduction

The end of the world has been predicted countless times over the centuries. However, despite all the dire predictions, various prophecies, and Biblical foretelling, the world is still going strong (or limping along, depending on one's perspective). One of the most prominent events that failed to deliver on the promise of the impending apocalypse was the Mayan calendar scare of 2012, which was "the most widely-disseminated doomsday tale in human history, thanks to the internet, Hollywood and an ever-eager press corps" (Little 2012). Propagators of this theory seized upon information that was incompletely presented and generally misunderstood. The scare was derived from the fact that one of the three calendars used by ancient Mayans, the Long Count Calendar, recorded time in five distinct blocks, one of which was scheduled to end around December 21, 2012. Though no documented Mayan prophecies actually predicted the world's demise, it did not stop conspiracy theorists from doing so. Though this may have been the most prominent publicized end-times conspiracy of the Internet era that failed to pay off, conspiracy theorists remain undeterred by such failed predictions and look to other calendar events to peddle this distinct brand of fear. Many end-of-world prophecies are influenced by, if not based on, religious influences, specifically, the Biblical Book of Revelations.

Biblical and Folkloric Influences

Even though most doomsday prophecies are based on Christian eschatological beliefs, many proponents of such theories are not even

Christian. "End Times believers are a huge swath of the population, and not limited to Christians. About a third of the world's current eight billion inhabitants are expecting Jesus to return" (Bodner et al. 2021, 118). This encompasses people of all religious beliefs, even those who do not follow a specific doctrine. Interestingly, this indicates that people are willing to believe a conspiracy theory, even if it goes against their religious beliefs. Under such fundamental Christian beliefs, end times scenarios occur in several different stages, including the rise of the false prophet and Antichrist, the establishment of a One World Religion, and a seven-year tribulation period. Many though not all Christian denominations believe in an end-time event called the Rapture, which would see all of Christ's followers, both living and dead, rise into the sky to meet the returning Jesus Christ. This second coming of Jesus Christ paves the way for the Millennium, a 1000-year reign of peace.

This Biblical end-times scenario was the driving force behind the 1990s Project Blue Beam, which emerged on the World Wide Web, foretelling an imminent end-of-the-world scenario perpetrated by NASA. This conspiracy theory, peddled initially by the late Canadian journalist Serge Monast, claimed that using an impressive array of satellite and hologram technology, the imminent, hoaxed second coming of Christ was being planned by NASA and other powerful, secret government entities. This powerful display would put the world in disarray, help establish a new-age religion, bring the Antichrist into power, and usher in a New World Order.* Monast may have died in 1996, but interest in Project Blue Beam has not. Due to the conspiracy's reference to epidemics, interest in the Project Blue Beam conspiracy resurfaced during the Covid-19 pandemic.

Examples of conspiracies during the internet era are numerous. World events sometimes trigger interest in old conspiracies, and the internet has enabled their mass distribution and spread. The death of Pope John Paul II in 2004 revived interest in "The Prophecies of St. Malachy,"† which was discovered in 1590 and predicted that only 112 popes would serve until the Last Judgment. John Paul II's death ushered in the era of the final two popes. More recently, the eccentric conspiracy theorist Paul Begley predicted that the end of days would occur on December 21, 2020, because of a rare planetary alignment. This prophecy coincided with one

---

*The New World Order, which focuses on secret societies operating behind the scenes to bring about totalitarian, global rule, is a detailed conspiracy theory integrated into many others, including Project Blue Beam. The theory will be explored in detail later in the essay.

†Many versions of this document exist online, even though most are similar, differences exist. For this discussion, the version found on Catholictradition.org is perhaps the most detailed.

by astrologer, syndicated columnist, and self-proclaimed psychic Jeane Dixon, who predicted Armageddon would occur in 2020. Harold Camping predicted the Rapture not once but twice in 2011. When May 21 passed without incident, he corrected himself, indicating that October 21 would be the day of reckoning. Camping is not alone in incorrectly predicting the rapture and subsequent end of the world. The late Kenton Beshore pinpointed 2021 as the beginning of the end times. These religious conspiracies are supplemented by more secular ones, the most bizarre of which is attributed to the French occultist and seer Michel de Nostredame, more famously known as Nostradamus. Words ascribed to him have been interpreted to predict a zombie apocalypse to occur in 2021, supposedly. "Few young people: half-dead to give a start … all the world to end" (Bardos 2021). Of course, false prophecies attributed to Nostradamus are plentiful on the internet, and no such zombie apocalypse occurred in 2021. Others have remained more believable with their predictions, focusing less on Evangelical teachings and more on secret government cabals. The conspiracy website ThreeWorldWars.com* predicts the coming of a third world war, which, if conspiratorial history is to be believed, has been planned for nearly a century.

The attraction to the end of the world prophecies and conspiracies has always been present. However, world events, especially the presidency of Donald J. Trump, a noted conspiracy theorist who spread the birther conspiracy regarding the legitimacy of President Barack Obama's citizenship, and the worldwide effects of the Covid-19 global pandemic, have only increased interest in such narratives. "Conspiracy theories reflect our human need to get a whole picture of an ambiguous phenomenon to feel control over nebulous circumstances" (Bodner et al. 2021, 42). While we may not be able to control the future, we comfort ourselves in at least "knowing" what will happen. People strongly desire to understand a phenomenon that, in many ways, is inexplicable. Prominent doomsday prophecies and conspiracies have focused on both religious and secular narratives. Project Blue Beam, "The Prophecy of the Popes," and the New World Order are among the strongest, most popular Internet-era conspiracies that reflect people's desire to eschew simple, rational explanations and believe complicated theories to explain phenomena outside their comprehension. These narratives represent modern folklore because they are "malleable," adaptable, changeable, and mostly anonymous (McNeill 2013, 9). Even centuries-old doomsday narratives continue to proliferate on the

---

*The website, though still operational, appears to have not been updated since 2006 and no longer accepts subscriptions to its newsletter. It still contains a wealth of documentation and resources dedicated to this conspiracy theory.

internet, though they have been adapted to fit a modern context. Examining such narratives in a folkloric context is essential to understanding their continued popularity and dissemination.

Project Blue Beam

One of the most detailed internet-era conspiracy theories centers on Project Blue Beam, a joint project between the United States government and NASA. Interest in Project Blue Beam was reignited during the Covid-19 pandemic, as some elements of the conspiracy refer to plagues. "He [the Antichrist] would be able to control and manipulate weather patterns, earthquakes, crop yields, epidemics, water resources, and many other things" (Brophilius 2012, 25). Despite this revival in interest, Project Blue Beam has failed to become a reality. Project Blue Beam was fueled by the emergence of new technology, including satellites and holograms, that would make staging such a hoax possible. It hews closely to Christian beliefs of a second coming of Jesus Christ, as foretold in the New Testament Book of Revelations. Canadian journalist Serge Monast presented this conspiracy in 1994. He died mysteriously of a heart attack in 1996 after the abduction of his daughter, despite no history of heart disease. While numerous web pages and YouTube videos discuss this conspiracy, access to actual primary sources is practically nonexistent. Those that do exist have apocryphal origins. Monast supposedly published a book about the phenomenon in 1994, republished in 2023 by Ethos Publishing, but this work is merely 30 pages. Being a new translation, it is hard to determine how much of this material is authentic or influenced by other translations that have surfaced over the years. It differs from what is believed to be the original text, which is archived on the website Educate-Yourself.org. The transcript of a 1994 lecture Monast gave is also archived here; it provides more depth and detail than Monast's book and appears to be the focus of many of the sources found on YouTube. In addition, The Internet Archive has curated several files from the late 1990s and early 2000s that discuss the theory. While these versions complement each other and were generated closer to the initial spread of the theory, they have not been verified as definitive texts.

Of course, this is true of any folkloric tests. According to Lynne McNeill (2013), "in order to identify something as folklore, we have to find it in more than one place" (12). Prominent folklorist Jan Brunvand (1994) supports this notion, stating that two critical characteristics of genuine folklore are that it exists in different versions and the elements become formularized (12). Despite differences in each source detailing Project

Blue Beam, several elements remain consistent. The conspiracy features a multi-stage plan that would systematically prepare people for a false second coming of Jesus Christ. Though at times preposterous, the detail and specificity in these documents lend credence to their believability. A study conducted by Shauna Bowles led to the conclusion that "closemindedness and certain social motives may contribute to individuals latching on to specific conspiracy theories … rather than abstract conspiratorial ideas" (Bowles et al. 2023, 283). Presenting a disturbing scenario, supported by specific details, makes such theories believable but not necessarily plausible. "Conspiracy theories … seek to explain upsetting events by identifying a supposed secret group of evildoers who must be opposed to bring the world back to a state of calm and order" (Bodner et al. 2021, 2). Project Blue Beam does just that—it provides a specific, identifiable perpetrator (NASA) that people recognize, providing a convenient enemy and an explanation that helps people understand a complex phenomenon, albeit in a convoluted way.

The first stage would see the world struck with multiple disasters and paradigm-changing discoveries that would disprove the foundational elements of all world religions. The second stage would employ holographic technology created by NASA that would portray the Second Coming in a blasphemous fashion. Representing key figures from several religions, this fake Second Coming would help usher in a new world religion and pave the way for the reign of the Antichrist.

> Then the projections of Jesus, Mohammed, Buddha, Krishna, etc., will merge into one after correct explanations of the mysteries and revelations will have been disclosed. This one god will, in fact, be the Antichrist, who will explain that the various scriptures have been misunderstood and misinterpreted, and that the religions of old are responsible for turning brother against brother, and nation against nation, therefore old religions must be abolished to make way for the new age new world religion, representing the one god Antichrist they see before them [Monast 1994].

In addition to this artificial Second Coming, the Rapture of Christ's church would be faked. This end-time event occurs when all Christian believers who are alive, along with resurrected believers, rise into the air to meet their returning savior. While this Christian view is pervasive and generally positive, other views exist. Tim LaHaye and Jerry Jenkins, authors of the Christian fiction book series *Left Behind*, focused on the sudden disappearance of Christ's followers and the struggles of those who were not raptured. Others believe that UFOs and aliens will be involved (McMillen 2004, 225). Project Blue Beam would require tractor-beams to abduct people, pulling them into the skies, to simulate the Rapture. Of course, tractor-beams have been depicted in science fiction films for decades, including famous blockbusters like *Star Wars*, but up until 2023, actual tractor-beam technology only worked on a microscopic level; a study finally proved that "laser pulling of a macroscopic object in rarefied gas" could work on an observable level (Wang et al. 2023, 2672). That is a long way from being able to pull millions of living people into the sky. These events, once completed, would usher in the New World Order, a term commonly used to describe a secret world government operating in the shadows to bring about totalitarian, global rule.

The third stage would employ "electronically augmented two-way communication" to make people believe that they hear their god speak to them telepathically. This psychological attack would remove independent thought and free will, placing people under an extreme form of mind control, leading to widespread destruction and chaos.

> Telepathic and electronically augmented two-way communication ... will reach each person from within his or her own mind, convincing each of them that their own god is speaking to them from the very depths of their own soul.... The rays will then interlace with their natural thinking to form what we call diffuse artificial thought [Monast 1994].

With people worldwide under the control of this technology, implementing mass societal and governmental changes could be accomplished quickly. The loss of autonomy and free thought constitutes significant components of many conspiracy theories, including ones featuring the nebulous New World Order. Project Blue Beam explains how this brainwashing will be accomplished conceptually (through telepathic and electronically augmented two-way communication) but fails to explain the mechanism to achieve this feat. In short, Project Blue Beam raises intriguing, albeit ludicrous, ideas but fails to explain the execution of such processes adequately.

The fourth step of Project Blue Beam, Universal Supernatural Manifestations via Electronics, occurs in multiple phases. The first orientation would prepare the world for an imminent alien invasion, forcing every country to deplete its nuclear arsenal in defense of this imaginary threat. The second would simulate the Rapture and the Second Coming. The third would create madness, leading to mass suicide, widespread murder, and mayhem, making people all over the world "ready for the new messiah to re-establish order and peace at any cost, even at the cost of abdication of freedom" (Monast 1994). Details of what follows this spectacle are scant, as Project Blue Beam focuses on how the end of the world as we know it comes about, paving the way for the emergence of the New World Order. This lack of specificity is typically written off as being by design. According to Aidan Brophilius (2021), author of the self-published *Project Blue Beam: The Quest for a New World Order*, that is because Project Blue Beam and its execution remain in shadows because they have been carefully hidden in shrouds of deception by its executioners (35). Explicit details of the technological show abound in these documents, but details of what these shadow groups hope to accomplish remain mysterious.

Perhaps, though, the origins of this nefarious project were not hatched in the dark, shadowy operations of some global cabal. One theory posits that Project Blue Beam was always a work of speculative fiction— specifically, it is believed to be the plot of a rejected movie script written by *Star Trek* creator Gene Roddenberry. "*Star Trek: The God Thing*" would have been the first *Star Trek* feature film in 1976, but Paramount Studios rejected it. Joel Engel (1994), Roddenberry's biographer, indicates that the proposed script included "a flying saucer, hovering above Earth, that was programmed to send down people who looked like prophets, including Jesus Christ" (165). The goal was to create confusion and doubt among the masses to destroy people's faith, making it easier for the aliens' religion to spread. The parallels to Project Blue Beam are impossible to ignore. Engel's biography was released the same year (1994) that Monast published his treatise on Project Blue Beam. Though diehard *Star Trek* fans are most likely familiar with this failed script, it is unlikely that the general public would be, making the idea seem new at the time. Though Roddenberry, who passed away in 1991, failed to bring this vision to the screen, parts of the story appear to have lived on in Project Blue Beam.

This desire to bring about the world's end illustrates the folkloric concept of ostension, which folklorist Carl Lindahl (2005) defines as "the process through which people live out legend, making it real in the most palpable sense" (164). Typically, ostension occurs when the events of a narrative are proven to be true because subsequent actions have made it so. For instance, the 2014 Slenderman stabbing in Wisconsin* occurred after dangerous tales of Slenderman had spread. The actions proved the rumors true because the perpetrators wanted it to be so. Similarly, spreading end-of-the-world scenarios with the detail expressed in Project Blue Beam illustrates a desire to bring about the final judgment. Contemporary legend scholar Bill Ellis (2000) further states, "if a narrative is widely known through oral or media transmission, individuals may become involved in real-life activities based on all or part of that narrative" (xviii–xix). While nobody has yet successfully brought about Armageddon, documents detailing such scenarios, like those that lay out the plans for Project Blue Beam, represent an extreme form of ostensive practice that could theoretically lead others to act.

---

*In 2014, Anissa Weier and Morgan Geyser, both twelve years old at the time, stabbed their friend Payton Leutner in what was believed to be a sacrifice to Slenderman, a character created on the internet (Piccotti 2023).

The Prophecy of the Popes

As intriguing and detailed as Project Blue Beam has proven to be, sometimes abstract, vague theories can attain a similar effect. The Vatican and the papacy have long been tied to end-time prophecies, with many popes considered candidates to be the Antichrist. Of course, the popes are not alone in this suspicion. They join the likes of many people whose identities have been shoehorned into the prophetic discussion, such as Bill Gates, Steve Jobs, Barack Obama, Vladimir Putin, and King Charles, to name a few. More interesting, and with a more extended history, are the supposed "Prophecies of St. Malachy," penned by an Irish saint and discovered in 1590, more than four centuries after his death. This document foretold the succession of 112 popes leading up to the final judgment. This conspiracy theory found new life in the internet era following the death of Pope John Paul II in 2005 and the resignation of Pope Benedict XVI in 2013.* Malachy's visions used vague, cryptic language open to any number of interpretations and have been, on occasion, twisted to fit a particular Pontiff. For example, the phrase attributed to John Paul II was "concerning the eclipse of the sun" (Lings 1984, 152). Believers in the prophecy point to Pope John Paul II being born and buried during solar eclipses as evidence of his fulfillment of the prophecy. However, eclipses occur two to five times yearly (Bakich 2023), and such a brief phrase is more likely to be a coincidence than proof of prophetic truth. Pope John Paul II certainly did not choose the day of his birth, but it is possible that his funeral was scheduled to coincide with an eclipse. If this were the case, such a practice would be considered an example of ostension.

According to this list, only two popes would follow John Paul II, with speculation being that the final pope would usher in the final judgment. John Paul's successor, Pope Benedict XIV, fit the phrase "concerning the glory of the olive" (Lings 1984, 153) in that the symbol of the Benedictine order is an olive branch; however, Pope Benedict XVI was not a member of this order (McHugh 2013, 46). If he chose the name to fit into the prophecy, it would be an act of ostension. Pope Francis, by Malachy's list, should be the final pope; however, the Argentinian does not fit Malachy's identifying phrase: "In the final persecution of the Holy Roman Church, Roman Peter will sit upon the throne ... the city of the seven hills will be destroyed and the terrible Judge will judge the people" (Lings 1984, 153). That has not stopped people who want to believe in the prophecy from concocting

---

*Interest in the "Prophecies of St. Malachy" was also revived by Pope Benedict XVI's death in 2022. However, since he had been retired for nearly a decade and no Papal election took place, it did not generate as much widespread interest.

convoluted explanations as to how Francis, despite his Argentinian heritage, somehow can be identified as Peter the Roman:

> The best the proponents of the prophecy have been able to do is point out that our good Cardinal Bergoglio took the name of St. Francis, whose father's name was Pietro. Of course! Plus, even though he is Argentinian, his parents are Italian [Staples 2013].

Of course, this explanation is nonsensical, obviously trying to fit a specific person to an obscure line written in a document found in the sixteenth century. Nevertheless, accepting notions like this illustrates people's strong desire to reconcile complex ideas with overly simplistic explanations. As Bodner points out, "Conspiracy theories can take on a shape similar to myth: a set of outsized but recognizable shapes that help simplify—and, more often than not, dangerously oversimplify—a complicated time" (Bodner et al. 2021, 2). These prophecies present a scenario in which the world presumably ends simply because the requisite number of popes predicted to serve has finally been reached. Such thinking ascribes the end of the world to an apocryphal four-hundred-year-old list while ignoring countless other factors that would have to occur to lead to such a catastrophe.

The theory spreads primarily through the desire to predict the unpredictable. Conrad Bauer (2022) states, "Folks are indeed often worried about the future. And some would appreciate it if there were those that might be able to see a little further down the road than the rest of us" (31). In addition, the prophecy continues to captivate people because of confirmation bias, which the American Psychological Association (2018) defines as "the tendency to gather evidence that confirms preexisting expectations, typically by emphasizing or pursuing supporting evidence while dismissing or failing to seek contradictory evidence." "The Prophecies of St. Malachy" provides vague phraseology that can be interpreted to fit whatever people want to believe. An apocryphal document they find online is more believable to them than religious scholars, church historians, and clergy members. These reputable sources have concluded that this prophecy is likely a forgery created to influence the pope's election in 1590. According to *U.S. Catholic* contributor Joseph McHugh (2013), the document allegedly identified Cardinal Girolamo Simoncelli as Malachy's prophesied choice, but Niccolò Sfondrati, who took the name Gregory XIV, was elected instead. The document is remarkably accurate until that particular election, after which the phrases become vaguer and more cryptic (46). Despite such expert testimony, the document still enjoys popularity online and resurfaces every time a change occurs in the papacy. Adding credence to its believability is that the entire papacy has seen its share of scandal over the centuries, and the papal selection process itself has been shrouded in secrecy since its inception.

The New World Order

The Vatican may have its share of secrets, and the Prophecy of the Popes illustrates that these can lead to speculative conspiracy theories. Despite being the center of various conspiracy theories, the Catholic Church is not typically considered to be a secret society. The pope is a popular figure worldwide, and he works to spread Catholic doctrine and pursue the Vatican's agenda, which is well-known and much publicized. Though some may bristle at church politics or deny the legitimacy of the Holy See or the Vatican, few would label them a secret society. However, as Arkon Daraul (1997) indicates, "not all secret societies are entirely secret" (9). As such, a secret society is more than just a society with secrets. As Daraul further points out, "Secret societies are generally considered to be anti-social; to contain elements which are distasteful or harmful to the community at large" (10). The most pervasive of these is the New World Order, "a conspiracy theory in which adherents believe that a cabal of powerful elites is secretly implementing a dystopian international governing structure that will grant them complete control over the global populace" (Flores 2022). The term New World Order originated in legitimate political discourse in the early twentieth century; however, New World Order conspiracy theories go back centuries.* This phrase has become synonymous with secrecy, world domination, and totalitarian control of the masses. The New World Order is central to Project Blue Beam and conspiracy theories.†

Shadow organizations like the Freemasons or the Illuminati are central to many conspiracy theories. According to the Institute for Strategic Dialogue (ISD) (2022), "While not synonymous, conspiracies about the 'New World Order' overlap with conspiracies about the Illuminati, the group of elites who are deemed to be behind the implementation of the 'New World Order'" (3). Regardless of what organization is trying to bring about a New World Order, certain narrative elements are typically present and often include forms of mind control, secret societies, and a limitation of freedom (ISD 2022, 5). Details of the New World Order have circulated around the World Wide Web since its inception. One of the most detailed accounts is a digital book released by Michael Nield titled *The Police State*

---

*The Knights Templar, whose origins date back to the 12th century, are featured prominently in conspiracy theories. According to the Institute for Strategic Dialogue (ISD), anti–Illuminati and anti–Masonic theories date back to the 1800s (ISD 2022, 3).

†Some of the most prominent conspiracy theories that feature a New World Order include QAnon and Reptilian theories. QAnon is a far-right extremist theory that focuses on a Deep State led by Satan worshippers and pedophiles. The Reptilian Conspiracy, pedaled primarily by author David Icke, supports the notion that the government has been infiltrated by alien reptiles.

Roadmap 2004,* which opens with the line "The New World Order is a clear, present and unparalleled danger to humanity" (5). Like many sources that discuss this conspiracy, Nield's book references the New World Order but never adequately defines it. Instead, the conspiracy theory draws upon the term's historical context and conflates it with conspiratorial ideas.

Separating the historical and political use of the term from the conspiratorial context is difficult, given the prominence of the conspiracy theory. The phrase New World Order has been used politically since the early twentieth century. In 1918, "President Woodrow Wilson put forth his vision for a new world order in his Fourteen Points for Peace—a plan that would profoundly shape international politics and America's status as a world leader for decades to come" (President Wilson's House 2023). During the Persian Gulf crisis, on February 1, 1991, President George H.W. Bush infamously invoked the term in remarks to community members in Fort Stewart, Georgia. "[T]here is no place for lawless aggression in the Persian Gulf and in this New World Order that we seek to create" (Qtd in McLaughlin 2016, 193). President Bush (1991) used the term again in a speech to Congress after the Gulf War: "Now, we can see a new world coming into view. A world in which there is the very real prospect of a new world order." Bush's use of the term was not conspiratorial in any way—it simply evoked similar phrasing used by Winston Churchill after World War II, who advocated that strong nations should protect the weak.

Even President Joe Biden used the phrase in 2022 about the war in Ukraine: "There's going to be a new world order out there, and we've got to lead it. And we've got to unite the rest of the free world in doing it" (Sadeghi 2022). These uses of political phraseology have led to those who utter it becoming targets of conspiracy theorists. As the Anti-Defamation League's Mark Pitcavage relates, "right-wing extremists have seized on the comments to suggest that they don't want a peaceful nation but rather 'a socialist one-world government' that would eliminate national borders, freedoms and liberty" (Sadeghi 2022). This type of paranoia and hate is a direct descendant of the anti–Semitic narratives from the early twentieth century that identified Jewish people "as the orchestrators of global events and accused of creating a supranational governing structure for nefarious purposes" (Flores 2022). Among the major world events that have been blamed on Jewish people include the Covid-19 pandemic, various terrorist acts, the drug trade,

---

*This book can still be found on many websites, including the Internet Archive. The information included on the publication page of the document, however, lists the original publication site as www.policestateplanning.com. Unfortunately, attempts to access this site result in a malware warning. It was available as a gift for subscribing to the website Threeworldwars.com, which is how I first acquired it. However, though the website still lists this document as a gift, the link to subscribe to the site's newsletter is no longer active.

multiculturalism, and even climate change (ISD 2022, 4). The conflation of the New World Order with conspiratorial thought makes it easy for such theories to spread. When political figures invoke the phrase, it proves that the phrase and concept of a New World Order are real; though the context is different, confirmation bias leads people to believe what they want; they see the term's use as proof of the conspiracy. Though it means something different from what followers of the conspiracy wish to believe, the continued use of the phrase in a political context lends legitimacy to conspiratorial ideas.

Conclusion

End-of-the-world prophecies are folkloric narratives that have been a staple of popular culture for centuries. Despite the long track record of failed end-of-the-world predictions, they still surface regularly—and people continue to believe them. While the Project Beam Conspiracy originated three decades ago, it has circulated on the internet consistently since then, and interest gets revived every time world events dictate. Most recently, the Covid-19 pandemic resulted in a resurgence of new materials that have updated the conspiracy to fit events of this century. Similarly, the Prophecy of the Popes, which has a much longer history, continues to generate widespread interest, especially every time a change occurs in the papacy. Since Pope Francis is an octogenarian and represents the last pope listed on St. Malachy's document, interest in this prophecy will likely remain prominent. Regardless of who is working behind the scenes to bring it about, the New World Order lurks in the shadows, comfortably fitting into many end-of-the-world scenarios. People's interest in such conspiracies represents a strong desire to understand a phenomenon they do not fully understand. The willingness to believe and spread such tales can represent an extreme form of ostension. Though people may not intend to bring about the Apocalypse by spreading rumors and theories about it, who is to say that doing so will not plant ideas that others may one day act upon? Regardless of what impact tales such as these have, one thing is certain: if you miss this end of the world this time, another opportunity will come around soon enough.

REFERENCES

American Psychological Association. (2018). "Confirmation Bias." *APA Dictionary of Psychology*, April 19. Accessed November 16, 2023. https://dictionary.apa.org/confirmation-bias.

Bakich, Michael. (2023). "How Often Do Solar Eclipses Occur? The Dates and Intervals of Annular, Partial, and Total Eclipses, Explained." *Astronomy*, July 18. Accessed November 16, 2023. https://www.astronomy.com/observing/how-often-do-solar-eclipses-occur/.

Bardos, Istvan. (2021). "Zombie Apocalypse in 2021? The CDC has You Covered." *ABC 24*, March 2. Accessed October 31, 2023. https://www.localmemphis.com/article/life/zombie-apocalypse-in-2021-the-cdc-has-you-covered/522-7d593de3-b297-4332-8817-b2ab690a0893.

Bauer, Conrad. (2022). *Conspiracies of the Vatican: Mysterious Conspiracies and Conundrums of the Catholic Church*. Self-published. Kindle.

Bodner, John, et al. (2021). *Covid-19 Conspiracy Theories*. Jefferson: McFarland.

Bowles, Shauna, et al. (2023). "The Conspiratorial Mind: A Meta-Analytic Review of Motivational and Personological Correlates." *Psychological Bulletin* 149 (5–6): 259–293.

Brophilius, Aidan. (2012). *Project Blue Beam—The Quest for a New World Order and the Rule of the Antichrist*. Self-published. Kindle.

Brunvand, Jan. (1994). *The Study of American Folklore*, Fourth Edition. New York: Norton.

Bush, George H.W. (1991). "George Bush's Speech After the Gulf War." Jerusalem Media and Communication Centre, March 6. Accessed November 30, 2023. http://www.jmcc.org/Documentsandmaps.aspx?id=341.

Daraul, Arkon. (1997). *A History of Secret Societies*. Secaucus: Citadel Press.

Engel, Joel. (1994). *Gene Roddenberry: The Myth and the Man Behind Star Trek*. New York: Hyperion.

Flores, Myles. (2022). *Middlebury Institute of International Studies*. Accessed November 28, 2023. https://www.middlebury.edu/institute/academics/centers-initiatives/ctec/ctec-publications/new-world-order-historical-origins-dangerous.

Institute for Strategic Dialogue (ISD). (2022). "New World Order." Accessed November 28, 2023. https://www.isdglobal.org/wp-content/uploads/2022/09/New-World-Order-ISD-External-August2022-.pdf.

Lindahl, Carl. (2005). "Ostensive Healing: Pilgrimage to the San Antoni Ghost Tracks." *Journal of American Folklore* 118 (48): 164–185.

Lings, Martin. (1984). "St. Malachy's Prophecy of the Popes." *Studies in Comparative Religion* 16 (2/3): 148–153.

Little, Jane. (2012). "Mayan Apocalypse: End of the World, or a New Beginning?" *BBC News*, December 19. Accessed October 31, 2023. https://www.bbc.com/news/magazine-20764906.

McHugh, Joseph. (2013). "What Is the Prophecy of the Final Pope?" *U.S. Catholic* 78 (9): 46.

McLaughlin, Greg. (2016). *The War Correspondent*, Second Edition. London: Pluto Press.

McMillen, Ryan. (2004). *Space Rapture: Extraterrestrial Millennialism and the Cultural Construction of Space Colonization*. PhD diss. University of Texas. Accessed December 30, 2023. https://www.proquest.com/openview/44317b134d60064d0f24a12e1094679a/1?pq-origsite=gscholar&cbl=18750&diss=y.

McNeill, Lynne. (2013). *Folklore Rules: A Fun, Quick, and Useful Introduction to the Field of Academic Folklore Studies*. Logan: Utah State University Press.

Monast, Serge. (1994). "Project Blue Beam." *Educate-Yourself*. Accessed October 31, 2023. https://educate-yourself.org/cn/projectbluebeam25jul05.shtml.

Nield, Michael. (n.d.). *The Police State Road Map 2004*. Self-published. Accessed November 15, 2023. https://famguardian.org/Publications/PoliceStateRoadmap/PoliceStatePlanning2004.pdf.

Piccotti, Tyler. (2023). "What Happened to the Key Figures from the Infamous Slender Man Stabbing?" *Biography*, September 18. Accessed November 28, 2023. https://www.biography.com/crime/a45191639/slender-man-stabbing-case-explained-and-updates.

President Wilson's House. (n.d.). "International Politics." Accessed November 21, 2023. https://woodrowwilsonhouse.org/wilson-topics/international-policy/.

"The Prophecies of St. Malachy." *Catholic Tradition*. Accessed November 16, 2023. http://www.catholictradition.org/Papacy/prophecies.htm.

Staples, Tim. (2013). "Is Pope Francis the Final Roman Pontiff?" *Catholic Answers*. Accessed November 14, 2023. https://www.catholic.com/magazine/online-edition/is-pope-francis-the-final-roman-pontiff.

Wang, Lei et al. (2023). "Macroscopic Laser Pulling Based on the Knudsen Force in Rarefied Gas." *Optics Express* 31 (2): 2665–2674. https://doi.org/10.1364/OE.480019.

PART II

Cultural Mythology and Social Media

Conspiring to Be an Ethical All-American

Hasmet M. Uluorta

Introduction

Nearly half of the U.S. population believes in at least one conspiracy theory (Sides 2015). This essay focuses on the underlying compulsion to disseminate and succumb to conspiracy theories in the context of the contemporary American techno-capitalist neoliberal political economy. In this essay I concentrate on two guiding questions: Which factors give rise to conspiracy theories in the United States? What functions do conspiracy theories serve?

To answer these questions, I center my analysis on an ideal-type of American citizenry—the ethical All-American (EAA) (see also Uluorta 2016, 2022). Drawing on Lacanian and Žižekian psychoanalytical approaches, I define the EAA as being an irrevocably divided subject that is constituted through identification with three hailing social discourses or mirrors that form the Symbolic order: the capitalist-market, national-patriotic, and religious-moral. The EAA has, within the contemporary era, come to identify themselves as inseparable from these mirrors. What is common across them is a belief in, and a *demand* for the belief in, American individual and national exceptionalism. When individual and national exceptionalism cannot be sustained, gaps develop between the EAA and the hailing from the three mirrors.

Yet these gaps do not necessarily mean a collapse of a particular Symbolic order or indeed of this one as there is a stuckness (Kapoor et al. 2023, 10–11) to the Symbolic order. It is within these growing gaps, or lack in the Symbolic order, that fantasies in the form of conspiracy theories are called upon to do their political work. They are meant to eliminate the fissures in the Symbolic order as a means to secure the EAA identification.

Conspiracies also seek to re-assert the power of the big Other's Symbolic order that once conferred recognition of the individual as the EAA.

I begin the essay with an overview of the formation of the subject through a Lacanian and Žižekian lens. In the second section, I discuss the establishment of the EAA that forms a partial barrier to the proliferation of conspiracy theories. In the third section, I examine the work of conspiracy theory production and consumption in upholding the EAA in a time of Symbolic decline. I conclude the essay by briefly reflecting on how a Lacanian and Žižekian psychoanalytical approach is useful as it reveals how the growing cracks and inconsistencies within the big Other's Symbolic order are the necessary triggers for conspiracy theories. More importantly it reveals, in an era of techno-capitalism, that conspiracy theories, their promulgators, and their widespread acceptance are a symptom of broader transformations in how the lacking Symbolic order is now maintained by a self-sustaining interpellated populace.

Split-Subjects and the Symbolic Order of the Big Other

In this section the aim is to explain subject formation and its tenuous nature, as it always remains beyond one's control and is permanently incomplete. This is where an understanding of conspiracy theories should begin as it is here that we locate a desiring subject finding enjoyment, or more precisely *jouissance* (pain-pleasure), in asserting their desire for completeness. This is not to suggest that all identities are equally representative within the Symbolic order. Only certain parts of our identities are acknowledged and therein arises the desire via fantasy and received *jouissance* to overcome lack. This forms the basis for conspiracy theories as they are a fantasy to overcome this void in the demanded identification.

Desire, within a Lacanian and Žižek framework, also requires modification as it does not simply emanate from the subject. While we often ask the question *what do I desire?* Lacanians note desire must be understood through the mirrors. In this sense, the question must be restated to *what is it that you (the big Other) desire of me?* As Žižek (1989, 132) writes,

> [f]antasy appears, then, as an answer to "Che vuoi?," to the unbearable enigma of the desire of the Other, of the lack in the Other, but it is at the same time fantasy itself which, so to speak, provides the co-ordinates of our desire—which constructs the frame enabling us to desire something.

The big Other forms an abstraction that is situated within language, norms, customs, and the law that casts its gaze upon us through the three mirrors and in so doing structures our desire (Žižek 1991, 6).

Subject formation, consequently, is better understood as identification rather than identity as it is found and maintained through the Symbolic order of the big Other. Lacan (1977, 1–7) explains this by stating that individuals understand themselves to be a subject only when they see themselves as exterior to themselves reflected in language (Symbolic order) and image (Imaginary order). Following Sigmund Freud, Lacan (1977) referred to this as the mirror stage. Lacan's twist to this is to emphasize that the mirrors are not to be taken literally but rather as language, gestures, moods, laws, norms and so forth that "mirror" back an ego-ideal. For Lacan what is also important is that this process of identification, with that which is exterior to oneself, is an on-going process that renders the subject's sense of wholeness impossible (Solomon 2014, 674).

It is in the reflective mirror that an individual understands themselves to take the form of an "I." One stands across from a mirror. A gap exists between us in the mirror and the us that stands before the mirror. That which we see externally to us, within the mirror, is an image. Is it us? Or is it an object like the other items we might see reflected such as a chair or clock? Contained within the mirror, then, is an idealized image, or an idealized-I. The gap between is the lack one feels between the eye that sees and the idealized-I with its returning gaze.

What is reflected in the mirror is not simply a reflection, but it is the ego forming a false self because the only way to experience selfhood is through this unbridgeable separation. What is seen through the mirrors is that which I desire everyone, including me, to recognize as me. It is ego that promotes and maintains this illusion of wholeness, coherence, and mastery (Homer 2005). In this sense, the idealized-I can be more readily understood as ideal-ego as legitimated by the big Other.

Two points of clarification are necessary at this juncture. First, this mis-knowing renders the subject as a rival to itself as it is introduced to lack, desire, and jouissance with the unbridgeable gap. The subject's experiences are alienated from their ideal-ego image making it equally likely to refer to them as a non-subject. Desire, in the form of fantasy, arises as we want to rid ourselves of this lack and be that complete and stable ego-ideal reflected in the mirror.

We experience jouissance in our attempts to overcome the lack through identification with the big Other and Symbolic order (Žižek 1989, 122). I refer to that identification as the Ethical All-American (EAA). I noted earlier there is not one but rather three overlapping mirrors that reflect back this idealized-I identification in the context of the contemporary United States: the free market capitalist, religious-moral, and nationalist-patriot mirrors. In short, and this is critical for an understanding of the production and consumption of conspiracy theory as the big

Other is essential to the non-subject's satisfaction (McGowan 2003). Žižek (2006, 4) describes it as

> the second nature of every speaking being: it is here, directing and controlling my acts, I as it were swim in it, but it nonetheless remains ultimately impenetrable, and I cannot ever put it in front of me and fully grasp it.

This becomes a more profound paradox, as this requires one to be the object of the big Other's desire without fully knowing what the big Other desires of one (Roberts 2005). An answer to the unanswered question of *what is it that you desire of me* might therefore be—"I am that there." The answer is most certainly not—"I am me." In short, identification requires us to be the object of the gaze of an unknowable big Other that structures our desire to be an EAA.

To make sense of the relevance of the big Other and Symbolic order, to the formation of the non-subject EAA and the political work of conspiracy theories we must understand how the Symbolic order folds in with two other orders: the Real and the Imaginary. The Real is that which cannot be represented since representation implies an immediate transference to the other orders (Lacan 1977, 53). The Real, when experienced, is best described as episodic irruptions into reality that are traumatic (Homer 2005, 83–84). One might consider the terrorist attacks of 11 September 2001, the Great Recession of 2008, or Covid, as examples of the Real.

The trauma that the Real represents curtails symbolization fixating and seizing the individual. It is only in the reflexive glance—the recognition of experienced trauma—that the Real is apprehended. In that moment, the Real is transferred to the Symbolic and Imaginary. Yet, it cannot be completely transferred and consequently it also becomes elusive, escaping our ability to define it completely. The mirrors therefore are also characterized by lack, as they cannot suppress the irruptions of the Real nor can they adequately represent it (Stavrakakis, 1999, 51–54). The threshold though is not a full translation of the Real, which is impossible. The threshold for upholding the Symbolic order or the big Other is the satisfaction of the desire to be the EAA. In those instances, when satisfaction is not possible, fantasy often in the form of conspiracy is required by the subject to maintain their ability to be the EAA.

The Symbolic order associated with codes, customs, language, rules and so forth is the authority and the law of the big Other. The importance of the Symbolic cannot be overstated as it is only through language that the EAA can identify as a subject. An understanding of the world—epistemology—is formed through the Symbolic and Imaginary as a means of translating traumatic experiences of the Real. In a phenomenological sense, the Symbolic and Imaginary are the means by which the big Other provides order, stability, and meaning.

The subject then is a divided non-subject caught between the Imaginary and Symbolic order and their desire for and experience of jouissance for subjective wholeness as the EAA. To restate the point, what this suggests is that what one desires is not internal to the self, but rather is inseparable from the unknowable desire of the big Other. In this way the term jouissance is apt as the enjoyment in desiring subjective completion is also accompanied by anxiety. This enjoyment combined with anxiety is productive as it is generative of Symbolic efficiency.

The Big Other's Symbolic Order: Ascendency of the Ethical All-American Identification

Symbolic efficiency forming the non-subject EAA provided a firewall that constrained the widespread proliferation of conspiracy theory production and consumption. It was the election of Ronald Reagan in 1980 that equated being an American with the EAA. The Reagan administration sought to re-assert American individual and national exceptionalism by establishing the EAA through re-symbolizing the trauma of the Real. These traumas included the defeat in Vietnam, a decade of stagflation, the Iran hostage crisis, and culminating in a supposed general American malaise. Desire, in this era, was constructed around the others' stealing of EAA jouissance. What is important to note is that the Symbolic order of the big Other proffered what could otherwise be defined to be conspiracy theories as official expert discourse.

The administration was effective in reflecting onto the public that this stolen jouissance was a consequence of the institutionalized gains made by social forces during the golden age of the welfare state. This included the collective representation of workers through trade unions as well as the race and gender-based gains that were the consequence of civil rights activists during the 1950s through to their institutionalization in the 1970s. It also came through the blurring of domestic and international with the anti-war protest movements that cast the United States as the enemy.

President Reagan (1981) assured Americans that, "[i]n this present crisis, government is not the solution to our problem; government is the problem." In so doing, he established the capitalist-market mirror as a national and individual identification. The Keynesian economic theory, of John Maynard Keynes, Alvin Hansen, and John Kenneth Galbraith, that had led to the "golden age of capitalism" (Esping-Andersen 1996), would be displaced by an individualizing free-market economics promoted by the likes of Milton Friedman, Gary Becker, and more broadly the Chicago school of economics.

The Reagan administration embraced the attainment of the "American dream" through individualized ambitiousness and enterprise within a "free" capitalist market. This was illustrated, in the everyday, by the applauding of so-called yuppies, or young urban professionals. Upwardly mobile, yuppies were perceived to be individuals who flaunted their wealth through hedonistic consumption. This identification received legitimation through the capitalist-market mirror as the ideal-ego's desire for autonomy, choice, happiness, health, sexual attractiveness, and wealth were within their grasp as seen in (their) mirror. Culturally, cable television programs such as *Dynasty* and *Dallas* provided the mirrored visuals for the fantasy of individualized subjective wholeness in fulfilling the desire of the big Other.

The nationalist-patriotic and religious-moral mirrors were initiated through the Iran hostage crisis and the intensification of the Cold War. These were represented as the other that had stolen EAA's jouissance of the United States as the exceptional and redeemer nation. President Reagan's (1983) "evil empire" speech hailed the EAA. Contained within the speech was the identification of the EAA as desirous of freedom, of freeing others. Its national leader became a clearer mirror, an ideal-ego, of the EAA. It also had an explicit religious-moral connotation with the other embodying evil and the EAA the good. In this way he affirmed the desire of the EAA as freedom loving and gifting the world with freedom.

Taken together, these were ethico-political reflections coupled with strategies that pointed the individual and the nation to see themselves within a collective future as EAAs. This, it should be noted, is in stark contrast to the current circumstances where vision and strategy have been replaced by the immediacy of tactics deprived of strategy and reflectivity as an EAA. The distinction is significant for understanding conspiracy theories as the response to the question of *what am I to the big Other* was undeniably clear and filled with individual and public purpose for the hailed EAA—I am "free" (Dean 2009, 56). I am on the side of "good." I can make others, in the world, be the "good and free." Collectively, the "I" would be replaced by the national "we" and "our." Our nation will make the world safe for those who are good and aspire to be free. Whether one believed or simply believed because the others, including the big Other believed, the outcome was the same. Namely, there was security and belonging in being desiring to be an EAA.

With these affirmations of identification, the three mirrors structured desire for the signifier of free—free trade, American democratic freedoms, and the individual's freedom of choice bestowed by God and fulfilled by the United States. It is this latter point of the promise of fulfillment by the nation, and as represented by President Reagan and his administration, that would resonate with a population seeking ontological security and belonging to something bigger (e.g., to the nation).

Domestically, the Reagan administration's actions, including the firing of unionized air traffic controllers (McCartin 2011), assaults on welfare recipients (Wilentz 2008), and attacks on racialized communities (Galbraith 1990, Soss et al. 2011) were signified to be the collectivist other (e.g., special interests) who stole the EAA's jouissance. Othering, by the big Other, is necessary for the EAA identification, and it was utilized continuously across party lines. During the economic downturn in the early 1990s a "new" Democrat President, Bill Clinton, introduced what was described as an objective and technologically-driven force to the American public—"globalization" (Amoore 2002). It was this, until now, invisible force that was obstructing the EAA's jouissance in the early 1990s. Commensurate with this idea, the Clinton administration reaffirmed the previous administration's call for intensifying free-market capitalism as a means of modernizing and thereby competing against other nations through a global free trade agenda. With adherence came the promise of the restitution from the other of the appropriated jouissance that rightfully belonged to the EAA identification.

As Jodi Dean (2009, 55–56) suggests, the fantasy promised by implementing free trade is that everyone benefits, and everyone wins because we are free. The Free Trade Agreement (FTA) of 1987 between the United States and Canada would be expanded under the Clinton administration to form the North American Free Trade Agreement (NAFTA) to include Mexico. No sooner had this been signed in 1993 than the Clinton administration sought the formation of a global institution (e.g., one that operated beyond the international level and included transnational corporations), the World Trade Organization (WTO), in 1995.

During the Clinton presidency the EAA identification would receive further affirmation with the technology boom along with the growing veneration of technology CEOs, such as Bill Gates and Steve Jobs. Technology CEOs quickly became household names, and the new technologies also generated the unidentified dot-com millionaires. Nameless, yet ever-present, these so-called techno-nerds watched, and were watched, as start-up ventures listed on the NASDAQ, or bought up by more established firms, led to instantaneous wealth.

As Ilan Kapoor (2014, 1118) notes, "late capitalism seduces"; it binds people to it libidinally by selling them not just "cool stuff" such as iPhones or TVs, but also alluring fantasies about the "good life." This structured desire (and fantasy) in a time when hyper-visibility, through cable television and the internet (including new video capacities), produced a disproportionate sense of abundance and simplicity. Questions such as *why them and not me? How can I get that?* would be answered with the emergence of electronic trading platforms, such as E*Trade Securities. What was promised was democratizing access to the abundance of capitalist wealth and the attainment of good life that was made possible by new technologies.

The Big Other's Symbolic Demise

The second term of the presidency of George W. Bush demarcates a turning point in the effectiveness of the big Other's Symbolic efficiency in maintaining the desire for the EAA and a shift to the proliferation and consumption of conspiracy theories. The increasing frequency of incursions of the Real would no longer be as successfully translatable within the Symbolic order. Rupturing, during the second term, was the claim that the big Other, in the form of capitalist, government, and military leadership, had access to reality as they failed to predict, prevent, successfully solve, or strategically plan for incursions of the Real.

For our purposes this also meant that they could not provide the demanded signifiers to contain the Real and affirm the desire of the EAA's identification. These incursions included the Enron bankruptcy (2001), the war in Iraq (2003), the hurricane Katrina response (2005), the Dubai Ports deal (2006), the housing foreclosure crisis (2006), the Troubled Asset Relief Program (TARP) (2008), and more broadly the expansion of government deficits (triggered by two tax cuts, two wars, and new unfunded government programs), in addition to unprecedented levels of (unwarranted) domestic surveillance.

These breaches could only be temporarily and only partially settled. With the failure of the big Other to adequately address the constancy of breaches across a spectrum of issues, fantasy, in the form of conspiracy, came to the aid of the big Other to maintain the Symbolic order. To restate the argument, the EAA identification would not be jettisoned for another identification, but rather would continue to be affirmed due to the stuckness of hegemony. As the gaps in the Symbolic order of the big Other became unconcealable, conspiracy would be required to salvage the possibility of maintaining the EAA identification. This was necessary as the big Other's future oriented vision and strategy would be replaced by reaction and a reliance on tactics without strategy that often failed, were contradictory, and more importantly amplified EAA insecurity. In this nothingness, and with the growing possibility of nonbeing, explanations of stolen jouissance would necessarily come from populist-based justifications that relied on the capacity to string together partial truths forming what we understand to be conspiracy.

The attacks of 11 September 2001, though, would temporarily offset this as they worked to both maintain and intensify the Symbolic order and the desire for the EAA identification. These horrific attacks would buttress the desire for the EAA with President Bush hailing Americans through signifiers such as terrorism, good versus evil, axis of evil, freedom loving people, and so forth. Consequently, when President Bush demanded that Americans resume their consumption of goods and services, despite hyper-inequality and burgeoning individual and public debt, he solidified the EAA identification. He declared,

> [n]ow, the American people have got to go about their business. We cannot let the terrorists achieve the objective of frightening our Nation to the point where we don't—*where we don't conduct business, where people don't shop*. That's their intention. Their intention was not only to kill and maim and destroy. Their intention was to *frighten to the point where our Nation would not act* ... [2001, emphasis added].

His was the authority of the big Other and through the three mirrors, the President reasserted the hegemony of the American techno-capitalist neoliberal political economy and the commensurate EAA identification. The command to enjoy one's consumption became not only a capitalist-market, but also a religious-moral and nationalist-patriotic desired duty.

As Žižek (2001) affirms, our consumption came at an opportune time as it reaffirmed the fantasy of the subject that lacks. For the EAA, the next purchase not only declared their desire to enjoy freedom as capitalist subjects, but it also upheld their jouissance as freedom loving patriots while enjoying a moral duty to defend freedom globally. Taken together, they were acting morally with each ringing of the cash register, signifying their desire to defend American and individual exceptionalism. The next purchase came with the fantasy of a purging of lack that is commensurate with capitalism (Böhm and Batta 2010), but it now included the supposed containment of unknowable future lack owing to the terrorist possibilities.

During the immediate aftermath of September 11, 2001, the Bush administration took the incursion of the Real, that included the real-time viewing of the downing of the Twin Towers in New York City, and efficiently translated them into a terrorist attack against freedom loving peoples. While he was quick to walk back the assertions of a civilizational war between Islam and Christianity, he approximated President Reagan, through the invoking of the religious-moral mirror by dividing the world into us and them as well as good and evil. With Americans hailed as

104 Part II: Cultural Mythology and Social Media

righteous in their demand for retribution for the attacks, what they sought was not merely justice. Pursued was also the removal of the barriers blocking Americans from the jouissance of being the EAA.

While this command of the big Other to enjoy their identification as EAA was transmitted through a multitude of media, it also demarcates an important and overlooked shift underway in the American way of life that would expand the limits of the possible for conspiracies. No longer could the command of the big Other to enjoy be disassociated from the multitude of bloggers, vloggers, social media sites, and AM conservative talk-radio shows that went well beyond the already saturated one-way broadcasts of pundits on 24-hour cable news networks such as Fox News. Indeed, even one-way broadcasters were now communicative flows, posting video clips or entire segments online that included extensive comments sections that would quickly see thousands of user generated comments and dialogue.

Endlessly transmitting and discussing across dial-up modems, broadband internet, fiber optic internet, radio waves and so forth the demand for the EAA identification was disengaging from a one-way determination. President Bill Clinton spoke about this transformation, which would intensify exponentially with the arrival of Web 2.0 in the aftermath of the dot.com bust of 2000 (Tim O'Reilly 2005). He (quoted in Cannon 1994) noted, "[a]fter I get off the radio with you today, Rush Limbaugh will have three hours to say whatever he wants, and I won't have an opportunity to respond, and there's no truth detector." What President Clinton omitted was that Limbaugh was but one example of conservative talk-radio programs that relied on callers as part of their daily nationally syndicated programming.

What President Clinton also missed were all of the means by which individuals could broadcast their opinions across media platforms before, during and after programs such as the Limbaugh AM radio program. My claim is what the President failed to note was a media format premised on the participation of a geographically dispersed, real-time user and user generated content that spoke with, before, and if need be, in the place of the big Other in support of the Symbolic order. It is to this latter point of speaking in place of the big Other that I now turn.

The Rise of the You: Conspiring to Be an Ethical All-American

By 2006, *Time* magazine designated "you" as the person of the year. The cover reads, "[y]es, you. You control the Information Age. Welcome to your world" (*Time* 2006). While the editors, like President Clinton in the late 1990s, could not have thought through the full consequences of this transformation, they were correct to point out the significance of "you." In 2003, websites such as 4Chan and Blogger were launched, in 2004 social media site Facebook and podcast downloader iPodder were founded, while in 2005 YouTube began hosting vlogs, and this was followed by other user-generated sites such as WordPress, Reddit, and Twitter.

The authority to uphold the fantasy of subjective completion as the EAA had shifted by the second term of the Bush presidency. This is undoubtedly the turning point for conspiracy theories as Symbolic inefficiency would come to dominate the institutions of political and economic governance in the United States. There have been other moments in American history of Symbolic inefficiency such as the Great Depression, Civil Rights protests and so forth. What was unusual in this instance is that the work of Symbolic efficiency had shifted to the generalized and largely anonymous and virtual "you" in place of the big Other.

By the time President Obama was elected in 2008, Americans would be shocked with yet another implosion of the Real that was unsatisfactorily translated within the Symbolic order as "the subprime mortgage crisis" or "the Great Recession" or "the global financial crisis." The Bush and Obama administrations would agree to the largest bailout of capitalist firms with the Troubled Assets Relief Program (TARP). The outcome would trigger online outrage and the coalescing of "you" in the form of the Tea Party Movement/Tea Party Caucus and later the Occupy Wall Street protests in 2011. The failure of these movements to re-shape the Symbolic order would give credence to theories that explained, once again, how the other had stolen the subject's jouissance as the EAA.

These theories insisted that the big Other (e.g., Democrats/Demoncrats and Republicans/RINOs—Republicans in Name Only) had succumbed to a globalist other and/or to corruption as the only truthful explanation of how it was possible that the subject's identification as the EAA had been stolen from them. Conspiracy theories come with a libidinal excess suggesting that their truths are validated by the anonymous "you" not because they are correct, but rather because these theories validate the desire to be the EAA.

The foregrounding of "you" as a structural change in the American techno-capitalist neoliberal political economy requires further elaboration. The War on Terror would be a total war fusing citizens-as-warriors on a battlefield that was believed to be everywhere. In this way "you" became central to the effort regardless of whether one was an actual active-duty soldier or not and whether one was in Topeka or Baghdad. From the "support the troops" stickers to being instructed to be vigilant, continuing to consume "you" would be central to the fighting of the *Global* War on Terror. The global meant that incursions of the Real were possible anytime and anywhere. The endless failures of the Bush administration in Afghanistan and Iraq presented daily meant that the state was no longer a credible guarantor of security. The nationalist-patriotic mirror now situated "you" not only as combatant but more importantly as expert strategist. "You" had an opinion on how the war should be fought and won.

Furthermore, the new techno-capitalism, inclusive of the Web 2.0 developments discussed above, situated "you" as both producer and consumer. In fact, anyone with an internet connection was a buyer, a resource, a producer and was also attempting to reproduce themselves and self-represent all at the same time (Harbison 2019). As the futurist Alvin Toffler (1980) argued the then emergent techno-capitalism came with a shift to prosumption. George Ritzer (2015, 413–414) explains, "the process of prosumption involves the interrelationship of production and consumption where it becomes difficult, if not impossible, to clearly and unequivocally distinguish one from the other." The significance of acknowledging "you" as both producer and consumer is that it implicates the subject as the boss, entrepreneur, creator, worker, and consumer thereby further blurring how "you" are situated with the big Other's capitalist-market mirror.

As such, it becomes significantly more challenging to say that individuals are acting against their interests (e.g., class). What are their interests if they are both employee and employer for example? What are their interests for calling for peace when they are both protective soldier and citizen? The challenge I am noting here is that the impetus to prosumption and protection of the homeland, unlike the celebratory *Time* magazine tribute, is that "you" are compelled to act in the face of Symbolic demise. Armed only with partial truths and the desire to ease the anxiety of an unattainable EAA identification conspiracy theories become compulsory in an otherwise complex and impossible world.

There is a coincidence in timing of course, as the incursion of the Real reinforces the notion of hyper-individualism and self-reliance that comes with the assumption of expertise and do-it-yourself (DIY) solutions that take shape as conspiracy theories. At issue is also the nature of "truth" and the ego-ideal of the EAA. The promotion of individualism, decline in the big Other as provider of security, coupled with the increasing communicative flow has led to the doubling-down on the EAA identification as the possessor of the "truth." As the bearer of the truth, "you" are only able to claim this with acknowledgment from the big Other. In this way, the desire for subjective completion remains feasible.

What stands, then, in the place of a failing big Other is an individualized and isolated "you" that conspires to believe that something other or someone else is in control of the big Other. This is the entry point for the prosumption of conspiratorial reason. Conspiracy theorists believe in a truth that something other, a person and/or an institution, is pulling the strings of American society and re-organizing daily life, preventing the jouissance that comes with the completeness of the EAA identification. The common question asked then within a conspiratorial reason is *who/what is responsible for my erasure when "you" is seen as the pinnacle of American society?* The answer is the Other's other that includes globalists, corrupted elites, and minorities.

The aim of these theories is to expose that other as that which is stealing the jouissance that comes from being an EAA. As Marasco (2016, 237) notes, conspiratorial reason is "an idealization of the state—and power, more generally—even as it works to unmask secret government plots and cover-ups." The prosumption of conspiracy theories works to reclaim power and the jouissance that has been foreclosed by the demise of the Symbolic order. Marasco is correct, noting that what is sought is not the displacement of authority but its reinstatement in order, but I would emphasize it is to alleviate the suffering of the desiring non-subject EAA.

Conclusion

Today, truths flow horizontally through mediascapes more than the one-directional flow from expert testimony, government press releases and so forth. In this way we can better make sense of individuals who have traditionally been assumed to be representatives of the big Other (e.g., presidents, CEOs) as they too manifest as prosumers of conspiratorial reasoning. This is precisely why conspiratorial prosumption should not be dismissed as crazy or belonging exclusively to "those" people. As alluded to throughout this essay, the jouissance associated with dismissal of the other, including the dismissal of the prosumption of conspiracy theories, should be understood to be the fantasy of subjective completion that requires its other to steal our enjoyment.

The fantasy of conspiratorial prosumption works in a similar way as it covers the gap that exists between the three mirrors of the Symbolic order and the attainment of the EAA identification. Sought are explanations of the unexplainable arising with the seemingly constant incursions of the Real and the inability of the big Other to successfully translate them through to the Symbolic order particularly during the mid-2000s. The resulting compulsion to fill the gap has been relegated to "you" as there is a stuckness to the American neoliberal techno-capitalist political economy and the desire to be the EAA.

Conspiratorial prosumption is made possible by the emergence of techno-capitalism generating the opportunity of partial truths to be connected from one to another with a simple tap of a screen. Yet, as I have argued, this should not be viewed as the primary cause for widespread acceptance of conspiratorial reasoning. These tools have made it possible to retain the desire to be the EAA identification in the face of Symbolic demise. Truths are no longer the domain of those that supposably know— the big Other. This is why, as reflected through and by the three mirrors of the Symbolic order, "you" conspire to be the EAA.

References

Amoore, Louise. (2002). *Globalisation Contested: An International Political Economy of Work*. Manchester: Manchester University Press.
Böhm, Steffen, and Aanka Batta. (2010). "Just Doing It: Enjoying Commodity Fetishism with Lacan." *Organization* 17, no. 3 (May): 345–361. https://doi.org/10.1177/1350508410363123.
Bush, George W. (2001). *Presidential New Conference*. October 11. Washington, D.C. https://georgewbush-whitehouse.archives.gov/news/releases/2001/10/20011011-7.html.
Cannon, Carl M. (1994). "Clinton Lashes Out at Falwell, Limbaugh on Radio." *The Baltimore Sun*, June 25. https://www.baltimoresun.com/news/bs-xpm-1994-06-25-1994176003-story.html.
Dean, Jodi. (2009). *Democracy and Other Neoliberal Fantasies: Communicative Capitalism and Left Politics*. Durham: Duke University Press.
Esping-Andersen, Gøsta. (1996). "After the Golden Age? Welfare State Dilemmas In a Global Economy." In *Welfare States in Transition: National Adaptations in Global Economics*, edited by Gøsta Esping-Andersen, 1–31. London: Sage.
Galbraith, John K. (1992). *The Culture of Contentment*. New York: Houghton Mifflin.
Harbison, Isobel. (2019). *Performing Image*. Cambridge: MIT Press.
Homer, Sean. (2005). *Jacques Lacan*. New York: Routledge.
Kapoor, Ilan, et al. (2023). *Global Libidinal Economy*. Albany: SUNY Press.
Kapoor, Ilan. (2014). "Psychoanalysis and Development: An Introduction." *Third World Quarterly* 35, no. 7 (October): 1117–1119. https://doi.org/10.1080/01436597.2014.926099.
Lacan, Jacques. (1977). "The Mirror Stage as Formative of the Function of the I as Revealed in Psychoanalytic Experience." *Écrits: A Selection*, translated by Alan Sheridan. London: Routledge.
Marasco, Robyn. (2016). "Toward A Critique of Conspiratorial Reason." *Constellations* 23, no. 2 (June): 236–243.
McGowan, Todd. (2003). *The End of Dissatisfaction? Jacques Lacan and the Emerging Society of Enjoyment*. New York: SUNY Press.
O'Reilly, Tim. (2005). What Is Web 2.0? *O'Reilly*. September 30. www.oreillynet.com/pub/a/oreilly/tim/news/2005/09/30/what-is-web-20.html.
Reagan, Ronald. (1981) *Inaugural Address*. January 20. https://www.reaganfoundation.org/ronald-reagan/reagan-quotes-speeches/inaugural-address-2/.
Ritzer, George. (2014) "Prosumption: Evolution, Revolution, or Eternal Return of the same?" *Journal of Consumer Culture* 14, no. 1: 3–24. https://doi.org/10.1177/1469540513509641.
Sides, John. (2015). "Fifty Percent of Americans Believe in Some Conspiracy Theory. Here's Why." *The Washington Post*, February 19. https://www.washingtonpost.com/news/monkey-cage/wp/2015/02/19/fifty-percent-of-americans-believe-in-some-conspiracy-theory-heres-why/.

Solomon, Ty. (2014). "Time and Subjectivity in World Politics." *International Studies Quarterly*, 58, no 4: 671–681. https://doi.org/10.1111/isqu.12091.
Soss, Joe, et al. (2011). *Disciplining the Poor: Neoliberalism Paternalism and the Persistent Power of Race*. Chicago: University of Chicago Press.
Stavrakakis, Yannis. (1999). *Lacan and the Political*. London: Routledge.
Time. (2006). "Person of the Year: You." *Time Magazine*, December 25. https://content.time.com/time/magazine/europe/0,9263,901061225,00.html.
Toffler, Alvin. (1980). *The Third Wave*. New York: William Morrow.
Uluorta, Hasmet. (2016). "The Tea Party: An Ethical All-American Performance." In *Dissent! Refracted: Histories, Aesthetics and Cultures of Dissent*. Edited by Ben Dorfman, 95–116. Oxford: Peter Lang.
Uluorta, Hasmet. (2022). "Beyond Post-Truth: I-War and the Desire to be an Ethical All-American." *Global Politics in a Post-Truth Age*. Edited by Stephen McGlinchey et al., 57–73. Bristol: E-International Relations.
Wilentz, Sean. (2008). *The Age of Reagan: A History, 1974–2008*. New York: HarperCollins.
Žižek, Slovoj. (1989). *The Sublime Object of Ideology*. London: Verso.
Žižek, Slovoj. (1991). *Looking Awry: An Introduction to Lacan Through Popular Culture*. Cambridge: MIT Press.
Žižek, Slovoj. (1999). *The Ticklish Subject: The Absent Centre of Political Ontology*. London: Verso.
Žižek, Slovoj. (2001). *The Fragile Absolute*. London: Verso.
Žižek, Slovoj. (2006). *How to Read Lacan*. London: Granta Publications.

From Candy to Contact Killer
Moral Panic and the Fentanyl Contact Overdose Myth

KAT ALBRECHT *and* ANDREW BURNS

Introduction

Urban legends are more than just campfire stories both in their origins and in their impacts. We argue that urban legends can actually promote unfounded fears of existential threats that reveal deep-seated prejudices and anxieties about social change. We take up one particular urban legend as the starting point for our analysis: the tall tale of poisoned Halloween candy. Generations of trick-or-treaters across the United States have grown up hearing the myth that Halloween candy may be poisoned or contain harmful objects. Myths of malevolent poisoners targeting children have existed throughout history. Still, specific myths about stranger-poisoned Halloween candy became especially entrenched in the United States beginning during the social upheaval of the 1960s. Reports of candy tampering were widespread in the media and by word of mouth, but research found virtually no events matching the stranger-candy-killer narrative (Best and Horiuchi 1985).

Despite being repeatedly debunked, potentially sinister sweets continue to make the news every Halloween. In 2022 reports of "rainbow fentanyl" went viral shortly before Halloween, thanks to an October announcement by the U.S. Drug Enforcement Administration (DEA) (Mann 2022). These claims coincided with another contemporaneous fentanyl myth—the belief that a person can overdose from mere incidental contact (i.e., touching) with near-trace amounts of the drug. Fentanyl contact overdose myths gained significant traction in recent years, largely fueled by official sources. Publicly released body camera footage of law enforcement officers collapsing ignited fears of fentanyl contact overdoses—spreading through various news media, and filtering into the Zeitgeist through popular culture and social media. Additionally, the CDC issued, and later retracted, guidance about incidental fentanyl exposure despite research finding that skin contact with even large volumes of fentanyl does not produce any effect (Feldman and Weston 2022).

In this essay, we trace the rise of contaminated candy mythology to the present concerns about rainbow fentanyl. In doing so we discuss the architecture of the myth, its appearance in news and popular culture, and the role of official agencies in legitimating otherwise unfounded moral panics. We consider how these candy conspiracies proliferate in the context of widespread misinformation about fentanyl contact overdoses. We place these myths in digital contexts, constructing a database of alleged incidents and tracing their spread across traditional and social media. In doing so we discuss the importance of belief in experts, political polarization in the evolution of moral panics, and the role of fear in studying conspiracy beliefs.

The History of Poisoned Halloween Candy

The exact origin of the Halloween sadist who poisons children with innocuous-looking candy on Halloween is debated, but the 1959 case of Dr. William Shyne is identified by experts as a key historical moment that fanned the flames (Kawash 2013, 278). The California dentist handed out candy coated laxatives on Halloween, with 30 children reporting illness. No one was seriously hurt (*New York Times* 1959). Another pivot in the spread of the poisoned candy mythology came on October 28, 1970, when the *New York Times* ran an op-ed titled "Those Treats Might be Tricks" that warned parents to watch out for contaminated candy and razor blades in apples (Klemesrud 1970, 83). By 1982, when cyanide in Tylenol capsules in Chicago led to the death of seven people, the poisoned candy fears were firmly entrenched in the American cultural Zeitgeist and continue to make headlines every October (Gutowski 2022).

Crucially, the Tylenol murders had nothing to do with Halloween. Even the deaths themselves took place in September. However, the police report records lows in trick-or-treating and 40 cities across the United States banned trick-or-treating altogether (Gutowski 2022). The Tylenol murders aren't alone in their tenuous real-world relationship to actual tampered candy. In fact, researchers find that very few cases of actual poisoned Halloween candy can be verified at all. Best and Horiuchi (1985) conducted an empirical study on Halloween sadism from 1959 to 1984, the heyday of poisoned candy myths, by examining news coverage from the *New York Times*, the *Chicago Tribune*, the *Los Angeles Times*, and the

Fresno Bee. They identified 76 alleged incidents and set out about trying to validate each incident (1985). They found that only 26.31 percent of those incidents even alleged injury, with only 2.86 percent of incidents resulting in deaths. The first of those was the 1970 case of Kevin Toston, who died from consuming heroin once claimed to be in his Halloween candy but later revealed as belonging to a family member (*New York Times* 1970). The second killing occurred in 1974, where Timothy O'Bryan died from cyanide-laced Halloween candy that was given to him by his father (Dexheimer 2016). Therefore, Best and Horiuchi conclude that "there were no reports where an anonymous sadist caused death or a life-threatening injury; there is no justification for the claim that Halloween sadism stands as a major life threat to U.S. children" (1985, 491).

In both of these cases, there was no stranger trying to kill random children on Halloween, but that does not mean the myth of poisoned Halloween candy did not play a role. In both cases, the responsible parties attempted to use an urban legend as a cover-up for a child's death. In both cases, the media disseminated the stories and stoked the fears of candy killers. In the case of Kevin Toston, the delayed reporting that it may not have been heroin-laced candy after all received substantially less news coverage and public interest (Best and Horiuchi 1985). This pathway tracks with other fear-based conspiracies, where underlying incidents were few and far between until the entrenchment of social fear led to crimes committed using the current fear-scape to instill further panic. Take as an example, the case of the Satanic Panic in the 1980s. Following the 1983 allegation of ritual satanic abuse at the McMartin Preschool, thousands of cases were brought forth based on uncritical and often unethically derived evidence, with news reporting fanning the flames (Goode and Ben-Yehuda 2010). A recent example is the creepy clown conspiracy in the mid– to late 2000s where tales of creepy clowns luring children into the woods that were never proven, led to a spate of actual threats to attack schools from fictitious internet clowns (Albrecht, Burns, and Bell, forthcoming). Not all examples of media-driven fear panics involve supposed satanists and movie villain clowns. In 1976, New York City saw a wave of fear awash the city after reports of a spate of violent crimes targeting elderly residents (Fishman 1988). However, it turns out that the number of elder homicides was actually lower in 1976 than it had been the year before. Instead, what had changed was the way the news was reporting incidents as part of a wave rather than isolated happenings (1988). This constitutes a subtler example of how even when some facet of an underlying incident is true, there can be substantial media driven distortion.

In later writings, Best and Horiuchi (1996) define urban legends as unconstructed social problems, things existing in a sort of pre-politicized void that may eventually become a politicized issue (2013). We argue that a version of the poisoned candy mythology is fast becoming a politicized issue as tales of drug-laced candy on Halloween cede ground to fears about drugs being intentionally designed as candylike to target children and further claims that merely touching drugs can lead to death. We build on theories of moral panic and urban legend by specifically considering the role of fear in facilitating the cultural entrenchment of false beliefs about drugs using the Fear Principle (Albrecht, Burns, and Bell, forthcoming). The Fear Principle postulates that overidentification with the social object of fear, combined with celerity via spread, and legitimation of the myths from trusted authorities can have long-lasting consequences for legal regulation and social understanding of false beliefs (Albrecht, Burns, and Bell, forthcoming; Albrecht, forthcoming).

We are not the first scholars to observe the connection between poisoned candy mythology and the rise of related mythology surrounding dangerous drugs that look like candy. Duncan (2022) notes that fears around newer versions of fentanyl dubbed rainbow fentanyl due to their candy-like appearance and brightly dyed color, quickly became associated with the poisoned Halloween candy mythology even though the warning from the DEA was made in August and has no mention of Halloween candy (DEA 2022). That did not stop other governmental actors from sounding alarms about the potential of rainbow fentanyl-laced Halloween treats. Florida attorney general Ashley Moody's office sent a news release warning parents that

> Halloween can be scary, but nowhere near as scary as rainbow colored fentanyl that looks like candy and can be lethal in minute doses. Whether these drugs are being transported in candy boxes or mixed with other common drugs and sold to unsuspecting users, the threat posed to the safety of kids and young adults is very real. Just one pill laced with fentanyl can kill, so parents please talk to your children about the dangers posed by this extremely lethal drug [Mason 2022].

At the same time, other legitimized news sources were reporting that "drug policy experts contacted by NPR agree there's no new fentanyl threat this Halloween" (Mann 2022). In their report NPR interviewed Dr. Brandon del Pozo who spoke on how fentanyl candy fears have become entrenched in the cultural mythos, saying, "Fentanyl's a very potent drug that's causing a lot of overdose death, but it's taken on a mythical life of its own" (Mann 2022). Rainbow fentanyl is not the only source of fentanyl mythology currently plaguing news cycles and America's fears: stories of fentanyl contact overdose—where merely touching fentanyl can kill you—having been making headlines since 2015.

This leaves regular citizens in a difficult position, where they have to navigate legitimate risk and overblown fears with competing information from conventionally legitimate sources. Notably, similar to the lack of stranger murders rightfully attributed to Halloween candy tampering, there have been no validated child deaths or injuries connected to rainbow fentanyl. Despite this, fentanyl fears are not illogical or easily dismissed, with the CDC reporting that over 150 people die each day from opioid related overdoses (CDC 2023). However, some particular fentanyl fears, like Halloween candy swapped for synthetic opioids, are further afield than others. In order to diagnose and disentangle fears and myths, we argue that you must consider the origin story of those myths. To do so, we trace the history of fentanyl in the United States to contextualize its currently mythology including fears about rainbow fentanyl targeting children and fentanyl contact overdose myths, with an explicit focus on fentanyl contact overdose myths as the most contemporary arena where we can negotiate conspiratorial or scientifically unproven beliefs.

The Mythology and Reality of Fentanyl

Long before the overprescribing of prescription opioid painkillers in the early 21st century sparked a massive overdose crisis, illicitly manufactured fentanyls (IMFs) first appeared in illegal drug markets masquerading as heroin under another name: China White. In 1980, several deaths in Southern California resembling opiate overdoses coincided with people seeking treatment for drug addiction in the area, only to test negative for heroin or any other known substance (Brittain 1982, 1123–1125). It would be months before DEA chemists identified what was sold as China White, a highly sought-after heroin originating from Southeast Asia, was a methyl analog of fentanyl—an opioid anesthetic registered under brand names Innovar and Sublimaze (1982, 1123–1125; King 1981, 21). This early appearance of IMF coincided with confusion about potency; whether "80 to 100 times" or "1000 to 2000 times more powerful than morphine," the latter estimate noted "when tested in rats" (1982, 1125). The many unknowns, confusion—since fentanyl subsequently took on the moniker of China White for years—and questions about potency plague public opinion and non-medical first responder knowledge about fentanyl to this day. In addition to these unknowns, some well-known and medically established facts remain misunderstood due to an active mythology surrounding the substance.

The fear of fentanyl continues to inspire new myths. Despite the unprecedented demand for opioids in the United States that followed the crackdown on overprescribing in the 2010s, Administrator Ann Milgram, head of the U.S. Drug Enforcement Agency (DEA), claimed in 2022 that multi-colored fentanyl products were being produced by cartels to deliberately entice children to fentanyl use and addiction (Best 2023; Burns and Albrecht 2023, 246–247). This, in turn, inspired a media narrative that so-called "rainbow fentanyl" would be in children's Halloween candy—a fearful expectation with no evidentiary basis that never came to pass (Best 2023, DEA 2022). When the Sacramento, California District Attorney's Office announced that "rainbow fentanyl" made it into the capitol area, their website claimed the pills "look exactly like Smarties candies, and they are designed to attract kids and teens" (SACDA 2022). The image, originating from the DEA, that the Sacramento DA and various other law enforcement and local news media agencies used to represent "rainbow fentanyl" was pressed to resemble Oxycodone, not Smarties. As Best (2023) points out, much like each of the last 35 years, Halloween 2022 ended without a single documented case of children exposed to poison, or "rainbow fentanyl," in their trick-or-treat candy.

This is not to say that fentanyl is not dangerous. Fatal and non-fatal overdoses alike are increasingly driven by the consumption of IMFs (Shealey et al. 2022). However, when mythical concerns overshadow rational concerns, level-headed attempts at reducing potential harms are hindered and replaced with reactions based on false premises. Consider, for instance, the myth of overdose through incidental contact—through indirect inhalation or skin contact—of fentanyl among members of the U.S. law enforcement community. Since most IMFs have greater potency by volume than heroin or morphine (though any estimate on how many "times" greater is likely an oversimplification), the chance of overdosing is greater with substances containing some form of fentanyl. This fact inspires irrational fears that fentanyl may be potent enough to kill simply by touching it or accidentally inhaling minute amounts if fentanyl powder becomes airborne, properties that fentanyl lacks. Signs of an overdose include:

- Weakness, difficulty breathing, or if breathing significantly slows or stops.
- Snoring, gurgling, or choking.
- Skin discoloration: including blue or purple tone, especially around lips or fingernails.
- Drowsiness, intense sleepiness, or loss of consciousness: unresponsive.
- Pulse weakens, becomes undetectable, or arythmic if detectable.

These signs are well-known among people who witness or experience an opioid overdose and are commonly found on government websites providing clear indicators for signs or symptoms of overdose. These signs also contrast sharply with the descriptions that follow.

Apocryphal Police Fentanyl Overdose

Within the occupational subculture of U.S. police officers, culturally specific mythology surrounding fentanyl developed as National overdose and associated death rates rose (Herman et al. 2020). To understand why some law enforcement officers (LEOs) experience what they believe to be fentanyl overdoses after perceived exposure to fentanyl, we locate and analyze distinct perceived overdose events. From January 1, 2015, to October 31, 2023, we located 28 distinct events. For each event, we seek and analyze digitally published news articles, television news segments, government documents, and any publicly released body-worn camera footage of the incident to develop an in-depth understanding of the events. Secondarily, we consider the collective spread of the mythology and the successful or unsuccessful attempts to impede that spread. Collectively, the progression of these events tells a story of mythology as it moves through the police occupational subculture.

In October 2015, the Centers for Disease Control (CDC) released their Health Alert Network message CDCHAN-00384. The document warned that fentanyl "poses a significant danger to public health workers, first responders, and law enforcement personnel that may unwittingly come into contact with fentanyl either by absorbing through the skin or accidental inhalation of airborne powder" (CDC 2015). To support their claim, the article follows with the story of two New Jersey officers exposed to fentanyl when conducting a narcotics field test of an unknown substance (CDC 2015). The two officers were later featured in the DEA Officer Safety Alert training video, *Fentanyl: A Real Threat to Law Enforcement* (DEA 2016). In the video, Detective Eric Price recalled, "I felt like my body was shutting down," adding that he thought he was dying. The other officer involved in the incident, Detective Dan Kallen, agreed he felt he was dying after a "minuscule amount" of fentanyl became airborne but added, "Everything you did was exaggerated in your mind, I guess." The DEA alert circulated nationwide, as did Price and Kallen's story. The *Washington Post* quoted both detectives in a September 2016 article when, in similar circumstances, eleven officers required medical observation after some officers complained of "lightheadedness, nausea, sore throats, and headaches" after raiding a suspected drug manufacturing facility, moving through a cloud of what they believed to be heroin and fentanyl in the air (Bever & du Lac 2016).

The belief that fentanyl could be absorbed through skin contact or in the form of aerial particulates spread among U.S. law enforcement. This, however, sparked a joint position statement in August 2017 from the American College of Medical Toxicology (ACMT) and American Academy of Clinical Toxicology (AACT), stating that incidental exposure to opioids is unlikely to have any effect; adding that nitrile gloves and "in extreme circumstances" an N-95 respirator mask would be sufficient protection (Moss et al., 2018). Despite this attempt at clarification, news stories continued to cover these for years without any attempt to clarify or provide context. Additionally, state health departments failed to understand the relevance of the statement. Consider the state of North Carolina's Department of Health and Human Services, which cited the joint statement while still claiming that fentanyl may be absorbed into the skin (NCDHHS 2017).

On August 12, 2021, the San Diego County Sheriff's Department released extended bodycam footage, dated July 3, of deputy-in-training David Faiivae collapsing after field testing several substances, including fentanyl (San Diego County Sheriff 2021). Six days before the extended bodycam footage was released, Los Angeles' Fox 11 News reported on the event, claiming "exposure to just a few small grains can have deadly consequences" (Fox 11 2021). The story was picked up by ABC News that same day, making the story national news. This story, however, became one of the first to be openly questioned in the news media. Two days after the Fox 11 story aired, the *San Diego Union Tribute* published a story online refuting the claims of the Sheriff's Office, quoting Dr. Lewis Nelson of Rutgers New Jersey Medical School, who stated, "I'm concerned that the officers themselves are being harmed." The harm, according to Nelson, does not originate from fentanyl but from the fear of fentanyl. Nelson continued, "I fear people won't rescue those who have overdosed because of the fear of being exposed" (La Ganga 2021).

Faiivae's fifty-four-minute bodycam video featured multiple directives to the trainee to be careful from his trainer, Cpl. Crane. Three seconds into the video, Crane can be heard saying, "be careful, don't get poked with a needle. Okay, bro." Two minutes later, Faiivae replaced his gloves for the first of several times after touching a crumpled piece of aluminum foil, later determined to be paraphernalia. Faiivae even grabs his box of nitrile gloves, prompting Crane to offer to take photos to avoid Faiivae changing gloves too often. This proximity between Faiivae and Crane initiates an ongoing dialog between trainer and trainee about what potential drugs and paraphernalia are uncovered during a search of a suspect's vehicle.

Faiivae repeatedly handles various items, including a bag of pills, aluminum foil with charred residues, and a glass pipe, over the ensuing half-hour before two of the samples test positive for fentanyl on a portable spectrometer. When this happens, Cpl. Crane appears agitated, yelling at a passerby after taking a photo of the spectrometry readout. Crane then appears to begin closely monitoring Faiivae, falling silent for several seconds before making a phone call. The call was clearly about the situation; "Hey, uh, the dope tested positive; it tested positive for fentanyl. Yeah, both of them did."

Crane's discussion over the phone becomes hushed as he walks away from Faiivae and the vehicle, and Faiivae turns toward Crane, falling quiet himself. As Crane returns, he can be overheard saying, "Yeah, I know, so that's where we're at. Alright. Yeah, well, we'll … once we … yeah, let me just hang out with him, and we'll, we'll be on our way. Alright, dude, later." Faiivae's bodycam moves up and down rhythmically, appearing to be breathing heavily as he tests the third and final sample: methamphetamine. Faiivae removes his gloves once again. Seconds before his collapse, field training officer Cpl. Scott Crane can be heard cautioning Faiivae, "[don't] put your face close to that shit." Crane continues, "That stuff is no joke, it's super dangerous … you gotta be really careful," adding, "I hate dealing with it." Faiivae, visibly rattled and holding his spent gloves in his right hand, bags the paraphernalia with ungloved hands. Faiivae pauses for a second, apparently noting that he has held the baggie of paraphernalia without his nitrile gloves on his hands, then folds the baggie, places it neatly in the trunk of the police vehicle he is using to conduct his field testing, and then collapses (San Diego County Sheriff 2021).

Faiivae's experience is illustrative of common elements found in most of the LEO fentanyl fear responses we identified. The LEO must be exposed to fear-based messaging about fentanyl that asserts, first, that fentanyl is dangerous or deadly upon contact or through incidental inhalation of particulate; second, that exposure is possible through incidental contact and, finally, that may have been exposed to fentanyl. Research shows that fentanyl misinformation is pervasive throughout U.S. law enforcement culture (Attaway et al. 2021). We can then assume that most LEOs have been exposed to fentanyl fears through culturally derived messaging (del Pozo et al. 2022). In the case of David Faiivae, he was primed by various environmental factors, including the apparent concern of a trusted expert within the field. Cpl. Crane, for his part, immediately perceives Faiivae's collapse to be a medical emergency, calling for an ambulance and immediately grabbing Narcan. Crane exemplifies an additional element, missing from print news articles and in the Price and Kallen story but apparent in all available police bodycam footage of these events: anxious behavior surrounding the substance, either by the person who later collapses, a fellow LEO or both. It has been regularly noted that these events are not consistent with an overdose but are consistent with anxiety, likely driven by contextual factors, some of which we discuss below (Nelson & Perrone 2018; del Pozo et al. 2022).

Understanding Fear and Moral Panics

Importantly, the evaluation of fear and potential harm from conspiracy-related objects requires nuanced consideration. In the case of fentanyl contact overdose myths, fentanyl is a legitimate and severe source of harm. However, it is not a legitimate and severe source of harm via contact overdose. This makes dispelling the myth more difficult, since the object itself is severely harmful and fear-worthy. However, it is important to clarify the legitimate sources of harm and fear precisely because illegitimate ones distract from true underlying social crises. That is, the opioid epidemic is real and worthy of attention, analysis, and regulatory action, but that energy and effort should be targeted properly.

The Fear Principle proposed by Albrecht, Burns, and Bell provides some leverage in understanding the regulatory risk of the entrenchment of fentanyl contact overdose myths (Albrecht, Burns, and Bell, forthcoming). The Fear Principle begins by employing a multi-dimensional theory of objects, considering that an object has tangible, legal, and social dimensions that should all be given considerable weight when trying to understand an object like fentanyl contact overdose (Madison 2005, 383–384, Smith 2012, 1961). Albrecht (forthcoming) advances a theory of objectification, whereby overidentification with one dimension of an object provides fertile ground for panic and reactionary regulation. Applying this to fentanyl contact overdose, the social fear around the idea of contact overdose (even if scientifically implausible) can overtake the other dimensions of the object.

The Fear Principle requires two more elements: celerity via spread and institutional legitimization. The fentanyl contact overdose myth has both of these in spades. The 28 cases identified here were found across both mainstream media and social media, two vessels specifically designed for spread. Previous studies of fear objects find that even media committed to factual recitation can produce false fear panics (Fishman 1988), much less unmoderated social media with no requirements around factual accuracy. In part, this can be attributed to the sociological work of creating news (Schudson 2011). The outcome of this satisfies on criteria of the Fear Principle in seeding misinformation, in this case, to a broad audience.

The Fear Principle also requires reification of the fear object via legitimating institutions. The fentanyl contact overdose myth accomplishes this in some canonical ways, but also in ways that pose significant complications to understandings of expertise. In warning the public about fentanyl overdose, governmental and other trusted institutional actors reify beliefs that fentanyl contact overdose is a real risk. The CDC report, DEA training video and cited beliefs of law enforcement are canonical examples of this legitimation. These are organizations who exist with a certain amount of social trust, and being seen to endorse fentanyl contact overdose myths primes already fearful individuals to take the myth more seriously, keeping in mind that this is far from the first drug scare imprinted into the social fear fabric of the United States.

Where the fentanyl contact overdose myth complicates and extends notions about the importance of legitimation is through its relationship to expertise. From discussions of poisoned candy to discussions of the plausibility of fentanyl contact overdose, we see the emergent importance of beliefs in scientific experts. Pointedly, non-experts speak with considerably more certainty than experts. That is, experts tend to qualify their opinions or lay out narrower boundaries within which to consider their expertise. This is generally good scientific practice. Take, for instance, a criminal trial with forensic scientists testifying to the likelihood of events. Because the legal standard for conviction is "beyond a reasonable doubt" it is necessary to illuminate the smallest hints of doubt and not over-speak in absolutes. However, the case of fentanyl overdose is not being litigated in a court of law, it's being litigated in the court of public opinion where fear is admissible. Where experts speak precisely in courtrooms, non-experts or pseudo-experts interface with an already panicked public without those qualifications.

After strong statements from the CDC, DEA, and police departments, an expert opinion from the American College of Medical Toxicology (ACMT) and American Academy of Clinical Toxicology (AACT), stating that incidental exposure to opioids is "unlikely to have any effect" while still advising precautions, pales as evidence sufficient to quell fear already in motion. Thus, the current climate of fentanyl contact overdose fears requires a careful consideration of how to leverage expertise, legitimation, and maybe even regulation to dispel harmful myths. In the case of fentanyl contact overdose, police officers fear-primed experience medical crises: just not ones brought on by fentanyl overdose.

In this way, the fentanyl contact overdose demonstrates how the Fear Principle needs to expressly consider the role of expertise and the agency of the individual expert within its understanding of belief in legitimating institutions. Importantly, this is an especially difficult thing to navigate in the context of conspiratorial beliefs because it requires building trust in scientific experts and their agencies in an era where there are often valid reasons to mistrust individuals or organizations. Similarly, it also requires a sorting mechanism to discern who is and who is not an expert. Only then can we critique or endorse them speaking with any level of confidence or authority. This is difficult to do in the calmest of situations but is even more difficult to contemplate in the midst of active crises or a wave of fear.

Conclusion

In this essay, we traced the history of poisoned Halloween candy mythology to the present crisis surrounding fentanyl contact overdose myths. In doing so we leverage Best and Horiuchi's (1996) pathway for considering how a socially constructed problem like poisoned treats can become a national drug scare based on misinformation and cultural entrenchment. We expressly consider the role of fear and the limitations of expertise in disentangling the fentanyl contact overdose myth from its very real consequences and the severe harm of fentanyl in the United States. We propose that this theoretical lens can be a useful pipeline to consider other urban legends and socio-cultural conspiracies, particularly before the entrenchment of potentially damaging legal regulation and intervention. This work sits in conversation with work on moral panics and work discussing the link between fear and regulation. Expanding on work by Albrecht et al. (forthcoming) that illustrates how the objects of fear need not be canonically real to affect regulation, we examine how entrenchment of false beliefs creates a fear-scape that is extremely hard to resolve. Importantly, we do not consider the fentanyl contact overdose myth to be a conspiratorial belief generated out of nowhere. Instead, we think about it as the next wave in a cognizable pattern of conspiratorial fear beliefs around drugs and contamination. Despite decades of evidence that these fear beliefs are unfounded, they persist.

References

ABC News. (2021). "Sheriff's deputy overdoses after exposure to fentanyl during arrest." https://abcnews.go.com/US/sheriffs-deputy-overdoses-exposure-fentanyl-arrest/story?id=79324033

Albrecht, Kat. (2024). "'If I See a Burmese Python I'm Gonna Kill That Shit': How Changing the Object of the Law Affects Support for Legal Regulation." *UC Irvine Law Review* 14, no. 3.

Albrecht, Kat, Andrew Burns, Sierra Bell. (2024). "Fear the Law: Codifying Fear Through the Objectification of the Law." *UCLA Criminal Justice Law Review* 8: 147.

Attaway, Peyton R., Hope M. Smiley-McDonald, Peter J. Davidson, and Alex H. Kral. (2021). "Perceived Occupational Risk of Fentanyl Exposure Among Law Enforcement." *International Journal of Drug Policy* 95: 103303.

Beletsky, Leo, Sarah Seymour, Sunyou Kang, Zachary Siegel, Michael S. Sinha, Ryan Marino, Aashka Dave, and Clark Freifeld. (2020). "Fentanyl Panic Goes Viral: The Spread of Misinformation about Overdose Risk from Casual Contact with Fentanyl in Mainstream and Social Media." *International Journal of Drug Policy* 86: 102951.

Best, Joel, and Gerald T. Horiuchi. (1985) "The Razor Blade in the Apple: The Social Construction of Urban Legends." *Social Problems* 32, no. 5: 488–499.

Bever, Lindsey, and J. Freedom du Lac. (2016). "Opioid Epidemic's Hidden Hazard: SWAT Officers Treated for Fentanyl Exposure During Drug Raid." *Washington Post*, September 14. https://www.washingtonpost.com/news/post-nation/wp/2016/09/14/eleven-swat-officers-treated-for-exposure-to-fentanyl-and-heroin-in-drug-raid/.

Brittain, Jerry L. (1982). "China White: The Bogus Drug." *Journal of Toxicology: Clinical Toxicology* 19, no. 10: 1123–1126.

Burns, Andrew, and Kat Albrecht. (2022). "Localized Syndemic Assemblages: COVID-19, Substance Use Disorder, and Overdose Risk in Small-Town America." *RSF: The Russell Sage Foundation Journal of the Social Sciences* 8, no. 8: 245–262.

CDC. (2015). "Increases in Fentanyl Drug Confiscations and Fentanyl-related Overdose Fatalities." https://emergency.cdc.gov/han/han00384.asp.

CDC. (2023). Fentanyl Facts. Centers for Disease Control and Prevention. https://www.cdc.gov/stopoverdose/fentanyl/index.html.

DEA. (2016). "Fentanyl: A Real Threat to Law Enforcement." https://www.justice.gov/opa/video/fentanyl-real-threat-law-enforcement.

DEA. (2022). "DEA Warns of Brightly-Colored Fentanyl Used to Target Young Americans." https://www.dea.gov/press-releases/2022/08/30/dea-warns-brightly-colored-fentanyl-used-target-young-americans.

del Pozo, Brandon, Josiah D. Rich, and Jennifer J. Carroll. (2022) "Police Reports of Accidental Fentanyl Overdose in the Field: Correcting a Culture-Bound Syndrome That Harms Us All." *The International Journal on Drug Policy* 100: 103520.

Dexheimer, Eric. (2016). "35 Years Later, Memories of Notorious Halloween 'Candyman' Murder Remain Vivid." *Austin American-Statesman*, October 14. https://www.statesman.com/story/news/2016/10/14/35-years-later-memories-of-notorious-halloween-candyman-murder-remain-vivid/9867992007/.

Duncan, Heather. (2022). "Fighting Misinformation about Halloween Candy Tampering." University of Albany. https://www.albany.edu/sph/news/2022-fighting-misinformation-about-halloween-candy-tampering.

Fishman, Mark. (1978). "Crime Waves as Ideology." *Social Problems* 25: 531, 538–540.

Fox 11. (2021). "California Deputy suffers Fentanyl Overdose After Exposure to Substance on Patrol." Los Angeles. https://youtu.be/Jd76HxqCPf0?si=xhmgITyvkhU1ualZ.

Goode, Erich, and Nachman Ben-Yehuda. *Moral Panics: The Social Construction of Deviance*. Chichester: John Wiley & Sons, 2010.

Gutowski, Christy. (2022). "The Tylenol Murders: Timeline of Key Events Before and After the 1982 Poisonings. *Chicago Tribune*, October 27. https://www.chicagotribune.com/investigations/ct-tylenol-murders-timeline-20221027-aqtsts4y7zd2hbcufzhlvfdwui-list.html.

Herman, Paul Alexander, Daniel Saul Brenner, Stewart Dandorf, Stephanie Kemp, Breann Kroll, Joshua Trebach, Yu-Hsiang Hsieh, and Andrew Ian Stolbach. (2020). "Media reports of Unintentional Opioid Exposure of Public Safety First Responders in North America." *Journal of Medical Toxicology* 16: 112–115.

Kawash, Samira. (2013). *Candy: A century of Panic and Pleasure*. New York: Farrar, Straus and Giroux.

King, Wayne. (1981). "Source of a Deadly Synthetic Drug Sought on Coast." *New York Times*, January 4. https://www.nytimes.com/1981/01/04/us/source-of-a-deadly-synthetic-drug-sought-on-coast.html.

La Ganga, Maria L. (2021). "Questions Arise Over Video of San Diego Deputy's Contact with Fentanyl." *San Diego Union Tribune*, August 8. https://www.sandiegouniontribune.com/top-stories/story/2021-08-08/im-not-going-to-let-you-die-deputy-overdoses-after-coming-in-contact-with-fentanyl.

Madison, Michael. "Law as Design: Objects, Concepts, and Digital Things, 56 CASE W. RES. L. REV. 381, 383–384."
Mann, Brian. (2022). "Is 'Rainbow Fentanyl' a Threat to Your Kids This Halloween? Experts Say No." NPR, October 11. https://www.npr.org/2022/10/11/1127168627/is-rainbow-fentanyl-a-threat-to-your-kids-this-halloween-experts-say-no.
Mason, Kyle. (2022). "Warning of Rainbow Fentanyl Ahead of Halloween." Florida Attorney General's Office. https://www.myfloridalegal.com/newsrelease/warning-rainbow-fentanyl-ahead-halloween.
Moss, Michael J., Brandon J. Warrick, Lewis S. Nelson, Charles A. McKay, Pierre-André Dubé, Sophie Gosselin, Robert B. Palmer, and Andrew I. Stolbach. (2018). "ACMT and AACT Position Statement: Preventing Occupational Fentanyl and Fentanyl Analog Exposure to Emergency Responders." *Clinical Toxicology* 56, no. 4: 297–300.
NCDHHS. (2017). "Fentanyl Safety for First Responders." https://www.ncdhhs.gov/documents/fentanyl-information-1st-responders-final/download.
New York Times. (1959). "Coast Dentist Hunted: Wanted in Halloween 'Treat' That Made Children Ill." *New York Times*, November 4.
New York Times (1970). "Boy, 5, Who Died of Heroin May Have Taken a Capsule." *New York Times*, November 10. https://www.nytimes.com/1970/11/10/archives/boy-5-who-died-of-heroin-may-have-taken-a-capsule.html.
Nelson, Lewis S., & Jeanmarie Perrone. (2018). "'Passive' Fentanyl Exposure: More Myth Than reality." https://www.statnews.com/2018/12/21/passive-fentanyl-exposure-myth-reality/.
NIH. (2023). "Drug Overdose Death Rates." https://nida.nih.gov/research-topics/trends-statistics/overdose-death-rates.
SACDA. (2022). "PUBLIC SAFETY ALERT: Rainbow Fentanyl in Sacramento!" https://www.sacda.org/2022/10/public-safety-alert-rainbow-fentanyl-in-sacramento/.
San Diego County Sheriff. 2021. "Deputy Faiivae Body Camera Video—San Diego County Sheriff's Department." https://vimeo.com/586551310.
Schudson, Michael. (2011). *The Sociology of News*. New York: Norton.
Shealey, Jalissa, Eric W. Hall, Therese D. Pigott, and Heather Bradley. (2022). "Systematic Review and Meta-Analysis to Estimate the Burden of Fatal and Non-Fatal Overdose Among People Who Inject Drugs." *medRxiv*: 2022-02.
Smith, Henry E. (2012). "Property as the Law of Things, 125 HARVARD L. REV. 1691, 1691."

It's a Bird, It's a Plane, It's a Manifestation of Grief

How Sightings of Mothman Reveal the Grief Behind Conspiracy

MICHELLE DRAKE

Introduction

On November 16, 1966, the *Point Pleasant* [West Virginia] *Register* would publish a story that would go on to have an unfathomable impact on the future of the town. The article headline read, "Couples see man-sized bird … creature … something!" and was featured above the fold of the newspaper (Sergeant 2021). The following story detailed the experiences of Steve Mallette, Roger Scarberry, and their wives who were not present for the interview. The men described a horrific sight near a World War II–era munitions plant at midnight, something "like a man with wings" that flew "about 100 miles an hour" (Sergeant 2021). This "thing" would soon be dubbed Mothman. Fear and confusion spread in Point Pleasant as locals tried to make sense of who or what this creature was.

Mothman could have been a fleeting story and a local legend grown stale if not for what happened next: the disastrous Silver Bridge collapse of 1967. This tragedy cemented Mothman as a mysterious story and allowed the sightings to obtain a larger value in local history. Mothman was said to have disappeared after this incident, yet sightings continue to be reported to this day, usually surrounding tragic events. This persistent reporting shows a potential for a grief-based story as a part of modern folklore. Right now, you can open your phone or computer and search for Mothman sightings and receive results as recent as last year. How are people still seeing this creature who has survived multiple major natural disasters, terrorist attacks, and a pandemic, as well as at least fifty-eight years of life?

There comes a time when a piece of folklore has the potential to cross over from cultural story to conspiracy. For Mothman this evolution caused his story to be separated from its tragic, folkloric origin and pushed even further into something removed of all history: a pop culture icon. The lifeblood of this story is rooted in something far deeper than mass hysteria; the story of Mothman is now a larger piece of folklore that has continued to spread through grief while also serving as a misaligned example of conspiracy.

It Definitely Wasn't a Flying Saucer

It was just before midnight on November 15, 1966, when the Scarberrys and Mallettes were approached by a mysterious being. In order to better understand future sightings and stories it is important to discuss the details of the original incident. The two men described "the thing as being about six or seven feet tall, having a wingspan of 10 feet and red eyes about two inches in diameter and six inches apart" (Sergeant 2021). The original location where they viewed such a terrifying being was by an old power plant, near the National Guard armory buildings. This location is also referred to as "the TNT area" due to the production of TNT at the address. After seeing the creature, the couples drove off as they had been frightened; however, this thing followed them. The men described a complicated path that they drove to get the "thing" to stop following them and yet "it seemed to be waiting on us." Mallette described the creature as flying across the top of the car. The men finished their interview by wondering if the thing lived in the vacant power plant: "There are pigeons in all the other buildings … but not in that one" (Sergeant 2021). This sensational headline came to Point Pleasant just five years after another strange and supernatural story from Barney and Betty Hill, a couple from New Hampshire who claimed to have been abducted by aliens while driving home one night. The Hills shared a story of a bright white light which followed them down the highway one night. Their story described an abduction as well as invasive medical procedures performed by their alien abductors. This was one of the first, and most well-known, alien abduction stories of the time. Even today it is sometimes credited as a first for alien abduction stories. Unlike the people in the Mothman story, the Hills were just one couple alone on a highway one night. While the two stories were vastly different, it is relevant to note the timeline of such amazing encounters with paranormal or extraterrestrial beings.

Despite Mallette and Scarberry stating they would return to the scene that day, there were no reports of significant findings at the time that they returned. Of course, if they had returned to the abandoned power plant and opened the abandoned boiler to discover a living, breathing Mothman, then this story likely would have a very different ending. What happened instead was an outpouring of reports over the course of the next year. Residents of Point Pleasant were seeing Mothman just about everywhere they could. Everyone from rowdy teenagers to well-respected community members were reporting sightings of a similar unidentified creature. The reports would rise higher and higher until December 15, 1967, when the community of Point Pleasant bore witness to one of the deadliest bridge collapses in United States history. On that day the Silver Bridge spanning the Ohio River collapsed due to structural failure while the traffic lights on each end of the bridge were red. As the bridge collapsed it took with it every stationary car that had been waiting for a green light. The sudden collapse resulted in forty-six fatalities.

While Point Pleasant residents paused their lives to address such a large tragedy there were murmurs around town. Suddenly, the town had a possible answer for such a horrific event. Many began to wonder if this mysterious figure could have been connected to the bridge collapse. One of the most curious facts was that some had reported seeing the unidentified flying man around the Silver Bridge during the days before the collapse and some even reported seeing him that very day. Perhaps, to this fearful community, this was the reason why their friends and neighbors died. Presented as a clean, straightforward explanation, this story of an ominous creature was something the citizens of Point Pleasant could point to. As this belief took root in the answer for the bridge collapse there was a rise in stories of a winged creature stalking the skies. Reports were technically still being made; however, they were only being made retroactively. It seemed, at least among most people, that there were no more sightings of the creature after the collapse. This led to the speculation of the Mothman's involvement in the bridge collapse to gain traction. However, the publication of initial Mothman research in 1975 would popularize this theory even further. For some, these sightings became a definitive explanation and the only reason they could see for the sudden and tragic death of their friends and loved ones. Some referred to Mothman as an omen or a harbinger of death. The community of Point Pleasant hoped and believed that he would not be seen again. By now, the Mothman represented more than a scary story for young people sneaking around at night. He was a symbol, an omen associated with the devastation of the town. There was something in their skies, something that everyone feared would show again. Thankfully, the community did not face another bridge collapse. However, the Mothman brought forward another surprising event. The result would push the Mothman into far more than a local legend and begin his journey to pop culture icon. Point Pleasant would be far from able to forget the events surrounding the Silver Bridge collapse. This folklore would soon be launched into conspiracy by the polarizing UFO-ologist John Keel.

In the 1970s John Keel would arrive in Point Pleasant in search of aliens. For Keel, this adventure was intended to boost his own career. As a UFO-ologist, he needed to find further proof or mystery to write about. What he would discover, instead, was the very creature first seen in 1966. Keel would then write about the stories of the creature with the ten-foot wingspan in the skies of Point Pleasant. *The Mothman Prophecies* would be released in 1975, putting Mothman into the public eye and available on shelves. This publication is noted as being responsible for the popularization of the Mothman story and, later, for the widespread new sightings of the creature as well as their attached conspiracies. Inside the book, Keel also connected Mothman to instances of UFOs and what he dubbed "ultraterrestrials" which were involved in the collapse of the Silver Bridge (Keel 2013). For Keel, and those who read his research, the Mothman had no association with grief. The creature was, of course, technically affiliated with the Silver Bridge and its collapse which gave the story a whisper of its tragic roots. For readers of Keel, however, there was no loss. Those fascinated with this mysterious creature cared far more about its existence, its connection to the ultraterrestrials, and what the men in black were covering up when they allegedly came to town. As time went on, Mothman himself would be further and further distanced from his very home. No longer a folkloric symbol of grief, he would become something far more popular.

Twenty-seven years later, in 2002, a film by the same name was released as an adaptation of Keel's novel. The film is a dramatization of alleged first-hand accounts and Keel's interpretation of the events in Point Pleasant. While the film received a variety of responses and criticisms, it grossed over $55 million and was considered a financial success (IMDB 2024). Now, Mothman was a pop culture symbol. He was a villain; he was the thing that goes bump in the night for anyone in the world who watched this film. He was a source of fear not because of his actual origin but because he caused fear due to his thriller movie presence or association with aliens. Despite this, the people of Point Pleasant noted a significant increase in tourism related to the film and, subsequently, Mothman himself. "Mothman was last reported seen in late 1968 but the creature has reappeared as a mysterious presence in the movie starring Richard Gere," Jennifer Bundy wrote for the *Appalachian Journal*. "Small business owners along Main Street hope the new notoriety brings prosperity to the town" (Keel 2013, 403). While the boost in the local economy was a welcome sight for Point Pleasant, the legacy of Mothman and Keel's novel would create a morally gray domino effect. Point Pleasant would go from an unknown West Virginia town to cryptozoological tourist destination.

Tragedy, Grief and Coping

We will all die, everyone we love, or hate, will die, and that's a simple fact we have all faced as long as there has been conscious life. Coping with those facts has taken countless forms for thousands of years as humans try to make sense of life, of death, and of what comes next. This attempt to cope has led to amazing discoveries in art, philosophy, science and more over the years. Grieving the loss of life or loss of loved ones is a common practice in many cultures around the world and takes on a variety of shapes. How do we describe the feeling of inexplicable tragedy or loss? There are no right or wrong answers to this question and the study of this subject would be enough to fill a library. For the purposes of this research, it is important to look at community trauma, grieving, and coping with that grief. However, these are not the only feelings or experiences that are hard to explain. Many stories of cryptids have also been born from the concept of the inexplicable.

In their essay "What Happens When the Pictures Are No Longer Photoshopped," researcher Andrea Kitta explores the legend of the Slender Man, a horror figure born in internet forums and falsified photos. Kitta explores the concepts of "experiences" that people have with stories. This research, in brief, explains that people have typical experiences and unusual experiences that can elicit specific feelings or reactions. Kitta infers that those who share the stories of Slender Man are sharing an "experience" and a group of feelings or culture. "The reason [Slender Man] 'feels real' to so many people is because he helps to give a voice to a real experience that is difficult to articulate otherwise.… Not only does Slender Man give us a place to assign value to these unacknowledged common experiences, he is standing there, acknowledging these experiences" (Kitta 87). In this research Kitta is presenting a vital concept to storytelling and folklore: assigning value to shared experiences. Things that cannot be explained, feelings that do not have a simple vocabulary, are the exact concepts that have sent poets down artistic spirals for thousands of years. One way that humans can feel closer to each other is communicating about relatable or shared experiences. In their discussion of Slender Man, as Kitta describes, the fictional being represents a feeling and a shared internet experience for those who "believe" in him.

Folklore is created by these shared experiences and the stories that go with them. Throughout oral histories, myths or folklore of creation, now-extinct creatures and important figures have reigned. These stories have formed the culture of their times and now we affiliate those very stories with those periods of time or cultures. Folklore is a vital ingredient to culture itself and to disregard folklore is to disregard the lived experiences of a past people. As people have learned to write and record their stories the folklore has continued to grow and expand; the written record allows the study of ancient cultures that otherwise would have died out with their oral traditions. As the research by Kitta shows, Slender Man has never truly been believed to be real. He started as a presumed and accepted fictitious piece of folklore and his story was spread for entertainment purposes. His popularity cemented him in pop culture and allowed him to be associated with emotions or shared experiences. Regardless of the reality of Slender Man, his fans or believers serve as a perfect example of this folklore and storytelling concept. As pointed out in Kitta's essay, people feel closer to each other and explore shared experiences by discussing Slender Man. This accepted symbol of internet culture serves as an example of folklore creation in the modern era and the importance of that form of storytelling. For the folklore of Mothman, the flying creature exists in a more firmly recognizable piece of history. His popularity was born from true tragedy that was organically associated with his existence.

Unlike Slender Man, Mothman does not only exist only on the internet. Mothman was born in the cultural quilt and deeply understudied region that is Appalachia. Within every corner of this region there are varying approaches to folklore, storytelling, and mourning. West Virginia, in particular, has suffered generations of isolating trauma and poverty. The result is a region with deeply rich history and stories, although many corners of academia have left the stone of Appalachia unturned. In their research "Complicated Grief in Rural Appalachia," Nancy Thacker and Melinda Gibbons describe the culture of rural Appalachia to better explore how grief manifests in the region. This essay explores the nature of "complicated grief" which the writers define as "an enduring and impairing grief response to the loss of a loved one" (Thacker and Gibbons 297). The research explores how the emphasis on community and individualism within Appalachia influences the experiences of complicated grief in the region. Thacker and Gibbons summarize this experience as "rural Appalachians' experiences of [complicated grief] also may be intensified because Appalachian cultural values are deeply rooted in community membership, familism, and egalitarianism" (302).

The concept of complicated grief or loss in Appalachia is vital to understanding any and all folklore that originates in the region.

Communal experiences, community grief, and shared experience are incredibly important to the cultural makeup of Appalachia. In an area greatly impacted by poverty, outsider distrust, and generational trauma, these shared experiences become even more important to the study of their local stories and myths. Kitta's previously mentioned research on Slender Man shows the desire to connect through these shared, inexplicable feelings or experiences. Seeing something in the skies of Appalachia fulfills this same category of shared experience. With this explanation of Appalachian culture in mind it is important to look at the full experience of grieving through folklore.

This desire to explain has resulted in endless avenues for the supernatural to fit within the narrative of tragedy and shared trauma by communities around the world. The lightest level of existence of this concept manifests itself in fortune telling or predicting events that will happen. Human beings inherently want to know what will happen to them; they especially have a desire to know about tragic or uncomfortable events so that they may prepare. During the heyday of Myspace or early internet online forums it was popular to share "prediction" posts where one could find out the day and method in which they would die. While this example is not very steadfast and was not taken seriously by most users, it is a perfect example of the human desire to know. Many famous psychics and fortune tellers around the world have been sharing their predictions of major events for centuries. One of the most popular psychics and source of many confirmations for conspiracy theorists is the 16th century French astrologer Nostradamus. Following the September 11, 2001, attacks, there were online forums in which commenters reacting to the tragedy mentioned Nostradamus and his alleged prediction of towers and brothers falling (MetaFilter 2001). These Nostradamus predictions have been used by many conspiracy theorists to discuss predictions of mass deaths, illnesses, and general chaos or even the end of the world.

It is not just the future or the retroactive fortunes that people are trying to explain. Tragedy, mourning, and grief can take many different supernatural forms for people around the world. On March 11, 2011, a historically catastrophic earthquake and tsunami brought death and destruction to Fukushima, Japan. This incident killed over twenty-five thousand people and devastated the residents of Japan and many people around the world. In a 2012 article, journalist Richard Lloyd Parry covered some of the after-effects of such a devastating incident. The journalist interviewed Reverend Kaneda who was performing exorcisms and helping people in the wake of the tsunami's destruction in their efforts to heal. Parry reported, "Victims of the disaster and those who simply witnessed its aftermath have reported the presence of ghosts and spirits and in some cases called on priests such as the Rev Kaneda to drive them away" (2012). This report followed the alleged ghost sightings and experiences with disturbed spirits that had no chance of being properly laid to rest due to the natural disaster. In the article, one man talked about visions of children and older adults standing together covered in mud. The reports are hair-raising and haunting, and the Reverend Kaneda attributes them in the article to the unrest and trauma of the event. Surviving this event has haunted the minds of those still living, and this report serves as just one example of how trauma can manifest after such a devastating disaster.

Despite these experiences with premonitions or ghosts and their seeming improbability, there are many people around the world that would argue these things are, in fact, possible. Even if they are not about to prove it scientifically, there are witnesses and survivors of great tragedy that will continue to argue the "truth" of the paranormal, supernatural, and extraterrestrial that surrounds their memories and experiences. And how could anyone tell them otherwise? What do we, as a society, gain from telling these survivors that they are wrong and that their tragic moments, the last breaths of their loved ones, or the events that keep them up at night are just everyday tragedies? Discussion of these strange beliefs or stories requires a level of respect and understanding in a group's reason for believing. To imply that nothing special has happened or interfered in the lives of those looking for reason or explanation is the psychological equivalent of stealing candy from a baby.

He Is Everywhere

The residents of Point Pleasant did not report seeing Mothman after the collapse of the Silver Bridge. As the years continued the popularity of the Mothman story grew and it seemed Mothman had moved to various locations around the world. There are rogue reports of Mothman sightings in various places over the last fifty years; however, the most notable sightings have been since the turn of the century. On September 11, 2001, both towers of the World Trade Center in New York City collapsed due to terror attacks resulting in the deaths of 2,996 people and the injuries of an estimated six thousand to twenty thousand people (Hartig and Doherty 2021). This was a devastating and horrifying day for the people of New York City as well as many people within the United States and around the world. While much of the country was discussing the current events and looking for loved ones, there was, at the same time, a murmur going around circles of conspiracy theorists and those interested in the supernatural. Sightings of Mothman near the Twin Towers had been retroactively reported around the time of the September 11 attacks. This story has since been largely discussed as falsified and is mostly still given life by online forums and social media. Theories around the connection between Mothman and the September 11 attacks were further "supported" by the discovery of a photo credited to Steven Moran. The photo features a figure alleged to be Mothman flying in the empty air space where the towers previously stood and flying toward the rubble (Wayland 2017). For the purposes of this research, it is important to discuss the story existing at all regardless of how believable it may be. During what is currently considered the deadliest attack on United States soil there are at least some people, retroactively, that have associated Mothman with the event.

The days surrounding the September 11 attacks would not be the last time Mothman was rumored to have appeared. On November 21, 2016, a sighting of Mothman was reported in Point Pleasant. The report came from an anonymous man who alleged he had seen the winged creature jumping between trees. Most notably, the report ends with a note from the journalist that reads, "Some believe that the Mothman is a bad omen and only appears when a tragedy is about to strike" (O'Neill 2016). This seemingly innocuous statement shows how the belief in Mothman's ominous qualities continue into the modern day.

From 2016 until 2020 Mothman seemed to have multiplied as there were a number of sightings reported across the United States. Most notable were sightings around Chicago that began in 2017 with fifty-five reported sightings in that year alone. Months before the global pandemic brought the world to a halt, there was a documentary released about these sightings titled *Terror in the Skies* which hoped to find evidence or reason for the new batch of Chicago Mothman episodes. Shortly after the documentary's release there grew a more popular belief that these sightings had been a warning about the pandemic itself. In a report published in 2020 journalist Dylan Hackworth covered the increased sightings in the Chicago area between 2017 and 2019. Hackworth's approach to the story also touched on the alleged omen that Mothman is claimed to bring with it. In the article a local professor, Tricia Hermes, is interviewed on the subject of Mothman's reputation. "Some say this is Mother Earth's way of taking revenge on humans. I think a belief in the paranormal—like Mothman—can be a kind of shield from the even harsher truths of the world" (Hackworth 2020). The article continues to discuss why people are affiliating Mothman with the global Covid-19 pandemic. Hermes continues their thoughts, saying, "Random violence and accidental death are frightening and something we cannot control. We look for meaning in the chaos" (Hackworth 2020). What Hermes is mentioning in this quote is important to the discussion of modern Mothman sightings. By this belief and standard, it is very explainable just why and how so many people have continued to associate Mothman with large-scale tragedy. This point is further shown by the more recent event of the Francis Scott Key bridge collapse in March 2024. Many were shocked when the Baltimore bridge was hit by a cargo ship; however, some people on the internet quickly began to discuss possible Mothman involvement. As reported on Politifact by Ciara O'Rourke, an image of Mothman on the Francis Scott Key bridge was published on Facebook along with a description claiming he had been seen three weeks before the collapse. This story was quickly dispelled as the shared image was from more than a decade before the post (O'Rourke 2024). How easily this story spread is a testament to the strong correlation between tragedy and Mothman in modern folklore.

Mothman as an Emblem of Grief

With the understanding of how grief and folklore are intertwined it is possible to better analyze and understand the tale of the winged creature from Point Pleasant. When the two couples were first facing the terror at the abandoned TNT yard, they had no clue what they saw. In the following days and interviews they gave it was apparent that whatever they saw just before midnight had scared them terribly, however, there was no name nor was there any specific paranormal descriptor for this creature. As previously mentioned, this sighting was also shortly after the highly publicized abduction story by Barney and Betty Hill. More recent scholarship has suggested that a major factor of the Barney and Betty Hill story was racism that the couple was facing (Blake 2023). While the Mallettes and Scarberrys were not facing the same issue, it does appear that the general mistrust of the government and fear surrounding the supernatural and extraterrestrials of the 1950s and 1960s could easily have been a factor at the time of the first reported Mothman sighting. Although the Mallettes and the Scarberrys do not seem to have been motivated by grief, the most important parts of the conspiracy—its lifeforce and longevity—were only possible due to the coming tragedy.

Hysteria, mania, and sensation are all terms that have been popularly used to describe the phenomena of increased supernatural and extraterrestrial encounters especially during this time period. The more than one hundred reported sightings of the creature between 1966 and 1967 could easily be attributed to these concepts of supernatural sensationalism and parallel many similar report trends of UFO sightings at the time (Keel 2013). After all, these UFO sightings are the very thing that brought

John Keel to the area and led to the popularization of the story of Mothman. However, would Mothman's story have continued to take flight over decades if not for the conspiracies started by Keel?

Forty-six people tragically died on December 15, 1967. According to population records that number accounts for nearly 1 percent of the total population of the town at that time (Health Statistics Center 2002). In the following decades, the town would see its population drop to its lowest point. An inexplicable and sudden tragedy such as the Silver Bridge collapse can drive a wedge into a community. At this same time more than one hundred members of the Point Pleasant community had reported seeing some strange creature in the skies that suddenly disappeared after the deaths of their neighbors, friends, and loved ones. The emotional impact of this tragedy would have been severe, and, as it took nearly a year to determine the cause of the collapse, there were many moments during which the residents of Point Pleasant could have shared their theories. With a desire to explain why this tragedy happened, the building tension of these sightings, and a small town, there was the perfect recipe for this folklore to become cemented permanently in the history of the town. Mothman would become synonymous with the local lore, and it was only a matter of time before someone such as John Keel could stumble upon this story-rich town in the quilt of Appalachia's folklore and utilize it for his own narrative, thus evolving a piece of grief-stricken folklore into an alien-adjacent conspiracy.

What If Folklore Becomes a Conspiracy

While something like the belief of Mothman would fit under the wide umbrella of conspiracy theory, it is not to say that Mothman is only a conspiracy or that he ever had to be associated with the term. The term conspiracy or conspiracy theory, which has been used throughout this essay, has a variety of definitions depending on which lens it is viewed through. One of the most comprehensive definitions comes from a 2023 article by Karen M. Douglas and Robbie M. Sutton in the *Annual Review of Psychology*:

> A conspiracy theory is a belief that two or more actors have coordinated in secret to achieve an outcome and that their conspiracy is of public interest but not public knowledge. Conspiracy theories (a) are oppositional, which means they oppose publicly accepted understandings of events; (b) describe malevolent or forbidden acts; (c) ascribe agency to individuals and groups rather than to impersonal or systemic forces; (d) are epistemically risky, meaning that though they are not necessarily false or implausible, taken collectively they are

more prone to falsity than other types of belief; and (e) are social constructs that are not merely adopted by individuals but are shared with social objectives in mind, and they have the potential not only to represent and interpret reality but also to fashion new social realities [282].

Although lengthy, this definition helps to show just how hard it is to clearly define a conspiracy theory. Regardless, the definition points out that a conspiracy theory is used to explain the reasoning behind an event and often creates a villain through a group of people or other source of power as part of that explanation. In the case of John Keel, he helped to fashion new social realities by using aliens and government as explanations for why ultraterrestrials were terrorizing the skies. This, as previously mentioned, made him investigate Point Pleasant and thus attached Mothman to the conspiracy theory. Using this definition, it can also be inferred that conspiratorial thinking is a line of thought powered by the concept or goal of discussing conspiracy. Conspiracy theories or conspiratorial thinking exist nearly in opposition to folklore or cultural storytelling as the latter do not have a goal of explaining wrongdoing by a source of power. Folklore exists as a means of telling a story, teaching a lesson, or sharing history.

It is important to understand the weight of exploring the unbelievable as it relates to evolution from folklore to conspiratorial thinking. For the people of Point Pleasant, Mothman is a piece of folklore, the thing that goes bump in the night and terrorizes the skies. He is a cautionary tale to young teens sneaking around abandoned waste facilities. To modern pop culture, Mothman is long since divorced from his tragic origin. In "Why Do People Believe in Monsters" authors Daniel Loxton and Donald Prothero look at the criteria that allow certain groups to believe in folklore, ghost stories, or even conspiracies. They suggest mistrust in the government, generational poverty, and regional trauma may all lead to belief in the unknown or paranormal. Groups with these qualities are more likely to believe in something other than pure fact or ordinary explanations.

As mentioned earlier, there is a desire to share experiences with others and connect a shared story. Slender Man, while having no basis in reality, serves as a representation of shared storytelling that can be used to process shared experiences or culture. For the story of Mothman, this shared experience is coupled with the criteria laid out by Loxton and Prothero to explain the reasoning behind this strong belief in monsters. When looking at these examples together, it becomes clear that the people of Point Pleasant were most certainly creating their own piece of folklore when the first sighting of Mothman was reported. They were already demographically predisposed to believe in something other than pure fact or fiction; they experienced a shared tragedy and then used a recent local story to explain the reasoning or find a way to cope with that tragedy. This was the creation of the folklore that is Mothman. It was a story that could have died out, yet it was made immortal by John Keel and his version of the events of the 1960s.

Shared stories and oral histories feel very real to their audiences. There is always a quasi-confirmation bias in the sharing of these stories due to alleged eyewitnesses. It was not the people of Point Pleasant that turned Mothman into a conspiracy. Instead, it was John Keel who entered the community in search of the unbelievable, a man who was looking for explanations to events that were already rooted in falsehoods or conspiracy. He sought answers to alien encounters, UFOs, and his own fear of the government covering up supposed ultraterrestrials. Using this predestined fear, he presented a new answer for something sinister and not something tragic. The difference between Mothman the folklore and Mothman the conspiracy is found in what he serves to become an answer for. When removing the tragedy or genuine desire to explain a massive cultural trauma, there is also the removal of the folkloric value of the story. This misalignment of folklore easily leads to a blurred line between cultural story and fearful conspiracy theory.

It feels natural that humans who have accepted one unbelievable idea as an explanation for trauma would be more vulnerable to turning to conspiracies as answers to the rest of their problems. Entertaining folklore is important as, regardless of content, its relationship to culture, and generational storytelling is vital to providing value to communities. It is also important to understand the power in not only entertaining folklore but changing that folklore from a coping mechanism to something more fearful or aggressive. A community or person that is predisposed to suspending disbelief could then, theoretically, accept a conspiracy that does not answer their own tragic experience but instead presents new fears. The mainstreaming of conspiracy theories in pop culture has made it difficult to differentiate between folklore and conspiratorial stories at times. The reality of exploring conspiracy and the "strange" is down to the informed researcher. It is important to understand the potential harm and issues of conspiracy thinking while also accepting that folklore is an inherently important part of cultural development and should remain a celebrated piece of generational storytelling or art.

Immortality

Despite the sharp and consistent decreases in population for Point Pleasant since the 1960 census data, there has been a significant increase in tourism and economic growth. The town hosts a yearly Mothman festival that brings out tens of thousands of attendees and many different vendors and stimulates the economy of the area annually. A search of online book retailers can show dozens of results for books about Mothman or featuring the name in the title. Some popular results include titles such as *I'm in Love with Mothman*, *Mothman's Merry Shadow*, and *Mothman Is Real*. Genres covering or including the creature range from nonfiction to romance to children's storybooks. If one had an endless budget, they could visit many popular gift-related websites such as Etsy and fill a home with Mothman plush toys, paintings, jewelry, and clothing. In a recent large-scale video game, *Fallout 76*, Mothman could be found as an enemy in the open world waiting to be fought. These examples show the pedestal Mothman has landed on and how widely known and beloved he has become. As time has passed, especially in the last fifteen years, the popularity of Mothman has helped pave the way for alternate cryptid spaces and more pop culture–centered interest in folklore. Instead of just terrifying tales of winged creatures and the men in black the internet is overrun with adorable art of everything from Chupacabra to Nessie to Fresno Nightcrawlers. Cryptids have gained immortal fame on the internet and in its culture.

Mothman is not the only supernatural entity or conspiracy to be born from great tragedy. Many ghost stories are born from forms of grief or after a mass casualty event. As previously mentioned, ghosts seen in the aftermath of the 2011 tsunami in Japan serve as an example of supernatural stories rooted in tragedy. The origins of the Jersey Devil were in a popular story of a woman dying tragically in childbirth. However, something about Mothman specifically, perhaps his large eyes and moth association, has allowed him to be the poster child for so-called cool cryptids. Much of his ominous presence or dark connotations have gone far away, or at least are not as present in the online discussions about the creature. Today, Mothman is immortal and worth a large sum of money. He has grown past both conspiracy and folklore into something else entirely: capitalism. He is a stuffed animal, a character in a children's cartoon, or something people on the internet want to have a romantic relationship with. You can fight Mothman in video games or share a meme about him on social media. Pop culture has firmly grasped Mothman with no sign of letting go, almost entirely divorcing him of his own story. He now holds a softer and warmer place in the hearts of thousands or even millions of people around the world. This development presents a very interesting yet concerning opportunity for conspiracies in pop culture. Instead of being fringe and unknown, the existence of Mothman is a cute story on the internet and the folkloric background of the creature is no longer a part of his story. By separating the cryptid from the conspiracy, pop culture has shown that this is equally possible for other cryptids or perhaps other conspiracy theories entirely. While the popularity of Mothman is not presenting noticeable negative impacts on society such as the racist fearmongering of other conspiracies, the wide acceptance of the story presents the potential for those more harmful stories to be accepted by mainstream society in the future should their stories evolve in the same way that Mothman's did.

Is Mothman Real?

In November of 1966, the Mallettes and the Scarberrys saw something that terrified them. It was large, it had red eyes, it chased them, and it horrified the four people beyond belief. As the months flew by so did reports of something haunting the skies, a creature with red eyes and a ten-foot wingspan that was unbelievable to behold. This creature terrorized a town of just under six thousand people for more than a year before, ultimately, their minds were shifted to the real-world horror of their friends and neighbors dying tragically. When the unthinkable happened on September 11, 2001, and the whole world was watching New York City, there were some who whispered sightings of the same winged creature around the time of the collapse of the World Trade Center. The number of reports was small and fell short of the much larger conspiracies born from that tragedy; however they are rumors still whispered about to this day. In the years and months leading up to what has been one of the deadliest epidemics in history, the creature was spotted again in the skies around Chicago. As Covid-19 took over the world it became clear to some online that the horrifying creature with the ten-foot wingspan was warning the world about something bigger than ever before. While reports of Mothman sightings came before and after each of these tragedies, their major discussions have largely lived on in the rumor that comes after a great tragedy. As new, unforeseen horrors struck the world time after time there were small groups around the world wondering if Mothman had been seen recently.

To the people online that post these threads, share photos, and discuss sightings over time, Mothman is very much alive. Much like the shared experience of Slender Man, as Kitta's research discovered, the truth of his origin does not matter. It is in the answers he provides and the grief that his existence soothes that makes Mothman alive to those looking for him. To some residents of Point Pleasant, in the aftermath of the Silver Bridge collapse the Mothman was an explanation. He held a purpose for existing and a reason for such a sudden tragedy. To those people, Mothman was very much real.

This research and analysis were not completed with the purpose of proving the existence of Mothman. The "true" existence or non-existence of Mothman is irrelevant to the study of folklore or anthropology that keeps such a figure alive. This is what John Keel and many conspiracy hunters since him have failed to realize. They were so busy creating fear and mistrust of communities that they missed the opportunity to truly relish what a beautiful thing it is to watch folklore form before your own eyes. What is important in this discussion is what Mothman represents. To many people Mothman represents the "why" and a shared trauma between themselves and their community members. He has been the omen that "we" all ignored and the reason that people needlessly died. Mothman is as real as you make him and that is the beauty of folklore and the shared stories of cultures.

Conclusion

When we think about the history of our family, community, or world we think about why and how things came to be. Those stories passed through history books and storytelling equally shape our views of where we live and why things work the way that they do. Many of the stories that shape our communities are born in tragedy, death, or horror. There are no simple explanations to why people suffer; that is a philosophical debate far beyond the realm of this essay. What we do know, intrinsically, is that storytelling can help humans cope and grieve. It can heal the pain of the "why" and provide comfort for moving on. Survivors of mass tragedies have continually sought answers as to why they suffered or why their loved ones are gone. The supernatural has fit the trauma-molded hole in the hearts of these survivors. Mothman exists as a reason why tragedy occurred to the community of Point Pleasant. He has become a vital part of the folklore of that region. In the modern day Mothman has served as a further comfort for those who do not have the same questions. He has become a part of modern folklore and stories to provide entirely unrelated comfort to those that speak about him online. If it were not for John Keel and his writing, then we might not be able to buy Mothman plush toys at the mall. It was after removing Mothman from his community, from his folklore, that pop culture accepted him. Mothman has become the poster child for loving cryptids and has healed much of the pain he previously caused for the community that bore him. Folklore is not inherently conspiratorial and there is no reason that each cultural story should ever be considered a conspiracy. In the case of Mothman, this creature and its story serves as an example of how local folklore can start as a reason, an

140   Part II: Cultural Mythology and Social Media

answer to why things happen only to later be removed from that origin entirely and open the door for conspiratorial thinking. When researchers and academics discuss conspiracy, it is important that we not simply push away these "alternative" theories and instead show due respect to them. By exploring folklore as a method of grief or coping we can further understand the modern developments of folklore, how to avoid developing them into more dangerous conspiracies, and how to analyze the evolution of our cultures through both.

REFERENCES

Blake, John. (2023). "Analysis: Barney and Betty Hill's UFO Abduction Story May Have Been More about Racism Than Aliens." CNN, October 19. https://www.cnn.com/2023/10/19/us/alien-abduction-betty-barney-hill-racism-race-deconstructed-cec/index.html

Bond, G.D., B. Pasko, F. Solis-Perez, C.S. Sisneros, A.F. Gonzales, A.J. Bargo, & W.R. Walker. (2021). "Remembering the Super-Typhoon: Some, but Not All, Qualities of First-Hand Survivor Memories of Natural Disaster Are Similar to Near Death Experience and Flashbulb Memory Accounts." *Psychological Reports*, 124(5), 2119–2138. https://doi.org/10.1177/0033294120957570.

Branson-Potts, Hailey. (2021). "How Wildfires Became Ripe Areas for Right-Wing Conspiracy theories." *Los Angeles Times*, January 30. https://www.latimes.com/california/story/2021-01-30/a-space-laser-did-it-gop-congressman-had-out-there-theory-on-deadly-california-wildfire,.

Breedlove, Seth. (2019). "New Film Explores Recent Sightings of Chicago's 'Mothman.'" *PR Newswire*, February 7. https://www.prnewswire.com/news-releases/new-film-explores-recent-sightings-of-chicagos-mothman-300791070.html.

Bundy, Jennifer. (2002). "Signs of the Times." *Appalachian Journal* 29, no. 4: 400–413. http://www.jstor.org/stable/40934190.

Daly, Jack. (2023). "Mothman, the Silver Bridge Collapse, and the Folklorization and Commemoration of Actual Events." *Journal of Scientific Exploration* 37 (1): 80–87. https://doi.org/10.31275/20232599.

Douglas, Karen M., and Robbie M. Sutton. (2022). "What Are Conspiracy Theories? A Definitional Approach to Their Correlates, Consequences, and Communication." *Annual Review of Psychology*, vol. 74, no. 1, Sept., pp. 271–98. https://doi.org/10.1146/annurev-psych-032420-031329.

Hackworth, Dylan. (2020). "Has the Fabled 'Mothman' Made Chicago home?" *DePaulia Online*, April 30, 1. https://depauliaonline.com/48132/artslife/48132/#comment-121288.

Hartig, Hannah, and Carroll Doherty. (2021). "Two Decades Later, the Enduring Legacy of 9/11." September 2. https://www.pewresearch.org/politics/2021/09/02/two-decades-later-the-enduring-legacy-of-9-11/.

Health Statistics Center. (2002). "A Look at West Virginia's Population by Decade, 1950–2000." May. https://www.wvdhhr.org/bph/hsc/pubs/briefs/008/default.htm.

IMDB. (2002). "The Mothman Prophecies." Accessed April 29, 2024. https://www.boxofficemojo.com/release/rl2825225729/.

Keel, John A. (2013). *The Mothman Prophecies*. New York: Tor.

King, Godfre R. (2008). *Unveiled Mysteries*. Schaumburg, IL: Saint Germain Press.

Kitta, Andrea. (2018). "'What Happens When the Pictures Are No Longer Photoshops?': Slender Man, Belief, and the Unacknowledged Common Experience." In *Slender Man Is Coming: Creepypasta and Contemporary Legends on the Internet*, edited by Trevor J. Blank and Lynne S. McNeill, 77–90. Denver: University Press of Colorado. http://www.jstor.org/stable/j.ctv5jxq0m.7.

Loxton, Daniel, and Donald R. Prothero. (2013). "Why Do People Believe in Monsters? The Complexity of Cryptozoology." In *Abominable Science! Origins of the Yeti, Nessie, and Other Famous Cryptids*, 296–336. New York: Columbia University Press, 2013. http://www.jstor.org/stable/10.7312/loxt15320.12.

Mallow, Gwen. (2021a). "An Ode to a Hometown Creature: Mothman of Point Pleasant, West Virginia." An Ode to a Hometown Creature: Mothman of Point Pleasant, West Virginia, June 7. https://folklife.si.edu/magazine/mothman-point-pleasant-west-virginia.

Mallow, Gwen. (2021b). "West Virginia's Mothman Leads Cryptid Renaissance." *Smithsonian*, October 21. https://www.smithsonianmag.com/blogs/smithsonian-center-folklife-cultural-heritage/2021/10/21/mothman-point-pleasant-west-virginia/.

MetaFilter. (2001). Comments on 10056, September 11. https://www.metafilter.com/10056/.

O'Neill, Kara. (2016). "Mythical 'Mothman' with 10ft Wings Spotted Jumping Between Trees by Baffled Driver; The Bizarre Creature—Said to Have Creepy Red Eyes—Had Not Been Spotted in Years Until Yesterday Evening." *Daily Mirror* [London], November 28. https://www.mirror.co.uk/news/weird-news/mythical-mothman-10ft-wings-spotted-9350447.

OregonBigfoot. (2009). "Couple Walking Reports Sighting, Odor." *OregonBigfoot*. https://www.oregonbigfoot.com/report_detail.php?id=04133.

O'Rourke, Ciara. (2024). "Photo Doesn't Show Figure on Key Bridge before Collapse." *Politifact*, March 29. https://www.politifact.com/factchecks/2024/mar/29/facebook-posts/no-this-isnt-a-photo-of-a-black-figure-on-baltimor/.

Parry, Richard. (2012). "Ghosts of the Tsunami Return in Survivors' Darkest Moments." *The Times* [London], March 10. https://www.thetimes.co.uk/article/ghosts-of-the-tsunami-return-in-survivors-darkest-moments-q66636xx830.

Rickard, Bob. (2002). "THE MOTH MAN COMETH: With Its Winged Aliens and Ghastly Premonitions, Can The Mothman Prophecies Call Itself a True Story? Paranormal Expert Bob Rickard Reports." *Guardian* [London], February 22, 14. https://www.theguardian.com/film/2002/feb/22/artsfeatures3.

Sergent, Beth. (2021). "'Couples see man-sized bird … creature … something!' … Mothman's 'appearance' to mark 55 years in 2021." *Point Pleasant Register*, January 8. https://web.archive.org/web/20210113155549/https://www.mydailyregister.com/top-stories/60370/couples-see-man-sized-birdcreaturesomething-mothmans-appearance-to-mark-55-years-in-2021.

Thacker, Nancy E., and Melinda M. Gibbons. (2019). "Complicated Grief in Rural Appalachia: Using Feminist Theory to Reconcile Grief." *Journal of Mental Health Counseling* 41, no. 4 (1 October): 297–311. doi: https://doi.org/10.17744/mehc.41.4.02.

Wayland, Tobias, and Emily Wayland. (2017). "Mothman and the Twin Towers." The Singular Fortean Society, June 22. https://www.singularfortean.com/singular journal/2017/6/22/mothman-and-the-twin-towers.

Zou, P. Hoideiniang, and B. Evangeline Priscilla. (2023). "Folklore: An Identity Born of Shared Grief." *Cogent Arts & Humanities* 10, no. 1. https://doi.org/10.1080/23311983.2023.2249279.

The Material Ephemera of QAnon "True Believers"
A Constitutive Rhetoric

Holly T. Hamby

Introduction

The United States presidential election season of 2020 was far more dramatic than expected. Under the shadow of a continuing pandemic, and significant loss of life, the incumbent President, Donald Trump, was controversial and combative. Flouting the social distancing rules imposed by his own government to prevent the spread of Covid-19, Trump held rallies and town hall meetings, arguing that his supporters would *ensure* his reelection. At the forefront of his followers hellbent on continuing his presidency were those members of the conspiracy group known as QAnon. As Will Sommer describes one such rally, "no one watching the Tampa rally could unsee it. A giant sign blocked Trump from view, leaving TV viewers to wonder why the president had been blotted out by the seventeenth letter of the alphabet" (Sommer 2023, 29–30). As the election season continued, QAnon members became a spectacle in and of themselves, often drawing attention from Trump, whose campaign outwardly discouraged the "Q" focus of Trump rally attendees. Yet, the influence of the QAnon ideology was always apparent during the election and was horrifically and prominently present during the January 6 insurrection. "Outside of Congress, the scene rippled with anger and open promises to commit violence if Trump wasn't reinstalled for four more years. Red hats and Trump flags featuring a muscular, armed–Rambo style Donald were popular. But there was another symbol in the swelling mob, too: a flag with a single letter. A Q" (Sommer 2023, 1). Visual symbols, both identifiable to lay people (such as the letter Q) and coded for members of the QAnon cult, had become emblems in the extremist, right-wing fight for the future of the country. Imperative in the world of adherents of the Q-Anon extremist conspiracy movement is defining who is a "true believer" or follower of the movement, and who is an outsider or group infiltrator. Constitutive rhetoric, a theoretical framework used to critically view any group's affiliation practices, is especially suited to analyzing the multimodal reach of this extremist ideology. This theory of discourse, while it presumes that identity always precedes persuasion, also presents a paradox which allows for markers of belief and identity to be established by the act of representation itself. One path by which conspiracy group membership is signaled and confirmed is through everyday material ephemera—including apparel, bumper stickers, and flags. These signals are often obvious, proudly displaying the Q symbol of this conspiracy group, while others are visual representations of both Q and the wider conspiracy and white nationalist communities, with intersections of belief in misinformation, distrust in government, and oppressive attitudes to anyone viewed as "outsider" to right-wing conceptions of the United States' heritage. This essay argues that the signaling and recognizing of conspiracy group membership in this way is a discourse of constitutive rhetoric, creating collective identity through popular, everyday textual objects.

Definition and Application of Constitutive Rhetoric

Constitutive rhetoric, as originated by James Boyd White, is a discourse theory that explores how language or symbols have the power to forge a shared identity among an audience, particularly through condensed symbols, literary works, and storytelling. Building on the concept of *symbolic action* argued for by Kenneth Burke in *Rhetoric of Motives*, White theorizes that this type of communication frequently requires taking steps to strengthen both the identity itself and the convictions associated with it. White explains that it denotes "the art of constituting character, community and culture in language" (White 1985, 37). This analytical lens, nestled within the realms of rhetorical studies, takes a different route compared to traditional viewpoints. It posits that language doesn't just reflect social realities but actively shapes them. Rather than being merely descriptive, language holds the power to construct and define our understanding of reality. This theory places significant importance on the role of rhetorical artifacts and texts in molding identities, power dynamics, and societal norms. Constitutive rhetoric underscores the performative aspect of language, where speech acts not only communicate information but also spark social actions and drive changes. Scholars delving into this area explore how language constructs group identities, challenges existing power structures, and catalyzes societal shifts. Recognizing the influence of context is pivotal, as the meanings and impacts of language depend on historical, cultural, and political contexts. Essentially, constitutive rhetoric disrupts the notion of language as neutral, presenting a theoretical framework that accentuates its active role in shaping societal identities.

The framework of constitutive rhetoric, as applied by scholars such as Maurice Charland, allows us to "examine how rhetoric effects what Louis Althusser identifies as the key process in the production of ideology: the constitution of the subject, where the subject is precisely, he or she who simultaneously speaks and initiates action in facilitates the rapid creation and discourse [...] and in the world" (Charland 1987, 133). In this expression of constitutive rhetoric, applied to my analysis here, the use of material displays is simultaneously a production of composite and recognized ideology, and a product of the *ideal* ideologically adherent subject. However, this deep theoretical construction has its problems—the practicality of real-world application. As Charland explains, "attempts to elucidate ideological or identity-forming discourses as persuasive are trapped in a contradiction: persuasive discourse requires a subject-as-audience who is already constituted with an identity and within an ideology" (Charland 1987, 134). This rhetorical approach is now part of the foundation by which we understand identity formation in scholarly spaces, and Charland articulates that constitutive rhetoric in particular "positions the reader towards political, social, and economic action in the material world and it is in this positioning that its ideological character becomes significant." This approach is far from static—those who are the rhetors must also act in "the material world [...] embodied subjects act freely in the social world to affirm their subject position" (Charland 1987, 141). Thus, those who take these identities and significantly, outwardly signify their identities, must *choose* to act, to affirm their "subject position" or adherence to the ideological group and identity. They may do this by representation through material objects, or literal embodied representation, such as in the form of tattoos or other body modification. This applies consistently in the land of QAnon, where even the most outwardly ordinary, everyday Americans choose to use coded material semiotics to signal to other people in the "cult" that they are bona fide followers of Q.

Roland Barthes introduced the concept of the "mythical" nature of objects in his seminal work *Mythologies*. Specific to the present argument, Barthes moved past Saussere's theory of the *signifier* and the *signified*, to articulate how everyday objects and cultural phenomena carry deeper symbolic meanings within society. According to Barthes, objects become imbued with cultural significance through a process of myth-making, where they are invested with ideological values and assumptions.

Barthes argues that these cultural myths serve to naturalize and reinforce dominant ideologies, often obscuring the social and historical contexts in which they arise. Through the analysis of various cultural artifacts, such as advertisements, magazines, and popular culture, Barthes reveals how objects are not merely neutral entities but are constructed and manipulated to convey specific ideological messages. Barthes' theory of the object explores how everyday objects are invested with symbolic meanings through cultural myths, which serve to reinforce dominant ideologies within society (Barthes 1972). However, I argue that Barthes' theories on the cultural act of making objects symbolic also translates to ideological reinforcement for any group, including QAnon, that relies on mythological creation to sustain themselves.

What Is QAnon?

QAnon is a far-right conspiracy theory that originated on online internet forums, specifically 4Chan, in 2017. QAnon revolves around "Q," an unidentified individual claiming access to privileged information regarding a global conspiracy targeting Trump. As detailed across many fields of contemporary scholarship and thorough media coverage, the core belief of QAnon is that a secret elite cabal, often referred to as the "deep state," is working against former U.S. president Donald Trump. The theory alleges that Trump is engaged in a covert battle against these individuals and that a figure known as "Q" has inside information about these activities. Central tenets of QAnon include allegations of a secretive "deep state" composed of influential figures engaged in illicit activities, interpretation of "Q" posts as prophetic, and ties to the discredited Pizzagate theory (which argues that an elite, secret cabal of Satan-worshipping pedophiles is kidnapping children to torture them, drain them of their blood, which they then synthesize into a substance called "adrenochrome," an elixir of eternal youth and life). The movement's proliferation occurs primarily through digital platforms, fostering virtual communities that reinforce its narratives. Despite attempts by mainstream institutions and fact-checkers to debunk QAnon claims and its classification as a domestic terrorism threat by the FBI, the movement persists and has real-world repercussions, including incidents of violence and terrorism.*

QAnon as a social movement was born digital, and the origin point,

---

*The Southern Poverty Law Center has kept a solid record of violent incidents related to the QAnon movement, both leading up to and after January 6. https://www.splcenter.org/hatewatch/2019/04/23/qanon-conspiracy-increasingly-popular-antigovernment-extremists.

the 4Chan website, itself functions as a shifting location of rhetorical identity-making and subverting. This digital platform, renowned for its unconventional and often controversial content, operates within a distinct ecosystem where the dissemination of disinformation is pivotal in shaping its culture and community dynamics. The intricate relationship between 4chan and disinformation is the confluence of several factors. The anonymity afforded by 4chan's platform fosters an environment conducive to the proliferation of disinformation, thus evading personal accountability. This anonymity grants individuals the freedom to fabricate or exaggerate information without fear of consequences, leading to the prevalence of false narratives and misleading claims. The decentralized structure of 4chan, coupled with its minimal content moderation, encourages use of the platform for the distribution of disinformation and propaganda. Unlike centralized social media platforms, 4chan operates on a model of user-driven content curation, allowing for unrestricted contributions to the discourse. Consequently, false information can propagate unchecked, gaining traction within the community before facing scrutiny. Furthermore, 4chan's openly recognized cultural ethos, characterized by irony, satire, and subversion, blurs the boundary between truth and fiction. Users often engage in acts of *trolling*, intentionally spreading misinformation to provoke reactions or sow confusion. This subversive culture not only normalizes disinformation but also complicates efforts to discern genuine content from deliberate falsehoods. Moreover, 4chan's emphasis on anonymity and pseudonymity fosters a sense of camaraderie and collective identity among users.

Disinformation can serve as a form of social currency, with individuals seeking attention, validation, and status within the community by crafting compelling narratives or participating in coordinated efforts. Thus, the circulation of disinformation becomes intertwined with the social dynamics of belonging and recognition, reinforcing its prevalence on the platform. 4chan thrives on disinformation due to its anonymous, decentralized nature, coupled with a culture that embraces irony, satire, and subversion. Disinformation serves as a mechanism for social currency and community bonding, facilitating its widespread dissemination within the platform's ecosystem. Significantly, as Meyer and Miller argue, the spread of disinformation poses significant risks due to its potential to incite widespread societal unrest and various forms of criminal behavior. At a broader scale, such misinformation campaigns have been linked to inciting riots, acts of violence, and other unlawful activities (Meyer and Miller 2023, 49). So, why would people be drawn into groups which employ misinformation, often to destructive ends?

Bradley Wiggins, in his review of the field of 4chan scholarship, explains that research, especially that of Crawford, Keen, and Suarez de-Tangil, have illustrated how individuals on 4chan employ unique language expressions aimed at hindering understanding by potential outsiders. Users on 4chan deliberately cultivate a sense of exclusivity, crucial in nurturing an extremist ideology. This phenomenon is partly attributed to the visual nature of the platform, which masks extremist content to those not well-versed in its conventions (Wiggins 2023, 383). In explaining what draws people to these groups, even in the face of obvious misinformation, Kelly-Ann Allen et al. argue that "the human need for belonging [...]and struggles to belong contribute to participation in antisocial groups such as gangs, cults, conspiracy groups [...] as people find and create meaning around shared and constructed identities" (Allen et al., 2023, 176). Furthermore, "group belonging can improve a person's social standing and influence, grant access to material resources, provide information, offer various forms of social support, and provide acceptance and a sense of meaning and identity" (Allen et al., 2023, 177). Reviewing the sociological literature, Allen et al. explains that "the self is constructed intrapersonally and interpersonally" with the people composing their identity based on the "values and norms of the people, often defined by the majority and those with influence or power" (Allen et al., 2023, 177). But, even when people are somehow outside of this mainstream culture, "the need and desire for belonging remains" (Allen et al., 2023, 177). These people who have constructed themselves as outcasts then must choose an alternate method of identity formation, and "people experiencing a lack of belongingness might not only seek alternative sources of belongingness, but they might also denigrate others, inflate their own self-importance, and engage in risky behaviors while doing so" (Allen et al., 2023, 177–178). Yet even among their fellow outcasts, Q followers must also assess the pathos of fellow group members accurately, and maintain an intergroup status quo, choosing which rhetorical moves to make to assert that their membership in the group is valid. Meyer and Miller support this, arguing that the research consensus on QAnon thus far points to one consistent conclusion: within group dynamics, members often adhere to group norms to maintain cohesion, frequently arriving at a consensus without thoroughly assessing alternative viewpoints. In the QAnon movement, conformity supersedes objective reality. Even when an individual follower harbors doubts and desires to voice dissent, they typically acquiesce to the majority to avoid social ostracism and repercussions (Meyer and Miller 2023, 54–55). Under duress, people will attempt to remain with the social groups that are consistent, dependable, and predictable.

A particularly unique stressor influencing the dynamics of QAnon was the ongoing Coronavirus pandemic. Not only were millions of people dying, controversy and misunderstanding of vaccine science fed into the disinformation machine of QAnon. "The global COVID-19 pandemic caused heightened perceptions of uncertainty, danger, and urgency, likely encouraging people to seek cognitive closure" (Meyer and Miller 2023, 53). This, combined with quarantine and isolation, naturally fed directly into the continued spread of QAnon, as more people depended on digital spaces for essential human interaction. As Allen suggests, individuals experiencing social concern may align themselves with a group that has faced threats of adverse events. This identification fosters a strong sense of belonging, leading them to perceive subsequent threats to the group as conspiracies (Allen 2023, 180). QAnon supporters gravitate towards Donald Trump as a symbol of a political outsider. Trump's unorthodox approach to politics, characterized by his outsider status in Washington and his confrontational style, resonated with the anti-establishment sentiments prevalent among QAnon adherents. Furthermore, Trump's rhetoric of "draining the swamp" and "challenging" entrenched power structures aligned with the narrative propagated by QAnon. This alignment between Trump's messaging and the conspiratorial worldview of QAnon provided fertile ground for the movement's supporters to view him as a champion against perceived corruption and conspiracy within the political establishment. Additionally, Trump's use of social media platforms to communicate directly with his supporters bypassed traditional media channels, allowing QAnon narratives to proliferate unchecked and reinforcing the perception of him as an outsider challenging the mainstream narrative.

While not all Trump supporters were/are also members of QAnon, they remain the most significant subculture of Trump-mania. Furthermore, even if many Trump followers were not avowed followers of Q, they may have still agreed with many overlapping areas of QAnon interest. As Mark O'Brien explains in his analysis of the legal regulation of digital QAnon,

> A significant aspect of Trump's unique, iconoclastic style was the cult-like devotion that he enjoyed—and at the time of writing, still enjoys—from certain sections of the United States population and his Republican Party voters. In the latter stages of his presidency, [the QAnon cult] was the subject of considerable media reportage, especially in the period from his loss of the Presidential election in November 2020, a result which he did [...] contest, up to and after the assault on the Capitol of 6 January 2021 by Trump supporters. This assault on the Capitol followed a speech made by President Trump as part of his continued campaign to dispute the election outcome. The assault has been closely connected by the media and others to QAnon, possibly in part due to the visibility of leading QAnon figures, QAnon imagery at the attack itself, and prior social and other media narratives [O'Brien 2023, 103].

The tendrils of QAnon influence pushed through even the most stalwart of traditional political boundaries, stretching the limits of how far so-called reasonable people could believe unbelievable conspiracy theories. To run as a Republican political candidate during this time was to be forced to confront the specter of Q. Miller argues for the dominance of QAnon to the right-wing political field, as it "is also unique because of the attention it gets from the media, the marketplace, and political leaders" Furthermore, "QAnon is not a typical conspiracy group because of the attention it is getting from high-level leaders. President Trump has called QAnon followers 'people who love our country' and has supported congressional candidates who support QAnon. In all, over a dozen congressional candidates on the ticket were QAnon followers to varying degrees" (Miller 2023, 10). QAnon became nearly inextricably linked to the right-wing of the 2020 election season, fulfilling its own predictions and Q-drops as politicians gravitated to the radical conspiracy side.

However, this is not to say Trump always openly supported his QAnon fan club. As Sommer details, during the 2020 election season, because of all the attention that then moved to QAnon instead of strictly Trump, Trump's campaign attempted to distance itself from QAnon formally, even though many Trump supporters were also adherents of Q. Remarkably, a ban was instituted by the Trump campaign in which staffers were quietly instructing Trump supporters who attended rallies to not wear T-shirts or fly Q-related flags, and would remove them if they displayed any material objects related to QAnon at the rallies, especially those that were televised. However, QAnon followers repeatedly found ways to skirt these rules, and would hold up Q shirts, and embedded cues, or QAnon-coded messages, inside of visual Trump rally items (Sommer 2023, 29–33). It seemed that no one, not even the highest officials on the side of Trump or other QAnon supported politicians, could stop the open demonstration of Q allegiance, or the display of associated visual materials.

Function and Form of the Material Ephemera

Since the January 6 insurrection, there has been an almost uncountable number of media segments and pieces covering the symbols of QAnon present in both the visual production and demonstration of QAnon adherence.* As Sommer explains in his observations of Trump rallies and the insurrection, "The first thing you notice about QAnon followers is the gear; clothing and poster covered in Qs, pictures of Trump, and

---

*A thorough analysis of the visual symbols of Q, along with allied symbols from other far-right insurrectionists, was published by the New York Times in the wake of January 6. https://www.nytimes.com/2021/01/13/video/extremist-signs-symbols-capitol-riot.html.

inscrutable acronyms" (Sommer 2023, 6). Most famously, the so-called QAnon Shaman, Jacob Chansley—resplendent in outlandish outfits and tattoos, complete with pseudo neo–Viking (or possibly Native American) headgear, and a Q inked in his flesh—became emblematic of the irrationality of both QAnon members and the insurrectionists as a whole. Yet, beside the most public manifestations of QAnon, material objects and ephemera, there is the everyday Q cult member who, in varying forms, continues to show their allegiance to what they believe to be the truth.* For example, on any given day in an American city, in parking lots of grocery stores and school pick up lines, one may find an array of bumper stickers, both obvious and more closely coded, which advertise a vehicle's owner will fight the *deep state* for the sake of Q and Donald Trump.

To demonstrate how these material objects form a constitutive rhetoric for QAnon followers, I will discuss four of the most used semiotic codes in these material objects.[†] To protect anonymity, I will not include personal examples that I have photographed; it is unnecessary to do so, when examples of each of these material objects are easily available with a quick Internet search and are also plentiful across types of items and shopping platforms. From T-shirts to ball caps to baby clothes, coffee mugs and car decals and bathing suits, there is a symbol of Q identity allegiance for both the most open and guarded of QAnon followers. The primary and obvious coded symbol used, and discussed throughout scholarship and media coverage,[‡] is a simple letter Q.[§] Before the rise of QAnon, seeing the letter Q may have symbolized to many English speakers an initial stand-in for the word "question," as in the term, "Q&A." However, the sheer volume of visual examples of this new use of the Q, especially after the deadly insurrection, would likely lead to the American public now assuming it refers to QAnon. This is likely the highest frequency photographed rhetorical symbol for QAnon, and would be a base level entry point for those adherents of the conspiracy theory who wish to

---

*We know of a long tradition of demonstrating political and personal affiliation with material objects/products. There has not yet been a study of the material objects of only the QAnon adherents, but there is a small body of scholarship focused on contemporary far-right ideologies, which are complementary to my study here, specifically Miller-Idriss, 2018, and Dionne, 2021.

†The Anti-Defamation League's "QAnon: A Glossary," serves as the foundation for my choice of the four symbols here. https://www.adl.org/resources/blog/qanon-glossary.

‡An excellent study, using critical discourse analysis of the frequency of online mentions of Q, is found in Wiggins, 2023. This study examined the posts made on 4chan/pol between January 3 and 9 of 2021; one of the highest frequency terms is the letter Q (Wiggins 386–387).

§There are many examples easily accessible via internet search. For one example from the January 6 insurrection, please see Platt, Stephen, Back of Q-Anon jacket with black hoodie, 2021, Getty Images, Web. 20 April 2024. https://www.timesofisrael.com/a-guide-to-the-hate-symbols-and-signs-on-display-at-the-us-capitol-riots.

signal to everyone, not just other members of their community, that they are followers of Q.

Another consistent symbol used by the movement as a rhetorical object is the number 17. This is primarily, and quite simply, because the letter Q is the seventeenth letter in the alphabet. While basic on its face as a symbol for the movement, without this explanation of its symbolic meaning, members of the public outside of the QAnon sphere wouldn't necessarily understand the significance. This takes the simplicity of using the letter Q itself in material objects to a slightly secondary, more esoteric level—enough to serve as a mark of identity for adherents to show to other adherents. A simple Internet search of the terms "17" and "QAnon merchandise" will bring up an array of items to purchase and display. One popular choice is a baby onesie with a combined graphic of a "Punisher" logo skull, with the number 17 embedded. This collage effect creates a type of portmanteau symbol, signaling that the baby who wears this onesie is a child fighting the deep state, or, more likely, her parents are.

Two more examples are significantly more coded, and their use would signify to members of QAnon that their bearers are no casual followers, but serious group members. These two signifiers are limited to those who are deeply invested in the full spectrum of textual interpretations and goals of this conspiracy theory. These examples are the visual image of a white rabbit, and an acronym: WWG1WGA. The white rabbit is a reference to the Lewis Carroll books, *Alice in Wonderland*, and *Through the Looking Glass*. Specifically, the so-called "Q drops" often included the symbol of the rabbit, with the phrases "down the rabbit hole," or "follow the white rabbit," as signposts to indicate where followers could start spiraling down the conspiracy theory by trying to interpret the cryptic messages contained therein.* Other Q followers in digital spaces would scour social media, and politicians' television appearances, in attempts to find references to both the white rabbit, and following the white rabbit, to validate the accuracy and authenticity of Q drops, and thus to indicate that Trump aligned with their goals. This particular symbol, transformed in digital memes and translated to merchandise, is an animal that usually reflects a wider dominant cultural narrative across world cultures of innocence and purity; now, the Q label has dramatically changed its perception in the conspiracy subculture. As Crawford et al. found in their CREST report on Chan culture and extremism, "the malleable meanings of memes, wherein several images may not be overtly extreme or promote violence but take on these connotations when situated within a wider context of extremism" (Crawford et al., 2020, 5). Thus, in the QAnon context, the white rabbit no

---

*https://www.adl.org/glossary/follow-white-rabbit.

longer calls for innocent allegiance but heralds a metaphorical and also literal call to arms.

WWG1WGA, an acronym for the phrase "Where We Go One, We Go All," became a metatextual rallying cry, an inside motto of those who were willing to lay down their lives to fight on the side of Trump. This specific acronym is a text that holds particular poignancy after the insurrection. This acronym signifies a closed rank, inside group among QAnon followers, and serves not just to establish a code for identity signaling, but also underscores a meta-mythology. These hard-core adherents, often sporting tattoos with this acronym, were flying flags with their chosen signifier at the insurrection, and indeed took bullets in a short-sighted attempt to do what they believed was right. They believed that, if President Trump thought the election was stolen, and he was on their side, then *Where* he (the *One*) went, there they *All* must go. As White frames in his theory of constitutive rhetoric, the symbols aren't just representations of identity, but an intricate part of establishing and reenforcing that identity. These group members assumed that they were doing the "right thing," and important, were *choosing* to defend their country from evil, and would secure a Presidential pardon once Trump was back in the Oval Office. In the days following the insurrection, self-identified Q followers in digital spaces praised these fellow QAnon members as martyrs for their cause, some laying down their lives for it, others yet to be prosecuted and imprisoned for their acts that day. This signifies agency in constructing a group identity and mythology, self-making the hardcore, self-labeled "elite" heroes of their ideological group. They continued to believe quite openly that these elite members of their group, rhetorically connected by their displayed symbolism, truly embodied the *WWG1WGA* slogan, and came to the aid of their greatest ally, former President Trump.

Conclusion

In the years since the January 6 Insurrection some of the sheen of QAnon has faded for former followers. Yet, the new presidential election cycle for 2024, and ongoing criminal trials of former president Trump at the time of this writing, will surely bring in new vigor and new members for this conspiracy group. Even with the years of wide media coverage, and public ridicule for Q and his followers, films and social media posts continue the conspiracy, and there remains a vibrant market for Q-related merchandise. While the 2020 U.S. presidential election showcased the significant influence of the QAnon movement, the aftermath has illuminated for the greater world stage how easily ideological groups can now capitalize on digital platforms to propagate disinformation and nurture a feeling of membership within its followers. Echoing Roland Barthes' study of the symbolic significance of objects, visual signposts of usually innocuous symbols are glazed with an extremist and potentially violent varnish, highlighting the complex interaction among digital culture, political discourse, and societal uncertainties. Furthermore, this underscores the challenges presented by QAnon's penetration into mainstream politics and its influence on democratic discourse. Future studies will surely reflect on a quickly shifting conspiratorial and extremist memetic space; yet, in each iteration of this conspiracy, it is predictable that the intricacies of group dynamics and the potency of symbols in shaping collective consciousness will continue to bolster the central *imago* Q.

REFERENCES

Allen, Kelly-Ann, et al. (2023). "The Need to Belong: The Appeal, Benefits, and Dangers of QAnon and Similar Groups." *The Social Science of QAnon: A New Social and Political Phenomenon*. Ed. Monica K. Miller. Cambridge UP, 176–191.
Barthes, Roland. (1972). *Mythologies*. Trans. Annette Lavers. Paladin.
Burke, Kenneth. (1959). *A Rhetoric of Motives*. U of California Press.
Charland, Maurice. (1987). "Constitutive Rhetoric: The Case of the Peuple Québécois." *The Quarterly Journal of Speech* 73.2.
Crawford, Blyth, Florence Keen, and Guillermo Suarez de-Tangil. (2020). *Memetic Irony and the Promotion of Violence Within Chan Cultures*. Centre for Research and Evidence on Security Threats.
Dionne, Laura. (2021). *Semiotics of White Supremacist Protest Wear*. fabricofcrime.ca. 20 May 2024.
Jobling, Paul. (2015). "Roland Barthes: Semiology and the Rhetorical Codes of Fashion." *Thinking Through Fashion: A Guide to Key Theorists*. Eds. Agnès Rocamora and Anneke Smelik. Bloomsbury, 132–148.
Meyer, Arial R., and Monica K. Miller. (2023). "Cognitive Processes, Biases, and Traits That Fuel QAnon." *The Social Science of QAnon: A New Social and Political Phenomenon*. Ed. Monica K. Miller. Cambridge University Press, 49–67.
Miller, Monica K. (2023). "The 'Who, What, and Why' of QAnon." *The Social Science of QAnon: A New Social and Political Phenomenon*. Ed. Monica K. Miller. Cambridge University Press, 3–13.
Miller-Idriss, Cynthia. (2018). "Trying on Extremism: Material Culture and Far-Right Youth." *The Extreme Gone Mainstream: Commercialization and Far Right Youth Culture in Germany* by Miller-Idriss. Princeton University Press, 24–50.
O'Brien, Mark. (2023). "The Coming of the Storm: Moral Panics, Social Media and Regulation in the QAnon Era." *Information and Communications Technology Law* 32.1: 102–121.
Sommer, Will. (2023). *Trust The Plan. The Rise of QAnon and the Conspiracy That Unhinged America*. HarperCollins.
White, James Boyd. (1985). *Heracles' Bow*. University of Wisconsin.
Wiggins, Bradley. (2023). "'Nothing Can Stop What's Coming': An Analysis of the Conspiracy Theory Discourse on 4chan's /Pol Board." *Discourse and Society* 34.3: 381–390.

Anti-Semitic Conspiracy Theories in Popular Culture
Blame It on "the Jews"

JAMES WEATHERFORD

One of the longest hatreds in human history is hatred against Jews. The origins and myths of anti-Semitism are rooted in conspiratorial thinking. Over the course of history, such conspiracy theories have inundated popular culture around the world. Wood carvings, paintings, cartoons, literature, and newspapers have propagated anti-Semitic myths for centuries. From the early church fathers that condemned Jews for their conspiracies to murder Christ, to Medieval blood libels alleging Jews steal the blood of Christian children, the history of anti-Semitism is rife with conspiracy theories. Rumors and conspiracy theories blamed Jews for poisoning the wells and starting the Black Plague, and such myths and fables about the sinister Jew, beset on destroying and controlling the world, have prevailed even to this day. As such, most conspiracy theories about Israel tend to be anti-Semitic. For example, the idea persists online that a "strategic alliance between the United States and Israel is part of a larger, global plot to push for one world government, designed specifically to be headed by the Jews" (Jane de Gara 2019, 100).

What can be deduced from the wide array of Jewish conspiracies and anti-Semitic myths is that such thinking is often untenable and illogical. By way of conspiratorial thinking, Jews are historically blamed for being Christ-killers and subsequently at fault for bringing Christianity into existence. Jews are blamed for being poor parasites of society while simultaneously being greedy elites who control the world. Conspiracy theories put Jews behind the origins of communism and contradictorily behind the ills of capitalism. In the early twentieth century, *The Protocols of the Elders of Zion* was published in a Russian newspaper then disseminated around the world in dozens of languages. Henry Ford republished an English translation in *The Dearborn Independent*. This proven forgery permeated popular culture with the anti–Semitic lie that a cabal of powerful Jewish leaders secretly control the world. In order to undermine and overthrow Christian civilization, the conspiracy theory holds that, Jews are pulling the strings behind the scenes in an effort to wipe out white Christianity in the West. Organizations such as the *Anti-Defamation League* have worked tirelessly for over a hundred years to stomp out and censor all anti–Semitic remarks made in popular culture and beyond.

This essay aims to accomplish three things. Primarily, the following will provide a general overview of the last 2,000 years of anti–Jewish hatred and conspiracy theories. Second, it will draw a clear connection between the historical anti–Semitism of times past and connect it to present examples riddled throughout popular culture, the mainstream media, and social media. Lastly, this essay will discuss why such conspiratorial thinking against the Jews has prevailed and how such thinking leads to continual violence against Jews. By way of a better understanding of the conspiracies, stereotypes, and hatred levied against Jews, the reader will be better equipped to understand the dangers of conspiratorial mythmaking and ways to undermine its prevalence in society.

The Dawn of the Common Era

In the early years of Christianity, Jews and Christians coexisted alongside each other without much conflict. The first Christians were ethnically Jewish, prayed in Hebrew, and gathered in the synagogues and temple. As it were, as time progressed, the rift between Christians and Jews widened as Christianity became an overtly Gentile religion rather than just another sect of Judaism. Christianity was declared the official religion of Rome in 380 CE, and Judaism was still considered a lawful religion. However, early Christianity was already rich with anti–Jewish sentiment. Around 284 CE, in referring to the Jews, Origen of Alexandria used very specific language that not only demarcated the differences between Christians and Jews but accused them of "conspiring" (ἐπιβουλεύσαντες) to kill God (deicide). He notes, "For they [the Jews] committed a crime of the most unhallowed kind, in conspiring against the Saviour of the human race" (Origen, *Against Celsus* 4.22). This notion of conspiracy will continue to expand across the centuries.

In 387–389 CE, the church father, John Chrysostom wrote a series of homilies against the Jews aptly titled, *Adversos Judaeos*. Going beyond mere anti–Judaism, he associated Jews with dogs, pigs, beasts, horses, goats, and Satan himself. This type of language may have served a rhetorical purpose, but such descriptions are manifested in Medieval and Reformation art. Referring to the synagogue, Chrysostom says that "demons inhabit the place ... the Jews themselves are demons" (Chrysostom, *Adversos Judeaos* 6.2). Chrysostom continues, "the godlessness of the Jews and the pagans is on a par. But the Jews practice a deceit which is more dangerous. In their synagogue stands an invisible altar of deceit on which they sacrifice not sheep and calves but the souls of men." This sparks the genesis of the trope of the animal-like, godless Jew that "sacrificed their own sons and daughters to demons ... [and] became more savage than any wild beast" (25). These ideas lay the groundwork for future superstitious and conspiratorial thinking against the Jews.

The Middle Ages and Reformation Era

In the Middle Ages, anti–Semites took to other sinister methods to make the Jews seem less-than-human. Namely, "depicting Jews as animals was a common method of dehumanizing Jews" (Aizenberg 2013, 26). In the Medieval and Reformation period, anti–Semitic visual representations portrayed Jews with cloven hooves, bird feet, and beaks. Wood carvings often depicted vile engagement with unclean animals such as swine. For example, throughout the Middle Ages, *Judensau* carvings "depicted Jews gorging on milk that they are sucking from the teats of a sow [pig]. On some, there was also the image of a Jew copulating with the pig, eating its feces, drinking its urine, or gazing into or caressing its rectum" (Smith 2021, 196). The flawed line of thinking held that "since swine symbolize the unclean and sinners, and since Jews are unclean and sinners, therefore swine can also symbolize Jews" (Geller 2011, 157). By the time the Nazis began their Final Solution during World War II, it was made known that "Jews are not human beings, but animals, indeed vermin. This is the dehumanization of the human being" (Manent 2013, 169). Over time, portraying Jews as animals became conflated with similar images of Satan. The agenda of such visual representation is clear. The Devil and the Jews are one and the same. "The identification of Jews and Satan was affirmed by the image that Jews—like Satan—had horns, a billy goat beard, and a tail" (Lupovitch 2009, 90). In fact, two notable Renaissance sculptures portray Moses with horns: Claus Sluter's *Well of Moses* (1395–1403) and Michelangelo's *Tomb of Pope Julius II* (1513–1516). Based on the mistranslation of the Latin Vulgate, Exodus 34:29–30 describes Moses descending Mount Sinai with "horns" instead of a "ray" of light. All of these stereotypes, myths, and superstitions about the Jews speaks to a grander conspiratorial idea that it is the inhuman, animal-like, satanic connection that drives Jews to control and dominate the world.

The old trope of conflating Jews with animals and the Devil reaches into contemporary popular culture as well. Fritz Berggren, a full time State Department employee, hosts a podcast called *Blood and Faith*. He is quoted as saying, "The Jews worship Satan and they're Satan's own children" (Scripps News 2023). Andrew Torba is the CEO of Gab, an alt-right social media platform. Torba has made numerous anti–Semitic comments that tout conspiracy theories about Jewish global domination and Jewish association with Satan. Torba's comments are dehumanizing and associate famous Jews with demons, animals, and other creatures. In an August 2021 newsletter, Torba calls Sheera Frenkel of the *New York Times* "a despicable gremlin of a woman." In his scathing screed, he refers to "her demonic friends at the ADL and Facebook's COO Sheryl Sandberg." In an April 2022 newsletter, Torba refers to Facebook as "Zuckerberg's demonic plantation." In a 2022 editorial titled "There Is No Freedom of Speech Without Freedom of Reach," Andrew Torba uses the phrase "vampire demons like Jonathan Greenblatt." Medieval anti–Semitism is rife with baseless Blood Libel accusations, so calling the Jewish Director of the ADL a vampire demon is more than mere rhetoric. It propagates an anti–Semitic myth and conspiracy theory that Jews drink blood.

Taking personal offense at Ben Shapiro from the *Daily Wire*, Torba's January 2023 newsletter brands Shapiro as the "Daily Wire Devil." In numerous other posts and rants, Torba calls Shapiro "controlled opposition" for conservatives, insinuating some kind of conspiracy that only permits some conservative voices to be heard in the media and popular culture. It is no mere coincidence that Shapiro is Jewish, and this only fuels those conspiratorial suspicions that Jews are controlling the media. Torba alleges that the *Daily Wire* employees "sell their soul" to Shapiro. In a January 2023 editorial called "Christians Must Enter the AI Arms Race," Torba asserts that every single AI platform "is skewed with a liberal/globalist/Talmudic/satanic worldview." Torba conflates globalism, the Talmud, and Satan in one fell swoop. More than mere rhetoric, such anti–Semitic slurs continue to fuel the fires of anti–Jewish conspiracy theories.

The Reformation era brought a renewed hostility toward the Jews. Martin Luther's seminal text on Protestant anti–Semitism, *On the Jews and Their Lies*, recommended that Jewish synagogues be burned, Rabbis harmed or murdered for teaching, and the Talmud burned in the streets (Luther 1543, 292). What likewise surfaces in Luther's writing is the conspiratorial tone that Jews cannot be trusted. Luther warns his Christian readers to "be on your guard against the Jews, who … are consigned by the wrath of God to the devil … they cannot be trusted and believed in any other matter ... even though a truthful word may drop from their lips occasionally ... wherever you see a genuine Jew, you may with a good conscience cross yourself and bluntly say: 'There goes a devil incarnate'" (Luther 1543, 164). Again, the theological connection is important because Jews are singled out as evil, synonymous with the devil, conniving, and untrustworthy. The mystery and enigma of this group of people who refuse to assimilate and conform to Christian society must be, as Luther asserts, the devil incarnate. This adds to the dehumanization that makes slaughtering the Jews in the Holocaust all the more possible.

Popular culture in recent years is a much different world than even ten years ago. The reach and platform that social media provides to anti-Semites and other forms of bigotry is astounding. Platforms such as X give a voice to the proponents of Luther. In a post from @DenizenDev on August 25, 2023, the user asserts, "Martin Luther was right about the Jews. No one who rejects Christ is a friend of God. Those who reject Christ are cursed." Anti Semites seem to have impeccable memories about the history of their tradition. Using the pop culture phenomenon of social media, everyone is given a stage and pulpit to preach from. Unfortunately, the message that permeates this realm of culture is a message of hate, fear, and distrust for the alleged untrustworthy and corruptible Jew.

"Antisemitism is a tradition which views the Jew as a threatening Other—powerful, well organized, omnipresent and evil. As such, it will almost inevitably function within a conspiratorial worldview" (Færseth 2021, 6). The ADL, along with some important figures in popular culture have sought to work together to dispel myths and conspiratorial thinking against the Jews. Comedian and actor Sasha Baron Cohen (Ali G, Borat) has spoken publicly about holding social media companies accountable for the anti–Semitic content on their platforms. In another humorous, yet pointed, video decrying the long history of anti–Jewish tropes in popular culture, cartoons, and films, the ADL and Jason Alexander (George Costanza from *Seinfeld*) produced a song and montage of the long history of anti–Semitic stereotypes. The stereotypes of Jews with hung backs, big noses, and greedy money hungry expressions and conniving riddle the short film. What is most shocking is the list of top comments on YouTube. The top comment is "All the stereotypes are 100% true" with over 200 likes accompanied by "imagine a group of people that are so unlikable they have to make laws that make it illegal to hate them" with over 450 likes. Other comments include mocking Holocaust denial and calling the ADL (a non-profit, 501[c][3] organization) "greedy" for asking for donations.

The Nazis effectively used popular culture as a tool to spread their anti–Semitism. Joseph Goebbels, the head of the Reich Ministry of Public Enlightenment and Propaganda, ensured that the Nazi message was communicated through various mediums such as art, music, theater, films, books, radio, and the press. Nazi propaganda campaigns created an atmosphere tolerant of violence against Jews, particularly during periods preceding legislation or executive measures against them. These campaigns aimed to encourage passivity and acceptance of the impending anti–Semitic measures by depicting the Nazi government as restoring order. The Nazis also used propaganda to mislead foreign governments, presenting their demands for concessions and annexations as understandable and fair. The pervasive nature of Nazi propaganda and its influence on popular culture contributed to the spread of anti–Semitism among the German population.

Perhaps one of the most flagrant works of popular culture the Nazis produced to further propagate the conspiratorial ideas infusing anti–Semitism is the film *Der Ewige Jude* (The Eternal Jew). "One of the film's most notorious sequences compares Jews to rats that carry contagion, flood the continent, and devour precious resources" (United States Holocaust Memorial Museum n.d.). Paradoxically viewing Jews as both greedy money-lovers and impoverished burdens to society is emblematic of the irrational and mentally dissonant nature of Jew-hatred. Where poor Jews may not be the focal point of contemporary anti–Semitism today, conspiracy theorists often allege that Jews are the masterminds behind the influx of poor minorities into the United States.

The contemporary "white replacement" conspiracy theory is popular among anti–Semites who blame the Jews for orchestrating the displacement of white Christians in America. According to this thinking, it would seem, the Jew has evolved from being the parasite that once devoured precious resources to becoming the mastermind behind an orchestrated invasion of immigrants and other people of color to destroy white America. According to the American Jewish Committee, "Great Replacement, also known as white replacement theory or white genocide theory, claims there is an intentional effort, led by Jews, to promote mass non-white immigration, inter-racial marriage, and other efforts that would lead to the 'extinction of whites.'" This concept of the great replacement is present on social media platforms and has been directly tied to anti–Semitic violence. In a Gab News email newsletter titled "The ADL's War on Free Speech" on April 11, 2021, CEO Andrew Torba laments, "Gab has been attacked and smeared by many different Jewish groups including the ADL for simply defending free speech online. Now today the ADL is trying to cancel Tucker Carlson for daring to speak the truth about the reality of demographic replacement that is absolutely and unequivocally going on in The West."

The horrific tragedy of the 2018 Tree of Life Synagogue shooting in Pittsburgh is but one example where replacement theory paranoia unfettered in the imagination of an anti–Semite led to violence against Jews.

The gunman, "Robert Bowers ... based his reasoning for his murder spree on a conspiracy theory that the migrant caravan currently working its way through Mexico is a Jewish plot intended to destabilize America" (Coaston 2018). According to this thinking, if the Jew is not personally subverting and supplanting white, Christian America, the Jew is orchestrating and manufacturing a replacement through a surging migrant crisis at the southern border.

"The 'great replacement' is a racist conspiracy narrative that falsely asserts there is an active, ongoing, and covert effort to replace white populations in current white-majority countries. In many versions—such as those rehearsed in the manifestos of mass shooters in Christchurch, New Zealand; El Paso, Texas; and Buffalo, New York—the purported replacement is being coordinated by Jewish people" (Wilson 2023). It should be noted that White Supremacists chanted "Jews will not replace us" in the Charlottesville protests in 2017. Angry neo-Nazis with tiki torches chanted such declarations as many had turned out to protest the removal of a statue of General Robert E. Lee. Scholar Jonathan Sarna points out the absurdity of this claim, noting that "only about 2,000 Jews live in Charlottesville, out of a total local population of 47,000. Nationally Jews number no more than 7.6 million, meaning that just over 2% of Americans are Jewish" (Sarna 2021). This fear rooted in conspiratorial thinking is unfounded and illogical but nonetheless prevails in the imagination of the anti-Semite.

Blood Libel, Host Desecration, and Well Poisoning

Blood libel conspiracies occurred throughout Europe in the Middle Ages, and there was also a baseless, twentieth-century blood libel case in Massena, New York, in 1928. Blood libel is the most insidious of all conspiracy theories and has resulted in extreme violence against Jews. Accordingly, "Jews, vampire-like, suck the blood out of Christians for their religious rites" (Biale 2009, 30–31). As such, "the ritual murder story is a critical ingredient in a specific genre of malicious myths about Jews" (Johnson 2012, 2). Among the most notable instances from history, there is the case of William of Norwich (1144), Hugh of Lincoln (1255), the Damascus Affair (1840), and the Beilis Affair (1911). Jewish ritual murder even found its way into thirteenth-century literature. Chaucer's *The Prioress's Tale*, included in the *Canterbury Tales*, narrates an instance of a blood libel case. Interest in these pervasive and insidious accusations are still alive and well in the twentieth century. "In 2014, the Anti-Defamation League appealed Facebook to take down a page titled 'Jewish Ritual Murder.' It took four years until the page was finally removed" (Teter 2020, 1). Therefore, for an advocate of "free speech" like Torba to call Greenblatt a "vampire demon," the long history of blood-related accusations and false conspiracies about Jews makes such name-calling all the more inflammatory.

Desecration of the host is another aspect of Medieval anti–Semitism that hinges on conspiratorial thinking about the Jews. "As early as the second half of the eleventh century ... rumors of Jewish Host profanation led to the slaughter of Jews across France" (Michael 2008, 71). The idea was that Jews sinisterly stole the bread wafer of Christ's "body" from Catholic churches to then pierce, stab, and crucify the body of Christ all over again. Jews were doomed to live under the charge of deicide. In the imagination of the anti–Semite, a Jew that could murder God cannot be trusted. Such untrustworthy god-killers will continue to kill God in whatever way they can. Stealing the host that is to undergo the supernatural miracle of transubstantiation during the Eucharist, is the same as killing the literal body of Christ (again).

Further conspiratorial thinking darkened the mind of Christian Europe especially when it came to the spread of infectious disease. Jews were blamed for poisoning wells and worse: "A sixteenth century chronicler, Johannes Avantin, records that in 1337 the Jews had planned to poison the entire Christian population of Germany, but their plan had miscarried" (Trachtenberg 2001, 102–103). Jewish doctors were blamed for poisoning their own patients. Jews were blamed for the Black Death in 1348, and unfortunately, "nine hundred Jews were burnt at the stake in Strasbourg on Valentine's Day 1349 for their alleged part in the Black Death, a particularly gruesome occurrence" (Harvey 2017, 64). Fast forward to the Covid-19 pandemic, rumors of how Jews were behind the spreading of the virus were found across social media platforms. In fact, in 2022, *The Jerusalem Post* reported that in Vancouver, B.C., there were "antisemitic flyers blaming Jews for the COVID-19 pandemic littering doorsteps, businesses and parked cars in their neighborhoods" (Jerusalem Post Staff 2022). In fact, "People in at least eight states found anti–Semitic fliers claiming Jews are responsible for COVID-19" (JNS 2021). Other "Modern manifestations of this include blaming the Jews or Israel for creating and spreading AIDS" (Fox and Topor 2021, chap. 5).

The Dreyfus Affair and the Protocols of the Elders of Zion

One significant event in the history of anti–Semitism is the 1894 case of Alfred Dreyfus, a French military officer who was falsely accused of passing military secrets to Colonel Max von Schwartzkoppen during

World War I. Dreyfus was charged and convicted, but his conviction was eventually overturned, and his honor was restored. Dreyfus was not shown the fairness and equality he deserved. The odds were stacked against him due to the long history of "anti–Semitic stereotypes of Jews as untrustworthy manipulators" (Harris 2010, 319). One need not look far to find contemporary interest in the Dreyfus Affair. Openly anti–Semitic Holocaust deniers riddle the internet with blogs, websites, and podcasts devoted to "revisionist" histories that affirm the guilt of Dreyfus, among other outrageous claims. A 2015 episode of the *Heretics' Hour* podcast titled "The Dreyfus Affair—Guilty!" proves this point.

One of the most pervasive and enduring conspiracy theories in popular culture centers on the false accusation that the Jews are controlling the world determined to destroy civilization and culture. The origins of this conspiracy theory are not clear, but it was certainly given an air of veracity when the *Protocols of the Elders of Zion* were published at the turn of the twentieth century. "Between 1897 and 1905 a specious collection of articles began circulating that focused on an alleged conspiracy by Jews to control worldwide finance, banking, and the newspapers" (Blakeslee 2000, 16). This falsified handbook of Jewish global domination was translated into numerous languages across Europe and the Middle East. In fact, one of the most notable English translations was endorsed by the founder of Ford Motor Company, Henry Ford. In Ford's own *Dearborn Messenger,* Ford "intensified the campaign against Jews.... Ford accused Jews with the fraudulent tract *The Protocols of the Elders of Zion*" (Korman 2022, chap. 10). Ford also published his own book on the subject (a compilation of articles from *The Messenger*), *The International Jew*, wherein he questioned Jewish trustworthiness and challenged every aspect of Jewish character and participation in society. Ford faced a libel case in which total incredulity served as his only defense. He claimed to have no idea such ideas had been printed in his name, and he was forced to recant his ideas and subsequently closed the newspaper down.

Ford's ideas would go on to influence Nazi anti–Semitism in the years that followed. Questioning Jewish loyalty to the nations in which they lived became an enduring conspiracy theory. With the establishment of the state of Israel in 1948, those suspicions flared. In fact, the Jewish Poles were expelled from Poland in 1968, mere decades after the Holocaust, for being a "fifth column." According to this accusation, the "fifth column" concept purports that "Jews cannot be trusted because they support Israel before the countries in which they live" (Maizels 2023). Divided loyalty is continually hurled upon the Jews. Generally, as a group of people that do not conform and assimilate enough, nationalists fear that Jewish citizens are not onboard with the security and prosperity of the countries they inhabit and are thus a threat to national security. Perhaps having their own nation will help quell the conspiracy theories. Unfortunately, this is not the case.

Holocaust Denial and Anti-Zionism

The Holocaust claimed the lives of approximately six million Jews due to illness, starvation, and extermination. Determining this figure has undergone the rigor of scholarly scrutiny, and official historians at the Auschwitz Museum and memorial adjusted their figures in the early 1990s to objectively establish actual deaths at the death camp. They officially changed the number inscribed on the memorial to reflect records revealed after the fall of the Iron Curtain. In full transparency, they determined that rather than four million deaths, the number is more closely aligned to one to one and a half million. Nonetheless, Holocaust denial still exists to this day and manifests itself in a myriad of ways. More than mere revisionist history, "Holocaust denial is a conspiracy theory that seeks to place Jews behind an international movement to promote a falsehood for monetary gain. In this way, Holocaust denial is no different than many other previous forms of antisemitism" (Knight 2003, 323). Variations of the conspiracy theory conclude that the entire thing is a fabrication invented by the Jews to influence and manipulate the world or that the Jews sacrificed their own people to influence the global opinion concerning Zionism.

In 2022, Amazon came under fire for allowing the documentary *Hebrews to Negroes: Wake Up Black America!* to be sold on their site. "This film has generated huge controversy for its antisemitic content promoting false claims about the reaches of Jewish power and the number of Jews who died in the Holocaust" (Zelizer 2022). Brooklyn Nets star Kyrie Irving was suspended and lost a deal with Nike for promoting the film on Instagram and Twitter. This documentary argues that "true Jews" are of black, African descent (a popular doctrine of the Black Hebrew Israelites), and many "false" Ashkenazi Jews were in fact slave traders who shipped Africans to their fate during the transatlantic slave trade. The ADL has vehemently condemned these statements.

As of October 2023, the outbreak of the Israel-Hamas conflict brought with it a surge of anti–Semitism on college campuses, city streets, and social media. Protesters took to the streets all around the world, often chanting "death to the Jews" (Delaney 2023; JTA and TOI STAFF 2023) and "from the river to the sea" (Lapin 2023; Basu 2023). The latter of these two phrases is somewhat ambiguous, but the heart of the meaning is the eradication of the entire nation of Israel. The removal of Israel altogether would mean the displacement (or death) of about nine million Israeli citizens. Many protestors on the streets of the United States and other countries exclaimed "Israel go to hell" (AGENCIES and TOI STAFF 2023). While genuine concern for the Palestinian people is understandable, using the Palestinians as a justification for reviving centuries old rhetoric about erasing Jews is problematic.

To add insult to injury, social media is frothing with a string of conspiracy theories that claim Israel allowed the Hamas attack to happen, that the IDF is responsible for the brutal attack on the Nova Music Festival, and that Israel created Hamas. By asserting that Israel allowed the Hamas attack to happen, it gives the appearance that the Jews sacrificed their own people so they could justify their assault on the Palestinians. Such ideas are so pervasive, they have even found their way into mainstream politics. The UK Labour party had to retract its backing for a parliamentary candidate over his remarks that propagated antisemitic stereotypes. Azhar Ali stated that Israeli prime minister Benjamin Netanyahu permitted the lethal Hamas assault on October 7 to deflect attention from his political challenges and enable the Israelis to act freely in Gaza. Additionally, Ali made antisemitic comments regarding Jewish influence in British politics and the media. Ali claims that Israeli prime minister Benjamin Netanyahu "allowed" the deadly Hamas attack on October 7 as a way to divert public opinion away from his political woes and give the Israelis "the green light to do whatever they bloody want [in Gaza]" (Sultan 2024). It is not uncommon to see such conspiracy theories about Israelis across the internet.

A November 1, 2023, article in the *New York Times* titled "Israel Knew Hamas's Attack Plan More Than a Year Ago" was certainly fodder for the anti–Semitic conspiracy theorists' minds. Steve Berman, with *The Racket News*, responded to how such reporting exacerbates a dangerous line of thinking, even if it does hold some kernel of truth. "Whether you believe the blindness was groupthink, incompetence or hubris, there's no evidence it was willful, in the sense that people who were aware of the operation simply turned a blind eye. That's a conspiracy theory, and a dangerous one" (Berman 2023). In fact, the feminist anti-war group Code Pink turned up at Nancy Peolosi's home shouting, "We know it was an inside job," "stop the genocide, stop the holocaust" (Mosley 2024).

As if the allegation that Israel allowed or caused the invasion to happen was not bad enough, outright denial that Hamas even invaded and attacked Israel has gained traction online. "Max Blumenthal, the editor of The Grayzone website, wrote a piece on October 27 that ... provided the basis for the now widespread conspiracy theory denying that Hamas murdered hundreds of Israeli civilians" (Perach 2023). Countless Reddit posts, Instagram, Facebook, and X posts are pushing narratives that the

Hamas attack was an "inside job." Similar conspiracy theories have been pinned on Israel such as being behind the September 11 attacks and mass shootings.

What Can Be Done?

The first step in understanding anti-Semitic conspiracy theories is determining why the Jews are the target of such relentless persecution and hatred. The ADL explains, "Jews are a convenient scapegoat for extremists and demagogues because of perennial anti-Semitic conspiracy theories that imagine evil Jewish puppet masters behind all of society's ills" (ADL 2020). At the core of it all, humans need someone to blame for their problems. Such mythic thinking is psychologically satisfying. On a deeper, archetypal level, the sinister, maniacal, conniving, Jew that is controlling the world and bringing the downfall of society, plays a necessary function in the mind of the anti-Semite. As Jonathan Sacks asserts, "Antisemitism is a sickness that destroys all who harbour it. Hate harms the hated, but it destroys the hater. There is no exception. Can the world be changed?" (Sacks 2015, 216). Theodore Isaac Rubin calls anti-Semitism "a malignant emotional illness" (Rubin 2014, preface). This disease of the mind is exactly that, a disease, but everyone is susceptible to such anti-Semitic thinking and conspiracy theories. However, there is disease prevention.

As humans, it is crucial to speak up when harmful conspiratorial thinking about the Jews arises. However, before anyone is equipped to quell what other people say, it is imperative that individuals take personal responsibility for their own actions and thoughts. If a stereotypical thought surfaces, take time to examine that thought critically and ask what purpose that thought serves. How is believing such conspiracy theories providing an easy answer and escape from the reality and complexity of the world's problems? Humans should refuse to engage in the conspiracy theories that rage online. Unfollow and report harmful content. While it may be impossible to change the world concerning anti-Semitism, one can commit to setting a standard for being free of anti-Semitism in all its manifestations. Discrimination, prejudice, and hate is always wrong, but hatred for the Jews seems to prevail in human history. Taking personal and social responsibility is the first step toward eradicating anti-Semitic Jew-blaming for the problems of the world.

As has been demonstrated here, anti-Semitism is an ancient form of hatred and discrimination that has endured, evolved, pervaded, and adapted across thousands of years. Whether it be the conspiratorial accusations that Jews plotted to kill God by crucifying Jesus, or the suspicion that

Jews are well-poisoners and disease carriers, a fundamental anxiety and distrust has always been projected on the Jewish people. Understandably, their culture, religion, and essential practices prevented them from fully assimilating into European Christian society, and that made them even more susceptible for suspicion and scapegoating when things went wrong in the world. Over time, the underpinning theological anti-Semitism morphed into a political form of anti-Semitism that saw Jews as disloyal to the state with a divided interest driven by Zionism. As it were, these sentiments have an enduring shelf-life and find themselves renewed and rekindled in every generation. The internet has given more force and reach to these suspicious accusations against Jews of all kinds and has even created a place for anti-Semites to gather and prattle on endlessly with impunity.

On the one hand, one should be optimistic and hopeful that a better tomorrow can exist where humans of all creeds, races, and religions get along and show each other mutual respect. On the other hand, the historical record does not seem to support the viability of this outcome. However, by taking responsibility for one's own thoughts, actions, and conspiratorial thinking temptations, this can push society toward a world of civility and respect. It is almost cliché to invoke the words of George Santayana who cautioned the world to know the past so as not to be doomed to repeat it, but there is something valuable to this idea. It seems that the loudest voices that want to condemn Holocaust awareness and teaching about anti-Semitism, are themselves anti-Semites. The only approach to solving the problem of anti-Semitism is awareness and education. It starts in the classroom and trickles down to the rest of society by equipping the mind of the learner, so they can go on to be empathetic and productive members of society. It is with this hope that a well-educated, thoughtful, and clear-thinking human being can navigate a world rife with hatred, suspicion, fear, and irrational distrust and discrimination towards others. Will anti-Semitism ever truly be eradicated? Probably not. However, sometimes it is the journey toward the good that is the good itself, rather than the desired destination. In this case, the good is a world free of anti-Semitism and irrational conspiratorial thinking against Jews. While this goal may never be fully achieved, it is a good thing to strive for.

References

ADL. (2020). "ADL Statement for the Record Before the House Subcommittee on Europe, Eurasia, Energy, and the Environment Regarding Resisting Anti-Semitism and Xenophobia in Europe." January. https://www.adl.org/resources/news/adl-statement-record-house-subcommittee-europe-eurasia-energy-and-environment

AGENCIES and TOI STAFF. (2023). "'Israel Go to Hell': Pro-Palestinian Activists Rally

in New York for 2nd Day." *The Times of Israel*, October 10. https://www.timesofisrael.com/israel-go-to-hell-pro-palestinian-activists-rally-in-new-york-for-2nd-day/.
Aizenberg, Salo. (2013). *Hatemail: Anti-Semitism on Picture Postcards.* University of Nebraska Press.
Basu, Brishti. (2023). "'Chilling Effect': People Expressing Pro-Palestinian Views Censured, Suspended from Work and School." *Canadian Broadcasting Corporation*, December 22. https://www.cbc.ca/news/canada/chilling-effect-pro-palestinian-1.7064510.
Berman, Steve. (2023). "Of Course Israel Knew." *The Racket News*, December 1. https://www.theracketnews.com/p/of-course-israel-knew.
Biale, David. (2009). "Blood and the Discourses of Nazi Antisemitism." *Varieties of Antisemitism: History, Ideology, Discourse*. Edited by Murray Baumgarten, Peter Kenez, and Bruce Thompson. Newark: University of Delaware Press, 29–49.
Blakeslee, Spencer. (2000). *The Death of American Antisemitism*. Westport, CT: Praeger.
Coaston, Jane. (2018). "How the Rise of Conspiracy Theory Politics Emboldens Anti-Semitism: Anti-Semitism Is a Form of Prejudice Rooted in Conspiracy." Vox.com, October 31. https://www.vox.com/identities/2018/10/31/18034256/anti-semitism-pittsburgh-synagogue-shooting-prejudice-right.
Delaney, Matt. (2023). "Masked Teens Yell 'Death to the Jews' at Florida Synagogue Congregants: Police." *The Washington Times*, October 30. https://www.washingtontimes.com/news/2023/oct/30/masked-teens-yell-death-jews-florida-synagogue-con/.
Færseth, John. (2021). *Conspiratorial Antisemitism*. Oslo: Antirasistisk Senter.
Fox, Jonathan, and Lev Topor. (2021). *Conspiracy Theories: Why Do People Discriminate Against Jews?* Oxford: Oxford University Press.
Geller, Jay. (2011). *The Other Jewish Question: Identifying the Jew and Making Sense of Modernity*. New York: Fordham University Press.
"Great Replacement Conspiracy Theory." (2024). *Translate Hate Glossary*. American Jewish Committee. https://www.ajc.org/translatehate/great-replacement.
Harris, Ruth. (2010). *Dreyfus: Politics, Emotion, and the Scandal of the Century*. New York: Metropolitan Books.
Harvey, Richard S. (2017). *Luther and the Jews: Putting Right the Lies*. Eugene, OR: Wipf & Stock.
Jane de Gara, Lisa. (2019). "Anti-Semitic Conspiracy Theories," in *Conspiracies and Conspiracy Theories in American History*, edited by Christopher Fee and Jeffrey Webb, 98–102. London: Bloomsbury.
Jerusalem Post Staff. (2022). "Antisemitic Flyers Blaming Jews for COVID Found in Vancouver, WA." *The Jerusalem Post*, February 14 . https://www.jpost.com/diaspora/antisemitism/article-696328.
Johnson, Hannah. (2012). *Blood Libel: The Ritual Murder Accusation at the Limit of Jewish History.* Ann Arbor: University of Michigan Press.
JNS. (2021). "Fliers Found in Illinois Blaming Jews for COVID-19." *St. Louis Jewish Light*, December 22. https://stljewishlight.org/news/antisemitism/illinois-among-goyim-defense-league-states-anti-semitic-fliers-blaming-jews-for-covid-19/.
JTA and TOI Staff. (2023). "'Death to the Jew:' Chants Heard at Berlin Pro-Palestinian Rally." *The Times of Israel*, April 12. https://www.timesofisrael.com/death-to-the-jews-chants-heard-at-berlin-pro-palestinian-rally/.
Knight, Peter. (2003). *Conspiracy Theories in American History: An Encyclopedia*. Santa Barbara, CA: ABC-CLIO.
Korman, Gerd. (2022). *This Was America, 1865–1965: Unequal Citizens in the Segregated Republic*. Brookline, MA: Academic Studies Press.
Lapin, Andrew. (2023). "Rutgers U Suspends Students for Justice in Palestine Amid Further Campus Uproar over Israel." *Jewish Telegraphic Agency*, December 12. https://www.jta.org/2023/12/12/united-states/rutgers-u-suspends-students-for-justice-in-palestine-amid-further-campus-uproar-over-israel.
Livingstone Smith, David. (2021). *Making Monsters: The Uncanny Power of Dehumanization*. Cambridge: Harvard University Press.
Lupovitch, Howard N. (2009). *Jews and Judaism in World History*. New York: Routledge.

168   Part II: Cultural Mythology and Social Media

Luther, Martin. (1543/1971). *On the Jews and Their Lies*, in *Luther's Works*, vol. 47. Philadelphia: Fortress Press.
Maizels, Linda. (2023). *What Is Antisemitism? A Contemporary Introduction*. New York: Routledge.
Manent, Pierre. (2013). *A World Beyond Politics? A Defense of the Nation-State*. Princeton,: Princeton University Press.
Michael, Robert. (2008). *A History of Catholic Antisemitism: The Dark Side of the Church*. New York: Palgrave Macmillan.
Mosley, Sterling. (2024). "WATCH: Nancy Pelosi Gets in a Shouting Match With Protestors in Resurfaced Clip—'Go Back to China!'" *Brandon Gill's DC Enquirer*, January 29. https://dcenquirer.com/watch-nancy-pelosi-gets-in-a-shouting-match-with-protesters-in-resurfaced-clip-go-back-to-china.
Origen of Alexandria, Against Celsus, Book 4, Ch. 22. (1894). *Ante-Nicene Christian Library: Translations of the Writings of the Father Down to A.D. 325*, eds. Alexander Roberts and James Donaldson. Edinburgh: T & T Clark.
Perach, Michal. (2023). "Opinion | Masterclass in Manipulation: Exposing Max Blumenthal's Lies About Israel and October 7." *Haaretz*, November 27. https://www.haaretz.com/israel-news/2023-11-27/ty-article-opinion/exposing-max-blumenthals-deceptive-claim-israel-is-responsible-for-most-october-7-victims/0000018c-102f-d65f-a7dd-f0ff7b550000.
Sacks, Jonathan. (2015). *Not in God's Name: Confronting Religious Violence*. New York: Schocken Books.
Sarna, Jonathan. (2021). "The Long, Ugly Antisemitic History of 'Jews Will Not Replace Us.'" *The Jewish Experience*. https://www.brandeis.edu/jewish-experience/jewish-america/2021/november/replacement-antisemitism-sarna.html.
Scripps News (2023). By Alexandra Miller, Posted: 7:57 p.m. EDT August 30. https://scrippsnews.com/stories/state-department-employee-shares-racist-remarks-on-podcast/.
Sultan, Abir. (2024). "Gaza War: Blaming Israel for October 7 Hamas Attack Makes Peace Less—Not More—Likely." *The Conversation: Academic Rigor, Journalistic Flair*, February 21. https://theconversation.com/gaza-war-blaming-israel-for-october-7-hamas-attack-makes-peace-less-not-more-likely-223934.
Teter, Magda. (2020). *Blood Libel: On the Trail of an Antisemitic Myth*. Cambridge: Harvard University Press.
Trachtenberg, Joshua. (2001). *The Devil and the Jews: The Medieval Conception of the Jew and its Relation to Modern Anti-Semitism*. Skokie, IL: Varda Books.
United States Holocaust Memorial Museum. (n.d.). "Der Ewige Jude," in *Holocaust Encyclopedia*. Washington, D.C.. https://encyclopedia.ushmm.org/content/en/article/der-ewige-jude.
Wilson, Jason. (2023). "Rightwing Personalities Use X to Bring Antisemitic Theories to Light in US." *The Guardian*, November 21. https://www.theguardian.com/technology/2023/nov/21/great-replacement-theory-antisemitism-racism-rightwing-mainstream.
Zelizer, Julian. (2022). "Opinion: Amazon's Recent Film Decision Reveals a Dangerous Trend." *CNN*, December 2. https://www.cnn.com/2022/12/02/opinions/amazon-antisemitism-film-sale-zelizer/index.html.

Memes, Schemes, and Conspiracy Machines

How Viral Disinformation Produces a Shadow-Marketplace of Ideas

CHELSEA L. HORNE

Introduction

From conspiracy theories about Area 51 and a flat earth to conspiracies such as Pizzagate and QAnon, or even those about the abominable snowman or Melania Trump's body double, it is clear that disinformation—and the mushrooming conspiracies that stem from it—thrives on the internet. While the stakes of each conspiracy theory vary greatly, there is an increasingly fraught relationship with disinformation both in news media and social media, with potentially devastating results for individuals and communities. And in some extreme cases, these conspiracies can impact the entire world. It is important to note that conspiracy theories and disinformation are not a new phenomenon, but the speed, spread, and overall viral potential for conspiracies in today's digital sphere have significant impact (Nahon and Hemsley 2013; Posetti and Matthews 2018; Horne 2021). Of particular interest to this essay is the conspiracy machine: the production, dissemination, and consumption of conspiracy theories online through social media networks. Further, this close examination of conspiracy theories online seeks to emphasize how conspiracies make the cyber-physical leap from the internet world to the "real" world, and the implications and consequences of how a convoluted information ecosystem riddled with disinformation is creating new challenges for speech online.

There are many interconnected factors that have given rise to popular conspiracy theories in the United States. Much of today's popular culture either develops on or is shared via social media platforms. Social media is also where half of Americans get their news at least sometimes, with Facebook the most popular platform for news gathering (Liedke and Wang 2023). In fact, globally, the average internet user has 8.5 social media accounts (Dixon 2022) and spends an average of 151 minutes on social media per day (Dixon 2023). Acknowledging the pivotal role of both the internet and social media platforms in the proliferation of conspiracy theories online, it is critical to consider the role of network effects, virality, and internet design and architecture in providing a forum for robust information sharing—of both "good" content like fact-checked and reliable information as well as problematic content like disinformation and conspiracy theories. In this analysis, the essay will address how the internet has reflected and amplified conspiratorial thinking.

A Burgeoning Shadow-Marketplace of Ideas

As a central thesis, I posit that today's digital sphere operates on what I suggest is a shadow-marketplace of ideas. A blending of two concepts—a shadow (or black) market and the marketplace of ideas—the premise of a shadow-marketplace of ideas seeks to emphasize two of the major current challenges of the online world in maintaining information integrity. First, the allusion to a "shadow market" of information refers to the mass proliferation and dissemination of disinformation online. These types of disinformation may range from false TikTok "life hacks" to troll farms creating "fake news" floods to deepfakes of revenge porn, and more. While some of these types of disinformation are definitively illegal, some are technically legal, but considered harmful. One of the current and pressing questions of new proposed policy and regulation is the need to distinguish and mitigate the potential harms of some types of content online. By invoking the concept of a "shadow market" in this essay, I mean less to focus on the illegality (or legality) of how these types of disinformation are created and spread, but rather to emphasize how these many and growing obstacles to information integrity are subverting the ideal of a marketplace of ideas, which has historically guided freedom of expression directives.

The second term, a marketplace of ideas, derives from the history of free speech laws. Truth and accuracy of the news are critical components in sustaining a democracy. To such an extent, in the United States, the First Amendment protects freedom of speech and freedom of the press. A driving principle behind interpretations of the First Amendment is the belief in the marketplace of ideas; the theory that in a competition, truth will eventually win out over falsehoods and that it is in fact this very competition of ideas that will separate the truth from the lies. This theory comes from John Stuart Mill's 1859 book *On Liberty*. In *Abrams v. United States* (1919), Supreme Court Justice Holmes invoked the first legal reference to the marketplace of ideas by stating, "that the best test of truth is the power of the thought to get itself accepted in the competition of the market, and that truth is the only ground upon which their wishes safely can be carried out" (D. Schultz 2023). Since then, the judicial system has invoked the concept of a marketplace of ideas countless times as a means to oppose censorship and encourage freedom of expression.

Fast forward to present day, and now people can find, share, and create information and engage and interact with other people instantly; an idea, an image, a video, a lie can circumnavigate the globe faster than one can type out "I can has cheezburger" or any other classic early internet meme. With a world population estimated at eight billion (Morse 2023) and a massive and increasing carbon footprint of the internet due to the necessary land, energy, and water to host the large servers and data centers required to make the internet function (Harding 2023), the marketplace of ideas is exponentially bigger than it ever was before. And while more ideas in the marketplace can lead to more knowledge and innovation, we are also seeing a spike in destructive, deceptive, and manipulative ideas. Underneath the ideal marketplace of ideas, a prospering shadow-market of false information has emerged. The affordances of internet technology and social media platforms allow for information to be disseminated with incredible speed, scope, and spread. Unfortunately, technological advances such as botnets and "fake news" troll farms can easily flood social media outlets with disinformation and then promote it through rigged engagements so that algorithms pick up the "trending" posts and as a result, disinformation sifts to the top of newsfeeds (Soares n.d.). And now with the accessibility and ease of AI generated content, it may be possible to generate falsehoods at literally a nonhuman scale.

The concern I raise with my concept of a shadow-marketplace of ideas is to suggest that new approaches to speech online may need to be considered, and urgently. We are at a critical juncture where information integrity is challenged daily, and citizens are constantly barraged with phishing attempts, hacks, disinformation, hate speech, extremist rhetoric, propaganda, dark patterns, and general information overload. Perhaps the truth will still "win out eventually" (or perhaps not, as conspiracy theorists may hold onto their theories even in the light of concrete evidence that refutes them), but in today's culture, where virality is strategic, it may not happen quickly enough. Or perhaps falsehoods, with the aid of quickly advancing and readily available technology combined with bad actors, may end up overturning the marketplace of ideas as we know it.

Power of Conspiracy Theories

There are conspiracy theories ranging from every subject imaginable: from mole and lizard people to a faked moon landing and even a recent popular conspiracy theory that causes many "teenagers [to] doubt the existence of Helen Keller" (Cosslett 2021). This last conspiracy became popular on the social media platform TikTok, which has a predominantly young user base. Recent studies have shown that misinformation and disinformation is rampant on TikTok: one report found that 20 percent of videos on the platform are misinformation ("Misinformation Monitor" 2022). While some proponents of this conspiracy theory denounce the existence of author, educator, and activist Helen Keller (1880–1968) entirely, the majority of believers do acknowledge that she was a real person, but question whether she was able to accomplish everything that she did, such as write fourteen books and fly a plane (Dapcevich 2020). It is possible that the TikTok account that first launched this conspiracy was making a joke or engaging in satire, but regardless, somehow the conspiracy has gained popularity and traction, and despite being widely debunked, is still a belief held by many teenagers (Cosslett 2021; Dapcevich 2020). A major worry about this conspiracy theory in particular is that it is rooted in profoundly ableist prejudice.

While certainly troubling and problematic, one might dismiss the conspiracy about Helen Keller as part of the folly of young people and the appeal of sensationalist ideas. What are the stakes, one might ask? What is at risk? Who does this hurt, really? Besides the obvious points about the worries of a misinformed public, reinforcement of ableist mindsets, and the erasure of history, it is possible to see how one might overlook and dismiss conspiracy theories such as this one as being insignificant in the larger scheme of things. To that end, in this section I will closely unpack the Pizzagate conspiracy theory, as I suggest that this specific conspiracy theory best encapsulates the role and power of conspiracies in our current digital world, and the overall implications of conspiracies on the media, technology, and democracy. Notably, the Pizzagate conspiracy theory later served as the foundation of the QAnon conspiracy, which falsely alleges that "the world is run by a cabal of Satan-worshiping pedophiles" and whose followers have been "charged with violent crimes, including kidnappings, assassination plots, and the 2019 murder of a mafia boss in New York" as well as participated in the January 6 insurrection at the U.S. Capitol (Roose 2021).

Pizzagate is the conspiracy theory that falsely alleges Hillary and Bill Clinton used the family pizza restaurant, Comet Ping Pong, in Washington, D.C., as part of a pedophile sex ring (Samuelson 2016). This conspiracy has been debunked and disproven by many major national newspapers and by the Metropolitan Police Department of the District of Columbia. The conspiracy began when in November 2016, WikiLeaks released the emails of John Podesta, the Clinton campaign chairman, which included mention of James Alefantis, the owner of Comet Ping Pong, in reference to potential fundraisers (Samuelson 2016). Users on 4chan, an anonymous internet messaging board, falsely claimed that there were coded messages in the emails referring to human trafficking and a child sex ring, and then began to trawl Alefantis' social media searching for photos and evidence (Wendling 2016). From there, the conspiracy quickly took off, spreading to Twitter, 8chan, Reddit, and other platforms including Alex Jones' talk show *Infowars*, which is known to spread misinformation.

There are several important points to highlight about the impact of the Pizzagate conspiracy theory. First, the timing: the conspiracy started to gain traction in early November 2016, coinciding with the U.S. presidential election on November 8, which was punctuated with a news cycle that was plagued with "fake news," disinformation, and the questioning of fact and truth. While the Pizzagate conspiracy mostly picked up after election day, WikiLeaks began releasing Podesta's emails on October 7, 2016, and *Rolling Stone* states that the original Pizzagate post appeared on Facebook on October 29 (Krawchenko et al. 2016; Robb 2017). It is possible that the burgeoning conspiracy theory may have had an impact on the presidential election, though it is hard to say definitively. Nevertheless, the acute timing of the emergence of this conspiracy right at the peak of a pivotal election emphasizes the powerful role conspiracies can play.

As a second key point, the cyber implications of the Pizzagate conspiracy had an immediate impact in the online world. Comet Ping Pong was bombarded with one-star reviews on Facebook and Yelp, causing the restaurant's overall rating to drop (Kurzius 2016; Delshad 2016). As restaurant ratings can be an important factor when potential customers are considering locales to frequent, the "review bombing" of a business can have significant impact on the financial output and could result in the decline of business. Yelp responded to the controversy by temporarily locking Comet Ping Pong's page and included the following note:

> This business recently made waves in the news, which often means that people come to this page to post their views on the news.... While we don't take a stand one way or the other when it comes to these news events, we do work to remove both positive and negative posts that appear to be motivated more by the news coverage itself than the reviewer's personal consumer experience with the business [LaCapria 2016].

Yelp's decision to suspend the restaurant's page is notable because it highlights the role, position, and power of online platforms to impact, either by amplifying or mitigating, online communication. Similarly, Reddit also stepped in and banned r/pizzagate—the subreddit where users were discussing and promoting the conspiracy—for violating Reddit's doxing policy, stating that r/pizzagate "was banned due to a violation of our content policy, specifically, the proliferation of personal and confidential information. We don't want witchhunts on our site" (Kurzius 2016; "Reddit–Dive into Anything" n.d.).

Thirdly, and crucially, the Pizzagate conspiracy theory made the cyber-physical leap from the digital sphere to the real world, in several critical and violent ways. There are certainly online harms to conspiracy theories as they spread across the internet, but some may overlook the potential of "real world" harms of conspiracies. In the first weeks of the conspiracy, as bad reviews poured in online for Comet Ping Pong, some protestors began to line the sidewalk of the restaurant, and in contrast, many people flocked to Comet Ping Pong to show support for the neighborhood pizza joint leading to forty-five-minute wait times (Delshad 2016; Wendling 2016). However, the situation quickly escalated when in December 2016, about a month after the Pizzagate conspiracy started, a North Carolina man arrived at Comet Ping Pong to "self-investigate," firing an assault weapon at least once, with the belief that he was on a rescue mission to save children after learning about the conspiracy theory (Siddiqui and Svrluga 2021; Fisher, Cox, and Hermann 2023).

And the fourth and final key point demonstrated by the Pizzagate conspiracy is longevity. Even after the original Pizzagate conspiracy had been thoroughly debunked by a variety of credible news sources, in 2020, the conspiracy picked up popularity again after a video of Justin Bieber adjusting his hat during an Instagram video was interpreted as a coded signal that he was a victim of Pizzagate (Kang and Frenkel 2020). Soon after on TikTok, posts with #Pizzagate received over 82 million views, and searches for Pizzagate soared on Google, Facebook, and Instagram (Kang and Frenkel 2020). Further, the conspiracy—which had previously remained localized in the United States—at this point had gained global reach and popularity, garnering millions of views in Italy, Turkey, and Brazil (Kang and Frenkel 2020). More recently, attention to the conspiracy spiked in late 2023, when Elon Musk boosted a meme about Pizzagate on X (formerly known as Twitter). A study showed that Musk's engagement resulted in a 9500 percent increase in Pizzagate posts on X, including over 81 million impressions (Bond and Peterka-Benton 2023). And still in 2023, Comet Ping Pong continues to receive bad reviews and comments on their Facebook page specifically in reference to the conspiracy theory. There is lasting power in conspiracy theories to linger and to continue to have currency. Overall, Pizzagate is an iconic representation of the impact and consequences of a shadow-marketplace of ideas.

Shifting Digital Landscapes

After suicide bombers killed more than 250 people in Sri Lanka on Easter 2019, the Sri Lankan government shut down social media (Facebook, Instagram, WhatsApp, and Viber) to stop the spread of "false news reports." The success of such a ban in quelling further violence was unclear, even when the ban was lifted more than a week later (K. Schultz 2019). The decision of the social media blackout was met with mixed responses and serves to highlight the involved nature of social media as a mode of information sharing—and by relation, of disinformation sharing—and the powerful effect it can have on a citizenry.

As technological advancements continue to increase, an interesting phenomenon has emerged: the more access we have to information and the availability of fact-checking software, the more disinformation and varying types of falsehoods and manipulative content emerge. From a technological perspective, not only is there a concern regarding the success of disinformation news stories to mislead the public, but there are also growing concerns about the sheer quantity of "fake news" that might bombard the Internet. For example, OpenAI has developed an algorithm that creates convincing "fake news," revealing that it might be possible to mass-produce "fake news" stories to promote propaganda or disinformation (Knight 2019). Simultaneously, attempts at artificial intelligence programs to detect "fake news," while improving, are not close enough in accuracy to be implemented in a mainstream fashion as a feasible defense against "fake news" yet (Hao 2018). There is a potential then, for computer generated disinformation to flood social media and other networks at an unmanageable scale. The sheer labor of having to sift through mass quantities of "fake news" shared through these networks could easily overwhelm and bury the "real" news. And even if most disinformation news stories are flagged and/or removed, even just one piece of disinformation news slipping through can cause incredible harm and lead to a cascade effect, including the rise of conspiracy theories. Already, being a constantly vigilant news consumer is exhausting for many due to information overload. Consequently, increasing the number of opportunities for consumers to be misled—especially susceptible communities such as elderly people (Guess, Nagler, and Tucker 2019)—is a very real threat. Further, the disinfodemic (Posetti and Bontcheva 2021) raises key additional questions about if and what role social media platforms should play in mitigating the spread of disinformation online, while still balancing out people's speech rights.

The affordances of social media have contributed to, and amplified, the shift in the way people share information with each other. Of particular interest in this context is the desire for media to "go viral." For advertisers and campaign managers the incentives to make certain media viral is obvious as it increases their access to consumers and opportunities to win over audiences. Researchers Karine Nahon and Jeff Hemsley identify that there is a notable difference between something that is "viral" and something that is just popular. For example, an instructional video that shows how to tie a tie might have millions of views that it has accrued steadily over a decade. This is merely a popular video. A viral video, on the other hand, will have a sudden surge of activity in a very short amount of time and then start to decay soon after in terms of activity; the overall number of interactions will follow an S curve (Nahon and Hemsley 2013). The key identifier of a viral item is the speed with which it spreads and its overall reach, leaping from network to network through shared connections (Nahon and Hemsley 2013). A viral event doesn't need to have lasting resonance (though it certainly can). Its main impact is its ability to engage media consumers to share the content. This is precisely what "fake news" is designed to do.

The speed and spread of "fake news" stories are two main components of their ability to influence. On the other hand, this same access to speed is one of the tools used to combat falsehoods. This speed is most effectively utilized in fact-checking speeches or other live events. In this context, "truth," or rather fact, is revealed immediately and distinguished from lies or half-truths. The marketplace of ideas prevails. However, the spread of this information can be limited. Only people who are interested in the truth will follow fact-checking updates, while those to which the speech or event was catered, most likely will not—they may not feel the need to. Here, confirmation bias and filter bubbles reveal the limits of the spread of "truth." Additionally, truth and speed often do not go hand in hand. There is frequently a delay in revealing the truth (to undergo the process of rigorous fact-checking and verification), and then sometimes an even longer delay in sharing this information to the public. Consider the security breaches in credit report companies, where it took years for these companies to reveal that consumers' information was at risk.

Alternative Facts, Misinformation, Disinformation, "Fake News," Junk News, Propaganda, and Other Sobriquets du Jour

Conspiracy theories are innately interconnected with disinformation, misinformation, and malinformation, which prosper on the shadow-marketplace of ideas. The prevalence and pervasiveness of disinformation contributes to a mis/disinformed public. A key concern of the "fake news" crisis is access to truth. Access to knowledge (A2K) and access to science are protected under Article 27 of the Universal Declaration of Human Rights ("Universal Declaration of Human Rights" n.d.). But what happens when the veracity, accuracy, and credibility of information—most of which is shared and disseminated via the internet and social media with incredible speed—is questionable or non-existent? Should access to accurate, objective, and truthful information be an inherent human right as well? Ultimately, all aspects that threaten information integrity such as "fake news," misinformation, disinformation, conspiracy theories, and propaganda may act as a threat to democracy.

Definitions of what constitutes "fake news" are widely varied, which complicates the discussion and consideration of the impact of "fake news" (Mansky 2018). Consider this historical example: on October 30, 1938 (Halloween Eve), in New York City, Orson Welles nationally broadcast on CBS Radio a fifty-two-minute chronicle of the Martian invasion of the United States, punctuated by news flashes and breaking updates (Henderson 2008). Rather than provide a simple dramatization of H.G. Wells' science fiction novel, *War of the Worlds* (1898), the twenty-three-year-old Welles instead decided on a realistic reportage (Flaherty 2018). Legend has it that the result was so effective and so realistic to listeners, that there was a mass panic during and immediately after the broadcast ended; however, more recent scholarship suggests that the legendary mass chaos may in fact be a myth, and the whole response may have been overblown (Pooley and Socolow 2013). Either way, Americans had just gotten their first experience of what some call the first "fake news."

A decade ago, if asked, "what is fake news?" many people would have probably thought of *Saturday Night Live*'s Weekend Update. As perhaps the original "fake news," both parody and satire are similar, but have a marked difference. Parody is the deliberate exaggeration of a style, genre, or story for comedic purposes. As one example: a 2018 *SNL* sketch parodied *It's a Wonderful Life* with then–President Trump (played by Alec Baldwin) reprising the role of George Bailey. A tweet from the real President Donald Trump in response to the skit implied that the intent of the sketch was to defame and suggested that *SNL* be "tested in court" (Entertainment 2018). Relatedly, news satire is similar in that it also uses humor to critique, mock, and contextualize real events and news. Popular examples of satire are *The Daily Show, Last Week Tonight, The Onion*, as well as *SNL*'s Weekend Update section. Both parody and satire are legally protected forms of expression under the First Amendment. The intent to deceive is low and as such constitutes little threat of misinforming the public of truth and/or facts. The effect is usually the opposite; by using humor, satire and parody often reveal more "truth" about an event or situation through a critical examination of the issue. As such, these humorous displays could even be considered symptoms of a healthy democracy.

In contrast, misinformation is "information whose inaccuracy is unintentional" (Jack 2017). This refers to mistakes in reporting information, possibly due to relying on faulty information, hasty reporting, or misunderstanding sources. These errors are typically retracted and/or remedied once identified. Rather than having an insidious design, misinformation highlights the need for following journalistic best practices. In contrast, disinformation "is information that is deliberately false or misleading" (Jack 2017). Disinformation campaigns include news examples such as Pizzagate conspiracy theory and the false claim of the Pope's endorsement of Trump (the latter blurs into propaganda as well).

In many countries, existing laws are not equipped to handle the amplification of mis/disinformation sharing through social media outlets, though there has been an increase in laws that seek to address the "fake news" crisis (Bradshaw, Nothhaft, and Neudert 2018). As a result, many have made calls for social media platforms and other content intermediaries to step in to moderate the dissemination of fake news. The concern though about this privatization of "fake news" regulation is that it can result in worrying levels of censorship. While there is no intent to deceive in misinformation and there is intent to deceive in disinformation, the consequences and effects are disturbingly similar. The information spreads with the same speed and ease through social media sharing and the implications of false information, regardless of intent, can be problematic.

The larger issue with a lack of a cohesive and universal definition of "fake news," is more than just miscommunication, it is that all these nuanced components get lumped together to mean anything that is a "falsehood" (regardless of intention) and/or "undesirable information." The consequences are significant as this erosion of truth can lead to a growing distrust in the news media (Marwick and Lewis 2017). Overall, media distrust can have disastrous impacts as "people who do not trust the media are less likely to access accurate information, which has civic and political ramifications" (Ladd 2012).

Conclusion

Just as the internet offers critical opportunities for innovation and access to knowledge, so too are there robust opportunities for conspiracy theories, disinformation, and manipulative content to flourish. This essay suggests a consideration of the ever-pressing reality of a shadow-marketplace of ideas, which warps and infuses disinformation into the information ecosystem in a manner that is difficult to combat. In particular, I examine conspiracy theories on a sliding scale ranging from benign to destructive. This distinction is important because it allows for a more critical consideration of the role and impact of conspiracy theories. All conspiracy theories can and do have impact, though the scale varies. For example, some may completely dismiss seemingly benign conspiracy theories such as the one about Helen Keller mentioned earlier. Certainly, while there may not be concrete real-world impact of this conspiracy, the acceptance and proliferation of ableist conspiracies could have longer cultural and societal influence over time. In contrast, there are also conspiracy theories with immense potential for destructive effects such as Pizzagate, which had both immediate and long-lasting consequences in both the digital and physical world, affecting the public, a business, political and public figures, and potentially democracy.

The case study of Pizzagate considers several of the key elements of conspiracy theories: their timing, their cyber reputational harms, their cyber-physical leap, and their longevity. The ability for false information to be spread at scale quickly across the internet, and the challenges of fact-checking, debunking falsehoods, and keeping up with the marketplace of ideas, creates problems in both the cyber world and the real world with potentially profound consequences and global impact. The growing prevalence of a shadow-marketplace of ideas in the digital sphere and how it feeds and is fed by a vigorous conspiracy machine is critical in illuminating the challenges and consequences of conspiracies and viral disinformation.

References

Bond, Benton, and Daniela Peterka-Benton. (2023). "Everything Old Is Q Again: X Activity About #PizzaGate Increased 9501.5% After Musk Boosted the Conspiracy." *Montclair State University*, November.

Bradshaw, Samantha, Howard Nothhaft, and Lisa-Maria Neudert. (2018). "Government Responses to Malicious Use of Social Media." NATO Strategic Communications Centre of Excellence, December 9. https://stratcomcoe.org/publications/government-responses-to-malicious-use-of-social-media/125.

Cosslett, Rhiannon Lucy. (2021). "Helen Keller: Why Is a TikTok Conspiracy Theory Undermining Her Story?" *The Guardian*, January 7, sec. Books. https://www.theguardian.com/books/2021/jan/07/helen-keller-why-is-a-tiktok-conspiracy-theory-undermining-her-story.

Dapcevich, Madison. (2020). "Did Helen Keller Fly a Plane?" *Snopes*, December 26. https://www.snopes.com/fact-check/helen-keller-fly-plane/.

Delshad, Carmel. (2016). "Tarnished By an Online Hoax, a D.C. Pizzeria Tries to Bounce Back." *WAMU* (blog), November 23. https://wamu.org/story/16/11/23/local_pizzeria_comet_ping_pong_faces_conspiracy_theories/.

180   Part II: Cultural Mythology and Social Media

Dixon, Stacy. (2022). "Global Social Media Account Ownership 2018." *Statista*, April 28. https://www.statista.com/statistics/788084/number-of-social-media-accounts/.

———. (2023). "Global Daily Social Media Usage 2023." *Statista*, August 29. https://www.statista.com/statistics/433871/daily-social-media-usage-worldwide/.

Entertainment, Legal. (2018). "Trump Says 'Saturday Night' Should Be 'Tested In Court' Over 'Wonderful Life' Parody." *Forbes*, December 17. https://www.forbes.com/sites/legalentertainment/2018/12/17/trump-says-saturday-night-should-be-tested-in-court-over-wonderful-life-parody/.

Fisher, Marc, John Woodrow Cox, and Peter Hermann. (2023). "Pizzagate: From Rumor, to Hashtag, to Gunfire in D.C." *Washington Post*, April 12. https://www.washingtonpost.com/local/pizzagate-from-rumor-to-hashtag-to-gunfire-in-dc/2016/12/06/4c7def50-bbd4-11e6-94ac-3d324840106c_story.html.

Flaherty, Michael. (2018). "'War of the Worlds' and the Manufacture of Panic." *National Review* (blog), October 31. https://www.nationalreview.com/2018/10/orson-welles-war-of-the-worlds-radio-broadcast-news-coverage/.

Guess, Andrew, Jonathan Nagler, and Joshua Tucker. (2019). "Less Than You Think: Prevalence and Predictors of Fake News Dissemination on Facebook." *Science Advances* 5 (1): eaau4586. https://doi.org/10.1126/sciadv.aau4586.

Hao, Karen. (2018). "Even the Best AI for Spotting Fake News Is Still Terrible." *MIT Technology Review*, October 3. https://www.technologyreview.com/2018/10/03/139926/even-the-best-ai-for-spotting-fake-news-is-still-terrible/.

Harding, Xavier. (2023). "The Internet's Invisible Carbon Footprint." Mozilla Foundation, August 3. https://foundation.mozilla.org/en/blog/ai-internet-carbon-footprint/.

Henderson, Amy. (2008). "Orson Welles and the 70th Anniversary of War of the Worlds." National Portrait Gallery, October 28. https://npg.si.edu/blog/orson-welles-and-70th-anniversary-war-worlds.

Horne, Chelsea. (2021). "Internet Governance in the 'Post-Truth Era': Analyzing Key Topics in 'Fake News' Discussions at IGF." *Telecommunications Policy, Norm Entrepreneurship in Internet Governance* 45 (6): 102150. https://doi.org/10.1016/j.telpol.2021.102150.

Jack, Caroline. (2017). "Lexicon of Lies: Terms for Problematic Information." *Data & Society*, August.

Kang, Cecilia, and Sheera Frenkel. (2020). "'PizzaGate' Conspiracy Theory Thrives Anew in the TikTok Era." *New York Times*, June 27, sec. Technology. https://www.nytimes.com/2020/06/27/technology/pizzagate-justin-bieber-qanon-tiktok.html.

Knight, Will. (2019). "An AI That Writes Convincing Prose Risks Mass-Producing Fake News." *MIT Technology Review*, February 14. https://www.technologyreview.com/2019/02/14/137426/an-ai-tool-auto-generates-fake-news-bogus-tweets-and-plenty-of-gibberish/.

Krawchenko, Katiana, Donald Judd, Nancy Cordes, Julianna Goldman, Reena Flores, Rebecca Shabad, Emily Schultheis, Alexander Romano, Steve Chaggaris, and Associated Press. (2016). "The John Podesta Emails Released by WikiLeaks." CBS News. November 3. https://www.cbsnews.com/news/the-john-podesta-emails-released-by-wikileaks/.

Kurzius, Rachel. (2016). "Reddit Bans Subreddit Dedicated To Harassing Comet Ping Pong." *DCist* (blog), November 23. https://dcist.com/story/16/11/23/reddit-bans-community-dedicated-to/.

LaCapria, Kim. (2016). "Is Comet Ping Pong Pizzeria Home to a Child Abuse Ring Led by Hillary Clinton?" *Snopes*, November 21. https://www.snopes.com/fact-check/pizzagate-conspiracy/.

Ladd, Jonathan M. (2012). *Why Americans Hate the Media and How It Matters*. Princeton: Princeton University Press.

Liedke, Jacob, and Luxuan Wang. (2023). "Social Media and News Fact Sheet." *Pew Research Center's Journalism Project* (blog), November 15. https://www.pewresearch.org/journalism/fact-sheet/social-media-and-news-fact-sheet/.

Mansky, Jackie. 2018. "The Age-Old Problem of 'Fake News' | History." *Smithsonian Magazine*, May 7. https://www.smithsonianmag.com/history/age-old-problem-fake-news-180968945/.

Marwick, Alice, and Rebecca Lewis. (2017). "Media Manipulation and Disinformation Online." *Data & Society*, May.
"Misinformation Monitor: September 2022." (2022). *NewsGuard* (blog), September. https://www.newsguardtech.com/misinformation-monitor/september-2022.
Morse, Anne. (2023). "Global Population Estimates Vary but Trends Are Clear: Population Growth Is Slowing." U.S. Census Bureau, November 9. https://www.census.gov/library/stories/2023/11/world-population-estimated-eight-billion.html.
Nahon, Karine, and Jeff Hemsley. (2013). *Going Viral*. Cambridge: Polity Press.
Pooley, Jefferson, and Michael Socolow. (2013). "Orson Welles' War of the Worlds Panic Myth: The Infamous Radio Broadcast Did Not Cause a Nationwide Hysteria." *Slate*, October 28. https://slate.com/culture/2013/10/orson-welles-war-of-the-worlds-panic-myth-the-infamous-radio-broadcast-did-not-cause-a-nationwide-hysteria.html.
Posetti, Julie, and Kalina Bontcheva. (2021). "Infodemic: Disinformation and Media Literacy in the Context of COVID-19." *Internet Sectoral Overview* 3 (September).
Posetti, Julie, and Alice Matthews. (2018). "A Short Guide to the History of 'Fake News' and Disinformation." *International Center for Journalists*.
"Reddit—Dive into Anything." (n.d.). Reddit. Accessed December 21, 2023. https://www.reddit.com/r/pizzagate/.
Robb, Amanda. (2017). "Pizzagate: Anatomy of a Fake News Scandal." *Rolling Stone* (blog), November 16. https://www.rollingstone.com/feature/anatomy-of-a-fake-news-scandal-125877/.
Roose, Kevin. (2021). "What Is QAnon, the Viral Pro-Trump Conspiracy Theory?" *New York Times*, September 3, sec. Technology. https://www.nytimes.com/article/what-is-qanon.html.
Samuelson, Kate. (2016). "What to Know About Pizzagate, the Fake News Story with Real Consequences." *Time Magazine*, December 5. https://time.com/4590255/pizzagate-fake-news-what-to-know/.
Schultz, David. (2023). "Marketplace of Ideas." The Free Speech Center, September 19. https://firstamendment.mtsu.edu/article/marketplace-of-ideas/.
Schultz, Kai. (2019). "Sri Lanka's President Lifts Ban on Social Media." *New York Times*, April 30, sec. World. https://www.nytimes.com/2019/04/30/world/asia/sri-lanka-social-media.html.
Siddiqui, Faiz, and Susan Svrluga. (2021). "N.C. Man Told Police He Went to D.C. Pizzeria with Gun to Investigate Conspiracy Theory." *Washington Post*, October 23. https://www.washingtonpost.com/news/local/wp/2016/12/04/d-c-police-respond-to-report-of-a-man-with-a-gun-at-comet-ping-pong-restaurant/.
Soares, Isa. (n.d.). "The Fake News Machine: Inside a Town Gearing up for 2020." CNN Money. Accessed December 21, 2023. https://money.cnn.com/interactive/media/the-macedonia-story/.
"Universal Declaration of Human Rights." (n.d.). United Nations. Accessed October 3, 2023. https://www.un.org/en/about-us/universal-declaration-of-human-rights.
Wendling, Mike. (2016). "The Saga of 'Pizzagate': The Fake Story That Shows How Conspiracy Theories Spread." *BBC News*, December 2, sec. BBC Trending. https://www.bbc.com/news/blogs-trending-38156985.

Part III
Film and TV

A Transmission of the Times
HIV/AIDS Conspiracies and Denialism in Historical Dramas

GORDON ALLEY-YOUNG

Introduction

In February 2021 the National Institutes of Health announced plans to study long Covid-19 while *It's a Sin*, about the lives of four gay Londoners at the beginning of the HIV/AIDS crisis, became a hit for HBO Max. As New York's Covid-19 travel restrictions lifted in June 2021, the series *Pose*, set in New York's queer ballroom scene, ended with emcee Pray Tell's death from AIDS related illness. In October 2022 *American Horror Story: NYC* depicted the devastation HIV/AIDS wrought on the gay community in early 1980s New York while the media reported the emergence of new dangerous Covid-19 subvariants. *Pose*, *It's a Sin*, *American Horror Story: NYC* dramatize the lack of answers and fear of the early HIV/AIDS era and speak to the current Covid-19 era.

Using Fiske's (2011) tri-level method, I examine how these programs attempt to balance entertainment with accurately capturing the early HIV/AIDS era including the transmission of conspiracy theories, denial, and misinformation without perpetuating them. Fiske's method examines television programs in terms of three levels that come together to create meaning for viewers. The first level is the program, the second level is the publicity and criticism of the program, and the third is the meanings audiences create from the programs. Using this method can identify how television producer's intended meanings can lead to audiences constructing divergent meanings.

Analysis will examine conspiracy theories within historical period dramas and how the HIV/AIDS and Covid-19 pandemics and related false information speak to a larger socio-cultural context of LGBTQIA+ (Lesbian, Gay, Bisexual, Transgender, Queer, Intersex, Asexual plus) and Black, Indigenous, People of Color (BIPOC) disenfranchisement. Programs will be examined for how they center and decenter the roles of LGBTQIA+, BIPOC, white, and female characters/perspectives and what potential meanings audiences can draw from this. Depictions of the HIV/AIDS and the misinformation, denialism, and HIV/AIDS conspiracy theories will be examined for their potential to inform and misinform audiences and for intertextual connections between HIV/AIDS representations and the recent Covid-19 pandemic. The concluding discussion will reflect on the cultural implication of these representations for public health, societal inclusion, and the potential implications of these representations for the individual and society.

Misinformation, Denialism, and Conspiracy Theories

Misinformation is defined as incorrect, misleading, or unproven information and even individuals not intending to misinform may still undermine public health efforts (Office of the U.S. Surgeon General 2021). For instance, websites promote unproven Covid-19 cures, folk remedies, or so-called immune boosters (e.g., coconut oil, air fresheners, antioxidants, colloidal silver) (Duetch 2020). HIV/AIDS misinformation observed in Sub-Saharan Africa (e.g., sharing space transmits HIV/AIDS, condoms are ineffective) resemble misinformation once commonly accepted in Canada (e.g., HIV/AIDS only affects homosexuals) (Jaffe 2009). Relatedly, denialism involves using elements of established knowledge (e.g., isolated facts, outdated information) to discredit scientific knowledge and using minor disagreements between experts to frame established facts as inconclusive evidence (Kalichman 2014). Denialists have rejected that HIV causes AIDS, citing poverty, drugs, or malnourishment instead (Kalichman 2014) or that Covid-19 vaccines work. The denialist is not a liar but someone who views the world through a reality ungrounded in established facts or a person engaging in a psychological defense strategy (i.e., after a recent HIV diagnosis) (Kalichman 2014).

Conspiracy theories have existed for centuries across political lines, and reject accepted explanations for events/phenomena, instead attributing them to sinister/powerful individuals/organizations working towards some anti-social goal (Anti-Defamation League 2022). Conspiracy theories emerge when people experience anxiety, frustration, massive cultural changes, loss of control or trust, negative health outcomes, and/or hardship often after natural disasters (e.g., pandemics, earthquakes) and societal crises (e.g., recession, war) (Kużelewska and Tomaszuk 2022; Lewandowsky, Jacobs, and Neil 2022; Miani, Hills, and Bangerter 2022; Sivelä 2015). Conspiracy theories are often connected into a larger belief network and thrive when societies lack reliable information and public trust (Heller 2015; Miani, Hills, and Bangerter 2022).

Conspiracy theories are shared by people who believe in and share them with good intentions or by bad actors attempting to sow discord, discredit critics/opponents, or distract from their ineptitude/malintent (Kużelewska and Tomaszuk 2022). Regarding believers with good intentions, research argues that individuals who are Black, Indigenous or Persons of Color (BIPOC) might subscribe more to HIV/AIDS conspiracy theories. In one study, 40 percent of those identifying as American Indian, Alaskan Native or First Nations believed that HIV/AIDS was created by the U.S. government, White people, or Christians (Gilley and Keesee 2007). African Americans who had perceived discrimination were found more likely to endorse the conspiracy theory that HIV/AIDS was created by the U.S. government to eradicate cultural minorities (Bird and Bogart 2005). BIPOC individuals' belief in HIV/AIDS conspiracy theories is influenced by a painful history that includes institutionalized abuse, experimentation, mistreatment, and murder including forced sterilizations, studying untreated illnesses (i.e., the Tuskegee study), forced experiments with chemical/biological agents, and cultural indoctrination (e.g., Native American and Aboriginal residential schools) (Bird and Bogart 2005; Mays, Coles, and Cochran 2012; Nattrass 2013; Oswald 2011; Sivelä 2015). LGBTQIA+ communities experienced damaging pseudo-scientific experiments called sexual orientation change efforts (SOCE) that included insulin comas, lobotomies, electroconvulsive therapy, shocks, antipsychotic drugs, induced vomiting, and chemical castration from the 1950s to the 1970s (Alley-Young 2022; Cobb 2022). Beyond the BIPOC and LGBTQIA+ communities, a representative survey of U.S. adults found that over half believed in at least one medical conspiracy theory (Miani, Hills, and Bangerter 2022).

Bad actors perpetuating conspiracy theories include the KGB who claimed that HIV/AIDS was a U.S. government bioweapon, a claim cited by former South African president Thabo Mbeki (Kramer 2020; Lewandowsky, Jacobs, and Neil 2022; Sivelä 2015). U.S. president Donald Trump claimed Covid-19 was created in a lab in Wuhan, China, and nearly 30 percent of Americans who were surveyed believed this as well (Jaiswal, LoSchiavo, and Perlman 2020). A website falsely claimed that Sacramento County was spreading Covid-19 to sell military-grade masks (Duetch 2020).

Conspiracy theories provide a counter narrative for disenfranchised and marginalized groups who are both blamed for and bearing the brunt of pandemics (Sivelä 2015). Conversely, conspiracy theories can be used to avoid managing a community's controllable HIV/AIDS risk factors (Nattrass 2013) and can reinforce feelings of helplessness and hopelessness (Heller 2015). Conspiracy theories that propagate mistrust in the government are negatively associated with testing (Ford et al. 2013) and can prevent use of available treatments (Shobowale 2021, 225). Some have suggested eschewing the language of HIV/AIDS conspiracy theories for lay/ folk theories or counter knowledge to avoid blaming communities bearing the brunt the pandemic and to acknowledge the personal experiences and histories of discrimination and institutional power at the heart of such theories (Dickinson 2013; Heller 2015; Jaiswal, LoSchiavo, and Perlman 2020).

Methodology: A Protocol for Reading Texts

John Fiske's (2011) method analyzes television on primary, secondary, and tertiary textual levels. Primary texts are read for content, (i.e., pandemics, HIV/AIDS conspiracy theories, denialism, and misinformation) leading this essay to focus on the second episode of *It's a Sin* where actor Ritchie denies the existence of HIV/AIDS and spouts HIV/AIDS conspiracy theories, episodes one through three of season eleven of *American Horror Story: NYC* where Dr. Wells encounters a deer virus and reporter Fran shares an HIV/AIDS conspiracy theory, and the series finale of *Pose* (i.e., season three, episodes seven and eight) that follows Pray Tell's end of life and AIDS related death as primary texts. Primary text analysis considers latent (i.e., symbolic or obscured) and manifest (i.e., readily available or surface level) content for meaning (Krippendorf 2004). Primary content is then read using secondary level texts (i.e., television criticism and publicity). Secondary texts will include popular sources of publicity (e.g., commercials, promos, actor interviews) and criticism (e.g., television reviews and criticism) as well as scholarly writings about conspiracy theories and representing diverse lives. Primary and secondary text content are then read through tertiary texts (i.e., audience discussion/responses). Analysis focuses on how these dramas balance entertainment with accurately capturing the early HIV/AIDS history including HIV/AIDS conspiracy theories, denial, and misinformation without perpetuating them.

It's a Sin: *Rejection, Protection, and the Politics of Trauma*

It's a Sin starts in 1981 as four gay men move to London. Actor Ritchie, teacher Ash, bartender Roscoe, apprentice tailor Collin, and their girlfriend Jill, also an actor, share a flat, The Pink Palace. Ritchie and Collin die from AIDS complications by series' end. Meanwhile the friends navigate romantic and family relationships, homophobic social policies, careers, and the anxiety and lack of HIV/AIDS information. Jill, Ash, and Roscoe band together in activism and in support of their dying friends.

It's a Sin episode two explores HIV/AIDS conspiracy theories, denialism, and misinformation. Roscoe kicks a man out of their gay pub for trying to post HIV/AIDS warnings. Ritchie delivers a monologue denying the existence of HIV/AIDS (i.e., "lies," "a pack of shit," "not true") claiming not to believe as he is not "stupid." Ritchie's denialism, as per Kalichman's (2014) research takes HIV/AIDS facts in isolation and inconsistencies to make HIV/AIDS seem to be theoretically incoherent. Gay cancer is illogical, Ritchie reasons, because cancer does not have a sexual orientation and furthermore, from his understanding, cancer cannot be transmitted. HIV/AIDS was initially called gay cancer because one of the first sign appearing on the gay men who contracted it was Kaposi's Sarcoma, a cancer that manifests as purple lesions on the skin. Ritchie also cites disagreements over transmission through semen or genital friction. Ritchie mentions several HIV/AIDS conspiracy theories (i.e., HIV/AIDS is from space, Russia, or a lab) and previously he tells a small-town sex partner who is nervous that Ritchie is from London that Americans, not Londoners, are the group to avoid, perhaps a reference to the U.S. government bioweapon HIV/AIDS conspiracy theory. Ritchie's denialism frames HIV/AIDS as a moral agenda meant to curtail gay sexuality and he cites conflicting HIV/AIDS conspiracy theories to secure a sexual partner, to support his denialism (i.e., all the HIV/AIDS conspiracy theories cannot be correct), and to reject the shaming and blaming of his gay community as the cause of HIV/AIDS. Conspiracy theories have been shown to provide a counter narrative that allow disenfranchised and marginalized groups to cope with blame when they bear the brunt of an epidemic (Sivelä 2015). As Ritchie's monologue ends, he dances below a neon sign reading *Heaven* to *Do You Want to Funk* recorded by Patrick Cowley and Sylvester, who both died of AIDS related illness.

Jill's friend Gregory subsequently expresses denial, as Kalichman (2014) notes it may be a psychological defense in the recently diagnosed. Gregory shows Jill inconsistencies, asserting, "But I'm getting better, and you don't get better from AIDS, do ya?" and incredulously citing the doctor's questionnaire that asked "have you ever had sex with animals?" and confuses them both. Gregory cements his denial by asserting, "I'm not [...] a slut" and he cites his doctor's initial diagnosis of tuberculosis claiming that he will "shake it off" in a month of sick leave.

Jill's storyline explores misinformation. As she cares for Gregory, they avoid being in the same room to avoid transmission. When Gregory unexpectedly has tea at Jill's flat she cannot sleep until she destroys and discards his tea mug. While getting birth control from her doctor Jill requests HIV/AIDS literature and the doctor asserts twice that HIV/AIDS does not affect her nor him, the implication being that they are both heterosexual. Jill, played by Lydia West, as a Black British woman, would be in a high-risk group for HIV/AIDS (Rutledge 2023). Jill finds one article in the gay press (*HIM Magazine*) and gives Collin money to buy as much HIV/AIDS literature as he can in New York when she can find no information in Britain. *It's a Sin* aired in early 2021 and the lack of HIV/AIDS information in the series comments on the struggles to find accurate and conclusive information during Covid-19 because living in a digital age contains both useful and fallacious information.

It's a Sin is not a history lesson, but audiences treat fictional period dramas this way (Brown 2015; Byrne 2014). Complications arise when the depiction of HIV/AIDS history suggests different realities. For instance, white characters Ritchie and Collin die of AIDS related illnesses, but Ash, Jill, and Roscoe as BIPOC and their communities bear more of the brunt of pandemics like HIV/AIDS and Covid-19 (Fields, Copeland, and Hopkins 2021). Media critic Taylor-Stone (2017) argues that media whitewashing of LGBTQIA+ history replaces the main protagonists who are people of color with conventional white males so that as time passes younger members of LGBTQIA+ community encounter whitewashed media versions of history like the Stonewall riots and the criticisms that the contributions of BIPOC people are missed. Taylor-Stone's (2017) point is well taken as on one *It's a Sin* discussion forum several members praised Randy Shilts (2007) HIV/AIDS history and the film that it inspired but only one respondent that I saw mentioned the fact that Shilts' (2007) work misrepresented a French-Canadian flight attendant as patient zero due to a misreading of a coding method used in a HIV/AIDS study.

Omari Douglas, who portrays Roscoe, notes in an interview that series creator Russell T. Davies initially pitched a longer series that included Roscoe contracting HIV but the network negotiated a shorter series (Bray 2021). Yet *It's a Sin*, by not killing off characters Jill, Ash, and Roscoe, who lovingly care for Ritchie and Collin and are subsequently depicted standing united at protests for better HIV/AIDS care, medicine and research, allows the series to avoid the overused trope of exploiting Black suffering and death (Mowatt 2018). Jill, Ash, and Roscoe appear to be depicted more akin to the Black love, activism, and community (BLAC) model as their activism is grounded in love and community that allows healing and resilience (Turner, Harrell, and Bryant-Davis 2022). Some critics felt that *It's a Sin* was exploitative of LGBTQIA+ suffering and death. During the *It's a Sin* series run, audience members of all generations flooded social media to post their emotional reactions to the series (Kelleher 2021). Mullin (2021) as a critic and a person with HIV argues that this is not what is needed as the protests that *It's a Sin* depicts were also meant to improve representations of persons with AIDS from images of suffering to be pitied to individuals with a voice needing to be heard.

American Horror Story: NYC: *The Death of Innocence and Rise of a Post-Truth Society*

American Horror Story: NYC begins in the early 1980s with NYC's gay community dying from a mystery illness and the Mai Tai killer. Dr. Wells discovers a virus in Fire Island deer which prompts their extermination while also finding increasingly rare illnesses in her gay male patients. Closeted Detective Read, his boyfriend Gino, a journalist, and Adam, whose roommate went missing, track the Mai Tai killer. Fran, a reporter at Gino's LGBTQIA+ newspaper, *The Downtown Native*, tells Dr. Wells that the United States created bio-weaponized ticks to destroy its enemies painfully. Fran argues that escaped ticks are killing the deer and potentially people before Dr. Wells rebukes Fran for spreading a conspiracy theory because it increases the spread of disease and infection rates.

Viewers question the HIV/AIDS and deer connection. Williams (2022) argues that the deer virus storyline is a plot device showing virus discovery. In 1981 Fire Island deer herds were being culled due to overpopulation, thus drawing pro and anti-culling groups into opposition. *American Horror Story: NYC*'s X account denied that the deer have HIV (The AHS Zone 2022) after fans took to social media expressing confusion and questioning the HIV/human/deer connection (Bubp 2022). This deer storyline likely references the monkey to human HIV transmission theory and the recent finding that humans likely infected deer with Covid-19 and now deer could be a potential reservoir for new Covid-19 variants (Feng et al. 2023).

Online audience members have interpreted killing the deer as representing wild innocence lost (Reddit 2022) as HIV/AIDS tempers the liberatory promise of Stonewall. Episode one shows bathhouse singer Kathy Pizazz, played by Patti Lupone, singing a siren song wearing a rhinestone crown resembling antlers as a young man follows a partner into the steam as Big Daddy, a masked representation of HIV/AIDS, looks on; this scene resembles an earlier scene where deer on Fire Island innocently walk towards the guns of a group of shooters. Critics argue that Big Daddy and the Mai Tai killer reflect the serial killer trope common to the *AHS* franchise but here this trope the ever-present threats to the LGBTQIA+ communities (e.g., recent anti-tran/drag/gay legislation) (King 2022). Media critic Huff (2023) observes that "reality can be scarier than any monster, ghoul, or serial killer." Of the potentially exploitive death and torture of gay characters in the series Taylor (2023) seemingly argues that it captures the horror resulting from the lack of help, apathy, anxiety and loneliness of the gay community at the time.

In episode two, Dr. Wells meets Fran in the park to share her bio-weaponized tic HIV/AIDS conspiracy theory. In episode three we see Fran meet Dr. Wells at a diner to convince the doctor that an actual post–World War II event (i.e., Operation Paperclip) also resulted in bio-weaponized tics escaping a government lab and infecting deer and endangering mankind. When the second episode aired on October 19, 2022, one review praising journalist Edward Hooper's book, *The River: A Journey to the Source of HIV and AIDS*, a book that promotes a debunked AIDS origin story (i.e., contaminated polio vaccines) was posted and another one was posted before the end of the series (GoodReads 2022). Between the airing of the second and third episodes a controversial HIV/AIDS denialism documentary, *House of Numbers: Anatomy of an Epidemic*, was reposted online on a documentary sharing website on October 24, 2022 (Leung 2009). These anecdotal examples might have no connection to the series' exploration of an HIV/AIDS conspiracy theory but they represent just a small part of what could be found online as part of the mainstream discourse by audiences as they watched the series. Fran urges Dr. Wells to go to the press, and this leads Dr. Wells to chastise Fran for spreading an HIV/AIDS conspiracy theory. Dr. Wells asserts, "With what? I don't have any proof of anything, and proof is everything. And a study could take years." Dr. Well's comments mark a beginning of a decline of the factual standards for the press, a degradation of standards on full display during both the first Trump presidency and the Covid-19 pandemic, two periods preceding and overlapping with the period of the series' original run where facts and the democratic standards that they support were most in peril.

Fran, who starts working at *The Downtown Native* to represent the lesbian community, likely symbolizes actual writer and HIV/AIDS denialist Neenyah Ostrom. Ostrom wrote for the *New York Native* that the series *American Horror Story: NYC* seems to be depicting in the fictional community newspaper *The Downtown Native* that Gino and later Fran, a conspiracy theorist, write for. Though the paper was among the first to publish HIV/AIDS information, critics cite *New York Native*'s subsequent focus on HIV/AIDS conspiracy theories as central to their downfall (Pogrebin 1997).

Charles L. Ortleb, the publisher of the *New York Native*, allegedly spent $200,000 to promote Ostrom's books that claimed that AIDS is chronic fatigue syndrome (CFS) (Lewin 1993). Ostrom's writings have claimed that HIV/AIDS drugs are toxic and are being foisted upon the Black and gay communities in what she likens to a modern-day Tuskegee Syphilis Experiment (Boswell Book Company 2023). When we look intertextually across texts, Jill in *It's a Sin* asks Collin to get her any American HIV/AIDS literature due to a dearth of information in the UK at the time. So, if the worlds of *It's a Sin* and *American Horror Story: NYC* existed they may have collided as Collin could have potentially provided a copy of the *TDN*, potentially containing an HIV/AIDS conspiracy theory article by Fran.

Pose: Writing LGBTQIA+ BIPOC Lives, Activism, and Success Back

In the 1980s Blanca, an HIV+ and trans Latina and former sex-worker, leaves the drag ball House of Abundance headed by Elektra, an African American transwoman, to form the House of Evangelista. The houses uplift BIPOC LGBTQIA+ youth through drag balls emceed by Pray Tell who is African American and HIV+. Across three seasons, house leadership and memberships shift with Elektra ultimately leaves the House of Abundance which she once led and joins Blanca's house. By the series' end, HIV/AIDS has ravaged the community and Pray Tell is hospitalized where Blanca, a nurse's aide, boyfriend Dr. Christopher, and nurse Judy work. Christopher and Judy advocate to get Blanca and Pray Tell into an HIV/AIDS drug trial. Pray Tell succumbs to AIDS related illness because he gives his trial drugs away. At the end of the series Blanca, now a nurse; Elektra, a businesswoman; and their drag children, now professionals, Lulu, an accountant, and Angel, a wife, mother, and model, both transwomen of color, are depicted as meeting for brunch to celebrate their success.

In the two-part finale, the characters are represented as living full lives of activism and love as opposed to being depicted as dying and marginalized. In episode seven, one of Blanca's white patients, Troy, gets into the drug trial. Blanca learns that only two of eighty people in the trial are BIPOC, so her boyfriend Dr. Christopher and Nurse Judy get Blanca and Pray Tell into the trial. Pray Tell gives his drugs to Ricky, a young African American dancer who is also HIV positive, and because of not having these life-saving drugs, Pray Tell dies shortly after performing one last time at the ball with Blanca.

In episode eight, Blanca Judy, on stage as part of a group of culturally diverse women at an Act Up planning meeting. Later we see video of the actual event where the ashes of those dead from AIDS related illnesses are sprinkled on the mayor's residence grounds interspersed with recreated scenes. Often white males are represented in portrayals of activism in the early HIV/AIDS era which is why having an ethnically diverse group of women leading an Act Up planning meeting is so significant. Activists like Sherman (2021) work to reveal the diversity and tactical sophistication of the organization beyond white media portrayals. Brown (2015) argues that certain period dramas are writing homosexual and hidden lives back into history. With scenes such as this, moreover the whole series, with its unprecedented harnessing of BIPOC and LGBTQIA+ talent both in front of and behind the cameras, is writing hidden lives back into early HIV/AIDS era history. More importantly the series is writing hidden lives into their rightful and necessary places within today's representational industries. HIV/AIDS conspiracy theories are only mentioned in the *Pose* episodes I examine when Blanca is nervous about the drug trial and cites the Tuskegee Experiment and Puerto Rico Birth Control Pill Trials. Later HIV/AIDS conspiracy theories are intimated when, working as a nurse, Blanca reminds a newly diagnosed patient to listen to her doctors and take her meds (i.e., do not listen to HIV/AIDS conspiracy theories and as a result, stop taking your medications). However, the fact that we are discussing writing marginalized lives back into popular history is, if not a result of a conspiracy of silence, or acts of denial of the fact that these lives existed and had impact, then the result of ongoing media misinformation. The question then becomes when does misinformation become something more insidious?

At the brunch where Elektra, Blanca, Lulu, and Angel reflect on their successes, they identify themselves as the anti–*Sex in the City* as the series reflected a wealthy white world seemingly devoid of BIPOC people. Duckels (2023) praises *Pose* for avoiding the exploitation of Black suffering and argues that it uses "cliché and excess along with real-life events to transcend racist and transphobic stereotypes" (126). The excess and success that *Pose*'s protagonists are shown achieving by series' end is within the realm of possibility given the attention that some of the queer ball scene's stars like Willi Ninja achieved because of *Paris Is Burning,* an early and controversial documentary about ballroom (Livingston 1990). Blanca is prophetic in noting that she does not believe in happy endings as those only happen in the movies, but she believes in happy moments that last an indeterminate amount of time and do not mean that everything bad is in the past. This both tempers the celebration of their success with reality, and it speaks to the current era in which the series airs and reminds viewers of the increasing changes faced by BIPOC and LGBTQIA+ communities (e.g., Covid-19, anti-gay/anti-trans/anti-drag bills and legislation).

Michaela Jaé Rodriguez, who portrays Blanca, after being the first trans actor to win a Golden Globe for her work on *Pose*, called out the *New York Times* for their transphobic behavior that she refers to as "constant disrespect" (Bergeson 2023). Other period dramas like Ryan Murphy's (also the creator of *Pose* and *American Horror Story: NYC*) *Hollywood* have written marginalized characters back in a way that exceeds what was possible at that time to rewrite our classist, racist, and homophobic social history (Alley-Young 2020). Blanca's activism is grounded in loving relationships and a community orientation to uplifting BIPOC and LGBTQIA+ youth through her belonging to the community of BIPOC and LGBTQIA+ people who walk and vogue in the ballroom scene, a community sustains her mental health in line with the Black love, activism, and community (BLAC) model (Turner, Harrell, and Bryant-Davis 2022). This model posits that Black activism is inspired and sustained by love and community and that resilience and healing for Black activists center on the four domains of relationships, spirituality, identity, and active expression. This model also affirms that one is loved by God and Blanca's church, also her source of expression and key to her identity as a house mother, is the ballroom as affirmed by Dr. Christopher who shares his first impression of ballroom with Pray Tell in episode seven, saying, "I didn't know what to expect, but it kind of reminded me of church. The costumes, theatrics, worshiping. I'm into it" and Dr. Christopher refers to those who walk ballroom as performing "ministry."

Discussion and Future Directions

It's a Sin, *American Horror Story: NYC*, and *Pose* were never meant to be taken as historical documents but research shows that audiences read them this way so media producers must get it right. This means providing a period drama grounded in verisimilitude, that is actively inclusive of the diverse voices of those whose lives are chronicled, where possible, and one that prepares audiences with some of the information that will keep them safe from conspiracy theories rather than just showing characters like Jill in *It's a Sin* seeking out their own information. Cook (2018) promotes inoculation theory, or pre-emptively telling people they might be misinformed and providing them with counterarguments to combat this misinformation. Just as everyone's experiences of Covid-19 were different depending on their risk factors, so too must media inoculation messages be tailored to different audiences. *Pose* speaks to this approach when we see how Blanca reaches a recently diagnosed transwoman who is a sex-worker because Blanca also shares she was once a sex-worker.

Hoyt et al. (2011) argue that different groups' mistrust might be inspired by different cultural histories, thus requiring that different intervention methods be created and tested. Similarly, Jaiswal, LoSchiavo, and Perlman (2020) argue that anti-racism education as well as training on research with and care for marginalized populations, be integrated into public health and medical education. Research tells us that social inequality/maltreatment, especially during immigration, can impact people adopting HIV/AIDS conspiracy theories (Ford et al. 2013). This is important to remember as we have failed to provide sustainable and equitable solutions to the international migration crisis, a crisis heightened by Covid-19 and its ongoing and varying outcomes.

The three series emphasize the value of good and accessible information. The educationally and economically disadvantaged groups most affected by HIV are the least equipped to critically evaluate online information (i.e., lower literacy levels, poorer reading comprehension) (Benotsch, Kalichman, and Weinhardt 2004). This is also true of the Covid-19 pandemic. Online HIV-related searches are laden with problematic information, but the highest quality information is often hard for a non-scientific audience to comprehend, and research shows that people living with HIV often cannot effectively distinguish quality from problematic information (Kalichman 2014). This suggests that we need to explore solutions such as partnering with public opinion leaders to transmit clear messaging while considering the idea of penalizing the spread of false information on social media (Shobowale 2021). Others have suggested a journalistic reliability scale for online news content (Duetch 2020). Heller (2015) argues that understanding a group's HIV/AIDS conspiracy theories, what he calls counter knowledge to avoid stigmatizing the people who hold them as ignorant, can help reveal their anxieties and this understanding can form the foundation for greater cooperation and trust between marginalized communities and the white gay community and public health institutions (Heller 2015). Popular cultural representations that emphasize the accomplishment of such cross-cultural cooperative partnerships would likely bolster such work.

Airing three HIV/AIDS period histories in close succession suggests a desire to relate to and learn lessons for dealing with Covid-19 from a past pandemic. This also suggests the popular belief that we are living in a post–HIV/AIDS age now we have antiretroviral drugs and an effective pre-exposure prophylaxis. Yet worldwide 39 million people are infected with HIV+ and an estimated 630,000 people died from AIDS complications in 2022 (World Health Organization 2024). Most of this devastation occurs outside of the West so it does not register with our popular cultural imagination. Covid-19 teaches us the risks of relegating any pandemic to the past. The issue of virus mutation aside, the conspiracy theories accompanying a pandemic, especially in a digital information age, can weaken the bonds of our societies and compromise the authority of our public institutions. Some characterize conspiracy theories as wars over meaning (Fassin 2012) while others cite the example of Covid-19 conspiracy theories spreading quickly on social media as exemplifying one of the single greatest threats to democracy (Kużelewska and Tomaszuk 2022). Creators of HIV/AIDS period dramas must recognize the unintended consequences of their work to perpetuate, reactivate and/or to continue circulating misinformation, denial and conspiracy theories and in so doing to call the authority of pro-social information agencies and authorities into question. Audiences perceiving period dramas as period fact is not a new phenomenon. However, in our digital world of unlimited online information, declining traditional news media, and incomplete/ineffectual information vetting, the stakes of where audiences source their health and/or historical facts from are considerably higher for both the individual and for greater society.

REFERENCES

The AHS Zone (@AHSZone). (2022). "The deer never had AIDS. Deer cannot carry or transmit HIV. There was a line in the finale stating they were infected with Lyme, but the necrotic lesions [...]." Twitter, December 16, 8:32 p.m. https://twitter.com/ahszone/status/1603926129819123712?lang=en.

Alley-Young, Gordon. (2020). "A Place to Call Home by Bevan Lee." [Review of the television series] *The Popular Culture Studies Journal* 8 (2): 279–282. https://www.mpcaaca.org/_files/ugd/5a6d69_35d1ba9a0e434005b02678e62d5c75c1.pdf?index=true.

Alley-Young, Gordon. (2022). "Bitter Living Through Science: Melodramatic and Moral Readings of Gay Conversion Therapy in A Place to Call Home." In *Diagnosing History: Medicine in Television Period Drama*, edited by Katherine Byrne, Julie Anne Taddeo, and James Leggott, 260–76. Manchester: Manchester University Press.

Anti-Defamation League. (2022). "Conspiracy Theories and How to Help Family and Friends Who Believe Them." August 23. https://www.adl.org/conspiracy-theories.

Benotsch, Eric G., Seth Kalichman, and Lance S. Weinhardt. (2004). "HIV-AIDS Patients' Evaluation of Health Information on the Internet: The Digital Divide and Vulnerability to Fraudulent Claims." *Journal of Consulting and Clinical Psychology* 72 (6): 1004–11. doi:10.1037/0022-006X.72.6.1004.

Bergeson, Samantha. (2023). "Michaela Jaé Rodriguez Calls New York Times a 'Transphobic' Publication: It's 'Constant Disrespect.'" *IndieWire*, March 31. https://www.indiewire.com/features/general/michaela-jae-rodriguez-calls-new-york-times-transphobic-1234824793/.

Bird, Sheryl Thorburn, and Laura M. Bogart. (2005). "Conspiracy Beliefs About HIV/AIDS and Birth Control Among African Americans: Implications for the Prevention of HIV, Other STIs, and Unintended Pregnancy." *Journal of Social Issues* 61 (1): 109–26. doi:10.1111/j.0022-4537.2005.00396.x.

Boswell Book Company. (2023). "The Real AIDS Epidemic: How the Tragic HIV Mistake Threatens Us All (Hardcover)." Accessed December 31, 2023. https://www.boswellbooks.com/book/9781510776715.

Bray, Abbie. (2021). "It's A Sin Creator Shares Heartbreaking Roscoe Storyline Cut from Show." *Metro UK*, June 2. https://metro.co.uk/2021/02/27/its-a-sin-creator-shares-heartbreaking-roscoe-storyline-cut-from-show-14157157/.

Part III: Film and TV

Brown, Lucy. "Homosexual Lives: Representation and Reinterpretation in Upstairs, Downstairs and Downton Abbey." In *Upstairs and Downstairs: British Costume Drama Television from The Forsyte Saga to Downton Abbey*, edited by James Leggott and Julie Anne Taddeo, 263–74. Lanham, MD: Rowman & Littlefield, 2015.

Bubp, Ashley. (2022). "American Horror Story: NYC Fans Are Already Confused by the Deer Storyline." *Looper*, October 20. https://www.looper.com/1064273/ahs-nyc-fans-are-already-confused-by-the-deer-storyline/.

Byrne, Kathleen. (2014). "Adapting Heritage: Class and Conservatism in *Downton Abbey*." *Rethinking History* 18 (3): 311–27. doi: 10.1080/13642529.2013.811811.

Cobb, Kayla. (2022). "'American Horror Story: NYC': 5 Things You Missed in Episodes 3 and 4." *Decider*, October 27. https://decider.com/2022/10/27/american-horror-story-nyc-episodes-3-and-4-cat-scratch-fever/.

Cook, John. (2018). "The Antidote to Fake News Is a Little Bit of Fake News." *Weber: The Contemporary West* 34 (2): 36–38. https://issuu.com/weberjournal/docs/spring_2018_book_for_web.

Deutch, Gabby. (2020). "How Misinformation Pays." *Newsweek* 174 (10): 18–19.

Dickinson, David. (2013). "Myths or Theories? Alternative Beliefs about HIV and AIDS in South African Working Class Communities." *African Journal of AIDS Research (AJAR)* 12 (3): 121–30. doi:10.2989/16085906.2013.863212.

Duckels, Gabriel. (2022). "AIDS Melodrama Now: Queer Tears in It's a Sin and Pose." *European Journal of Cultural Studies* 26 (July): 122–28. doi:10.1177/13675494221097134.

Fassin, Didier. (2021). "Of Plots and Men: The Heuristics of Conspiracy Theories." *Current Anthropology* 62 (2): 128–37. doi:10.1086/713820.

Feng, Aijing, Sarah Bevins, Jeff Chandler, Thomas J. DeLiberto, Ria Ghai, Kristina Lantz, Julianna Lenoch, et al. (2023). "Transmission of SARS-CoV-2 in Free-Ranging White-Tailed Deer in the United States." *Nature Communications* 14 (1): 4078. doi:10.1038/s41467-023-39782-x.

Fields, Errol L., Raniyah Copeland, and Ernest Hopkins. (2021). "Same Script, Different Viruses: HIV and COVID-19 in US Black Communities." *Lancet* 397 (10279): 1040–42. doi:10.1016/S0140-6736(20)32522-8.

Fiske, John. (2011). *Television Culture*. 2nd ed. New York: Routledge.

Ford, Chandra L., Steven P. Wallace, Peter A. Newman, Sung-Jae Lee, and William E. Cunningham. (2013). "Belief in AIDS-Related Conspiracy Theories and Mistrust in the Government: Relationship with HIV Testing among at-Risk Older Adults." *The Gerontologist* 53 (6): 973–84. doi:10.1093/geront/gns192.

Gilley, Brian Joseph, and Marguerite Keesee. (2007). "Linking 'White Oppression' and HIV/AIDS in American Indian Etiology: Conspiracy Beliefs among AI MSMs and Their Peers." *American Indian & Alaska Native Mental Health Research: The Journal of the National Center* 14 (1): 44–62. doi:10.5820/aian.1401.2007.48.

GoodReads. (2022). "The River: A Journey to the Source of HIV and AIDS." Accessed December 21, 2023. https://www.goodreads.com/en/book/show/1159147.

Heller, Jacob. (2015). "Rumors and Realities: Making Sense of HIV/AIDS Conspiracy Narratives and Contemporary Legends." *American Journal of Public Health* 105 (1): e43–50. D oi:10.2105/AJPH.2014.302284.

Hoyt, Michael A., Lisa R. Rubin, Carol J. Nemeroff, Joyce Lee, David M. Huebner, and Rae Jean Proeschold-Bell. (2012). "HIV/AIDS-Related Institutional Mistrust Among Multiethnic Men Who Have Sex with Men: Effects on HIV Testing and Risk Behaviors." *Health Psychology* 31 (3): 269–77. doi:10.1037/a0025953.

Huff, Lauren. (2022). "American Horror Story: NYC Finally Reveals Big Daddy's Identity in Devastating Finale." *Entertainment Weekly*, November 16. https://ew.com/tv/american-horror-story-nyc-big-daddy-reveal-finale-explained/.

Jaffe, Gita. (2009). "Bringing HIV and AIDS Awareness Home." *Education Canada* 49 (3): 22–25. https://www.edcan.ca/wp-content/uploads/EdCan-2009-v49-n3-Jaffe.pdf.

Jaiswal, J., C. LoSchiavo, and D.C. Perlman. (2020). "Disinformation, Misinformation and Inequality-Driven Mistrust in the Time of COVID-19: Lessons Unlearned from AIDS Denialism." *AIDS & Behavior* 24 (10): 2776–80. doi: 10.1007/s10461-020-02925-y.

Johnson, Brian, D. (2019). "How a Typo Created a Scapegoat for the AIDS Epidemic." *Maclean's*, April 17. https://macleans.ca/culture/movies/how-a-typo-created-a-scapegoat-for-the-aids-epidemic/.

Kalichman, Seth C. (2014). "The Psychology of AIDS Denialism: Pseudoscience, Conspiracy Thinking, and Medical Mistrust." *European Psychologist* 19 (1): 13–22. doi:10.1027/1016-9040/a000175.

Kelleher, Patrick. (2021). "It's a Sin Leaves Queer People in Tears—and Brings Back Painful Memories of the Worst Years of the AIDS Epidemic." *PinkNews*, Jan 23. https://www.thepinknews.com/2021/01/23/its-a-sin-russell-t-davies-olly-alexander-twitter-reaction-fans-channel-4/.

Kramer, Mark. (2020). "Lessons From Operation 'Denver,' the KGB's Massive AIDS Disinformation Campaign." *The MIT Press Reader*, May 26. https://thereader.mitpress.mit.edu/operation-denver-kgb-aids-disinformation-campaign/.

Krippendorff, Klaus. (2004). *Content Analysis: An Introduction to Its Methodology*. 2nd ed. Newbury Park: Sage.

Kużelewska, Elżbieta, and Mariusz Tomaszuk. (2022). "Rise of Conspiracy Theories in the Pandemic Times." *International Journal for the Semiotics of Law = Revue Internationale de Sémiotique Juridique* 35 (6): 2373–89. doi:10.1007/s11196-022-09910-9.

Leung, Brian, dir. (2009). *House of Numbers: Anatomy of an Epidemic*. Rocky Mountain Pictures. Accessed December 10, 2023. https://www.documentarytube.com/videos/house-of-numbers/.

Lewandowsky, Stephan, Peter Jacobs, and Stuart Neil. (2022). "Conspiracy Theories Made It Harder for Scientists to Seek the Truth." *Scientific American* 326 (3): 72–77. https://www.scientificamerican.com/article/the-lab-leak-hypothesis-made-it-harder-for-scientists-to-seek-the-truth/.

Lewin, Jonathan A. (1993). "Publisher Alleges AIDS Hoax: Spends $200,000 to Publicize Book About Conspiracy Claims." *The Harvard Crimson*, October 29. https://www.thecrimson.com/article/1993/10/29/publisher-alleges-aids-hoax-pa-new/.

Livingston, Jennie. (1990). *Paris Is Burning*. Off White Productions, Inc.

Mays, Vickie M., Courtney N. Coles, and Susan D. Cochran. (2012). "Is There a Legacy of the U.S. Public Health Syphilis Study at Tuskegee in HIV/AIDS-Related Beliefs Among Heterosexual African Americans and Latinos?" *Ethics & Behavior* 22 (6): 461–471. doi:10.1080/10508422.2012.730805.

Miani, Alessandro, Thomas Hills, and Adrian Bangerter. (2022). "Interconnectedness and (in)Coherence as a Signature of Conspiracy Worldviews." *Science Advances* 8 (43): 1–9. https://www.science.org/doi/full/10.1126/sciadv.abq3668.

Mowatt, Rasul A. (2018). "Black Lives as Snuff: The Silent Complicity in Viewing Black Death." *Biography: An Interdisciplinary Quarterly* 41 (4): 777–806. doi: 10.1353/bio.2018.0079.

Mullin, Brian. (2021). "It's A Sin Brings Viewers to Tears—But AIDS Activists Never Wanted Pity." *Them*, March 4. https://www.them.us/story/its-a-sin-aids-activists-essay.

Office of the U.S. Surgeon General. *Confronting Health Misinformation: The U.S. Surgeon General's Advisory on Building a Healthy Information Environment*, 2021. Washington, D.C.: U.S. Department of Health and Human Services. https://www.hhs.gov/sites/default/files/surgeon-general-misinformation-advisory.pdf.

Oswald, Alina. (2011). "A Look Back at 30 Years of AIDS and AIDS Conspiracy Theories." *Out in Jersey* 17 (1): 10–11.

Pogrebin, Robin. (1997). "Controversial Gay Magazine Shuts Down." *New York Times*, January 9. https://www.nytimes.com/1997/01/09/nyregion/controversial-gay-magazine-shuts-down.html.

Reddit Inc. (2022). "SPOILER: The Deer on Fire Island are a Metaphor for Wild Innocence Lost." Accessed December 31, 2023. https://www.reddit.com/r/AmericanHorrorStory/comments/y9hsrp/spoiler_the_deer_on_fire_island_are_a_metaphor/.

Rutledge, Jaleah D. (2023). "Exploring the Role of Empowerment in Black Women's HIV and AIDS Activism in the United States: An Integrative Literature Review." *American Journal of Community Psychology* 71 (3/4): 491–506. doi:10.1002/ajcp.12644.

Schulman, Sarah. (2021). *Let the Record Show: A Political History of ACT UP New York, 1987–1993.* New York, Farrar, Straus and Giroux.
Shilts, Randy. (2007). *And the Band Played On.* 20th ed. New York: St. Martin's Press.
Shobowale, Oluwakemi. (2021). "A Systematic Review of the Spread of Information during Pandemics: A Case of the 2020 COVID-19 Virus." *Journal of African Media Studies* 13 (2): 221–34. doi:10.1386/jams_00045_1.
Sivelä, Jonas Samuel. (2015). "Silence, Blame and AIDS Conspiracy Theories Among the Xhosa People in Two Townships in Cape Town." *African Journal of AIDS Research (AJAR)* 14 (1): 43–50. doi:10.2989/16085906.2015.1016984.
Taylor, Reece. (2023). "American Horror Story: NYC Was Exploitative—and That Was the Point." *CBR*, March 20. https://www.cbr.com/american-horror-story-nyc-exploitative/.
Taylor-Stone, Chardine. (2017). "Whitewashing Our History." *Diva*, February, 44–4.
Turner, Erlanger A., Shelly P. Harrell, and Thema Bryant-Davis. "Black Love, Activism, and Community (BLAC): The BLAC Model of Healing and Resilience." *Journal of Black Psychology*, 48, no. 3–4 (May 2022): 547–68. doi:10.1177/00957984211018364.
Williams, Jordan. (2022). "What's Up with the Deer in American Horror Story: NYC?" *Screen Rant*, October 22. https://screenrant.com/american-horror-story-season-11-nyc-deer-fire-island/#:~:text=Hannah%20Wells%20(Billie%20Lourd)%20tests,if%20it%20 hasn't%20already.
World Health Organization. (2024). "People Living with HIV." Accessed December 30, 2024. https://www.who.int/data/gho/data/themes/hiv-aids#:~:text=Global%20 situation%20and%20trends%3A,people%20have%20died%20of%20HIV.

Gendered Extremism and Horror Cinema
Immersive Depictions of Far-Right Radicalization in Soft & Quiet

TARA HEIMBERGER

Introduction

Within the horror genre, the dynamic interplay between victim and villain has been a recurrent theme, exploring multifaceted manifestations of evil while employing traditional sequencing and montage techniques to maintain a narrative distance from the horrors depicted on screen. However, Beth de Araujo disrupts this paradigm in her debut film *Soft & Quiet*, employing an innovative long-take style that renders the spectator helplessly complicit for the entire 91-minute run time as they bear witness to a group of female white nationalists radicalizing one another to a home invasion, to assault, and eventually murder. This cinematic strategy engenders a novel experience of horror that the *New York Times* aptly characterizes as "distressingly immersive" in its portrayal of realistic violence and the threat of white nationalism.

The long-take methodology eradicates any discernible demarcation between reality and its cinematic representation, intensifying the phenomenological and immersive nature of the physical and sexual violence displayed on the screen. de Araujo's narrative extends beyond the realm of cinematic analysis to encompass the contemporary socio-cultural landscape, with a specific focus on the alt-right "TradWife" movement and the weaponization of white female victimhood, as exemplified by the Central Park Birdwatching Incident of 2020, which inspired the concept of the film (Sarachan 2022). In this exploration of the relationship between extended scenes of violence and the ethics of spectatorship, de Araujo adeptly unfolds a narrative that realistically exposes the insidious undercurrents of "soft" and "quiet" white nationalism among suburban white women in the United States. This essay seeks to contextualize the ideological implications embedded in *Soft & Quiet* by investigating the socio-cultural backdrop of the women of the alt-right in the 2020s.

The Alt-Right and the Internet

In recent years, the political landscape has witnessed the emergence and proliferation of various ideological movements, reshaping the traditional contours of the political spectrum. Among these, the Alternative Right, often abbreviated as the alt-right and used interchangeably with far-right, has garnered significant attention for its white supremacist ideologies and recruitment via digital platforms. Understanding the alt-right necessitates a nuanced exploration of its defining characteristics, ideological underpinnings, and place within the broader political spectrum. The distinction between the far right and conservative spectrum "is not meant to disregard potential overlaps between conservatism and the far right—that boundary has become increasingly blurred through the recent mainstreaming of far-right ideas into conservatism since Donald Trump's rise—but rather to identify that the far right is fundamentally and overtly supremacist in its dehumanization efforts" (Leidig 2023, 2). In an interview with American neo–Nazi and white supremacist Richard Spencer, Canadian YouTuber and far-right influencer Lauren Chen categorizes the alt-right into four specific tiers of increasing extremism. Those who fall under Tier 1 are described as Western Nationalists who are "pro–Western" but not necessarily "pro-white." Those who fall under Tier 2 are pro-white Nationalists who believe in "white pride." Those who fall under Tier 3 believe in racial homogeny and determinism. Lastly, those under Tier 4 believe in white supremacy and antisemitism. A comprehensive overview and close examination of the intersections of gender and far-right ideology in the digital age, Eviane Leidig's book *The Women of the Far Right: Social Media Influencers and Online Radicalization* classifies the alt-right "as a *reactionary* movement, with the core of this reaction as the reproduction of far-right ideology ... [which] includes three elements: nativism, extreme nationalism, and authoritarianism" (2023, 23–24). This reproduction of far-right ideologies is facilitated on the internet, with the most notable and long-lasting being the American neo–Nazi website Stormfront.org, which was founded in 1996. The website remains active and features a women-centric bulletin board called "The Women's Forum: Sugar, Spice, and Everything Nice." The board features shopping, fashion, parenting, current events, and recruitment threads. Though it seems this particular forum is not as active as others on the site, with most posts or replies being as recent as 2022, there are still a few posts as recent as this year (2024). Online platforms such as these remain crucial to alt-right groups for spreading propaganda and networking with other extreme conservatives. Leidig emphasizes the role of digital platforms in radicalization, stating, "Far-right supporters don't dramatically adopt far-right views overnight. The process of radicalization and recruitment (or vice versa) into far-right movements often happens incrementally" (2023, 45). In the 2010s, social media spaces became a more mainstream opportunity to disseminate white supremacist ideology and propaganda, particularly visual-based platforms such as Instagram, YouTube, and Facebook. Later, TikTok would serve a similar purpose in the popularization of the Tradwife movement, as women of the alt-right found these platforms to be influential in their goal of "rebranding" perceptions of supremacist ideologies. By blending lifestyle choices such as homeschooling, homesteading, fashion, and cooking recipes, with subtle political messaging, alt-right Tradwives are able to disseminate their ideologies and enact this "rebranding" as a means of recruitment under the guise of connecting with fellow women.

The "Soft" and "Quiet" Rebranding of Women in the Alt-Right

The title of de Araujo's film, *Soft & Quiet*, stems from the methodology enacted by the main character, kindergarten teacher Emily, and her approach to spreading white supremacist ideology. The far-right women play a key role in "normalizing and legitimizing far-right ideology for mainstream appeal" (Leidig 2023, 3). When the press mentions or shows images of the alt-right, there is an automatic assumption that the group is predominantly male, which disregards the fact that some of these men have wives who support and propagate the same ideals. Beth de Araujo sought to subvert this stereotypical notion of those in the alt-right entirely by depicting the more insidious and realistic nature of white supremacy, through the female lens. Women who subscribe to this ideology have been intentionally "rebranding" (a term used by de Araujo) white supremacy for years, crafting an image of intelligence and palatability to spread their agenda. This form of white nationalism is described by Emily early in the film during the women's first meeting of the "Daughters for Aryan Unity." She states, "We are the best secret weapon that no one checks at the door because we tread quietly" (de Araujo 2022). They intend to radicalize through the softness of traditional gender roles, and quietly following expectations of femininity. Though the characters in the film are not influencers, they still use an internet forum to find one another and conduct this meeting, which begins the chain of events that leads to the violence depicted in the film. Emily as the leader, can thus be seen as a type of influencer, with her goal of creating a children's book rife with white supremacist ideologies and forming the "Daughters of Aryan Unity."

In *Soft & Quiet*, the unyielding manifestation of prejudiced ideologies becomes palpable in the first assembly of the "Daughters of Aryan Unity." Within this setting, the women's motivations for joining unveil a shared foundation of victimization. Emily, the group's organizer, prompts the women to divulge their reasons for affiliating with the organization, often encouraging them when they use outright hate speech and slurs. Marjorie, initially reticent until encouraged by Emily, attributes her perceived professional setback to concepts like "diversity," and "inclusion." Jessica, whose familial ties include her father's role as a KKK chapter president, professes a commitment to recruitment and to "talk common sense." Kim, a mother and store owner, attends in pursuit of homeschooling materials, aiming to shield her children from perceived indoctrination in public schools. Leslie, emerging as the group's instigator and the most violent, seeks community and guidance following her release from prison. As de Araujo guides the audience through this diverse array of rationales, a microcosm of radicalization unfolds, illustrating the women's progression from hate speech to murder over the course of a single evening. The inaugural meeting strategically delineates community action items, encompassing "Matchmaking," "Recruitment," and a "Newsletter" which Emily describes as "soft on the outside, so vigorous ideas can be digested more easily" (de Araujo 2022).

Tradwives: Networked Intimacy and Traditional Ideologies

de Araujo's choice to represent white nationalism in this manner is rooted in a contemporary right-wing movement called the TradWife movement. Leidig states that "far-right women hence see the opportunity to be involved in trad culture because it seemingly lacks any political ideology," but the movement can serve as an insidious vehicle for white supremacist ideology to be commodified and spread (2023, 100). In their article "Tradwives: The Housewives Commodifying Right-Wing Ideology," Sophia Sykes and Dr. Veronica Hopner investigate the phenomenon of the "Tradwife" movement, which they define as "an influential online community of right-wing women who espouse a highly traditional heteronormative rendition of the 'wife and mother' role that is equal parts ideology and aesthetic" (Sykes & Hopner 2023). Although this movement does have ties to alt-right-wing beliefs, not all who adopt the TradWife lifestyle are affiliated with extremist ideologies. In their study, Sykes and Hopner found that there are three right-wing positions in the "TradWife Landscape," the "Conservative Right Tradwives," the "Alt-Lite Tradwifes," and the "Alt-Right Tradwives." The Conservative Right Tradwives "advocate for a #Tradlife within the home, supporting their husbands and children ... [with] clear conservative values on politics and religion, but, on the whole, did not overtly engage with issues of race" (Sykes & Hopner 2023). The Alt-Lite Tradwives, acting as a bridge of radicalization to the alt-right, often project "the continuation of Eurocentric culture, as opposed to the continuation of the white race," a key ideological belief of the alt-right (Sykes & Hopner 2023). The researchers consider how these women not only embody traditional gender roles but also how some within the movement leverage social media and online platforms to commodify and disseminate right-wing beliefs, which are often rooted in white supremacist ideologies. The Alt-Right Tradwives present "an ideological online personal rooted in Alt-Right identities which enshrined value systems such as white supremacy, heteropatriarchy, and anti-feminism" (Sykes & Hopner 2023). These women are often conventionally attractive, college-educated white women who depict a sophisticated and meek demeanor in order to present "a softer and more palatable voice for right-wing ideology" (Sykes & Hopner 2023).

Women in the TradWife movement are meant to "preserve" a traditionally conservative lifestyle, and they do this by spreading their agenda as softly as possible, either through their roles as teachers, nurses, or other public-facing roles, most often through their roles as mothers. Sykes and Hopner analyze the intersection of domesticity, gender norms, and political ideology within the context of the Tradwife movement, highlighting how these women contribute to the propagation and popularization of right-wing ideas, blurring the lines between personal lifestyle choices and political engagement, most often through visual social media platforms such as TikTok or Instagram. They found that the movement is "rooted in a perceived decline of patriarchy and the undermining of the imperative role of women within the family unit" and that these Tradwife influencers "used commodification to encourage societal reinvigoration of conservative religious and fundamental heteronormative values of sex and gender" (Sykes & Hopner 2023). Sykes and Hopner conclude their study with the implications of this commodification, stating that Tradwives use "their position of influence to perpetuate contentious perspectives on wifely submission, abortion rights, birth control, racism, and the LGBTQIA+ community ... actively contribut[ing] to societal shifts towards more conservative, more traditional living." In its most extreme manifestation, "Tradwife culture commodifies the politics of division and intolerance that inevitably threatens social cohesion," further contributing to the fracturing of society (Sykes & Hopner 2023). This fracturing of society is epitomized through the January 6 insurrection on the United States Capitol Building, a historic event and riot in which the extreme manifestation of the radicalization to violence pipeline facilitated by social media came to fruition.

Mediation, Conspiracy, and Radicalization

Dr. Jenny Gunn's article "Theorising Digital Self-Mediation and the Smartphone as Filmic Apparatus after 6 January 2021" discusses the significance of the insurrection not only politically but also in terms of media history and visual culture studies due to its highly mediated nature. Gunn emphasizes the pervasive use of smartphone cameras by participants in documenting the storming of the Capitol, which has led to ongoing identification and arrests by the FBI. The article argues that the event provides a thorough document of smartphone usage as a filmic apparatus, blurring the lines between objective and subjective modes of mediation. She states, "This elaboration is necessary to understand participation in the storming of the Capitol as a simultaneously lived and mediated experience" (Gunn 2021). The spectatorial experience of the insurrection in witnessing the escalation of violence is similar to what is represented in de Araujo's *Soft & Quiet*. As more and more insurrectionists documented and even live-streamed the event, the sheer scale of right-wing radicalization becomes evidentiary of how quickly and easily these ideologies can be disseminated and turned to action. Gunn suggests that the hyper-mediated nature of the insurrection, facilitated by smartphones, contributes to the fragmentation of consensus and the proliferation of conspiracy theories in contemporary media and politics. Although the insurrectionists are typically presented as the same stereotypical demographic as the alt-right, white cisgender heterosexual men, the "martyr" and face of the insurrection is part of a demographic often underrepresented in the media as being a key figure in the far-right, a woman.

Ashli Babbitt, an avid Donald Trump supporter, was killed during the insurrection on the United States Capitol on January 6, 2021. According to Michael Biesecker, an investigative reporter for the Associated Press, "Babbitt, 35, was fatally shot while attempting to climb through the broken window of a barricaded door leading to the Speaker's Lobby inside the Capitol, where police officers were evacuating members of Congress from the mob supporting Trump's false claim that the 2020 presidential election was stolen." Prior to the insurrection, Babbitt was a known conspiracy theorist, with her social media accounts consistently referencing QAnon, "which centers on the baseless belief that Trump has secretly battled deep-state enemies and a cabal of Satan-worshiping cannibals that includes prominent Democrats who operate a sex trafficking ring" (Biesecker 2022). Babbitt has since become a martyr and symbol of resistance of the alt-right and white supremacy groups, with the white supremacist National Partisan Movement Telegram channel posting a memorial image of Babbit's face along with the phrase "Rest in White Power." The police officer who shot Ashli Babbitt was cleared of any wrongdoing, yet she remains a symbol of the alt-right's worst fears, a confirmation of their conspiracy of an all-powerful leftist cabal who seek to silence the alt-right. Although Babbitt's violent actions in the insurrection seem to defy the "soft" and "quiet" depictions of female members of the alt-right, the martyring of Babbitt does emblemize the growing prevalence and role of women in these more radicalized groups. The manner in which her likeness and presence on social media is now being used as both a recruitment tool and means to farm outrage upholds the idea of white women in particular being used as the "new" and "rebranded" image of the alt-right. The alt-right's weaponization of Babbitt as a symbol of injustice indicates their perceived victimhood and feelings of injustice, particularly white female victimhood, with some Telegram users referring to her as "the white man's George Floyd," a clear erasure of the prevalence of police violence against people of color. The year 2020 witnessed heightened media scrutiny surrounding the calculated deployment of white female victimhood, which sets the sociopolitical context for figures like Ashli Babbitt to rise to prominence in the alt-right in the years following. This focus was particularly pronounced in the emergence of a viral trend documenting white women needlessly calling law enforcement on people of color, notably initiated by the Central Park Birdwatching Incident (Jerkins 2023).

Weaponizing White Female Victimhood

The conception of *Soft & Quiet* occurred during the 2020 global pandemic, and de Araujo cites the Central Park Birdwatching Incident of 2020 as the direct inspiration for the characters depicted in the film. She refers to the incident involving Amy Cooper and Christian Cooper (no relation), which gained widespread attention in May 2020. Christian

Cooper, a Black man and avid birdwatcher, asked Amy Cooper, a white woman, to leash her dog in an area of Central Park where it was required. When she refused, he began recording the encounter. Amy then called the police and falsely claimed that a Black man was threatening her life, a move widely criticized as an example of racial profiling and a potentially dangerous escalation, especially in the context of the national reckoning with the murder of George Floyd by police. As described in an article for *The Guardian*, reporter Morgan Jerkins outlines the danger and intentionality of weaponized white victimhood, stating, "In that instant, a white woman made a false accusation that could have led to his death. She knew the stakes, which is why she feigned hysteria on the phone with the cops. Christian Cooper knew the stakes too." The incident sparked discussions about racism, false accusations, and the misuse of emergency services, leading to Amy Cooper facing consequences such as losing her job and facing public backlash. In an interview with *Fangoria*, de Araujo says the film "came from [her] greatest fears and nightmares" and the incident "reminded [her] of someone that I have encountered in my life. A surge of emotion took over and [she] just started frantically writing" (Bernstein 2022). Amy Cooper's strategic manipulation of white female victimhood marked the genesis of a viral video trend capturing similar instances of false accusations steeped in overt racism. Leidig refers to the response of women in the alt-right to the Black Lives Matter protests in 2020, stating:

> In the United States and around the world, protestors took to the streets calling for action against institutional racism and police brutality. Far-right women influencers, in contrast, responded to these protests with disdain, highlighting instances of looting and violence as representative of the largely peaceful protests, especially connecting the protestors to antifa (short for "antifascists") for inciting disorder. Their social media feeds were full of videos, photos, and media headlines sensationalizing the "anarchy" unfolding on the ground, some of which was revealed to be disinformation [2023, 118].

The alt-right women's digital response to racial injustice further emphasizes the prevalence of dehumanization of all they deem as "other" for the sake of centering white female victimhood.

In the pivotal scene where the women confront Anne and Lily, two Asian American sisters who visit Kim's store for a bottle of wine, their assertion of white victimhood takes center stage. Despite instigating verbal harassment and violence, the women assert Anne and Lily as the aggressors, expressing feeling threatened and disrespected. Notably, the camera maintains the perspective of a spectator throughout the encounter, offering a glimpse into the film's evolving dynamics. The audience becomes privy to the women's overt harassment of Lily and Anne, witnessing the simultaneous victimization of themselves as they initiate violence, setting a poignant tone for the trajectory of the narrative. de Araujo skillfully employs the long-take technique, compelling the viewer to remain immersed in the unfolding atrocities without respite or diversion. This deliberate choice prompts a critical examination of the ethics of spectatorship, challenging the audience to grapple with the implications of witnessing violence on screen in a realistic manner. The film strategically questions the ethical nuances inherent in observing such horrors and delves into how the horror genre intentionally incorporates these elements to construct an immersive and unsettling cinematic experience.

Disrupting Viewer Complicity in Soft & Quiet

In traditional cinema, the deployment of editing can serve as a narrative pause, a breath that affords the spectator a crucial detachment from the unfolding on-screen events. Beth de Araujo's deliberate adoption of the one-take style fundamentally disrupts this established cinematic convention, unapologetically compelling the audience to share an unbroken continuum of experiences with the characters on screen. In the context of *Soft & Quiet*, this unique stylistic choice subverts the traditional cultivation of sympathy due to the fact that the characters are white supremacists, thereby engendering a distinctly horrific viewer experience. Describing the filmmaking process, de Araujo, in an interview with *Filmmaker Magazine*, details the execution of the film entirely through handheld camera work over a compressed four-day period. The daily repetition of the entire film by the cast and crew mirrors the performance style of a play, albeit complicated by the management of multiple locations and logistical intricacies such as seamless transitions, vehicular sequences, and set clearance for shooting. Ultimately, approximately 85 percent of the film comprises footage from the fourth day, with the remaining 15 percent derived from the third day of filming (Macaulay 2022). The result is a measured and deliberate narrative that denies the audience any opportunity for escape. In a sense, the audience is both the invader and the invaded as a result of the unwavering and realistic nature of the camera work. The camera, serving as the surrogate eyes of the audience, assumes the role of a complicit spectator or participant, contributing to the hate crime. This inescapable engagement renders the spectator a present yet powerless observer, caught in a state of helplessness, as the women perpetrate acts of physical and sexual violence against Anne and Lily. The single-take methodology thrusts the viewer into involuntary complicity, akin to the home invaders depicted on screen, fostering an unsettling sense of silent spectatorship and implicating the viewer in the crimes the women enact. The film's commitment to a realistic depiction of alt-right women and radicalization to violence is heightened through the long-take style, accentuating the horrors presented on screen. de Araujo's deliberate choice of using long takes contributes to a willfully horrific viewing experience, acknowledging and confronting the stark realities depicted within the narrative. The immobile status of the spectator further amplifies the sense of guilt, underscoring the film's impact on shaping the audience's affective engagement with the disturbing events unfolding on screen.

Affective Engagement and Narrative Proximity

In "From the Semantic to the Somatic: Affective Engagement with Horror Cinema," Adam Daniel navigates the complex terrain of affective engagement within the realm of horror cinema. Daniel initiates his exploration by scrutinizing the viewer's affective response, emphasizing the significance of identification with the characters and narrative in shaping emotional engagement, how this dynamic functions, and is often subverted, particularly within the horror genre. Daniel states that "horror film as a genre ... is dependent on a specific consideration of the monster's transgressive qualities by the spectator" (2020, 14). While the antagonists in *Soft & Quiet* are undeniably monstrous, the film introduces a subversive affective engagement through its distinctive long-take style. This stylistic choice enforces a narrative proximity to the antagonists, cultivating a deeply uncomfortable and immersive experience with their monstrosity. Daniel's exploration of how emotion is typically elicited through "prolonged cognitive identification" takes a turn as de Araujo deliberately subverts the conventional application of the long-take style (2020, 17). Rather than fostering empathy through shared time and space with the protagonist, the film utilizes this technique to evoke horror and disgust, compelling the audience to share every experience with the antagonists for the entire runtime. Spectators are unable to escape the women's hate speech and their actions, making the spectator sit with this deeply realistic representation of white nationalism. Adam Daniel extends its examination to instances where cinematic experiences transcend semantic comprehension, delving into the realm of involuntary somatic reactions. Emphasizing the visceral responses elicited in horror audiences, Daniel underscores somatic reactions such as startle or freeze responses, offering insights into the affective nuances at play in unconventional horror experiences. This framework becomes relevant in the context of *Soft & Quiet* and its immersive techniques, notably the long-take shot style, which diverges from traditional horror tropes and aligns with Daniel's exploration of affective engagement and phenomenological response. The film's departure from the traditional jumpscare-and-release paradigm is exemplified in the scene depicting Lily's anaphylactic shock after the women torture her and force-feed her peanuts.

Once Anne is freed from the duct tape gag, she pleads for them to retrieve Lily's Epi-Pen or she will die, and a cacophony of panic ensues. Leslie willfully takes her time retrieving the Epi-Pen, escalating the violence from torture to murder. The spectator, confronted with Lily's agonizing final moments, experiences a brutal and nauseating affective engagement, prompting contemplation on the ethics of spectatorship and the visceral witnessing of physical, and later, sexual violence, on-screen through the intentional use of the long-take. The film's ability to elicit such affective responses has sparked critical discourse, exemplifying the nuanced ethical considerations inherent in the intersection of cinematic techniques and audience engagement.

Ethical Witnessing and Cinematic Technique

Oliver Kenny's work, "Beyond Critical Partisanship: Ethical Witnessing and Long Takes of Sexual Violence," engages in a critical examination of the stylistic attributes associated with the use of long takes and extended scenes in cinematic depictions of violence, with a specific focus on sexualized violence and the ethical implications and audience impact of such stylistic choices. Kenny's exploration centers on the deliberate usage of long takes and extended scenes, eschewing traditional montage or editing techniques, and their profound impact on the audience's phenomenological experience. He critically assesses the stylistic choices in the representation of extreme situations on screen, emphasizing the intensified horror resulting from the absence of temporal breaks. Kenny introduces the concept of an "ethical witness," or "a form of spectatorship which encourages the viewer of a *spectacle* of violence to assume the ethical responsibilities of the witness of *actual* violence" (2022, 165). Though he acknowledges "this ethical witness is an inherently problematic form of spectatorship ... it is important and productive *because of* rather than *despite* these difficulties" (Kenny 2022, 165). Though some audiences may see extreme representations of violence on screen as wildly problematic and exploitative, Kenny's framework suggests that depictions of violence that occur in reality can offer progressive potential for interpretation and discussion regarding actual violence. Regarding the use of long-takes, he finds that "new extreme films draw particular attention to processive duration by removing aspects a film which can distract our attention away from the passing of time" such as "camera movements, dialogue, changes in the depicted acts, changes in focus, zooms, and extra-diagetic music," and that if these elements are muted or erased entirely, "processive duration can be emphasised" (2022, 167). *Soft & Quiet* minimizes these elements with its complete lack of non-diegetic music, no clear evidence of cuts or editing, and realistic, sometimes cacophonous and improvised dialogue. Though the camera moves constantly, the effect is closely aligned to that of found-footage, first-person perspective films, positioning the audience as a bystander or member of the women's group, and thus a witness to their crimes.

Oliver Kenny finds the long-take style to craft a "feeling of temporal authenticity, and thus the feeling of time passing at the same pace as for the characters, evoked by being privy to the processive duration of events: were we actually there, we could not edit any parts out or condense them into a few minutes of film" (2022, 168). de Araujo's intentional crafting of temporal authenticity aligns with Kenny's assertion that such a technique evokes the feeling of being a witness to the depicted events. The film's unbroken continuity from the initial meeting of the Daughters of Aryan Unity in the afternoon to the disposal of the bodies in the lake that night eliminates any temporal pause, rendering the audience unable to escape the unfolding events. Within Kenny's framework, this stylistic choice "evoke[s] the feeling of being a witness to these events. Real-life witnessing conventionally holds significant legal and moral weight, with witnesses called to courts of law, and testimonies of atrocities used to warn against their recurrence" (2022, 168). The positioning of spectator as accomplice through the long-take style evokes this feeling of witnessing what is framed to be an incredibly realistic hate crime and murder in *Soft & Quiet*. The style constructs a viewing experience in which one can feel as though de Araujo is demanding that the spectator witness and recognize the increasing prevalence of these types of women, the ease at which they can be radicalized, the violence they can enact, and the "soft" and "quiet" nature of white nationalism in the United States.

Related to his concept of ethical witnessing, Kenny discusses representations of sexually oriented violence, a subject fraught with ethical complexities. Many critics, as cited by Kenny, state that off-screen depictions of rape are the only ethical depiction possibly being that they do not visualize the act itself (2022, 174). This resonates significantly with *Soft & Quiet*, which employs the single-shot extended-take style to depict racially motivated physical and sexual violence. To make their crimes appear to be perpetrated by a man and with physical evidence of rape, the women believe they will not be incriminated. To create this physical evidence, Leslie assaults Anne with a carrot. The assault occurs just off-screen, and it is one of the few instances in which the camera remains static for an extended period. With no evidence of temporal manipulation, as Kenny states, "we experience the same processes of duration as the characters" (2022, 169). The rape scene serves as a stark juxtaposition to the cacophonous dialogue and chaotic camera movements during the previous torture scene. It is quiet, unmoving, and unflinching as the spectator is once again forced to endure and watch. In discourse regarding scenes of extended violence such as this, there are often questions of ethics and intentionality. Kenny's framework finds a dichotomous interpretation of violence as both regressive and progressive. Extended scenes of violence can be both "a problematic glamorisation of a woman's abused sexualised body ... *and* a reminder and reinscription of the material corporeal elements of (sexual) violence" (2022, 170). The scene serves as a powerful reminder of the visceral consequences of far-right radicalization and the dehumanization of the victim, Anne, who becomes a symbolic representation of the violence women can perpetrate under the radicalized ideologies depicted in the film. As a result of their radicalization into white supremacist ideologies, they have dehumanized Anne both physically and psychologically based on her race. The women see this act of sexual violence as not only a means of hiding their involvement in Lily's murder, but also a symbolic summation of what they have been taught through their alt-right ideologies, the white race dominating all "others." Although the film grants viewers the knowledge that Anne has survived the hate crime as she emerges from the lake, they are left with an ambivalent sense of justice, unsure if these women will actually receive punishment for their crimes in a justice system built to protect them, and the legacy of white supremacy in the United States.

Conclusion

The emergence of the alt-right as a distinct ideological movement, characterized by white supremacist beliefs and facilitated by digital platforms, is represented in de Araujo's film *Soft & Quiet* as a real and present threat in contemporary society that requires unflinching attention to the violence this ideology can enact, as evidenced through the use of the long-take filming style. The mechanisms through which the alt-right operates, particularly in its recruitment efforts and dissemination of extremist ideologies, demonstrate the alt-right's adaptability in leveraging digital spaces to advance its agenda. The discussion on the ethical implications of spectatorship in cinematic depictions of political and racially motivated violence, as exemplified in *Soft & Quiet*, highlights the importance in critically engaging with media representations of extremism.

Ultimately, the alt-right's exploitation of digital platforms and the normalization of extremist ideologies among certain segments of society underscore the urgent need for comprehensive strategies to counteract and mitigate the influence of far-right extremism. This includes proactive measures to address online radicalization, promote media literacy, and foster inclusive communities that reject bigotry and hatred in all its forms. In navigating the complex landscape of the alt-right and its nexus with the internet, it is imperative for society to combat the insidious spread of far-right extremism. By immersing viewers in the unsettling realities of radicalization and hate-driven violence, works like *Soft & Quiet* provoke introspection and challenge audiences to confront the prevalence of white supremacy in the United States, the role of gender in disseminating alt-right beliefs, and how quickly these ideologies can be radicalized into devastating actions.

References

Aldana Reyes, Xavier. (2013). "Violence and Mediation: The Ethics of Spectatorship in the Twenty-First Century Horror Film." *Violence and the Limits of Representation*, 145–160. Palgrave Macmillan UK.

Bernstein, Abbie. (2022). "Soft & Quiet Writer/Director Beth de Araujo Wants to Get Under Your Skin." *Fangoria*, 15 November. https://www.fangoria.com/original/soft-quiet-writerdirector-beth-de-ara%C3%BAjo-wants-to-get-under-your-skin/.

Biesecker, Michael. (2022). "Ashli Babbitt a Martyr? Her Past Tells a More Complex Story." *Associated Press News*, 3 January. https://apnews.com/article/ashli-babbitt-capitol-siege-a15c7e52a04d932972b7a284c7a8f7df.

Chen, Lauren. (2017). "Richard Spencer Interview | What is the Alt-Right? (Pt. 1)." YouTube video, 20:14, May 2. https://www.youtube.com/watch?v=mlOv3BXSyJM.

Daniel, Adam. (2020). "From the Semantic to the Somatic: Affective Engagement with Horror Cinema." *Affective Intensities and Evolving Horror Forms*, 13–29. Edinburgh: Edinburgh University Press.

de Araujo, Beth, dir. *Soft & Quiet*. Blumhouse Productions, 2022. 1 hr., 32 min. https://www.netflix.com/title/81649833.

Jerkins, Morgan. (2023). "'She Doesn't Have the Power': Central Park Birdwatcher Christian Cooper on Why Racist 'Incident' Won't Define Him." *The Guardian*, 19 June. www.theguardian.com/environment/2023/jun/19/christian-cooper-central-park-birdwatcher-racism.

Kenny, Oliver. (2022). "Beyond Critical Partisanship: Ethical Witnessing and Long Takes of Sexual Violence." *Studies in European Cinema* 19, no. 2: 164–78.

Leidig, Eviane. (2023). *The Women of the Far Right: Social Media Influencers and Online Radicalization*. New York: Columbia University Press.

Macaulay, Scott. (2022). "'There Has Been a Deliberate Rebranding of the Alt-Right Women to Have the Veneer of Smart, Sophisticated Instagram Influencers': Director Beth de Araujo and DP Greta Zozula on *Soft & Quiet*." *Filmmaker Magazine*, 23 March. https://filmmakermagazine.com/113776-beth-de-araujo-and-greta-zozula-soft-quiet/.

Sarachan, Risa. (2022). "'Soft & Quiet' a Chilling and Timely Indie Horror Film." *Forbes*, 9 Nov. www.forbes.com/sites/risasarachan/2022/11/08/soft—quiet-a-chilling-and-timely-indie-horror-film/?sh=478e43abb80a.

Sykes, Sophia, and Dr. Veronica Hopner. (2023). "Tradwives: The Housewives Commodifying Right-Wing Ideology." *Global Network on Extremism and Technology*, 7 July. gnet-research.org/2023/07/07/tradwives-the-housewives-commodifying-right-wing-ideology/.

How Conspiracy Theories Manifest Anthropocenic Anxieties
A Post-Human Critique of Humanism Through the Lens of Inside Job

SUTIRTHO ROY

Introduction

Conspiracy theories, aptly named because of their seeming existence on the fringes of known science and mainstream thought, abound in popular culture. For instance, card games like *Illuminati* (Somerlad 2021) as well as Dan Brown's best-selling novel *Angels and Demons* (Brown 2000), among others, offer a fictive spin on the idea of a shadowy organization that secretly puppeteers major events and government agencies. Similarly, cryptids like the giant simian Bigfoot and the elusive sea monster, Nessie, feature in countless tales of science fiction and fantasy. While most instances use conspiracy theories as elements of speculative storytelling and science-fiction settings, others do not. In fact, the speculative documentary series *Ancient Aliens* is being increasingly critiqued for its subtle colonial tendencies as well as the racist and xenophobic implications of equating non–Western feats of engineering and architecture with extraterrestrial intervention (Osegueda 2019).

As such, fringe theories permeate through a spectrum ranging from speculative storytelling to degrees of believability. One piece of media that acknowledges this spectrum through a self-aware gaze is *Inside Job*, an 18-episode show on Netflix that posits a "what-if" scenario in a world where almost all fringe theories exist, through the creation of a fictional organization named Cognito Inc. that regulates such theorizations amongst the general populace. However, throughout, the show consciously places these theories in the realm of fiction, never claiming the truth behind any of these theories. Despite having entire episodes dedicated towards the celebration of these theories centered on JFK's assassination, reptilian shapeshifters, the Flat Earth, claims of the faked Moon landing, and more, the show simultaneously attempts to tell a relatable emotional story through its central cast of characters who take the shape of various human and non-human entities.

This emotional story at the heart of absurd science fiction was the brainchild of creator Shion Takeuchi. While coming to know of the shadow government as a collection of "hyper mysterious, incredibly competent people, manipulating global events beyond our comprehension, with how advanced they were" (The Collider & Takeuchi 2021), Takeuchi soon realized otherwise as she remarked in an interview:

> And that idea became funny to me, because if there was a shadow government, there would have to be people running it. And from what I know of people, we really can't get our shit together. So I imagined that if there was a shadow government, it would be just as chaotic and stressful as any job that you or I would have. And I thought that'd be a really funny office comedy [Ibid.].

The purpose of this study is to look at the narrative of *Inside Job* and analyze how the portrayed humanness of protagonist Reagan Ridley and her co-workers serve as a counter-gaze to the cryptic aura of intimidation and mystery that surrounds many fringe theories in popular parlance. Additionally, this essay analyzes the semiotic elements of *Inside Job* to gauge how it employs elements of parody, satire, and absurd humor to delegitimize the seriousness behind conspiracy theories in a self-reflexive and carnivalesque manner. Such a carnivalesque depiction, in turn, poses a meta-narrative counter-gaze to the very insecurities which lead people to formulate, propagate and cling to fringe theories.

This essay hopes to posit how these very insecurities arise from not only intraspecies, but also interspecies power differentials—arising from mankind's uneasy relationship with the Other entities of the environmental, societal, cultural and political sphere. As such, this essay explores the various ways in which the show visually explores more-than-human spaces across space, time and other dimensions, where the role, responsibility, power and agency of the human(ist) subject is mediated across the familial, socio-political and ecological spheres through the use of conspiracy theories. Finally, this essay gauges how fringe theories function as a contemporary form of mythopoeic storytelling that stems from the human(ist) self's desire for individual and/or collective power in the Anthropocene.

Anxieties about Human/Human Interactions and Institutions as Portrayed in Inside Job

From the beginning of the first episode, *Inside Job* meta-narratively paints a picture of the archetypal conspiracy theorist through the ramblings of a drunken old man.

> Listen up, kids. Everything they teach you at school is a lie. The world is controlled by shadowy elites and shapeshifting lizard people.... Am I the only one who cares that the president is a robot? Wake, up sheeple. The evidence is real [Takeuchi 2021a].

While seemingly inviting audiences to laugh at him, the show self-reflexively subverts expectations by revealing that this old man, Rand Ridley, is, in fact, Reagan's father and the co-founder of Cognito Inc., a megacorporation which functions as the shadow government of the United States. The function of Cognito Inc. (a tongue-in-cheek rephrase of the word "incognito"), is to actively dupe the general populace and alter their perception of major historical and/or contemporary events through media manipulation, subliminal messaging, mind control, holograms, and almost every other conceivable conspiracy-theory-turned-sci-fi-trope.

Expectations are subverted once more as Reagan enters a dark room with hunched figures sitting around a round table, which initially lends a mysterious ambience as suspenseful music plays in the background. Reagan switches on the lights and all the characters groan collectively. Revealed to be her coworkers, this ensemble crew is revealed to have been in the dark, not because they were plotting in the shadows, but because they were victims of a hangover, and the lights hurt their eyes. Through this humorous double subversion based on incongruity, the show ascertains its self-reflexive, authorial stance on conspiracy theories—that, while useful and interesting ideas for speculation, these theories hold no merit in reality since the shadow government is bound to be "just as dumb as the real government" (Ibid.). Reagan reiterates this idea comically when she sharply retorts to her coworkers, they should try to take their job seriously because their occupation literally involved shadow-running the free world (Ibid.).

However, both Reagan and her coworkers consistently succumb to anthropogenic incompetence, to paraphrase Takeuchi's words. Their inability to "get [their] shit together" (Ibid.), provides the major source of humor as the characters' personal lives absurdly intersect with their mission to run the world, reducing world-changing events to the self-serving whim of eccentric office workers.

In the pilot, Reagan digs up dirt on her colleague Brett to defame him because she believed that the latter did not deserve to co-lead her team. The B-plot of this episode parodies the very act of formulating conspiracies by having Reagan use a conspiracy wall, board, and red tape to maniacally chart out the reasons as to why Brett is a secret sleeper agent from elsewhere, possibly a rival company. Despite portraying its protagonist as a rare genius in every other aspect, *Inside Job* portrays Reagan's paranoid claims about Brett in the same comedic light as the rants of a group of militant Flat-Earth believers in a future episode (Takeuchi 2021a).

Reagan's conspiracy against Brett stems from anxieties about the loss of her power and control, which, in a microcosm, mirrors the American public's anxieties and fears about a secret clandestine organization (the deep state) controlling their seemingly elected government. That is exactly what the A-plot of the pilot is about, as Cognito attempts to replace the U.S. president with an easy-to-control robotic one—even as they attempt to dupe the general populace, the characters of the show are ironically susceptible to the very human tendency to create and believe in their conspiracies. While using the interlinking A- and B-plots to satirize fringe theories and theorists, Episode 1 of *Inside Job* also subtextually highlights how conspiracy theories are themselves borne of individual and collective anxieties about one's perceived lack/ loss of power.

Despite the origin of the term "deep state" at a later instant, the concept entered the popular imagination in the 1950s (Wills 2017). Since then, a variety of demographics including professors (Michael Glennon as quoted in Smith 2020) and journalists (Ambinder 2017) have used or critiqued the idea of a covert shadow government that secretly runs the world. Of this theory, Sonam Sheth states:

> But soon after the possibility of the beginnings of an American deep state was first raised by the mainstream media, the idea took hold of the far-right media, quickly reaching a fever pitch [Sheth 2017].

During his presidency, Donald Trump's government and right-wing media outlets had claimed that the U.S. Department of Justice was a part of the deep state (Lucey & Superville 2021) and that Barack Obama was using this same deep state to coordinate resistance against Trump's government (Weigel 2017). The deep state became synonymous with right-wing conspiracies which arose out of anxieties by the government and its supporters about the perceived loss of power by the elected representatives. The supporters of Trump's regime even began using the very term "deep state" to refer to how secret intelligentsia and officials were clandestinely influencing policy (Gordon 2017), thereby highlighting the fact that the very tendency to believe in these conspiracies partially originate from fears and insecurities about one's place in the contemporary political climate.

Despite acknowledging conspiracy theories as a global phenomenon that was exacerbated by the Covid-19 pandemic (Farinelli 2021, 4), a study has shown a positive correlation between right-wing extremism, conservatism and the tendency to believe in fringe theories:

> Extremist groups use conspiracy theories as a tool for recruitment and to advance their radical agendas exploiting uncertainties, fears, socioeconomic issues and mental health disorders amongst vulnerable people. In recent years, right-wing extremism has proven to be active and efficient in the dissemination of conspiracy theories aimed at targeting individuals or groups blamed to be responsible for the evil in society [Ibid.].

As such, the very notion of the deep state itself becomes a right-wing fantasy, which the characters in the show refer to by way of tongue-in-cheek humor, calling even their own actions "evil," as they disregard the collateral damage they cause while trying to succeed in their mission.

The self-serving origin of certain conspiracy theories, insofar as they prey on the gullible's anxieties, is shown more overtly in Episode 6 of Part 1 when Rand Ridley is regarded as the in-universe cause for starting rumors that the Earth is flat. According to him, he had made a bet with his co-worker J.R. that there was no idea that could be dumb enough for people to not believe it. To prove his point, he had concocted the idea of the Flat Earth Theory, which had gained a cult following among certain people (Takeuchi 2021f). Rand's shenanigans put the characters in danger as he uses the Flat Earthers to hitch a ride to his ex-wife's wedding, following which, they militarize the entire boat by keeping everyone hostage. In the end, the leader of this cult forces Reagan to take him to the edge of the Earth, during which Reagan convinces him that the very notion that he has dedicated his life to is a selfish ploy designed to manipulate him. While the actual Flat Earth conspiracy is not associated with militant extremism for the most part, Reagan's speech and later, the sentient mushroom Myc's ironic comment—"Most conspiracies are just capitalism" (Ibid.)—allows the show to critique not only the gullibility of those who believe in conspiracy theories but also the selfishness of the ones who consciously perpetrate the same.

The episode with the Flat Earthers accomplishes this by portraying Cognito Inc., its workers, and the rich people in power as self-centered capitalists who have their own idiosyncrasies and cut-throat methods to climb the corporate/political ladder. In this regard, Cognito Inc. (including Rand's actions) becomes a microcosm of the real Western world, where the interlinked political and the corporate spheres feature "assholes all the way down" (Takeuchi 202a). That does not however imply that all conspiracies arise out of conscious political manipulation, and *Inside Job* specifically explores different fringe theories in different ways. Actual beliefs about the Flat Earth, a historical misconception about a belief in the Middle Ages (Russel 1997) which in the modern ages holds relevance as a form of anti-science propaganda, is revealed to be a concept too ridiculous even in the wacky world where the story is set—in fact, the Earth is hollow, where monsters of various kinds thrive till the present day.

Real-world beliefs that the Earth is flat likely stem from other anxieties—anxieties about mainstream knowledge and the consequent desire to formulate one's version of events. Proponents of the Flat Earth society were involved in claims that the moon landing was faked, and, in 1980, actively sought to defame NASA by claiming that the evidence behind this supposed achievement was a creative and collaborative effort among animator Walt Disney, science fiction writer Arthur C. Clarke, and filmmaker Stanley Kubrick (Schadewald 1980). *Inside Job* mocks this sensational idea in two related ways. Firstly, it shows that not only was the moon landing real, but the real cover-up was done to hide the fact that there remains an elite, functioning society on the moon which was founded by Buzz Aldrin and Neil Armstrong. However, the characters soon find that this supposed moon society, though elite, was succumbing to the same anthropogenic pressure affecting the world, and that Buzz Aldrin was a dictator and a murderer who wanted to wage war on the Earth. In his place, Buzz Aldrin on Earth who gained media coverage is revealed to be a "crisis actor." Crisis actors, according to conspiracy theorists, are deemed to be hired performers who are privy to historical events from a close perspective (Wilson 2018); such a belief delegitimizes the very scale of the historical events and their impact on people by proclaiming the said event to be staged. However, the B-plot of this episode, dealing with this crisis actor, humorously satirizes this very idea of government-employed crisis actors being responsible for contemporary tragedies to absurdly mock the attempts of theorists to delegitimize the realness of actual incidents.

The actual faked-moon-landing conspiracy was the brainchild of Bill Kayesing who worked as a technical writer for NASA's Apollo Moon missions (Knight 2019). Kayesing's claims about his inside knowledge of a political conspiracy to fake moon landings evolved into full-blown murmurs seeking to dig up dirt on various aspects of the event photographs believed to be a spectacle with its roots in the Cold War (Ibid). Intended to dupe and defeat the Soviet Union in the Space Race, the conspiracy truly took hold in mid–1970s America "in large part due to a wider crisis of trust in the country at the time" (Ibid.), fueling a shift "from a belief in external enemies, such as Communists, to the suspicion that the American state was itself conspiring against its citizens" (Ibid). Currently, opinion polls dictate that around 5 to 10 percent of Americans, 12 percent of Britons, and

20 percent of Italians believe in the faked moon landing, though the prevalence of subconsciously national views and anti–Western conspiracy theories in Russia showcase that more than half of the Russian population were firm adherents to the theory and highlight how the tendency to trust in fringe theories is far from being limited to the United States or even the West (Ibid.).

This belief and fear of internal enemies can be tied to rumors surrounding the assassination of President Kennedy, whose murder was tied to the activities of both covert arms of the shadow government as well as the CIA due to perceived conflicts over Cold War policies and geopolitical issues. The JFK assassination does play a role in *Inside Job* as well, particularly in the second episode, where a plague of JFK clones is unleashed, forcing the erstwhile president's murderer—the oldest employee of Cognito, Grassy Noel Atkinson—to come out of retirement and take up arms again. The sight of an aged sniper rushing headfirst into a pile of JFK clones, which merge to form an eldritch monster of flesh and goo, creates an absurd spectacle on screen and delegitimizes the genuinely held belief of JFK's murder through parody, low comedy and absurd humor based on incongruity.

Whether it be a fake moon landing, ideas of the deep state, or a president's murder, conspiracy theories arise from a person or a group's feeling that things are not what they seem, and that the truth is being hidden from them consciously or otherwise. Even believers in the Flat Earth do so often because of a partial or complete distrust in the official version of events, the government, contemporary scientific evidence and/or mainstream media. Dr. Karen Douglas, in an interview at the American Psychological Association, highlights three specific psychological factors which motivate people to believe in conspiracy theories—the epistemic (the need for knowledge and motive to possess information), the existential (the need to feel safe and secure in the world and the wish to have more power over intangible factors affecting them) and the social/individual (the desire to feel good about oneself through potential access to information denied to others) (Mills & Douglas 2021). This is evident in the very rhetoric used by the actual fringe theorists—the formulators and the believers.

Rachel Runnels analyzes how the narrative of these theories are framed in a pattern derived from the hero's journey monomyth, where the reader-audience is the hero who has access to secret information, the formulator/propagator is the trusty mentor providing same access, while the entities with perceived power serve as the villains or antagonists. In doing so, she analyzes the rhetoric and framing of MUFON (Mutual UFO Network), the Flat Earth Society, and 911truth.org—three major websites dedicated to the uncovering of conspiracy theories:

All three organizations use different types of language to frame themselves as credible in what I call the "reliability frame." The Flat Earth Society uses words associated with intelligence and freedom.... MUFON repeatedly uses words associated with scientific validity to prove their worth as a credible member of the scientific community ... 911truth.org highlights their media exposure to build credibility [Runnels 2021].

While playing on the people's epistemic need to possess information and consequently agency over their lives, these theories also capitalize on the existential need to feel safe and secure in the world through the possession of more knowledge. Finally, the social and/ or individual need to feel good about oneself is highlighted because the theorists portray the reader-audience as the chosen one who can understand and/or receive information denied to other members of their society.

Anxieties about Human/Non-Human Interactions as Portrayed in Inside Job

These anxieties do not remain confined to humanistic institutions (one's own government, other countries, secret human populations, etc.) but spill over to other entities as well. The bizarre and colorful world of *Inside Job* is populated by a range of different entities. Along with Cognito, five other groups work in tandem to manipulate major world events— the Reptoids, the Atlanteans, the Juggalos, the Illuminati, and the Catholic Church—with the presence of all six groups directly corresponding to a well-known conspiracy theory and consequent anxiety. *Inside Job* critiques the acts of the Catholic Church in the same vein as it mocks fringe theories, and even has an episode where the current Pope (exemplified by how he allows for gay dog marriage) is regarded as far too liberal, and, using a mind-control device due to the protagonists' interventions, has his conservative attitudes raised (Takeuchi 2022d). By continually portraying Cognito and its actions as evil and unethical through a self-aware lens, *Inside Job* automatically uses this episode—filled with an artificially constructed hell with animatronic demons—to critique the fanatic actions of orthodox Christianity and its conservative views as borne of the same anxieties which give rise to conspiracy theories.

Anxieties about losing power and agency to both human (Jews) and non-human (reptiles) entities manifest in the form of the Reptoids (Anonymous columnist 2024, *https://www.varsity.co.uk/comment/11782*). The conspiracy of the Reptoids upholds that the people in power are shape-shifting reptilians who secretly manipulate major events and hope to take over the world someday (klunder.2, 2019). The Reptoids which appear in Episode 3 of *Inside Job* aspire to do the same thing, but, like elsewhere, the show uses gross humor (through the means of a reptilian orgy) and elements of the carnivalesque to poke fun at the idea of high functioning lizard people. The idea of the Reptoids was popularized by David Icke who claimed that the people we know, especially people in positions of power, are in fact, shapeshifting aliens from another dimension (Greenspan 2021). Despite the outlandishness of the theory, the theory finds many believers even in the present day. Icke's claims have been largely regarded as anti-Semitic because of his own endorsements of the anti-Jew publication *The Protocols of the Elders of Zion*, as well as his claims' evocativeness to "the centuries-old blood-libel conspiracy theory, which alleged that a cabal of Jews were controlling the world and drinking the blood of Christian children" (Ibid.).

However, these notions also tie into erstwhile and contemporary anti-Semitic narratives in the United States, expressing the anxieties of a certain section of the population through the seemingly disturbing idea that "our sinister rulers are at least disproportionately Jewish" (klunder.2, 2019). The idea of creating reptilian overlords which serve as caricatured Jewish analogues becomes a successful metaphor in the eyes of these people, as they serve to enmesh political and religious anxieties about certain sections of the population with humanity's inherent and evolutionarily adaptive, psychological repulsion towards reptiles (Stanley 2008). Often regarded as an evolutionary mechanism that had developed as a form of self-defense against potential danger (such as venomous snakes), this psychological distaste has culturally manifested in Western media in different forms, taking the shape of the Biblical serpent, the Medieval dragon, and so on. Reptoids become just the most recent addition in that one long lineage.

Similarly, the presence of the Atlanteans points to another recurrent anxiety. According to the lore of *Inside Job*, Atlanteans are amphibious merpeople from the famed underwater city Atlantis, who are involved in the shadow-running of the government. The Atlanteans are not the focus in any of the episodes, but the show reveals that they are involved in keeping Cthulhu away from human beings and that NASA actively photoshops their civilization out of photos of the Earth. Their relationship with human beings has been hostile to semi-hostile in the past, showcased by the fact that they had sent an invasion fleet to attack humanity which was sunk by the members of the elusive Shadow Board—this, consequently, was linked to the sinking of the *Titanic* in mainstream media. While not much is known about them due to their limited screen time, their temporary appearances—such as during their participation in a gathering of secret societies—reveal them to be as comically inept and self-serving as the other factions.

The presence of the Atlanteans combines several anxieties in one package, foremost of them being the fear of the deep water, which, in extreme cases, leads to thalassophobia (Cherry 2023). The very city of Atlantis itself has crossed the line from mythical stories to actual contemporary belief, with popular culture capitalizing on the sensational nature of this sunken city—the story of this city has often been associated with fearfully world-ending and apocalyptic events (CBC Radio 2023) and has even been co-opted by Nazi narratives (Ratner 2022). However, the most pressing anxiety comes from nowhere but the very appearance of the Atlanteans themselves. Stories of merpeople seducing and dragging people below the oceanic depths point to a recurrent fear of the dark, the deep, and the agency of the uncanny Other. By resembling us in certain ways, but through their vast differences, merpeople and amphibious entities are believed to dwell in an entirely different world. Even through their very appearances (human-like gait, faces, expressions but fishlike features on other parts), these entities are regarded to inhabit the realm of the uncanny Other, who threaten not only human victims but also the very idea of what it means to be human (Dominguez 2022).

In fact, not only the Atlanteans but also the Reptoids are depicted as the uncanny Other, being born from humanity's collective anxiety about beings who lack a clear boundary between the human and the non-human body. *Inside Job* tackles complex issues regarding humanity and personhood, raising questions about what constitutes a person, with the idea of personhood often being linked to dimensions of the Self/Other dynamic (more so in cases where non-human entities feature as sentient characters). Is Glenn Dolphmann, the human-dolphin hybrid super soldier, who took on his current appearance as a result of his patriotic fervor, a person? While Glenn's antics and jingoistic drive are mocked in-universe as products of militant brainwashing, so is his appearance. This is especially evident in Episode 11 when Glenn is forced to retire to a separate section of the Burning Man–style gathering, designated for beings unpleasant to look at—an area where he co-inhabits with Reptoids, Atlanteans and Myc, the sentient mushroom. Not only does Glenn perceive himself as unnatural, but time and again, his being a freak of nature is played for laughs (Takeuchi 2022a). The show does not seem to condone this. Still, it uses Glenn's existence and occasionally heroic actions to critique the very anthropocentrism that leads people to ostracize Other beings (whether *Homo sapiens* or otherwise) who, in their eyes, do not deserve the same moral considerations or empathy.

If Glenn can be considered human because of his *Homo sapiens* genes, Myc Celium, the sentient mushroom from Hollow Earth, is certainly not. An assortment of fringe theories intersect in the character of Myc. There is a recurring joke about the fact that he is often equated with an extraterrestrial, because of his outlandish design (something that is often attributed to alien lifeforms in popular culture). An episode spoofing Steven Spielberg's *ET the Extra-Terrestrial* even goes as far as to liken him to an alien who must be saved by small-town kids who, while trying to save him from government agents, ultimately realize that Myc's abrasive personality does not make him a good companion and try to abandon him. The director subverts his character (and thereby the popular reconstruction of an alien) from an otherworldly or superhuman being to an entity as foulmouthed, selfish, and petty as a human being; one who is no less prone to cracking sexual jokes than any individual *Homo sapiens*. Of course, Myc's identity shifts throughout the series, and he refuses to identify with the fact that everybody likens him to an extraterrestrial alien, instead choosing to call himself a sentient mushroom from Hollow Earth. This is proven partially false, as Myc's species is later revealed to have arrived on Earth via an asteroid—this entire altercation satirizes the anthropogenic idea of labeling anything alien to common knowledge as belonging to an extraterrestrial race. In doing so, the show uses tongue-in-cheek humor to critique the very Eurocentric and racist knowledge that the foundation of *Ancient Aliens* (as discussed above) is based upon.

Myc's perversion and the narrative's choice to deem his tentacles as sexual organs (which Cognito milks to get their mind-erasing fluid) employs vulgar (often scatological) humor based on incongruity to debase or disassociate his character from any form of intimidating, extraterrestrial presence. In the world of *Inside Job*, the Stoned Ape Hypothesis (Lamb & Henderson 2023)—or the idea that human beings only achieved sapience after a tribe of apes consumed mushrooms to expand their minds—is true. While this idea still finds traction in some parts of the scientific community (Ibid.) the show plays around with the idea humorously, showing a sort of revenge-themed alien-invasion arc, where the very human beings, after becoming sentient, drove the mushroom to the center of the Earth where they remain and bide their time till they can take over the world again (Takeuchi 2022c). However, revenge does not pan out. In a series of mishaps as is characteristic of *Inside Job*, the show makes it clear that no matter how alien, mushroom or telepathic Myc's kind is, they are no higher or superior beings, but as susceptible to petty foibles as the humans whom his species helped evolve. Nowhere is this more evident than in the episode where Myc returns to his Hive. Rather than posing a serious, apocalyptic threat to the characters as is common of many extraterrestrial invasion stories, the series focuses on Myc's high school reunion and his attempts to fit into the numerous groups, which resemble cliques in different high school dramas. The alien mushrooms are subdued, not by the protagonists' superior power or resilience, but through a series of subversive events where Reagan and her team remind Myc of his narcissistic selfishness and rude humor, which are characteristic of his individual self. This goes on to motivate him to break out of the Hive Mind and take control of it, in effect, becoming the archetype of the cool kid that he had always hoped to be (Takeuchi 2022c).

Through its absurd, chaotic and carnivalesque setting, where even the most somber occasion can give way to black comedy, *Inside Job* portrays a complex world where the Mothman is the head of Human Resources and has an addiction to lamps and where the Sasquatch is a violent and unintelligible entity with no dialogue. These *Inside Job* versions of these cryptids portray far tamer characters than the eerie and threatening real-world counterparts who lurk at the fringes of civilization and are claimed to be violent and/or malevolent non-human entities. In the world of *Inside Job*, Sasquatch and Mothman might be real—albeit caricatures—of their cryptid selves, but others like the Chupacabra and the Loch Ness Monster are no more than machines or robotic equipment who are designed to carry out hoaxes to perfection. Despite their differing depictions in the show, the predominance of all these cryptids (and the discipline of their study, aka cryptozoology) can be traced to our belief systems, arising not only out of epistemic anxiety with one's relationship with the natural world but also through a form of morbid fascination. Teresa Coppens likens our desire and tendency to believe in monsters to a "fear that something might lurk in the depths of the ocean or the vast wilderness" (Coppens 2021), threatening the human understanding of our known world.

Paleontologist Darren Naish looks at cryptozoology as more of a cultural phenomenon than a zoological one with cryptids serving as cultural archetypes "embedded in the way people imagine the world" (Naish 2022). Despite arising out of proto-scientific enquiry and a curiosity to understand the world (which manifested in folkloric and mythology in the absence of advanced/ contemporary scientific enquiry), the discipline has, in modern times, veered into associations with paranormal entities and unidentified flying objects:

> discussions about cryptozoology in the popular sphere now overlap with those on UFOs, demons and paranormal phenomena. All are suspected by aficionados to be related branches of the same big picture. What we're seeing here is a disregard for (or ignorance of) the zoological roots of cryptozoology, and a downhill slide to belief in a demon-haunted world. Archaeologist and anthropologist Jeb Card terms these overlapping beliefs the Paranormal Unified Field Theory, or PUFT [Ibid.].

Additionally, while noting that genuine scientific enquiry still persists in parts of the community, with several proponents not being "misguided, woefully naïve or anti-scientific" (Ibid.), studies have located this interest "to be connected to fringe beliefs such as creationism and conspiracy theory, and it is not difficult to find anti-scientific tones in sectors of the cryptozoological community" (Ibid.). As far as conspiracy theories go, the perceived threat to one's way of life does not always derive from political unrest and clandestine governments, but from human/non-human hybrids, extraterrestrial aliens, or even primitive monsters, albeit in different ways.

Conclusion: Fringe Theories as the Modern Myth

Whether they are overt or subtle (transnational apprehensions with the Soviet Union versus the portrayal of Jews as blood-thirsty lizard people), related to human endeavors or non-human entities (apprehensions of the deep state versus the presence of aliens and cryptids), fringe theories become a form of storytelling designed to reflect humanistic anxieties about the "other" and the unknown. Here, the very idea of what it meant to be "human" comes under question, as Francesca Ferrando suggests, with the very signifier being a privileged marker that people in power have co-opted to marginalize or dehumanize other individuals or groups of *Homo sapiens* whom they deem less than human (Ferrando 2021 80). Such dehumanization is complex on the individual level, where a strong self/other dynamic crops up among members of different ages, sexes, political beliefs and religions regarding other groups. Case in point: while there is not adequate proof to highlight that the believers of the reptilian theory are all haters of Judaism, the very anti–Semitic origin of lizard people links the believers' deep-rooted fears about Jews with the disgust associated with cold-blooded reptiles. As such, consumers and perpetrators of fringe theories involving non-human entities (aliens, cryptids, shape-shifters) as well as human-built political structures (like the deep state and communist governments), create narratives where groups of *Homo sapiens* and non-humans (who, in different ways pose a threat to the believers' coveted ways of life and perceived safety through their presence or active interference) are framed as the antagonistic other. Such anxiety is often tempered with morbid fascination about possessing exclusive information that other members of their group do not have, a phenomenon that equates the possession of said knowledge with a different kind of power.

These fringe theories become a means to explain hitherto-believed-to-be-unknown phenomena through otherworldly/supernatural phenomena. In this respect, such a conspiracy theory becomes a myth of the contemporary world, with the idea of the myth referring to a traditional story ... explaining some natural or social phenomenon, and typically involving supernatural beings or events ("Myth" n.d.). These ideas draw power from their potential to be passed on among the public through oral or other means—often defying empirical science—and act as a form of confirmation bias about a believer's/group of believers' anxieties about the Other, by filling up self-perceived knowledge gaps with fictive scenarios that somehow seem more believable than the established dominant narrative. Many of these new myths do not seek to explain the phenomena of lightning or sea storms (of which early *Homo sapiens* were afraid of/revered) but hope to uncover deeper secrets beneath political or social events (which *Homo sapiens* in our day are anxious about). Other myths, however, reflect ancient fears which however manifest differently—for instance, the fear of snakes and/or reptiles is not new, but can be owed to an evolutionary adaptation that can be traced back to the time when the ancestors *Homo sapiens* were still primates and were at risk of being poisoned/constricted to death (Stanley 2008). When ancient civilizations began narrativizing these serpents in their stories, the fear manifested, albeit in different ways. While ancient Greco-Roman faiths began portraying them as monsters who deserved revulsion and disgust (case in point, Medusa or Echidna), others looked on at them in a mixture of reverence and healthy respect born of apprehension (the ambivalent depiction of Nagas in Hindu mythology [*Symbolism and importance of snakes in Hinduism and mythology*] 2023). The portrayal of lizard people as coldblooded and cunning shapeshifters is just one extension of the Eurocentric reptile narrative that also had the villainous medieval dragon and the Satanic serpent as its proponents.

As such, whether it be in ancient myths or contemporary fringe theories, the fears leading us to formulate these stories and believe in them can be deemed as arising from anthropocentric apprehension, where the role and agency of the humanist subject are perceived as coming under attack by unknown forces beyond our individual or collective control. In ancient myths, the hero was structured as an extremely masculine person setting out to conquer the unknown (which appeared in the form of non-human or hybrid monsters who allegorized anthropogenic fears regarding the place of the Self in the world) (Campbell 2020). This act of conquest is present in the narrative structure of contemporary fringe theories as well, where the believer is the protagonist seeking to know the truth (as analyzed in the previous section). This very learning process towards truth is analogous to the hero's journey. Instead of a physical defeat of one's enemies, the act of knowing the hidden truth is deemed analogous to the hero's triumph; a triumph they achieve by thwarting their enemies' (perpetrators of the dominant narrative) plans.

The article *Conspiracy Theories and Anxiety in Culture* analyzes how this very act of formulating fringe theories is a psychological attempt to deal with threat-related misinformation (Palecek & Hampel 2023) through the humanistic ability of mythopoeia (mythmaking). Additionally, it is also this very act of myth-making that *Inside Job* satirizes through the absurdly humorous and carnivalesque portrayal of the entities whom we perceive are secretly withholding information and/or power from us; these beings are no overwhelming or omniscient force of nature but lack as much control over their own (and, in cases, even our) lives as we do. Their petty troubles get in the way of their job of duping the public—in most cases, they end up duping each other. In other words, the gravitas and might associated with the idea of mysterious and all-powerful beings controlling our world (which is a major characteristic of fringe theories) is thwarted by showcasing how, even if such organizations/entities/shapeshifters/cryptids exist, they are not divine, all-powerful or even well-adjusted, but as susceptible to anthropogenic foibles as the rest of us.

References

Ambinder, Marc. (2017). "Opinion | Five Myths about the Deep State." *The Washington Post*, March 10. https://www.washingtonpost.com/opinions/five-myths-about-the-deep-state/2017/03/10/ddb09b54-04da-11e7-ad5b-d22680e18d10_story.html.

Anonymous columnist. (2024). "Your Conspiracy Theory Is Anti-Semitic." *Varsity Online*, March 11. https://www.varsity.co.uk/comment/11782.

Bloom, David. (2021). "Netflix's '*Inside Job*' Plumbs the Deep State One Joke at a Time." *Forbes Magazine*, October 18. https://www.forbes.com/sites/dbloom/2021/10/14/netflixs-inside-job-plumbs-the-deep-state-one-joke-at-a-time/?sh=77cae3fa1c98.

Brown, Tracy. (2021). "'*Inside Job*' Showrunner Thought a Shadow Government Would Be Scary. Reality Was Scarier." *Los Angeles Times*, October 23. https://www.latimes.com/entertainment-arts/tv/story/2021-10-23/inside-job-netflix-shion-takeuchi-conspiracy-theories.

Campbell, Joseph. (2020). *The Hero with a Thousand Faces*. Los Angeles: Joseph Campbell Foundation.

CBC Radio. (2023). "Atlantis and the Apocalypse: The World of Fringe Archaeology | CBC Radio." *CBCnews*, November 20. https://www.cbc.ca/radio/ideas/atlantis-and-the-apocalypse-the-world-of-fringe-archaeology-1.6757733.

Cherry, Kendra. (2023). "Coping with Thalassophobia (Fear of the Ocean)." *Verywell Mind*, May 12. https://www.verywellmind.com/thalassophobia-fear-of-the-ocean-4692301.

The Collider, and Shion Takeuchi. (2021). "'*Inside Job*': Shion Takeuchi on Creating Her Wildly Imaginative (and Just Plain Wild) Netflix Animated Series." *The Collider*, October 28.

Comedy Central Stand Up. (2019). "'Ancient Aliens' Is the Most Offensive Show on Television—Devin Field." *YouTube*, December 25. https://www.youtube.com/watch?v=2a65Q0X8R6A.

Conway, Lucian Gideon, Alivia Zubrod, Linus Chan, James McFarland, and Evert Van de Vliert. (2020). "Is the Myth of Left-Wing Authoritarianism Itself a Myth?" *Frontiers*, December. doi:10.31234/osf.io/frcks.

Coppens, Teresa. (2021). "Why Do We Love to Believe in Monsters?" *Science Alcove*, August 17. https://sciencealcove.com/2015/03/why-we-love-to-believe-in-monsters/.

Part III: Film and TV

Disney Advertising. (2023). "Let's Get Animated: Reaching the Adult Animation Audience—Disney Advertising Insights." *Disney Advertising Insights—A Collection of Data-driven Insights across the Disney Advertising Portfolio*, March 21. https://insights.disneyadvertising.com/thought-leadership/lets-get-animated-reaching-the-adult-animation-audience/.

Dominguez, Alicia. (2022). "Lessons about Humans You Can Learn When Researching Mermaids, Sirens and Other Sea Creatures." *Medium*, August 6. https://medium.com/mindful-mental-health/lessons-about-humans-you-can-learn-when-researching-mermaids-sirens-and-other-sea-creatures-bedb4c5b74b0.

Farinelli, Francesca. (2021). "Conspiracy Theories and Right-Wing Extremism—Insights and Recommendations for P/CVE." *Radicalisation AWareness Network*, 1–28.

Fortuna, Paweł, Zbigniew Wróblewski, Arkadiusz Gut, and Anna Dutkowska. (2023). "The Relationship Between Anthropocentric Beliefs and the Moral Status of a Chimpanzee, Humanoid Robot, and Cyborg Person: The Mediating Role of the Assignment of Mind and Soul." *Current Psychology*, November. doi:10.1007/s12144-023-05313-6.

Fox, Nick, and Matt N. Williams. (2023). "Do Stress and Anxiety Lead to Belief in Conspiracy Theories?" *Routledge Open Research* 2 (September): 30. doi:10.12688/routledgeopenres.17925.1.

Friedman, George. (2017). "The Deep State Is a Very Real Thing." *HuffPost*, March 16. https://www.huffpost.com/entry/the-deep-state_b_58c94a64e4b01d0d473bcfa3.

Goodman, David G. (2005). *The Protocols of the Elders of Zion: Aum and Antisemitism in Japan*. Jerusalem: Vidal Sasson International Center for the Study of Antisemitism.

Gordon, Rebecca. (2017). "What the American 'Deep State' Actually Is, and Why Trump Gets It Wrong." *Business Insider*, January 20. https://www.businessinsider.com/what-deep-state-is-and-why-trump-gets-it-wrong-2020-1?IR=T.

Greenspan, Rachel E. (2021). "The Bizarre Origins of the Lizard-People Conspiracy Theory Embraced by the Nashville Bomber, and How It's Related to QAnon." *Business Insider*, January 8. https://www.businessinsider.com/lizard-people-conspiracy-theory-origin-nashville-bomber-qanon-2021-1?IR=T.

Halmhofer, Stephanie. (2022). "Did Aliens Build the Pyramids? And Other Racist Theories." *SAPIENS*, October 24. https://www.sapiens.org/archaeology/pseudoarchaeology-racism/.

Hobbs, Thomas. (2019). "The Conspiracy Theorists Convinced Celebrities Are Under Mind Control." *WIRED UK*, May 9. https://www.wired.co.uk/article/mkultra-conspiracy-theory-meme.

Hriddo, Abhoy. (2021). "Netflix's *Inside Job* Confirms All Your Conspiracy Theories." *The Daily Star*, November 25. https://www.thedailystar.net/shout/editorial/news/netflixs-inside-job-confirms-all-your-conspiracy-theories-2901086.

Jacobson, Mark. (2013). "50 Years of Conspiracy Theories—CIA Mind Control—New York Magazine—Nymag." *New York Magazine*, November 25. https://nymag.com/news/features/conspiracy-theories/cia-mind-control/.

KennyB. (2023). "Magic Myc from *Inside Job*." *The Ultimate Cartoon Character Resource*, July 14. https://cartoonvibe.com/magic-myc-from-inside-job/.

King, Jade. (2022). "*Inside Job* Shows That Blunt Satire Is Often the Most Necessary." *TheGamer*, November 29. https://www.thegamer.com/inside-job-satire-politics-conspiracy-theories-season-2/.

klunder.2. (2019). "Behind the Belief: Lizard People." *The Psychology of Extraordinary Beliefs*. The Ohio State University, February 12. https://u.osu.edu/vanzandt/2019/02/12/behind-the-belief-lizard-people/.

Knight, Peter. (2019). "How Moon Landing Conspiracy Theories Began and Why They Persist Today." *How Moon Landing Conspiracy Theories Began and Why They Persist Today*. University of Manchester, July 12. https://www.manchester.ac.uk/discover/news/moon-landing-conspiracy-theories/.

Lamb, Robert, and Austin Henderson. (2023). "Stoned Ape Theory: Magic Mushrooms and Human Evolution." *HowStuffWorks Science*, September 29. https://science.howstuffworks.com/life/evolution/stoned-ape-hypothesis.htm.

Little, Becky. (2023). "How the Bigfoot Legend Began." *History.com*, July 25. https://www.history.com/news/bigfoot-legend-newspaper.
Lofgren, Mike. (2021). "Essay: Anatomy of the Deep State." *BillMoyers.com*, April 13. https://billmoyers.com/2014/02/21/anatomy-of-the-deep-state/.
Los Angeles Times, and Shion Takeuchi. (2021). "'*Inside Job*' Showrunner Thought a Shadow Government Would Be Scary. Reality Was Scarier." *Los Angeles Times*, October 23.
Lucey, Catherine, and Darlene Superville. (2021). "Trump Accuses DOJ of Being Part of 'Deep State.'" *AP News*, April 22. https://apnews.com/article/8720fde079e84237b8e6cca4219aafb2.
Michael. (2008). "Why Are Dirty Jokes Funny?" *Daily Writing Tips*. December 13. https://www.dailywritingtips.com/why-are-dirty-jokes-funny/.
Miller, Liz Shannon. (2021). "'*Inside Job*': Shion Takeuchi on Creating Her Wildly Imaginative (and Just Plain Wild) Netflix Animated Series." *Collider*, October 28. https://collider.com/inside-job-shion-takeuchi-interview-netflix/.
Mills, Kim, and Karen Douglas. (2021). "Speaking of Psychology: Why People Believe in Conspiracy Theories, with Karen Douglas, PhD." American Psychological Association. Accessed February 12. https://www.apa.org/news/podcasts/speaking-of-psychology/conspiracy-theories.
Moklytsia, Mariia. (2017). "Mythical Allegories of Fear (a Psychoanalytic Aspect)." *Accents and Paradoxes of Modern Philology* 1. doi:10.26565/2521-6481-2017-1-6.
"Myth." (n.d.). *Oxford Reference*. Accessed February 13, 2024. https://www.oxfordreference.com/display/10.1093/oi/authority.20110803100220460.
"Mythopoeia." (2024). *Oxford Reference*. Accessed March 14, 2024. https://www.oxfordreference.com/display/10.1093/oi/authority.20110803100220548.
Naish, Darren. (2022). "A Cultural Phenomenon." *RSB*, September 12. https://www.rsb.org.uk/biologist-features/a-cultural-phenomenon.
Needham, George C. (2000). *Angels and Demons*. Chicago: Moody Press.
Osegueda, Hector. (2019). "'Ancient Aliens': A Damaging Perspective." *The Liberator Magazine*, February 28.
Oto, Berk. (2022). "Animated Show '*Inside Job*' Parodies Conspiracy Culture." *U-High Midway*, January 24. https://uhighmidway.com/14244/arts/animated-show-inside-job-parodies-conspiracy-culture/.
Palecek, Martin, and Václav Hampel. (2023). "Conspiracy Theories and Anxiety in Culture: Why Is Threat-Related Misinformation an Evolved Product of Our Ability to Mobilize Sources in the Face of Un-Represented Threat?" *Philosophy of the Social Sciences* 54 (2): 99–132. doi:10.1177/00483931231210335.
Ratner, Paul. (2022). "Why the Nazis Were Obsessed with Finding the Lost City of Atlantis." *Big Think*, April 19. https://bigthink.com/the-present/why-the-nazis-were-obsessed-with-finding-the-lost-city-of-atlantis/.
Roberts, David. (2015). "Why Conspiracy Theories Flourish on the Right." *Vox*, December 10. https://www.vox.com/2015/12/10/9886222/conspiracy-theories-right-wing.
Runnels, Rachel. (2019). "Conspiracy Theories and the Quest for Truth." Digital Commons @ ACU, Electronic Theses and Dissertations. Paper 180. https://digitalcommons.acu.edu/etd/180.
Russel, Jeffrey Burton. (1997). *Inventing the Flat Earth: Columbus and Modern Historians*. New York: Praeger.
Scahill, Jeremy. (2017). "Donald Trump and the Coming Fall of American Empire." *The Intercept*, July 22. https://theintercept.com/2017/07/22/donald-trump-and-the-coming-fall-of-american-empire/.
Schadewald, Robert J. (1980). "The Flat-out Truth: Earth Orbits? Moon Landings? A Fraud! Says This Prophet." *Science Digest* 9 (April).
Schager, Nick. (2021). "Inside the Netflix Series Skewering QAnon Nuts-and Joe Rogan." *The Daily Beast*, October 21. https://www.thedailybeast.com/netflixs-inside-job-gleefully-skewers-qanon-nutjobs-and-joe-rogan?ref=scroll.
Sheth, Sonam. (2017). "'This Gets to the Fabric of the Nation': Inside the Dark

232 Part III: Film and TV

Conspiracy That Made Its Way from the Fringe to the White House." *Business Insider*, May 6. https://www.businessinsider.in/this-gets-to-the-fabric-of-the-nation-inside-the-dark-conspiracy-that-made-its-way-from-the-fringe-to-the-white-house/articleshow/58551208.cms.

Smith, Jordan Michael. (2020). "Vote All You Want. The Secret Government Won't Change." *BostonGlobe.com*, September 16. https://www.bostonglobe.com/ideas/2014/10/18/vote-all-you-want-the-secret-government-won-change/jVSkXrENQlu8vNcBfMn9sL/story.html.

Somerlad, Joe. (2021). "The 1990s Card Game That 'Predicted' 9/11, Donald Trump, Covid and the Capitol Riot." *The Independent*, April 29. https://www.independent.co.uk/news/world/americas/us-politics/illuminati-card-game-trump-covid-b1839470.html.

Spielberg, Steven, director. *ET—The Extra-Terrestrial*. Amblin Entertainment, 1982.

Stanley, Jonathan W. (2008). "Snakes: Objects of Religion, Fear, and Myth." *Electronic Journal of Integrative Biosciences* 2 (2): 61–76. http://altweb.astate.edu/electronicjournal/stanley_snakes.htm.

Still Watching Netflix. (2021). "The Lizard People Conspiracy | Inside Job | Netflix." *YouTube*, October 25. https://www.youtube.com/watch?si=uUJNZUQCTT1GJ_BZ&v=lw7tZ2z9krE&feature=youtu.be.

"Symbolism and Importance of Snakes in Hinduism and Mythology." (2023). *KARIGAROFFICIAL*, April 9. https://www.karigarofficial.com/blogs/blog/symbolism-and-importance-of-snakes-in-hinduism-ayurveda-and-mythology.

Takeuchi, Shion, director. (f). *Inside Job*. Part 1, Episode 1, "Unpresidented." Aired October 22. https://www.netflix.com/watch/81050646?trackId=255824129.

Takeuchi, Shion, director. (2021b). *Inside Job*. Part 1, Episode 2, "Clone Gunman." Aired on October 22. https://www.netflix.com/watch/81120865?trackId=255824129.

Takeuchi, Shion, director. (2021c). *Inside Job*. Part 1, Episode 3, "Blue Bloods." Aired on October 22. https://www.netflix.com/watch/81120866?trackId=255824129.

Takeuchi, Shion, director. (2021d). *Inside Job*. Part 1, Episode 4, "Sex Machina." Aired on October 22. https://www.netflix.com/watch/81120867?trackId=200257858.

Takeuchi, Shion, director. (2021e). *Inside Job*. Part 1, Episode 5, "The Brettfast Club." Aired on October 22. https://www.netflix.com/watch/81120868?trackId=200257858.

Takeuchi, Shion, director. *Inside Job*. (2021f). Part 1, Episode 6, "My Big Flat Earth Wedding." Aired on October 22. https://www.netflix.com/watch/81120869?trackId=200257858.

Takeuchi, Shion, director. (2021g). *Inside Job*. Part 1, Episode 7, "Ghost Protocol." Aired on October 22. https://www.netflix.com/watch/81120870?trackId=200257858.

Takeuchi, Shion, director. (2021h.) *Inside Job*. Part 1, Episode 8, "Buzzkill." Aired on October 22. https://www.netflix.com/watch/81120871?trackId=200257858.

Takeuchi, Shion, director. (2021i). *Inside Job*. Part 1, Episode 9, "Mole Hunt (Part 1)." Aired on October 22. https://www.netflix.com/watch/81120872?trackId=200257858.

Takeuchi, Shion, director. (2021j). *Inside Job*. Part 1, Episode 10, "Inside Reagan (Part 2)." Aired on October 22. https://www.netflix.com/watch/81120873?trackId=200257858.

Takeuchi, Shion, director. (2022a). *Inside Job*. Part 2, Episode 1, "How Reagan Got Her Grove Back." Aired on November 18. https://www.netflix.com/watch/81148959?trackId=200257858.

Takeuchi, Shion, director. (2022b). *Inside Job*. Part 2, Episode 2, "Whoas-Feratu." Aired on November 18. https://www.netflix.com/watch/81148960?trackId=200257858.

Takeuchi, Shion, director. (2022c). *Inside Job*. Part 2, Episode 3, "Reagan & Mychelle's Hive School Reunion." Aired on November 18. https://www.netflix.com/watch/81148961?trackId=200257858.

Takeuchi, Shion, director. (2022d). *Inside Job*. Part 2, Episode 4, "We Found Love in a Popeless Place." Aired on November 18. https://www.netflix.com/watch/81148962?trackId=200257858.

Takeuchi, Shion, director. (2022e). *Inside Job*. Part 2, Episode 5, "Brettwork." Aired on November 18. https://www.netflix.com/watch/81148963?trackId=200257858.

Takeuchi, Shion, director. (2022f). *Inside Job*. Part 2, Episode 6, "Rontagion." Aired on November 18. https://www.netflix.com/watch/81148964?trackId=200257858.

Takeuchi, Shion, director. (2022g). *Inside Job*. Part 2, Episode 7, "Project Reboot." Aired on November 18. https://www.netflix.com/watch/81148965?trackId=200257858.
Takeuchi, Shion, director. (2022h). *Inside Job*. Part 1, Episode 1, "Appleton." Aired on November 18. https://www.netflix.com/watch/81148966?trackId=200257858.
TEDx Talks. (2020). "Conspiracy Theories and the Quest for Truth | Rachel Runnels | Tedxtexasstateuniversity." *YouTube*, April 14. https://www.youtube.com/watch?v=LZoXb1WDpls.
Thomson, Jonny. (2023). "A Soviet Doctor's Wild Experiment to Create Hybrid Human-Ape Super Warriors." *Big Think*, October 2. https://bigthink.com/the-past/soviet-human-ape-super-warriors-humanzee-ivanov/.
Today I Found Out. (2018). "The Origin of the Bigfoot Legend." *YouTube*, October 19. https://www.youtube.com/watch?v=J50Ba7psR-Q.
Uscinski, Joseph E., and Joseph M. Parent. (2014). "Conspiracy Theories Are for Losers." *American Conspiracy Theories*, September, 130–53. doi:10.1093/acprof:oso/9780199351800.003.0006.
Weigel, David. (2017). "Trump and Republicans See a 'Deep State' Foe: Barack Obama ..." *The Washington Post*, March 7. https://www.washingtonpost.com/news/powerpost/wp/2017/03/07/trump-and-republicans-see-a-deep-state-foe-barack-obama/.
Wills, Matthew. (2017). "The Turkish Origins of the 'Deep State.'" *JSTOR Daily*, April 10. https://daily.jstor.org/the-unacknowledged-origins-of-the-deep-state/.
Wilson, Jason. (2018). "Crisis Actors, Deep State, False Flag: The Rise of Conspiracy Theory Code Words." *The Guardian*, February 21. https://www.theguardian.com/us-news/2018/feb/21/crisis-actors-deep-state-false-flag-the-rise-of-conspiracy-theory-code-words.

"We're now living in a post-cover-up, post-conspiracy age"
The X-Files *and the Changing Forms of Conspiratorial Culture*

BETHAN JONES

Introduction

What comes to mind when you think of conspiracy? The assassination of JFK? Vaccines as a method of controlling the population? The faking of the moon landing? Or maybe it's something a little more offbeat: the idea that the U.S. government has stored alien technology at Area 51 since 1947; Bigfoot is alive and well in the forests of the Pacific Northwest; Elvis faked his own death? Each of these, from the somewhat believable to the off-the-wall, has appeared in *The X-Files*, a show ostensibly about alien abduction and the paranormal but which has become most notable for its recurring themes of conspiracy and government cover-ups. Debuting in 1993, the series was created by Chris Carter, former editor of *Surfing Magazine* who—inspired by *Kolchak: The Night Stalker*—wanted to "create a wildly entertaining show that would scare the pants off you" (quoted in Hyman 1993). Carter was inspired to center the series around the search for a paranormal "truth" by two events: a 1991 Roper poll which found that four million U.S. citizens had some form of alien-related experience, such as seeing unusual lights or missing time; and the 1973 Watergate scandal, which he referred to as "the most formative event" of his youth (quoted in Graham 1996, 57). While combining these two elements to create a TV series that focuses on the existence of a global conspiracy to colonize Earth may not have been immediately obvious, it is testament to Carter's understanding of the cultural moment of the early 1990s. As David Lavery, Angela Hague, and Marla Cartwright point out, the American public's interest with UFOs, which had begun with reports of a UFO crash landing in Roswell in 1947, had transformed into a fascination with abduction that placed *The X-Files* in a larger historical, cultural and mythical context, while the 1993 release of records pertaining to secret human radiation experiments conducted by the U.S. government forced the public to come to terms with the fact that their government could not only perform experiments without their knowledge but would also cover them up. Discussing these converging themes midway through the show's first season, Carter noted that not only had believers in alien abduction become a core audience for the show but "the thing that was really surprising in my research and in the tests of the pilot (episode), was how pervasive the belief is that the government acts in secretive ways" (quoted in Hyman 1993).

The X-Files came to an end in 2002, two years after the Millennium—with its own conspiracy theories which never came to pass—and a year after the terrorist attacks of 11 September 2001. As I have argued elsewhere it seemed that, almost overnight, "the world of *The X-Files* was no longer reflective of the one Americans lived in" (Jones 2023a, 32). While the show's debut nearly a decade earlier had coincided with reports into covert experiments on human subjects, a similar season 8 plot line, which saw the U.S. government creating "super soldiers" by experimenting on U.S. citizens, seemed out of touch with the mood of the post-9/11 United States, in which the government protected its populace from external forces rather than spying on them from within. When discussions about a reboot of *The X-Files* began circulating online some 12 years after its cancellation the world had seen yet another shift in global politics. Fake news, the spread of disinformation and the widespread belief in conspiracy theories involving government actors were as pertinent to the show's concerns in 2016 as Watergate and the end of the Cold War had been to the original. In the years since *The X-Files*—both original and revival seasons—has aired, scores of articles in the popular press and academic scholarship have considered its legacy. Its impact on television (Johnson 2005) and fandom (Romano 2016) has been notable, and the topic of numerous articles, but its emergence in the context of Trump, QAnon and fake news has perhaps garnered the most—and most controversial—attention. This essay is interested in the various contexts *The X-Files* emerged in, cultural, political and mystical, and how its central questions of what do we believe and who can we trust have remained relevant over the last three decades. It begins by examining the cultural context in which *The X-Files* emerged and the particular political, social and economic factors that contributed to the conspiratorial narratives that underlined its success. It then examines the conspiracy theories that emerged following 9/11 and their increasing prominence, before exploring *The X-Files*' impact on popular culture and the symbiotic relationship between the show and the broader culture it exists within. Ultimately, this essay argues that *The X-Files* was not responsible for the increasing visibility and attractiveness of conspiracy thinking, but instead reflects the political and social moments in which it exists, reflecting a mirror onto society and asking whether we can still trust no one.

"Do you believe in the existence of extraterrestrials?": Cover-Ups, Conspiracies and the Cold War

Although stories of UFO and extraterrestrial beings have circulated through the ages—indigenous rock art thousands of years old feature what some consider other-worldly being while some claim ancient art like Aert De Gelder's 1710 *The Baptism of Christ* depicts UFOs—modern interest in aliens really began in 1947. In June of that year, a pilot named Kenneth Arnold reported seeing a formation of nine batwing-shaped objects flying at high speed in Washington state; in July reports of strange wreckage being uncovered in Roswell, New Mexico, which were subsequently taken to a nearby Army Air Base for examination, were published. By that August, a Gallup poll revealed that nine out of ten Americans had heard of "flying saucers" (Clarke 2023). These reports coincided with the beginning of the Cold War, a period of intense paranoia where, concerned by the threat of Communism and worried that Communists and left-wing sympathizers inside America might work as spies in order to bring down the country, the government began spying on its own people. Positioning the Soviet Union as the ultimate evil, its Communist manifesto taking hold through the infiltration of the U.S. government and pro–Communist ideology being spread through film, granted unprecedented power to the likes of the FBI and Congress. Under Senator Joseph McCarthy nine days of hearings were held into the Communist Party's influence in Hollywood with over 300 industry professionals ultimately being blacklisted by studios, while J. Edgar Hoover authorized the FBI to surveil, wiretap, and infiltrate groups that he thought posed a threat (the subject of the season five episode "Travellers"). Given both the overt and covert monitoring of the U.S. population, reports of flying saucers and test-flights of prototype aircraft at top secret U.S. military bases, it is no surprise that paranoia became *de rigueur* during the Cold War years and left its mark on both politics and popular culture.

As well as the continuing legacy of the Cold War, which ended in the early 1990s, one of the other key inspirations for *The X-Files* was the Watergate scandal. The arrest of several burglars who had broken into the

Democratic National Committee office ultimately led to then-president Richard Nixon's resignation when it was revealed the burglars were linked to his re-election committee and he had not only taken steps to cover-up the break-in but swore to the public that none of his staff had been involved. Commenting on the scandal, Carter noted, "I was about 15 or 16 years old when Watergate happened and I think that ruined me forever as far as my belief in institutions and in authority and agendas of government" (quoted in Beale and Caruso 1998), and Watergate is referenced implicitly and explicitly throughout the show. Mulder's first informant was named for the real-life Deep Throat, while we see Mulder watching a news report about the scandal in a flashback to the night of his sister's abduction. Gregory Frame refers to the period between the 1963 Kennedy assassination and Watergate as "the nation's 'traumatic decade'" (2023, 136) and argues that *The X-Files* represents these

> as part of its wider suggestion that the nation's post-war history, contrary to conventional wisdom, has been consistently subject to denial, cover-up, manipulation and subversion by powerful forces existing outside the nation's democratic mechanisms [2023, 136].

This is perhaps most evident in season four's "Musing of a Cigarette Smoking Man," in which we find out that the Cigarette Smoking Man (CSM)—one of the series' most prominent and enduring villains—was responsible for orchestrating and carrying out the assassination of John F. Kennedy for the 1961 Bay of Pigs disaster. The importance of events such as the Cold War, Watergate, JFK's assassination and the like for *The X-Files* is that they showed that the American government was willing to lie to its people to preserve power at any cost, and if it could lie about domestic espionage and murder, it could also lie about the existence of extraterrestrials.

This theory had actually been proposed in the 1950s by retired U.S. Marine Donald Keyhoe. Keyhoe—who had also published stories in pulp fiction magazines in the 1920s and 1930s—claimed that a secret war was being waged between the U.S. military and extraterrestrials that overlapped with the Cold War (Clarke 2023). This becomes part of *The X-Files* mythology in season one's "E.B.E." when Deep Throat tells Mulder about his role in the conspiracy and how far back it stretches:

> After the Roswell Incident in 1947, even at the brink of the Cold War, there was an ultra secret conference attended by the United States, the Soviet Union, the People's Republic of China, Britain, both Germanies, France, and it was agreed that should any extraterrestrial biological entity survive a crash, the country that held that being would be responsible for its extermination.

UFOlogist Stanton Friedman coined the phrase "cosmic Watergate" in the 1980s after examining leaked documents which purported to offer evidence of the creation of the Majestic 12 group, designed to control evidence related to extra-terrestrial life, and a comprehensive government cover-up of such (Salla 2005). Friedman was one of the co-founders of NICAP, an organization—referred to in *The X-Files* episode "Fallen Angel" among others—which investigated reports of UFOs and attempted to discover the truth about what the U.S. government was hiding about them. Aaron John Gulyas suggests that "within the UFO community, politicized rhetoric such as the phrase 'Cosmic Watergate' indicated a shift toward a conspiratorial style of thinking that was closer to the parapolitics of John F. Kennedy assassination theories and paranoia about the Federal Reserve System than ufology had previously occupied" (2015, 6). Combining the extraterrestrial with the political allowed Carter and his fellow writers to explore the changing fears of the American populace as the country entered the final decade before the millennium. The show's referencing of real organizations dedicated to the investigation of UFOs and the paranormal included contemporary publications such as *Omni*, which was published until 1995, and the Committee for the Scientific Investigation of Claims of the Paranormal (CSICOP), which still exists as a program within the U.S. Center for Inquiry under the name the Committee for Skeptical Inquiry. David Clarke argues that Carter "successfully combined horror and conspiracy themes from 1970s television and 1950s science fiction movies to create *The X-Files* at a moment when popular belief in UFOs made the leap from fringe to mainstream" (2023, 106) but it is also important to recognize the contemporary political and cultural climate of the early 1990s. I have argued elsewhere (Jones 2023a) that *The X-Files* has always spoken to its contemporary climate and its debut in 1993 coincided with Bill Clinton becoming President, marking the end of more than a decade of Republican leadership. The end of the Cold War and growing economic and cultural divisions within American society saw fears about immigration, globalization and technology emerging. M.A. Crang suggests that the show's emergence during the Clinton era can be seen "as a response to the *beginning* of a world no longer characterized by the same political certainties" (2015, 11)—although the same scandals and cover-ups were in evidence under the Democrat Clinton as they had been under Regan and Bush. Indeed, the *Washington Post* claimed that Clinton's first term "marked the dawn of a new age of conspiracy theory" (Thomas 1994) which included theories such as the Clinton Body Count and the alleged coverup of drug smuggling and money laundering in Mena, Arkansas.

Douglas Kellner argues that *The X-Files* instilled "distrust toward established authority, representing institutions of government and the established order as highly flawed, even complicit in the worst crimes and evil imaginable" (1999, 169) though as I have argued elsewhere it is "less that the show instilled distrust and more that it leveraged the growing number of reports about the government's secretive activities to inspire its storylines" (2023a, 22–23). During Clinton's terms in office events like the siege of the Branch Davidian compound in Waco, Texas, and the Oklahoma City bombing carried out by Timothy McVeigh made their way—explicitly or implicitly—into the franchise. The spread of new technology like artificial intelligence and nanotechnology also appeared in episodes like "Ghost in the Machine" and "SR 819," further addressing real-world fears about government control and the show's resident conspiracy theorists, the Lone Gunmen, maintain a watchful eye on goings-on in government. *The X-Files* had long been considered a subversive show, suggesting if not implicitly encouraging viewers to distrust authority and the government. In fact, one of Carter's intentions had been to "jolt people out of their complacency" by showing them "that in the absence of political or public mindedness, the people who wield the power will wield it in dangerous ways" (quoted in Soter 2015, 124). For the first eight seasons of the show questioning the government and encouraging television audiences to not only distrust authority but to "trust ourselves" (Bellon 1999, 152) was accepted and acceptable. Enrica Picarelli and M. Carmen Gomez-Galisteo argue that this was because *The X-Files* was broadcast at a time when the United States seemed safe from international terrorism. With the events of September 11, 2011, however, the show's central tenet that the government can't be trusted was a message it seemed no one wanted to hear. As Picarelli and Gomez note, the attacks "demanded a strong government to protect citizens and restore their trust in their very safety—notions at odds with the distrust *The X-Files* promoted" (2013, 82). While the show's earlier seasons had touched a chord with audiences, the events of 9/11 understandably turned viewers' attention away from the skies and across the seas. With Bush declaring a "war on terror" and increasing support for the American government evident with the public display of American flags, the increasingly convoluted storylines featuring super soldiers and Earth's colonization seemed far removed from everyday fears of more terrorist attacks and soon after *The X-Files* was cancelled.

"You believe what you want to believe—that's what everybody does now": Fake News, Mainstream Conspiracy and the Twenty-First Century

For a show which had been so adept in picking up on the nuances of political, cultural and mythical events and turning them into highly rated storylines it seems strange that its ratings dropped following 9/11. In Mulder and Scully's world this type of event—and more importantly the government's reaction to it—was not unusual. The Patriot Act, introduced in October 2001, expanded the surveillance abilities of law enforcement; authorized the indefinite detention without trial of immigrants; and gave law enforcement permission to search property and records without a warrant or even the knowledge of the owner (Jones 2023a). These were precisely the kinds of activities *The X-Files* had been warning about. Yet shows like *24*, which followed counterterrorism agent Jack Bauer as he protected U.S. senator David Palmer from assassination, "consciously spoke to the nation's anxieties and uncertainties" in a way *The X-Files* could not (Mooney 2017, 163). Cantor suggests that "Perhaps *The X-Files* did not generally receive the credit it deserved for modelling the post-9/11 world because media pundits did not want to face up to a disturbing truth—the show had actually predicted a new age of international terrorism with uncanny accuracy" (2012, 80). In fact, *The X-Files* spinoff *The Lone Gunmen* appeared to predict the events of 9/11 with uncanny accuracy. The pilot episode, which aired on March 4, 2001, saw a hacker taking control of a Boeing 727 with the intention of crashing it into the World Trade Center. The three Gunmen—John Fitzgerald Byers, Melvin Frohike, and Richard Langly—prevent the attack but discover it was organized by a group within the American government who planned to blame it on foreign dictators in order to start a profitable war for the United States. Discussing the episode *The X-Files* co-producer Frank Spotnitz said:

> We were really upset, and worried that somehow we had inspired the plot. But we were relieved to discover that the plot pre-dated *The Lone Gunmen*, and that 9/11 had nothing to do with our work. And then once we realized that, my next thought was how the government hadn't known about this plot [quoted in Newitz 2008].

This was the question conspiracy theories asked after 9/11, proposing that not only did the government know about the attacks but that they had been orchestrated by the government to justify the invasions of Afghanistan and Iraq (Smallpage 2019). In the years since 9/11 and the end of *The X-Files*, new forms of conspiratorial culture have emerged and conspiracy theorists are no longer on the fringe but have become part of the mainstream. One important technological development has contributed to this mainstreaming: the internet. Although the early days of the internet converged with the debut of *The X-Files*, the years since have seen tremendous growth in access to, and use of, the world wide web. While Langly may have been "hopping on the internet to nitpick the scientific inaccuracies of *Earth 2*" in season two's "One Breath," today's netizens are debating everything from last night's television to whether the Covid-19 pandemic was a hoax or if the British royal family are actually all lizard people. Clarke suggests that "UFO conspiracy narratives have spread beyond the confines of UFOlogy because they appeal to a wider audience of conspiracist thinking that emerged in the aftermath of the 9/11 terrorist attacks" (2023, 116). Among the theories that have been put forward in the last twenty years and which have gained ground in the mainstream are the 9/11 Truth movement, whose adherents argue against the official explanation of the attacks; birtherism, which argues that Barack Obama was not born in the United States and is therefore ineligible to be President; that vaccines cause autism; and that a clandestine network, including members of the FBI, finance and industry, exercises control within the U.S. government. Many of these were endorsed by Donald Trump not only during his run for President but also during his time in office, which began the same year that season ten of *The X-Files* aired.

News of *The X-Files*' return had been circulating online since 2014, with fans and critics alike divided over whether the show could capture the mood of the twenty-first century in the same way it had the late twentieth. As one fan noted, "crazy" conspiracy theories had become mainstream and Carter was going to have to up his game (Jones 2023a, 46). As had been the case during the original seasons, Carter took inspiration from the world around him, the news, and the internet and conspiracy theories were a growing topic of discussion along with an anti-intellectualism that argued the truth was what we *felt*. That *The X-Files* was firmly situated in twenty-first-century politics and culture was made clear in the first episode of season ten. Mulder is called back to the X-Files by Assistant Director Walter Skinner who wants him to meet with a right-wing web-show host, Tad O'Malley. O'Malley is clearly based on real world conservative personalities such as Alex Jones and Glenn Beck, a point Mulder makes in the episode when comparing him to then–Fox news host Bill O'Reilly (O'Malley responds, saying, "What Bill O'Reilly knows about the truth can fill an eyedropper"). In a 2015 interview with *The Guardian* Carter pointed out that "right now in the internet there are 500 conspiracy sites, and there are people like Tad O'Malley out here who have got the public's attention" (quoted in Dredge 2015) and indeed his show, *The Truth Squad with Tad O'Malley*, rails against "a mainstream liberal media lying to you about life, liberty and your God-given right to bear firearms" in a similar way to the real life O'Malleys. Although only the first and last episodes of season ten deal with the show's mythology the underlying tensions between what is true, who can we trust and how much is the government lying to us that emerged in the early 2000s are evident. As Ben Lindbergh (2018a) writes, the season "nodded in the direction of recent political trends" despite being "conceived before 'fake news' became a buzzword and a conspiracy theorist became president." Season eleven, premiering two years into Donald Trump's term as president, "emerged into a political climate where multiple versions of the truth were out there, and conspiracy theories were wilder than even Mulder could have imagined" (Jones 2023b, 156).

If season ten demonstrated that conspiracy theories had moved away from the fringe, season eleven cemented the fact that they were now mainstream. Lindbergh (2018b) argues that it "is steeped in 2017, when once disreputable and easily dismissed movements monopolized mainstream attention and staged a cultural (and Constitutional) coup," referring in part to the QAnon movement which emerged in 2017 in support of Trump. These political and cultural changes are highlighted at various points throughout season eleven, including in the opening montage of episode one which featured footage of Trump's inauguration, Black Lives Matter protestors, Russian president Vladimir Putin and robed Ku Klux Klan members as CSM provides the voice-over. More explicitly, in "Plus One" Mulder tells Scully that "the world is going to hell [...] The president working to bring down the FBI along with it," but it is "The Lost Art of Forehead Sweat" which really reflects the paranoid distrust of the contemporary moment. Written by Darin Morgan the episode introduces us to Reggie Something, a conspiracy theorist more akin to the "conspiracy nuts" of the 1980s than the smooth-talking O'Malley of season ten. Through Reggie we discover that a scientist is manipulating people's memories in order to blur the lines between what is real and what is fake. Mulder's confrontation with the scientist—Dr. They—highlights the role that fake news played not only in the episode but in the real world as well:

> Dr. They: Your time has passed.
> Mulder: Okay. So, what is or what was my time?
> Dr. They: Well, it's a time when people of power thought that they could keep their secrets secret, and were willing to do anything to keep it that way. Those days are passed. Gone. We're now living in a post-cover-up, post-conspiracy age....
> Mulder: As long as the truth gets out.
> Dr. They: They don't really care whether the truth gets out. Because the public no longer knows what's meant by the truth.
> Mulder: What do you mean?
> Dr. They: No one can tell the difference anymore ... between what's real and what's fake.
> Mulder: There's still objective truth, objective reality.
> Dr. They: So what [...] They won't know whether to believe it or not.

Morgan pointed to Trump as an inspiration for the episode, saying: "The initial thing was trying to find some sort of Trump thing. I wanted to write something about it because [the show's] whole premise is 'The Truth

Is Out There,' and now your fictional characters work for someone for whom the truth is a bit fuzzy" (quoted in Coggan 2018). Morgan here references Trump's presidential campaign, in particular the assertion made by White House Press Secretary Sean Spicer that the crowds at Trump's inauguration were the largest inaugural audience ever. While this was easily disproved, Trump's counselor Kellyanne Conway defended the statement as Spicer simply offering the press "alternative facts." David Smith argues that this "these formed the original sin of the Trump presidency, culminating in his coronavirus and election denialism" (2020) but combined with the term "fake news" they also shaped much of the discourse of the late 2010s. Morgan's episode thus seemed, not only to reflect the contemporary political and cultural moment, but scarily prescient as the second decade of the twenty-first century drew closer.

"Mulder, the Internet is not good for you": Encouraging Conspiracy Culture, Media Effects and Audience Agency

Thus far I have focused on the ways in which *The X-Files* reflected the overarching concerns of its time, both during the original nine seasons and in the revival episodes. There have, however, been criticisms of the show, in particular the suggestion that, rather than simply reflecting conspiracy culture, it encouraged it. Jason Diamond, discussing the show's twentieth anniversary, alludes to this, while not quite pointing the finger of blame at Carter:

> I'm not saying that *The X-Files* bears the majority of responsibility for that shift [in attitudes toward the government], but a television show that (at its peak) pulled in nearly 20 million viewers per episode, and took every opportunity to drive home the point that everything we believe in and take for granted is a lie, had to play some role in bringing different and potentially extreme ways of thinking to the masses [2013].

Diamond's concerns are not new: while *The X-Files* was still on air organizations, including CSICOP and the Council for Media Integrity, argued that it was contributing to a declining belief in science (Yeema 1996) and scientists like Richard Dawkins criticized its fans for being gullible, paranoid conspiracy-theorists who believed willy-nilly in ghosts, UFOs and hidden government agendas. Giving the 1996 Richard Dimbleby Lecture he said:

> soap operas, cop series and the like are justly criticised if, week after week, they ram home the same prejudice or bias. Each week *The X Files* posts a mystery

and offers two rival kinds of explanation, the rational theory and the paranormal theory. And, week after week, the rational explanation loses. But it is only fiction, a bit of fun, why get so hot under the collar?

Imagine a crime series in which, every week, there is a white suspect and a black suspect. And every week, lo and behold, the black one turns out to have done it. Unpardonable, of course. And my point is that you could not defend it by saying: "But it's only fiction, only entertainment."

Let's not go back to a dark age of superstition and unreason, a world in which every time you lose your keys you suspect poltergeists, demons or alien abduction.

Dawkins' concerns that the series promoted suspicion have been superseded in the twenty-first century by concerns that it promotes conspiracy theories. Alison de Souza asked James Wong and Glenn and Darin Morgan if *The X-Files* had helped steer conspiracy theories into mainstream culture. Wong reframed the question in his response, saying:

I think your question was, "Do you feel a little responsible for creating (today's) conspiracy theories?" We may have brought them into more of the mainstream because it is a network television show. But those theories and their proponents have been in existence since we began doing the show. It's just that I think we had a chance to reach a larger audience and, maybe, if you're saying, "Does that allow the audience to more readily accept conspiracies?," I guess so. But if you look at All The President's Men (1976) and other suspense movies…, I think that idea has always been around, even with president John F. Kennedy's assassination in the 1960s. So I think what we did was tap into something that was more or less hidden in the beginning when we were doing it, but I don't believe that we're at the forefront of what's happening today [quoted in de Souza 2018].

Glenn Morgan agreed, pointing out that the conspiracy theories that circulate now on platforms such as InfoWars are "so beyond anything we were even proposing as entertainment." You know, what InfoWars is saying. I used to check out Alex Jones back in the day and go, "This is too weird even for us" (quoted in de Souza 2018).

Alex Jones has referred to *The X-Files* and the conspiracy theories that constituted its storylines, Carter acknowledging that "someone told me last night that Alex Jones was talking about how *The X-Files* actually was talking about spiked viruses long before we ever heard about the coronavirus—or were made more aware of it. I've got serious cred on Info Wars, apparently" (Wax 2021). Carter's "serious cred" on InfoWars is not that surprising: Mulder might have been paranoid, but he was paranoid for a reason, as we see repeatedly. It is not too much of a leap to suggest that some viewers might recognize aspects of Mulder's paranoia and apply it to the real world, especially given the government abuses, cover-ups and surveillance that have come to light over the last several decades. This kind of thinking is, however, rather simplistic and suggests that audiences lack the agency to understand and interpret texts; they are "injected" with various theories or ways of thinking by the media and blindly accept these. An examination of fan discourse over the last thirty years demonstrates how varied reactions to the show were, and how much thought was put into analyzing its storylines. Gulyas notes that "the question of extraterrestrial life, government cover-ups of its existence, and the manner in which the show presented these topics were routine subjects of discussion" in online forums (2015, 62), however what is particularly interesting are viewers' suggestions that the show was either created to prepare the public for disclosure about the truth of extraterrestrial life, or that it was produced in collaboration with dark government forces. These flip the idea that the series *encouraged* conspiratorial thinking on its head. Conspiracy theories were already in existence, *The X-Files* becoming the subject of one which said the show was "part of a wider disinformation campaign aimed at derailing truthseekers" (Gulyas 2015, 63). rather than the show encouraging conspiracy theorists to find the "real" truth off-screen. For most viewers, however, the show was nothing more than entertainment and as it began to develop its own internal conspiracy theories to serve the narrative it left the wider conspiracy culture of the time behind (Gulyas 2015).

Its return in 2016 was firmly situated in the contemporary moment, including a storyline related to vaccines which caused controversy among some viewers. During the show's early seasons, a vaccine was developed to fight against the alien virus that would lead to the colonization of Earth; in season ten it was revealed that the smallpox vaccination every American received would strip their immune systems, spreading the Spartan Virus and wiping out 90 percent of the population. Ostensibly this is in order to save the earth for mankind: CSM tells Mulder that we have just had the hottest year on record, megafauna has been decimated, over 40 percent of bird life has been lost, referring to current reports about climate change. Yet neither this, nor Scully's attempts to create a vaccine using her own DNA were mentioned in reviews and critiques of the episode. Rather it was this exchange between Scully and Agent Einstein that received the most attention:

> SCULLY: I was given a smallpox vaccine as a child, as I'm sure you were as well. It was standard practice in America at the time.
> EINSTEIN: If you are suggesting that there is more in that shot than-than a vaccine....
> SCULLY: It's actually not that far-fetched and within the realm of accepted science. Something entering the germ line, something that would be passed down hereditarily.

Reflecting on the episode, Sophie Gilbert, Megan Garber, David Sims, and Lenika Cruz wrote,

> Vaccines? Seriously? Do you know what the public-health ramifications are of having Dana Scully (of all people!) reveal that the smallpox vaccine actually contains a secret virus that allows the government to destroy our immune systems (enhanced by releasing radiation and phosphorus into the air), at which point the other vaccines we've received over time will kill us? [2016].

In a similar fashion, fans also criticized the way "the episodes promoted fear of government and especially government health initiatives" (quoted in Jones 2023, 43). That the foregrounding of vaccinations as the source of the problem was highlighted by viewers, rather than the fact that vaccinations also offered the antidote, speaks to the ideas still put forward in the media that what we watch affects what we think. While of course television *can* have an impact (see, for example, the "Scully effect"—the impact the character of Scully had on encouraging women to enter STEM fields) this has to be considered with other factors such as class, gender, race, social status, social and cultural background and a myriad of others. While *The X-Files* may have encouraged viewers to question authority, only those already predisposed to conspiratorial thinking are likely to have been swayed into believing the theories expounded by the likes of Alex Jones, Tucker Carlson and Michael Flynn.

Conclusion

Despite its focus on aliens and the paranormal, *The X-Files* has always excelled at picking up on the pertinent questions, issues and concerns of the times it finds itself in. From the increasing use of AI in the early 90s to New Religious Movements in advance of the Millennium and the increasing surveillance powers awarded by the U.S. government following 9/11, it reflected a mirror back on society. This was still evident during the revival seasons, despite the varying quality of some of the newer episodes. The 2008 financial crash had led to political instability, economic austerity, and a polarization between the left and the right, but rather than being limited to the United States, as had been the case with earlier inspirations for the show, these reverberated across the globe. An increasingly connected world—technologically, economically and politically—saw conspiracy theorists emerging from the fringe to inhabit spots on primetime television and within government itself. Revelations such as Wikileaks and the use of the Patriot Act to surveil American citizens reinforced the belief—expressed in earlier seasons of *The X-Files*—that no government could be trusted while theories that 9/11 had actually been instigated by the U.S. government and that Barack Obama was a Muslim who was planning to bring down the United States from the inside monopolized mainstream attention. Given *The X-Files*' attention to political, cultural and social mores, that these formed the bedrock for the revival of the show in 2016 hardly seems surprising. In fact, Carter highlighted the changing political and cultural moment as an inspiration for the revival, pointing out that "*The X-Files* has gotten to deal with a lot of political realities, and I'll always think it's given the show a lot of its life" (quoted in Thomas 2018) and noting that what the conspiracy world of the 2010s "[has] done for me and the writers it has given us a whole new open field [in] which to run. It's given the show an interesting new life and context that it might not have had in 2002" (quoted in Hibberd 2016).

Critics of both the original and revival seasons may condemn the series for encouraging a turn towards a conspiratorial culture but as I have argued through the course of this essay, this is a simplistic understanding of both the show and its viewers. *The X-Files* cannot be understood simply in terms of a subversive/progressive binary or as a reactionary text. It may subvert televisual systems of seeing which have taught viewers to look at established institutions such as the government positively, but viewers who subscribe to the idea that the government is not sharing all of its information with its citizens (even if they do not engage with the idea that the government is conducting secret tests on its citizens or spying on the general population through the internet) will not necessarily see it is a progressive text. Similarly, arguments that the series is reactionary and "demonstrates the infantilism of the American psyche, where the loss of faith in a political vision has given way to an ingenuous belief in everything else" (O'Reilly 1996, 6) fail to grant viewers the agency to think critically about the media they consume. *The X-Files* ultimately holds a mirror to society rather than a gun: it does not force viewers to accept conspiratorial thinking or encourage them to adopt conspiracy beliefs; rather it asks the question if the real world is like the world of *The X-Files*, who can we trust and what can we ultimately believe.

REFERENCES

Beale, Lewis, and Michelle Caruso. (1998). "'x' Drive Chris Carter Brings His 'X-Files' Passions And Obsessions To The Big Screen." *New York Daily News*, 14 June. Available at https://www.nydailynews.com/x-drive-chris-carter-brings-x-files-passions-obsessions-big-screen-article-1.797964.
Bellon, Joe. (1999). "The Strange Discourse of *The X-Files*: What It Is, What It Does, and What Is at Stake." *Critical Studies in Media Communication* 16.2, pp. 136–154.
Cantor, Paul A. (2012). *The Invisible Hand in Popular Culture: Liberty Vs. Authority in American Film and TV*. University Press of Kentucky.

Clarke, David. (2023). "'I want to believe': How UFOs Conquered *The X-Files*," in James Fenwick and Diane A. Rodgers (eds.), *The Legacy of The X-Files*. Bloomsbury, pp. 105–120.
Coggan, Devan. (2018). "*X-Files* Writer Breaks Down His Trump-Inspired Episode 'About Truth and Lying.'" *Entertainment Weekly*, 24 January. Available at https://ew.com/tv/2018/01/24/x-files-writer-darin-morgan-trump-inspired-episode/.
Crang, M.A. (2015). *Denying the Truth: Revisiting The X-Files after 9/11*. CreateSpace.
Dawkins, Richard. (1996). *Science, Delusion and the Appetite for Wonder*. Available at http://www.edge.org/3rd_culture/dawkins/lecture_p12.html.
de Souza, Alison. (2018). "How X-Files Brought Conspiracy Theories into Mainstream Culture." *The Straits Times*, 31 January. Available at https://www.straitstimes.com/lifestyle/how-x-files-brought-conspiracy-theories-into-mainstream-culture.
Diamond, Jason. (2013). "The Truth Is Still Out There: An Appreciation of *The X-Files* on Its 20th Anniversary." *Flavorwire*, 10 September. Available at https://www.flavorwire.com/414229/the-truth-is-still-out-there-an-appreciation-of-the-x-files-on-its-20th-anniversary.
Dredge, Stuart. (2015). "*X-Files* Revival Inspired by Surveillance Revelations, Says Show's Creator." *The Guardian*, 6 October. Available at https://www.theguardian.com/tv-and-radio/2015/oct/06/return-of-the-x-files-inspired-by-nsa-surveillance-revelations.
Frame, Gregory. (2023). "The End of History? Contesting the Legacy of the 1960s and 1970s in *The X-Files*," in James Fenwick and Diane A. Rodgers (eds.), *The Legacy of The X-Files*. Bloomsbury, pp. 135–148.
Gilbert, Sophie, Megan Garber, David Sims, and Lenka Cruz. (2016). "*The X-Files*: Do We Still Want to Believe?" *The Atlantic*, 23 February. Available at https://www.theatlantic.com/entertainment/archive/2016/02/the-x-files-do-we-still-want-to-believe/470541/.
Graham, Allison. (1996). "'Are You Now or Have You Ever Been?' Conspiracy Theory and *The X-Files*," in David Lavery, Angela Hague and Marla Cartwright (eds.), *Deny All Knowledge: Reading The X-Files*. Syracuse University Press, pp. 52–62.
Gulyas, Aaron John. (2015). *The Paranormal and the Paranoid: Conspiratorial Science Fiction Television*. Rowman & Littlefield.
Hibberd, James. (2016). "Fox's 'X-Files' Revival Has Controversial New Theories." *Entertainment Weekly*, 11 January. Available at https://ew.com/article/2016/01/11/x-files-revival-conspiracy/.
Hyman, Jackie. (1993). "'The X Files' May Really Exist Says Show's Creator." *Roanoke Times*, 25 December. Available at https://scholar.lib.vt.edu/VA-news/ROA-Times/issues/1993/rt9312/931225/12250171.htm.
Johnson, Catherine. (2005). "Quality/Cult Television: *The X-Files* and Television History," in Michael Hammond and Lucy Mazdon (eds.), *The Contemporary Television Series*. Edinburgh University Press, pp. 57–74.
Jones, Bethan. (2023). *The Truth Is Still Out There: Thirty Years of The X-Files*. Columbus: Fayetteville Mafia Press.
Jones, Bethan. (2023). "'You Believe What You Want to Believe—That's What Everybody Does Now': *The X-Files*, Fake News and the Rise of Qanon," in James Fenwick and Diane A. Rodgers (eds.), *The Legacy of The X-Files*. Bloomsbury, pp. 149–168.
Kellner, Douglas. (1999). "*The X-Files* and the Aesthetics and Politics of Postmodern Pop." *Journal of Aesthetics and Art Criticism* 57 (2), pp. 161–175.
Lindbergh, Ben. (2018a). "'The X-Files' in the Post-Conspiracy Age of Trump." *The Ringer*, 3 January. Available at https://www.theringer.com/tv/2018/1/3/16843804/x-files-season-11-age-of-trump.
Lindbergh, Ben. (2018b). "A Conversation with 'X-Files' Legend Darin Morgan." *The Ringer*, 24 January. Available at https://www.theringer.com/tv/2018/1/24/16928880/the-x-files-darin-morgan-q-a.
Mooney, Darren. (2017). *Opening The X-Files: A Critical History of the Original Series*. McFarland.
Nera Kera, Myrto Pantazi, and Oliver Klein. (2018). "'These Are Just Stories, Mulder':

Exposure to Conspiracist Fiction Does Not Produce Narrative Persuasion." *Frontiers in Psychology* 9, article 684, pp. 1–17.
Newitz, Annalee. (2008). "Chris Carter Says 9/11 Killed X-Files, But America Is Ready for It Again." *Gizmodo*, 23 February. Available at https://gizmodo.com/chris-carter-says-9-11-killed-x-files-but-america-is-r-360044.
O'Reilly, John. (1996). "A Jump-Cut Above the Rest." *The Independent*, 5 September. Available at https://www.independent.co.uk/arts-entertainment/a-jumpcut-above-the-rest-1361967.html.
Picarelli, Enrica, and M. Carmen Gomez-Galisteo. (2013). "Be Fearful: The X-Files' Post–9/11 Legacy." *Science Fiction Film and Television* 6 (1), pp. 71–85.
Romano, Aja. (2016). "Canon, Fanon, Shipping and More: A Glossary of the Tricky Terminology That Makes Up Fan Culture." *Vox*, 7 June. Available at https://www.vox.com/2016/6/7/11858680/fandom-glossary-fanfiction-explained.
Salla, Michael E. (2005). "The History of Exopolitics: Evolving Political Approaches to UFOs and the Extra-terrestrial Hypothesis." *Exopolitics Journal* 1 (1), pp. 1–17.
Smallpage, Steven M. (2018). "Conspiracy Thinking, Tolerance, and Democracy," in Joseph E. Uscinski (ed.), *Conspiracy Theories and the People Who Believe Them*. Oxford University Press, pp. 187–198.
Smith, David. (2020). "Alternative Facts, Witch-Hunt, Bigly: The Trump Era in 32 Words and Phrases." *The Guardian*, 28 December. Available at https://www.theguardian.com/us-news/2020/dec/28/alternative-facts-bigly-witch-hunt-trump-era-words-phrases.
Soter, Tom. (2015). *Investigating Couples: A Critical Analysis of The Thin Man, The Avengers and The X-Files*. McFarland.
Thomas, Kenn. (1994). "Clinton Era Conspiracies! Was Gennifer Flowers on the Grassy Knoll? Probably Not, but Here Are Some Other Bizarre Theories for a New Political Age." *The Washington Post*, 16 January. Available at https://www.washingtonpost.com/archive/opinions/1994/01/16/clinton-era-conspiracies-was-gennifer-flowers-on-the-grassy-knoll-probably-not-but-here-are-some-other-bizarre-theories-for-a-new-political-age/52f44fe4-ba8e-4f9a-a119-c1d526fad4b4/.
Thomas, Leah Marilla. (2018). "'The X-Files' Is Going to Give Donald Trump the Government Conspiracy Treatment." *Bustle*, 3 January. Available at https://www.bustle.com/p/trump-references-in-the-x-files-season-11-emphasize-the-shows-obsession-with-government-conspiracies-7764495.
Wax, Alyse. (2021). "Chris Carter on the Continued Prescience of *The X-Files*, 28 Years After Its Premiere." *Paste*, 10 September. Available at https://www.pastemagazine.com/tv/x-files-anniversary-conspiracies-predictions-chris/.
Yeema, John. (1996). "Aliens Capture Uncritical Media, Debunkers Claim." *Boston Globe*, 1 July. Available at https://www.nasw.org/sites/default/files/sciencewriters/html/sum96tex/aliens.htm.

About the Contributors

Kat **Albrecht** is an assistant professor in the Andrew Young School of Policy Studies at Georgia State University. She is a legally trained sociologist and computational social scientist studying how complex data can inform policy, with particular emphasis on the nexus of fear, criminal data, and the law. She received her PhD and JD from Northwestern University. She is a fellow with the Criminal Justice Administrative Records System.

Gordon **Alley-Young** is a professor of speech communication at Kingsborough Community College, City University of New York, where he has also served as the chairperson of Communications & Performing Arts and the dean of faculty. His research, including works published in Spanish, Turkish, and English, focuses on qualitative media analyses of topics including whiteness, LGBTQAI+ identity, MENA feminism, popular education films, journalistic hoaxes, terrorism and social media, and historical drama.

Andrew **Burns** is a research associate at the Social Research and Evaluation Center. He received his PhD in sociology from Louisiana State University. He specializes in qualitative methodology focusing primarily on opioid use and conspiracy beliefs. His research is forthcoming or has been recently published in the *Journal of Qualitative Criminal Justice* and the *Russell Sage Foundation Journal of the Social Sciences*, among others.

Daniel P. **Compora** is an associate professor in the Department of English at the University of Toledo, where he specializes in undergraduate education. An interdisciplinary scholar, he has publications in various areas, including literature, folklore, popular culture, and educational technology. Recent publications include "Toxic Nostalgia in Stephen King's IT"; "Dystopian Literature at a Distance"; and "The Ties That Bind: Familial Burdens in a Zombie Apocalypse."

Michelle **Drake** is a postgradaute academic literary researcher and essayist from Paradise, California. Holding a master's degree in multicultural literature from Heritage University, Michelle has a varied background in topics related to literary research and criticism. They have presented at international conferences dedicated to women, gender, and sexuality studies, comparative literature, Shakespeare, and more. They have also published on topics related to poetry, queer theory, feminism, and Gothic literatures.

About the Contributors

Holly T. **Hamby** is an associate professor of English and the director of the Center for Teaching and Learning at Fisk University. She is a member of the advisory committee of the John R. Lewis Center for Social Justice. Her central research focuses on religious literature and rhetoric, specifically early medieval English literature and the use of medieval topoi in contemporary white supremacist propaganda.

Matthew N. **Hannah** is an associate professor in the School of Information Studies at Purdue University and was a Fulbright specialist to Morocco in 2022. His research focuses on the political economy and public impact of online information, conspiracy theories, and social media. He has published in *Journal of Information Literacy*, *First Monday*, *Social Media + Society*, and *The Journal of Magazine Media*.

Tara **Heimberger** is in the Film & Media Studies PhD program at Georgia State University in Atlanta. Her master's thesis defines the "Good for Her" genre of horror, examining the genre's development through internet discourse and cinematic depictions of female rage and catharsis. She also has a publication in the *Sigma Tau Delta Review*. Her research focuses on the intersections of horror cinema, feminism, and cultural studies.

Chelsea L. **Horne** is a senior professorial lecturer in the Department of Literature at American University and a faculty fellow at the Internet Governance Lab. Horne's areas of research encompass disinformation, privacy, digital rhetoric, communication, information literacy, and Internet governance. Recent work has appeared in *Telecommunications Policy*, Routledge Studies in Shakespeare, and *Writing Spaces*. She regularly presents her work at ICA, AoIR, GigaNet, NeMLA, and other international conferences.

Bethan **Jones** is a postdoctoral research associate and lecturer at Cardiff University, where she researches the way the past is remediated/animated through algorithmic systems, and with what consequences. She has written extensively about fandom, gender and participatory cultures, and she has been published in *Television and New Media* and *Convergence*, among other journals. She is on the board of the Fan Studies Network and co-editor of the journal *Popular Communication*.

Colin **McRoberts** teaches courses on business law and conspiracy theories at the University of Kansas. His published commentary includes articles about pseudolaw, the belief in complex and false sets of legal rules, and the teaching of religious creationism in public schools. Before joining academia, Colin worked as a litigator and then an expert in negotiation, advising professional negotiators in dozens of countries around the world.

Sean Thomas **Milligan** has taught English courses at SUNY Oswego and Cayuga Community College. He studies the intersection of narrative and illness and is particularly interested in the ways in which comics and graphic novels incorporate visual elements, along with the interplay of text and image, to represent non-normative bodies and minds. He incorporates service learning and civic engagement into many of his courses.

Sutirtho **Roy** works full-time with the Israeli-based Vault AI, where his research concerns the means by which artificial intelligence might improve upon the understanding of visual media, especially speculative fiction, postcolonial literature, animal autobiographies and children's literature. His research interests intersect at the juncture of popular culture, children's literature, post-humanism and critical animal studies, the last of which he has attempted to decolonize highlighting Indian and Japanese perspectives.

Julia **Siwek** is a research fellow and PhD candidate in medieval German literary studies at the University of Passau, Germany. As a part of the project SKILL. de, she develops innovative seminar concepts in teacher training, addressing the intersections of disciplinary, didactic, and digital competencies as well as information and media literacy. Her teaching and research look for ways of fostering future skills through the engagement with medieval German literature.

Robert **Spinelli** is a librarian and independent scholar located in Nashville, Tennessee. He holds an MA (philosophy) and an MS (information sciences). He has presented at conferences speaking about conspiracy theories and their connections with religion and social media and has co-presented on African American funerary traditions. He has books in the publication process on various topics including death commemoration/memorialization and the role of grief in the construction of archives.

Hasmet M. **Uluorta** is an associate professor of political studies and international development studies at Trent University in Peterborough, Canada. His scholarly interests include globalization, theories of international relations, global political economy, and employment/work strategies as well as the impacts of new technologies and speed on subjects, societies, and world order. Recent research focuses on the U.S. political economy, seeking to clarify why consent may be forthcoming domestically despite hyper-contradictions.

James **Weatherford** has a PhD in theology and an MA in the history of ideas. As an instructor for various postsecondary institutions in the Dallas-Fort Worth area, he teaches humanities courses which survey cultural and artistic development in the west and diversity in contemporary society. His research interests include Christian-Jewish relations, the Holocaust, and the theological and philosophical frameworks of anti–Semitism.

Florian **Zitzelsberger** is a PhD candidate in American studies at the University of Passau, Germany. His research is situated at the nexus of queer theory, performance studies, and narrative theory. His dissertation focuses on narrative impossibilities in the American film musical from the perspective of queer narrative theory. He has published on viral media, influencer culture, hashtag activism and information and media literacy, among other topics.

Index

AIDS 5, 161, 185–200
alien 1, 35, 37, 55, 84–86, 89, 125, 127, 134, 136, 140, 215, 223, 225, 227, 234–236, 244–246
alt-right 6, 157, 201–208, 210, 213, 214
American exceptionalism 20
antichrist 81, 83, 84, 87
Appalachia 127, 129, 130
apocalypse 13, 80, 82, 91, 251

belief 1, 4, 11, 13, 15, 17–19, 25, 32, 35, 40, 43, 60, 64, 66, 70, 74–76, 80, 81, 95, 110, 111, 113, 114, 117, 120, 121, 126, 131, 133, 135, 138, 143, 145, 171, 172, 174, 187, 196, 205, 207, 213, 214, 219–221, 224, 226, 227, 235, 237, 238, 246, 247
blood libel 154, 157, 160
Blue Beam 5, 81–87

cabal 5, 51, 56, 60, 61, 66, 67, 77, 82, 86, 89, 145, 155, 172, 207, 223
Campbell, Joseph 4, 42, 48
capitol 52, 76, 115, 148, 149, 150, 172, 206, 207
Clinton, Hillary 4, 20, 21, 101, 104, 105, 172, 173, 238, 239
comic 5, 60–62, 65, 68–80, 217, 223
conspiracism 5, 40–42, 44–46, 48–50, 55, 56
conspiracy narrative 4, 15, 40, 42–58, 160
conspiratorial thinking 2, 4, 5, 62, 76, 78, 135, 136, 140, 154, 155, 158, 160, 161, 165, 166, 170, 245, 246
contact overdose 110, 111, 119–121
contaminated candy 111
Covid-19 5, 34, 56, 60, 81–84, 90, 91, 132, 138, 142, 148, 161, 185–187, 190–193, 195–197, 219, 240
cryptid 128, 137–139, 215, 226, 227, 229
cultural trauma 136

Deep State 54, 55, 61, 70, 77, 89, 145, 150, 151, 218, 219, 221, 227
devil 12–19, 63, 64, 137, 156–158
disinformation 6, 10, 11, 22, 146, 148, 153, 169–172, 175, 176, 178, 179, 208, 235, 245

EAA (ethical All-American) 95–108
extremism 57, 151, 153, 202, 213, 214, 219

fake news 170, 171, 175,-178, 235, 241–243
fantasy 68, 77, 96–108, 215, 219
fear 5, 19, 26, 33, 54–56, 61, 69–74, 77, 78, 80, 110–121, 124, 126, 133, 138, 139, 146, 158, 162, 166, 185, 207, 208, 218, 219, 221, 224, 226, 227, 228, 238, 239, 246
fentanyl 5, 110–123
fiction 4, 5, 11, 18, 27, 29, 35–37, 41, 42, 47, 57, 60–65, 77, 84, 86, 128, 135, 137, 146, 177, 215, 216, 238, 243, 244
First Amendment 170, 177
folklore 2, 18, 28, 32, 63, 82, 83, 124, 125, 127–130, 133–140

gender 14, 15, 18, 22, 99, 202, 204, 205, 214, 246, 251
great replacement 33, 40, 51, 52, 56, 60, 74, 159, 160
grief 4, 124–140

Halloween 110–115, 121, 177
Hellfire Club 60–79
HIV 6, 185–197
Holocaust 73, 158, 159, 162–164, 166
horror 6, 128, 138, 139, 185, 188, 191–193, 195, 201, 209–211, 238

Illuminati 5, 51, 52, 54, 56, 61, 77, 89, 179, 215, 222
information studies 42

Jew (also Jewish) 13, 15, 26, 33, 56, 67, 74, 90, 137, 154–166, 222, 223, 227

Keller, Helen 172, 179
Ku Klux Klan 25, 26, 28, 29, 242

literacy 9–11, 22, 196, 214
literary studies 57

Marvel 60, 61, 65, 68, 69, 70, 72, 73, 77, 79
meme 137, 151, 153, 169, 171, 174
Middle Ages 13, 15, 156, 160, 220
misinformation 2, 60, 111, 118, 119, 121, 143, 146, 147, 172, 176–178, 185, 186, 188, 189, 194, 195, 197, 229
moral panic 5, 110, 111, 113, 119, 121
Mothman 5, 124–127, 129, 131–140, 226
Mulder, Fox 3, 33, 34, 237, 240–245

narrative theory 42
Nazi 25, 26, 32, 156, 158, 160, 162, 202, 224
New World Order 61, 70, 77, 81, 82, 85, 89–91
9/11 2, 3, 6, 51, 52, 140, 232, 235, 239–241, 246–249

opioids 114, 117, 120
ostension 86, 91

Pizzagate 4, 20, 21, 145, 169, 172–175, 178, 179
Propp, Vladimir 44–47
Puritanism 17–20

QAnon 2, 4, 5, 21, 52, 53, 55, 56, 66, 71, 89, 142, 144, 147–153, 169, 172, 203, 235, 242

St. Malachy 81, 87, 88, 91
Salem 17–19, 69
Satanic Panic 51, 56, 112
secret societies 5, 61, 61–63, 68–71, 77, 81, 89, 91, 223
Stone Mountain 27, 28
superheroes 60, 72, 76
Superman 5, 25, 26, 28–32, 36–39, 75

techno-capitalism 96, 106, 108
Trump, Donald 2, 21, 47, 51, 54, 82, 142, 145, 148–152, 169, 177, 178, 187, 192, 202, 206, 218, 235, 241–243
truth 2–4, 29, 30, 34–37, 40, 48, 54, 61–64, 71, 75, 87, 103–109, 131, 132, 138, 216, 221, 228, 234, 238, 240–243

virality 6, 170, 171

white nationalism 6, 201–205, 210, 212
white supremacy 5, 26, 202, 203, 205, 207, 213, 214
witch 5, 10–24, 69, 174
witch-hunt 10, 12, 15, 16, 18, 19, 21, 22

X-Files 1, 6, 33, 234–247
X-Men 5, 61, 65, 66, 68, 69, 71, 73–77